I0815096

BUD WILKINSON AND THE RISE OF OKLAHOMA FOOTBALL

BUD WILKINSON

AND THE RISE OF OKLAHOMA FOOTBALL

JOHN SCOTT FOREWORD BY JOSEPH HARROZ JR.

UNIVERSITY OF OKLAHOMA PRESS : NORMAN

Publication of this book is made possible through the generosity of Edith Kinney Gaylord.

Library of Congress Cataloging-in-Publication Data

Names: Scott, John Prosser, 1946– author.
Title: Bud Wilkinson and the rise of Oklahoma football / John Prosser Scott; foreword by Joseph Harroz Jr.
Description: Norman : University of Oklahoma Press, [2021] | Summary: "Tells the story of how, in 1947, thirty-one-year-old Bud Wilkinson was named head coach of the University of Oklahoma's football program and led the team on its meteoric rise from mediocrity to its present status as a perennial powerhouse. Includes vignettes of Wilkinson's closest coaching friends (Royal, Bryant, Leahy, Sanders, Blaik, Tatum) and serves as an authoritative and entertaining history of the sport that will appeal to all college football fans."—Provided by publisher.
Identifiers: LCCN 2021013928 | ISBN 978-0-8061-7554-6 (hardcover)
Subjects: LCSH: Wilkinson, Bud, 1916–1994. | Football coaches—United States—Biography. | University of Oklahoma—Football—History—20th century. | BISAC: BIOGRAPHY & AUTOBIOGRAPHY / Sports | HISTORY / United States / State & Local / Southwest (AZ, NM, OK, TX)
Classification: LCC GV939.W48 S36 2021 | DDC 796.332092 [B]—dc23
LC record available at https://lccn.loc.gov/2021013928

The paper in this book meets the guidelines for permanence and durability of the Committee on Production Guidelines for Book Longevity of the Council on Library Resources, Inc. ∞

10 9 8 7 6 5 4 3 2 1

To my father, who taught my brother, my sister,
and me an abiding love of sports,
and
To my mother, who cared nothing at all for sports,
but who loved us enough that she tolerated—
and supported—our enthusiasm

Contents

Foreword

JOSEPH HARROZ JR.

There are many honors and privileges that accompany being president of the University of Oklahoma, and I count being asked to write the foreword to John Scott's book *Bud Wilkinson and the Rise of Oklahoma Football* among these. As a native Oklahoman and an OU graduate and administrator, I've spent half my life on this campus. Over the years, I've stood in the middle of Owen Field and looked up at the majesty of the Palace on the Prairie soaring around me and reaching to a clear-blue western sky. Countless times, I've heard the deafening roar of the crowd in the loudest stadium in college football. Like my predecessors, and all of us who serve at OU, I love this university and its traditions of success, innovation, and excellence—traditions that underlie the relationships of a very personal and intimate community. Bud Wilkinson also loved this university, and the story told here is as much about OU as it is about football and Coach Wilkinson.

Innovation and excellence at OU are evident in the long-standing success of our football program, which has always reflected the aspirations and ambitions of the university and of the people of Oklahoma. In the wake of Wilkinson's first national title, my predecessor Dr. George Lynn Cross was asked by a state senate appropriations committee, "Why do you need so much money?" Cross replied with a smile, "I would like to build a university of which the football team could be proud."

Cross wasn't telling tales out of school. OU's football program had already emerged as a national force, on par with Notre Dame and Army. To have similar aspirations for a public university in a state still recovering from the Dust Bowl was bold and, to some, ludicrous. However, Wilkinson's proven success, coupled with Cross's political acumen and good humor, set the course for the persistent and enduring growth of OU as the state's beacon of learning, research, and leadership.

Bud Wilkinson and the Rise of Oklahoma Football reflects the tradition of its subject and the spirit of our university. It is the product of careful work, meticulous attention to detail, constant innovation, and a great deal of patience and persistence in pursuit of success. John Scott has combined compelling play-by-play descriptions of the great games of the Wilkinson era with the stories of recruiting and relationship-building with staff, players, and Oklahomans, while laying out the strategy on both sides of the ball and in recruiting—establishing OU football as a dominant force amidst the changing times and circumstances of college football in the postwar era.

The result is the definitive story of Bud Wilkinson and the creation of the winning tradition of OU football. How great were Wilkinson's teams? The tale of the tape is telling. When the 31-year-old assistant took over from departed OU coach Jim Tatum in 1947, the Sooners began a period of unprecedented success. During Wilkinson's first 72 conference games, the Sooners were never defeated (70 wins, 2 ties). They did not lose a conference game until 1959, when they were finally beaten on the road by Nebraska. In the process, Wilkinson claimed 13 straight conference titles and would win a 14th in 1962. Wilkinson owns both the first- and ninth-longest winning streaks in college football history, winning 31 straight games from 1948 to 1950, and then a likely unbreakable 47 straight games from 1953 to 1957. OU also claimed three consensus national titles from 1950 to 1956. In 1963, Wilkinson ended his collegiate coaching career with a record of 145–29–4.

From generation to generation, the legend has been told many times: of championships and winning streaks and Heisman winners. But the greater story is the one of relationships, innovation, and risk. Wilkinson was one of the fathers of the modern game, coaching through the difficult transition from one-platoon to two-platoon football. He helped create the modern role of the quarterback, and he spent his career pursuing a "triple option" offense, which was ultimately perfected by Houston's Bill Yeoman with the veer. Wilkinson actively worked to break down racial barriers at OU and in our football program, and in this book, Scott details Wilkinson's efforts to recruit, enroll, and mentor future Hall of Famer Dr. Prentiss Gault.

Wilkinson's "coaching tree" reflects the creation of deep and personal relationships built on a singular quality of honesty and trust. His mentorship and friendship with Darrell Royal is just one example of the very personal relationships he built with players and staff that Scott recounts. These relationships are a hallmark of OU and other OU coaching legends, such as Chuck Fairbanks, Barry Switzer, and Bob Stoops. And across the OU family, it is this spirit of genuine goodwill that unites our community, transcending the generations.

But Wilkinson's story in creating OU football is, more than anything else, one of loyalty to this university that we love. Serving my alma mater and our state's flagship university as its president is an immense honor. When I was named the fifteenth president of OU, I said that this position was more than a promotion or a dream job. It was a chance to pay back the debt I owed our university. OU changes lives every day. I knew this firsthand because OU changed my life. I wouldn't be who I am if not for the education my father—the son of Lebanese immigrants—received at OU, and the education that I also received from this extraordinary institution.

After his retirement in 1963, Wilkinson went into politics and then broadcasting. He returned to the sidelines, briefly coaching the Cardinals in the NFL in the late 1970s. However, he never roamed a college sideline as coach after OU. Neither did Barry Switzer or Bob Stoops. Wilkinson's college football legacy begins and ends at Owen Field. OU took a chance on Wilkinson, and he paid it back.

Preface

If you look at a list of the top ten college football teams at the end of World War II, the schools you find are largely the same as in the upper echelon of teams today: Alabama, Notre Dame, Georgia, Ohio State, USC, Michigan, Texas. However, one school missing from that list in 1945 is now a mainstay in the top ten: Oklahoma.

Central to Oklahoma's rise to college football prominence is one man—Bud Wilkinson. In his seventeen years as the head football coach at Oklahoma, his teams won three national championships and once won forty-seven straight games (a record that still stands after more than sixty years). During his tenure, Wilkinson laid the groundwork that enabled OU to become a national football power, a tradition since carried on by Barry Switzer, Bob Stoops, and Lincoln Riley.

Bud Wilkinson and the Rise of Oklahoma Football chronicles Wilkinson's years at Oklahoma and outlines the personal beliefs and coaching tenets that enabled Wilkinson to become the preeminent football coach of his time. The story is told in narrative style, so events unfold as Wilkinson experienced them. Furthermore, the accuracy of the events described in this book was verified by Wilkinson himself, who reviewed the first draft of the manuscript before his death in 1994.

Let me explain how this can be true. In 1986 I began research and writing of *Bud Wilkinson and the Rise of Oklahoma Football*, a project funded by Tribune Swab/Fox (TSF, the owners of the *Tulsa Tribune*) under the direction of G. Douglas Fox, Howard Barnett, and Bob Craine. The concept was to create a distinctive coffee table book (with illustrations by artist Jay O'Meilia) that would be a highly desirable corporate gift and a keepsake coveted by OU fans. In the summer and fall of 1986 I spent five full days interviewing Wilkinson at his office in St. Louis. I created the first draft of the book in 1987 and sent a copy of the manuscript to Wilkinson for his review. He finished reading the manuscript and approved it in February 1988.

During that period, the price of oil had dropped below eleven dollars a barrel during the summer of 1986 and stayed below fifteen dollars for much of the next eighteen months. As a result, TSF decided the market for a luxuriously illustrated coffee table book no longer existed and chose to shelve the project. TSF retained rights to the manuscript until 1997, when I was able to purchase those rights.

In writing *Bud Wilkinson and the Rise of Oklahoma Football*, my primary source was Wilkinson himself, but there were two published sources that were key to creating this book. These were *47 Straight* by Harold Keith (1984) and *Bud Wilkinson: An Intimate Portrait of an American Legend* by Jay Wilkinson (1994).

In that regard, let me note the encyclopedic nature of *47 Straight*. Keith, the sports publicist during Wilkinson's years at OU, was privy to all that went on during that seventeen-year period. He knew Wilkinson. He knew Gomer Jones and other members of the coaching staff. He knew the players. He took copious notes (often written on the backs of his own business cards). At the time I was doing my research, that remarkable font of information was located in the files of OU's Sports Information Department. Of great assistance in that regard were former OU sports information director Mike Treps and his staff (particularly Jan Burton). They provided me access to OU's files of newspaper clippings, magazine articles, and photographs related to the Wilkinson years at OU.

Similarly, I am grateful to Jay Wilkinson for providing significant details regarding his father's personal life. Jay's insights complete the picture of Charles Burnham Wilkinson as a person, not merely as a coaching legend.

In addition, there are four other books I read to gather information for *Bud Wilkinson and the Rise of Oklahoma Football*. These include *Presidents Can't Punt* by Dr. George L. Cross (1977); *The Undefeated* by Jim Dent (2001); *I Remember Bud Wilkinson* by Mike Towle (2002); and *The Sooner Sidelines* by Jay C. Upchurch (2003).

I am also grateful to the more than two dozen OU players who were gracious enough to spend time with me to discuss their experiences playing for Wilkinson. Others providing meaning insight were OU president Dr. George L. Cross, OU sports business manager Ken Farris, and Jeanette Jones, the widow of Gomer Jones.

Amid other demands in my life during the past twenty or more years, I have worked through more than a dozen revisions of the manuscript, all of them oriented toward focusing the narrative more narrowly on Wilkinson himself (a suggestion made by Sally Dennison, one of the former owners of Council Oak Books, now an imprint of Chicago Review Press). At the same time, I have added profiles of several famous coaches who were Wilkinson's friends and among the most successful coaches of the 1940s, 1950s, and 1960s. Those profiled include Bear Bryant (Kentucky, Texas A&M, and Alabama), Darrell Royal (Texas), Frank Leahy (Notre Dame), Earl Blaik (Army), and Jim Tatum (Maryland and North Carolina).

A word about quotations: I will readily admit I was not present to hear the actual words said by Wilkinson or any of the other characters in the OU drama. But next to accuracy—which was my foremost consideration—I created *Bud Wilkinson and the Rise of Oklahoma Football* with readability in mind. Thus, the last thing I wanted to do was burden a remarkable story with a plethora of footnotes or kill its immediacy by relying on nothing but indirect quotes. On top of that, the conversations documented in this book took place twenty-five to forty years before they were relayed to me, making it virtually impossible for anyone to remember them word for word. As a result, I have abided by the following guidelines in documenting conversations:

- When Wilkinson related conversations to me, he did so trying his best to recall what was said. In many cases, he spoke as if he remembered the exact words spoken. Other times, it was clear he was recalling—if not in the exact words—the gist of conversations. In general, I have put these conversations in dialogue form for readability's sake. In some cases—notably in comments made directly to the Sooner players—I have quoted them as they were quoted by Harold Keith, who was there and put them in *47 Straight*. Many players recounted conversations with Wilkinson as if they were recalling his exact words. I have placed those conversations in direct quotes as well.
- The conversations among Billy Vessels and Charles and Kitty Rountree came from my interview with Vessels in December 1986.
- Conversations between players and coaches were generally reported as they were described in *47 Straight*. In a few cases, players I interviewed attempted to reconstruct conversations with coaches or other players. I have placed those conversations in direct quotes, as well.

- Conversations involving Dr. George L. Cross and Wilkinson came from my interview with Dr. Cross in November 1986.
- The quotes regarding Tommy McDonald's natural athleticism were from an interview with Jack Santee in January 1987.
- Newspaper and magazine stories written during the Wilkinson years often contain direct quotes from Wilkinson and others. I have trusted that the journalists who wrote those stories and articles were diligent in their work and that conversations presented in direct quotes were an accurate reflection of what was said. Accordingly, I have kept them as direct quotations.
- Mickey Mantle never played football at OU, but he was a high school star in Commerce, Oklahoma, during Wilkinson's early years in Norman. As a result, Mantle makes a couple of Dickensian appearances in the story of OU football. The most significant of these occurs when his shin was accidentally kicked during football practice. The leg began to swell and turn red, and the doctors talked about amputating the leg. "Like hell you are," Mantle's mother said. I am indebted to Jane Leavy for preserving that response. (Jane Leavy, *The Last Boy: Mickey Mantle and the End of America's Childhood* [New York: HarperCollins, 2010], 61.)

Acknowledgments

I want to thank the following Sooner players who were kind enough to visit with me about their experiences playing for Bud Wilkinson at OU: David Baker, Dick Bowman, George Brewer, Carl Dodd, Leon Cross, Eddie Crowder, Tom Emerson, Wayne Greenlee, Jimmy Harris, Bob Harrison, Leon Heath, Bill Krisher, Tommy McDonald, Jack Mitchell, Harry Moore, Benton O'Neal, Jay O'Neal, John Pellow, Jerry Pettibone, Billy Pricer, J. D. Roberts, Jack Santee, Byron Searcy, Clendon Thomas, Bob Timberlake, Jerry Tubbs, Billy Vessels, and Jim Weatherall.

I also want to thank John Hadl, who for a brief time verbally committed to playing for Wilkinson before choosing to attend the University of Kansas.

Two individuals instrumental in helping me understand the administrative and logistical aspects of the Oklahoma football program were Dr. George L. Cross, president of the university during Wilkinson's tenure as head coach, and Ken Farris, sports business manager.

Four friends were vital in making sure the narrative was compelling—and grammatically correct. They are David Braun, Tom Huberty, Gary Liess, and Troy Niles. Other friends who were instrumental in giving me continuing encouragement in the writing of this book—and occasional nudging, if necessary—are Nolene Niles, Chad Corbitt, Beth Corbitt, and Sharon Haworth.

Finally, no author can be successful without that greatest of assets—a diligent editor. In my case, I was fortunate enough to have the help of Kerin Tate, a freelance copyeditor from Kansas City. She was sensitive to subtle choices in grammar, syntax, and punctuation. Beyond that, she was a bulldog in correcting mistakes I made. We worked through all her corrections and suggested changes, and this book is the result. It was made better by her involvement.

Part I
THE VICTORIOUS VETERANS

1947

The silver locomotive steamed through the Virginia countryside, the beam from its single, penetrating headlight knifing through the cold January night. The train had completed half its journey from Jacksonville to New York and, after passing down from the rolling Piedmont plateau to the broad Tidewater plains, seemed to be continuing its northward trek with renewed strength. The rhythm of the cars speeding over the rails echoed through the darkened passenger cars and the still-lighted club car, where incorrigible night owls sought solace in the company of others.

Farther back in the train, another man found sleep a stranger. Bud Wilkinson lay awake in his Pullman berth, staring at the ceiling. As the night wore on, Wilkinson would occasionally pull back the curtains and look out at the scattered, lonely lights faintly visible across the fallow fields. But mostly Wilkinson gazed at the ceiling in contemplation, just as any man might who knows a secret and has the opportunity—and the will—to act upon it. Wilkinson's secret was simple. He could be the next head football coach at the University of Oklahoma. The choice would be his. Dr. George Cross, the university's president, had told him so.

"Bud," Cross had said, "there's been some talk about Jim Tatum leaving Oklahoma and becoming the head coach at Maryland. If he does, I know there will be the opportunity and the temptation to leave with him. I don't know if we can resolve the situation with Jim or not, but I have been authorized by the regents to tell you that if Jim does leave, we want to offer you the head coaching job at OU."

Wilkinson thanked Cross for the vote of confidence and said he would be interested if the opportunity presented itself. Then he gave the matter little thought. At the time, he was preparing for the Sooners' Gator Bowl game against North Carolina State the next day. The Sooners, who had won the Big Six championship and finished the season with a 7–3 record in Tatum's first year as head coach, seemed destined for victory if the players and coaches kept their attention focused on the matters at hand. And Wilkinson, who firmly believed in keeping one's goals in perspective, believed that preparing for North Carolina State took precedence over contemplating a situation he knew was far from resolved.

To be sure, Tatum's interest in the coaching job at Maryland was not news to Wilkinson. Tatum had already told Wilkinson about his discussions with Curley Byrd, the president of the University of Maryland, himself a former Terrapin football coach. Tatum's discussions with Maryland had been encouraging, but his selection remained in doubt, so he had used the situation as a negotiating wedge with the OU regents. He knew they wanted the university to have a football powerhouse, and he could provide it. But if he were to do so, he expected to be well paid. And his assistants would be well paid, too. That is, if he chose to stay.

Tatum relished the situation. He simply could not lose. Wilkinson had quietly assented that his friend did indeed seem to have everything going his way, but Wilkinson knew that was the way Tatum always worked. Full speed. Hit 'em hard. Keep 'em off balance. Press for any edge. Anything to get what he wanted. And what Tatum wanted was to be the greatest football coach in America.

"Come with me to Maryland, Bud," Tatum, the master recruiter, urged Wilkinson. "We make a great team."

Tatum had used the same reasoning to convince Wilkinson to accompany him on a trip to Norman, Oklahoma, in early 1946 for his interview for the head coaching position at Oklahoma. The two had become friends when both were assistant coaches at the U.S. Navy's Iowa Pre-Flight training center during World War II. At Iowa Pre-Flight, they had studied under Don Faurot (in peacetime, the head coach at Missouri), who had devised a stunning new offensive formation—the Split T—that was revolutionizing football.

In the 1930s, when Wilkinson had played football at Minnesota, most teams used the single wing formation. A few had been successful with Clark Shaughnessy's T formation, in which the center snapped the ball directly to the waiting hands of the quarterback rather than through the air to the tailback. The formations were different in appearance, but similar in concept. To make yardage, both required the offensive line to charge forward and push opposing linemen to the side to make a hole for the ball carrier to run through. Faurot's modification was elemental but ingenious. By spacing the players in the offensive line three to four feet apart, rather than sandwiching them shoulder-to-shoulder, you could force the defense to spread out to cover its flanks. The holes offensive linemen had formerly fought to open now already existed. All a lineman had to do was make one quick block to keep the hole open, and the ball carrier could speed through before the defense recovered.

Tatum and Wilkinson had learned their Split T lessons well. With the war over, both were eager to put those lessons to work as college coaches. The regents at Oklahoma were equally hopeful of luring an ambitious young coach to the university to develop a football team that could earn national prominence and dispel the state's Dust Bowl Okie image. Tatum, three years older than Wilkinson, seemed perfect for the job. Loud. Verbose. Demanding. He was everything a football coach was supposed to be. Plus he had a salesman's gift for convincing young men that wherever *he* was, they should be, too. And once they got there, he could make them win. At least, they'd damn well better. He'd get them so scared of him, they would overcome any opponent on earth rather than face him after losing. You bet your bottom dollar, Jim Tatum could make a football program a winner!

In truth, Tatum was but one of several coaches the regents considered seriously. One of the others was Red Drew, the head coach at the University of Alabama. Another was a gruff southerner named Paul "Bear" Bryant, who had played at Alabama at the same time Tatum was playing at North Carolina. Bryant had become the head coach at Maryland in 1945 and had turned the school's football fortunes around with a nucleus of players he brought with him from North Carolina Pre-Flight.

The OU regents believed the same type of magic could be worked at Oklahoma if they could hire Tatum or Bryant, either of whom could bring a corps of experienced players they had coached in the navy. Unknown to Tatum, he was the favorite for the position, having known OU athletic director Jap Haskell at Jacksonville Pre-Flight and having been recommended over Bryant by Tom Hamilton, the respected football coach at the U.S. Naval Academy. Tatum wanted the Oklahoma job so badly he refused to take any chances. He prevailed upon Wilkinson, who had a strategic mind better than his own, to accompany him to Norman for his interview.

"If we go in together, show them the kind of team we make, they can't turn us down," Tatum assured Wilkinson.

Tatum was right. The OU regents liked what they heard and signed Tatum as the head coach, provided Wilkinson came as his assistant. At twenty-nine, Wilkinson had spent seven years as an assistant coach, and he was beginning to think he might be better off in the mortgage banking business with his father, C. P. Wilkinson. After all, he now had a family to support, and a career as a football coach was hardly lucrative—and far from secure. Still, Wilkinson could not say no. He loved coaching. He liked Jim Tatum. And so for one year, he would give it his best.

When Tatum and Wilkinson arrived at Oklahoma, the task confronting them seemed monumental. At the time, OU was anything but a national power. In fact, Oklahoma was no better than the third best team in the state. Oklahoma A&M, victorious in the 1946 Sugar Bowl, was viewed by some as the best in team America in 1945. The Aggies still had Bob Fenimore and were considered a preseason favorite for the national title in 1946. Even Tulsa, which had appeared in bowl games for five straight seasons, was more highly regarded than the Sooners. In the previous five years, Snorter Luster's OU teams had won two Big Six championships and finished second three times, but they had lost five straight to Texas and twice to Tulsa.

It did not take Tatum long to assess where he and Wilkinson stood.

"There are two things I've learned about his job," he said to Wilkinson. "One, we better beat Texas before long. Two, we better beat A&M immediately."

Eagerly, Tatum and Wilkinson went to work. By spring, they set up tryout camps for prospective Sooners. More came during the summer. No one knows how many hopeful prospects came and went. Maybe two hundred. Maybe three hundred. They had to show what they could do quickly, or they would be gone. Tatum's assistants took the names of those who showed promise. Those who did not were cast aside. Among the casualties were most of the Sooners from 1945, which caused some to complain that Tatum had intentionally eliminated Luster's players. The truth was not so brutal. College players who had been good by Luster's standards could not measure up to the finest Tatum could assemble. The veterans—taught by the finest coaches in America and survivors of a world war—were simply better and tougher.

To find good players, Tatum would search anywhere: Small town high schools. Family farms. Railroad depots. Tatum's zeal was unflagging, and in being so motivated, he wrote the book on modern-day recruiting. To him, any able-bodied male with size, speed, and college eligibility remaining was fair game. He was so energetic, so thorough, it was surprising to many that he did not try to recruit his celebrated cousin, Army's Doc Blanchard, who won the Heisman Trophy in

1945 and had one year of eligibility left. Those who knew Tatum well were certain the idea had not escaped him.

Together, Tatum and Wilkinson accomplished everything Tatum promised they would. The two planned, organized, and recruited. Then they drilled their recruits relentlessly through the summer of 1946. When they were finished, they had molded three dozen players—mostly returning veterans attending college on the GI Bill—into a football team the regents and the State of Oklahoma could be proud of.

Using Faurot's revolutionary Split T, Tatum and Wilkinson's Sooners tied for the Big Six championship. They beat Missouri and their mentor Faurot. They avenged a 45–0 loss inflicted by the Oklahoma Aggies in 1945. They almost beat archrival Texas and played Army, led by Heisman Trophy winner Glenn Davis, to a virtual standoff before succumbing. The season was a success by almost anyone's standards. Oklahoma had gone seven years without a single All-American player. In 1946 there were three—guards Buddy Burris and Plato Andros and center John Rapacz. All would be back for the 1947 season. In one year, Tatum and Wilkinson had produced a football team of national stature.

Everything should have been fine, but Tatum was a man who refused to sit quietly and let opportunity pass him by. And in coaching, opportunity can be reduced to two ingredients—the schedule you play and how many games you win. Nothing more. So when the University of Maryland came to Tatum offering a coaching position that seemed to offer greater security, greater exposure to the New York media, and a free hand in the operation of the football program, he felt compelled to listen.

The more Tatum listened, the better the Maryland offer sounded. Tatum shared his interest in Maryland with all of his assistants because he wanted them to accompany him to College Park. And, Tatum reasoned, if his entire staff went to Maryland, wouldn't some of the better players also be interested in changing schools?

Cross and the regents had heard rumors that Tatum intended to take the entire coaching staff to Maryland for a visit after the Gator Bowl game. It was those very rumors that caused Cross to fly five hours from Norman, Oklahoma, to Jacksonville, Florida, in a small company plane provided by regent Lloyd Noble in order to talk face-to-face with Wilkinson. It was a mission Cross was glad to perform. He and other regents had preferred Wilkinson to Tatum from the beginning.

The evening after Oklahoma's 34–13 victory over North Carolina State, Wilkinson boarded the train that would carry him from Jacksonville to New York and the

American Football Coaches Association (AFCA) convention. As the train rolled northward, Wilkinson finally took time to consider his alternatives. Should he go with Tatum to Maryland? Or should he stay at Oklahoma?

As was his habit, Wilkinson tried to consider the matter carefully. Mentally, he enumerated the pros and cons of each alternative to make sure he overlooked nothing important. Unlike Tatum, Wilkinson was not given to emotion or flashes of inspiration. He preferred to analyze situations logically, and so he weighed his own future in that light.

Wilkinson believed he could equal what Tatum had accomplished, maybe even exceed it, but he would have to do it his own way. He knew a coach can be no one but himself and be successful. A football season is too long, the schedule too demanding, the sources of conflict too great to allow anyone to hide behind a mask. A coach must be himself, win or lose, because his ability to win depends upon selling his players on his way of doing things. And that means selling them on himself.

Staring into the darkness, Wilkinson weighed the situation. On the plus side, he counted his playing and coaching experience. At Minnesota, he played for Bernie Bierman, one of the greatest coaches of all time. He played in the line and in the backfield as a single wing blocking back. He even played in the defensive secondary. He was an All-American at guard and called the signals for the College All-Stars against the professional champion Green Bay Packers. And his signal calling—combined with the passing of TCU's Sammy Baugh and the efforts of a number of exceptional college players—enabled the collegians to beat the pros, the first time the feat had been accomplished. After that, Wilkinson spent five years as an assistant to Ossie Solem at Syracuse, a year at Minnesota under George Hauser, and another year as an assistant to Faurot at Iowa Pre-Flight.

Yes, Wilkinson decided, he had the proper bloodlines to succeed in coaching. He knew the fundamentals of football. He knew how to teach those fundamentals, and he knew how to organize. That was perhaps the greatest skill of all. Without it, time—the most vital commodity in putting together a winning team—would slip through your fingers as surely as a muddy football. Without organization and discipline, success could not be sustained. It was, in essence, no different from his experiences as hangar deck officer on the USS *Enterprise*. Without organization, without training, without discipline, coaching football was like launching airplanes under the same conditions—a haphazard and risky undertaking.

Great coaches come up through great programs—*that* Wilkinson knew. He also knew Oklahoma had seen that kind of program in action and seemed to like the results. Biff Jones, an Army captain with blue ribbon coaching credentials, had brought the fundamentals of modern football to OU in the mid-1930s to rescue the program from years of stagnation. Tom Stidham and Snorter Luster continued the quest for football success that Jones had initiated, but except for Stidham's 1938 team, which had played in the 1939 Orange Bowl, none of their teams had achieved recognition outside the borders of the Big Six Conference.

Tatum and Wilkinson had changed that. In one year, they had brought OU more national recognition than it had enjoyed ever before. Yes, Wilkinson thought, Oklahoma was a school ready for winning football and aware of the steps necessary to reach that goal.

Negatives? Wilkinson could think of only one. His own age. At thirty, was he really ready to take control of an entire football program? Recruit players? Hire coaches—and fire them, if necessary? Organize practices? Motivate players? Satisfy the expectations of the administration, faculty, regents, alumni, and the press? Might he be better off to follow Tatum to Maryland, ingrain himself further in the techniques needed to create a winning football program, and then be selected as a head coach in three or four years? Perhaps even as heir to Bierman's throne at Minnesota?

And then there was the matter of being a coach at all. For years, Wilkinson's father had been after him to give up this football foolishness and get a real job.

"No matter how able or successful he may be, every coach eventually reaches a point where a lot of people want somebody else," his father would warn him.

Maybe his father was right that football coaching was really a knockabout profession, if profession was even the right word. Several times since he finished college, Wilkinson had worked for brief periods at Wilkinson Home Finance to please his father, but he had never been satisfied. Without a doubt, he could become a prosperous mortgage banker, but that prospect did not excite him. After all, had he spent his spare moments on the *Enterprise* talking about the future of the mortgage banking business? No, he had spent it talking football and diagramming Split T plays on scraps of paper. That was what he loved.

Lying in the darkness, Wilkinson made his decision. If Tatum did leave Oklahoma, he would stay and become the head coach at Oklahoma. Success was far from assured, but if he wanted to be a football coach, it was time he learned how good he really was.

Once Wilkinson returned to Norman from the AFCA convention, events moved swiftly. If Tatum had been interested in Maryland's overtures before the Gator Bowl, he became even more captivated when George Cross discovered the missing $6,000. Technically, the money was not missing. It had been spent by the athletic department, but the reason for the expenditure was unaccounted for in the department's records. The oversight concerned Cross. The freestanding athletic department, never the model of accounting decorum, had become even more freewheeling since Tatum's arrival. If the football program needs it, buy it. That was Big Jim's motto. And athletic director Jap Haskell, who did not insist on carefully kept records, had been either an ally or an unwitting victim of Tatum's dreams of glory.

Shortly after the team returned from the Gator Bowl trip, Cross happened to see Joe Golding, the Sooners' star halfback, walking on campus. Cross suspected that Tatum might have violated conference rules and used the $6,000 to buy gifts for the team. He hoped Golding could shed some light on the matter.

"Joe, how were the gifts to players handled at the Gator Bowl?" Cross asked. "Did all who made the trip receive presents or were they given only to those who actually played in the game?"

"President Cross, the squad voted on that," Golding said. "We voted that all who made the trip would be treated alike."

"What was the gift? Tatum talked about the possibility of shotguns or sets of golf clubs."

"We voted on that, too. We decided to take cash for our personal out-of-pocket expenses—$120 apiece."

The mystery was solved. Fifty players, $120 each. A total of $6,000. Cross called Tatum to his office to discuss the matter. The propriety of giving players "spending money" was questionable according to Big Six Conference rules, and such behavior could not be tolerated in the future, Cross told Tatum. The incident strengthened Tatum's resolve to leave Oklahoma. Any school that would quibble over $6,000 certainly did not have the same desire to win that he did.

By January 19, it was official. Tatum announced he was leaving OU to become the head coach of the University of Maryland. The same day, Oklahoma announced the appointment of Wilkinson as his successor. Wilkinson's only security was a four-year contract, which gave him time to bring one freshman class he recruited through its senior year of competition. Three months short of his thirty-first birthday, Wilkinson emerged from relative obscurity to meet his destiny.

Just as majestic oaks take decades to grow, coaching philosophies mature with time. Seldom consciously derived, they develop slowly until the moment a coach takes responsibility for an entire football program. Only then, when his values become the standards for others to follow, must a coach be able to articulate his beliefs clearly. Even before accepting the job, Wilkinson had crystallized his core philosophy in his own mind. To be successful, a football team must have discipline, preferably self-discipline. Everything else follows from that. Add organization, conditioning, morale, and instruction. Those were the essential elements. All the rest is window dressing.

One coach who influenced Wilkinson's thinking was one he had never even seen on a football field—Red Sanders. After the end of World War II, Wilkinson had been transferred from the *Enterprise* to the staff of the Naval Air Training Command at Pensacola, Florida. There he found Sanders, who had been the head coach at Vanderbilt before the war. Technically, their assignment was a misnomer. With the war over, there was no naval air training, so Wilkinson and Sanders filled each day talking football and playing golf. From Sanders, Wilkinson absorbed much, not the least of which was Sanders's recommended reading list for aspiring coaches.

"If you want to be a football coach, read Machiavelli," Sanders suggested.

From the base library, Wilkinson checked out *The Prince*, a classic of Western civilization Wilkinson remembered from his college studies. Written in the sixteenth century by a political theorist named Niccolo Machiavelli, *The Prince* outlined Machiavelli's principles for governing successfully: Armies must be kept disciplined and well supplied. The people respond more rapidly to humanity and gentleness than to cruelty. A ruler is better served to be feared than loved. As Wilkinson read, he came to understand Sanders's wisdom. *The Prince* was a political textbook. And as Wilkinson already knew, there was no shortage of politics surrounding a college football program.

Also on Sanders's reading list was *The Art of War*, written about 300 B.C. by a Chinese general named Sun Tzu. Similar to Machiavelli's book, Sun Tzu's was not about football, but his discussions of military tactics were just as germane: Soldiers who are not accustomed to rigorous drilling will be hesitant in battle. All warfare is based on deception. Pretend inferiority and encourage an enemy's arrogance. Keep the enemy under strain and wear him down. Invincibility lies in defense; the opportunity for victory in attacking. Attack where an enemy is unprepared. Here, Wilkinson thought, is the greatest football primer ever written. Football *is* warfare reduced to a rectangle 120 yards long and 53 1/3 yards wide.

With the fate of the Oklahoma football program now in his hands, Wilkinson's first priority was to find a line coach, and he wanted the best available. Without a doubt, the best line the Sooners faced during the 1946 season was Nebraska's, coached by a former All-American from Ohio State named Gomer Jones, who had coached at St. Mary's Pre-Flight during the war. Jones was a simple, straightforward man whose greatest joy was teaching the fundamentals of line play to young men who loved to block and tackle. As a lineman himself, Jones knew only too well that a personal sense of accomplishment and a pat on the back might be the only rewards a lineman would receive. The glory and headlines go to the backs.

At Ohio State, Jones excelled as a player before becoming an assistant coach at John Carroll and then a high school head coach in Martin's Ferry, Ohio. When the war came, he applied for duty in the Pre-Flight program. Unlike Wilkinson, who was only a coach, Jones played as well. As an "old" twenty-eight-year-old, Jones had to lose forty pounds to get back in shape to play, but with the war on and money scarce, Jones's wife would not let him buy new clothes after he lost the weight. She was afraid he would gain the weight back if he stopped playing, so Jones spent the summer of 1942 walking around in baggy pants cinched up by his belt.

After the war, Jones was offered a job as the line coach at Nebraska. The caliber of line play the Cornhuskers demonstrated against the Sooners was not lost on Wilkinson, who made a point to see Jones at the AFCA convention after the Gator Bowl. Shortly thereafter, when Wilkinson was finally named the Sooners' new head coach, he called Jones and arranged for them to meet in Kansas City. When Wilkinson described what he hoped to accomplish at Oklahoma, Jones was enthralled. Yes, he told Wilkinson, he would come to Oklahoma.

In addition to Jones, Wilkinson hired Dutch Fehring, another of Tatum's assistants in 1946, to form the nucleus of the new OU staff. In the spring, Wilkinson elevated Bill Jennings, a part-time assistant under Tatum, to full-time status and added Walter Hargesheimer (Wilkinson's former teammate at Minnesota) to complete his staff.

With the line in capable hands, Wilkinson began to consider how he would organize Oklahoma's offense. As Tatum's quarterback coach the fall before, Wilkinson taught Jack Mitchell and Darrell Royal the rudiments of the Split T, but he believed further refinement was needed. Wilkinson knew that defenses employed by college football teams were becoming increasingly sophisticated. Plays that had worked during the halcyon days of the single wing no longer were successful. You simply could not fool—or overpower—defenses the way you could during the 1930s. Against good teams, there simply were no weaknesses to be exploited. Defensive schemes—and players' abilities—matured so quickly that game plans used little more than a decade before would be doomed to failure.

Wilkinson analyzed the Split T as Faurot had designed it. A Split T offense could go to the left or right with equal facility, but biased, of course, by the fact that most quarterbacks—and hence, most teams—are right-handed. The halfbacks and fullback were runners or blockers, depending upon which particular play was called, and the quarterback was generally expected to be a passer and the dispatcher of the ball to the designated ball carrier. But why be limited to only three runners? Faurot had included a quarterback keeper and a quarterback option play in his original vision of the Split T, but Wilkinson believed those plays had never been exploited fully by Faurot. Why, Wilkinson asked himself, could you not make the quarterback—the man who gets the ball first and is closest to the line of scrimmage—a primary ball carrier, too? Thus, the quarterback option became a fundamental part of the Sooners' playbook, which was far from voluminous and did not need to be, Wilkinson believed. By repeating a small number of plays with precision and deception, a Split T offense could move the length of the field through a series of short but consistent gains. And if a team could maintain that kind of offensive pressure on the opposing defense long enough, it would eventually score.

A good offense, Wilkinson knew, would not be as essential as a good defense, however. If you keep the other team from scoring, the worst you can get is a tie. If he had to choose, Wilkinson would take a good defense and a good kicking game. If you have those, you can always gain field position and find a way to score enough to be victorious.

During spring practice in 1947 the Sooners learned for the first time how life would be playing for the tall, rangy Wilkinson and the short, rotund Jones, both pleasant perfectionists who demanded total dedication on the field but allowed the players considerable freedom away from it. Wilkinson was keenly aware that virtually all of the Sooners were war veterans eager to finish college so they could pursue their careers. The last thing they needed was childish harassment from coaches barely older than they. Wilkinson understood that, just as he understood that education was the reason they were at the university in the first place. They played football merely because they—like Wilkinson himself—loved the game.

In that regard, there seemed to be no one who enjoyed the game more than Jones. In addition to his knowledge of line play, Jones's most valuable contribution was his sense of humor. From the beginning, Jones entertained Wilkinson and the other members of the staff with his seemingly endless supply of humorous stories. Among the staff's favorites were his stories about Francis Schmidt, head coach at Ohio State when Jones played for the Buckeyes. One that amused the Sooner coaches most—particularly because it contrasted with the open atmosphere at Oklahoma—was the story of Schmidt's obsessive secrecy regarding The Playbook.

Fearful that his assistants would appropriate his plays, go to another school and use them against him, Schmidt never let his assistants see the book. The only way his players learned the plays was when he diagrammed them one at a time on the blackboard and told the players to memorize them. Schmidt was the only person allowed to see The Playbook, although one of the student managers was assigned to carry it around the practice field like an acolyte.

One afternoon as the Buckeyes were practicing a play they recently learned, an offensive guard pulled from his assigned spot and moved along the line of scrimmage to block the defensive end at the other end of the line. When he did, Schmidt charged out from the sideline.

"You idiot. You're not supposed to do that!" Schmidt screamed.

"Yes, I am, Coach. That's the way it's drawn up. I know I'm supposed to do it," the player said.

Schmidt summarily called for The Playbook, in which the plays were kept in no particular order. The manager knelt on the ground and flipped through the pages as quickly as he could to find the proper play.

"Coach, here it is!"

Schmidt and the player looked down at the play as diagrammed in The Playbook.

"See, Coach, I told you I was right!"

"Even the playbook's wrong!" Schmidt shouted and kicked the book.

The pages flew loose from the binder and began to fly all over the field. Schmidt, seeing the work of a lifetime blowing away, became hysterical.

"Quick," he screamed to the managers and the players. "Grab those pages! Don't let the coaches get those plays!"

Just as Jones's sense of humor masked his demanding nature on the practice field, his thick frame and slouched shoulders belied his remarkable physical quickness. More than a decade after his last college football game, Jones remained tremendously agile—a trait that enabled him to demonstrate the value of the techniques he insisted the Sooners use. What bothered Jones most was wasted motion.

"You must gain ground with every step," Jones preached to the Sooner linemen. "When you pull, take your first step in the direction you're going. Don't ever lift a foot and put it down in the same place. If you step wrong, you've lost two steps."

Among the first Sooners to receive the benefit of Jones's wisdom was Burris. Over the years, Burris had developed a stance that Jones believed was improper. Jones tried to correct Burris's stance, but the stubborn Burris resisted.

"Try it my way for two or three weeks," Jones said. "Then if you don't like it, we'll go back to your way."

Burris quickly found that by following Jones's suggestion, he had better lateral control, better balance, and more power straight ahead. The other Sooners knew Burris was slow to make new friends or change his habits in any way, so when Burris became one of Jones's early converts, it gave Jones immediate credibility with the other members of the team.

Another who was quick to appreciate Jones was Wade Walker, a tackle who had played at Jacksonville under Tatum. Walker achieved some degree of notoriety among the Sooners the year before by committing a minor faux pas when he first arrived in Norman. At the time, Tatum was staying at Jap Haskell's house until his belongings arrived. Walker drove to Norman from his home in Gastonia, North Carolina, pulled into Haskell's driveway, and went inside. There, Walker was introduced to the youthful-looking Wilkinson. He greeted Tatum's chief assistant in his friendliest southern manner.

"And what position do you play?" Walker asked Wilkinson.

What gave Walker further status among the other Sooners was that he was already proficient in the Split T before he arrived in Norman. After a season with Tatum in the navy, he knew more of the theory and application of Split T line play than did any of the other linemen. As it turned out, he also knew more than Jones, whose grounding was in the single wing. When Jones began to ask Walker questions about the Split T, Walker and the other Sooners gained tremendous respect for Jones. They knew few coaches so sure of themselves that they would ask a player how something was supposed to be done.

Before the Sooners ever took the field under Wilkinson, he was hit with a setback he had feared but hoped would not happen. Two of the Sooners chose to turn pro rather than stay at Oklahoma. What made the matter worse was who they were—Plato Andros and Joe Golding, the Sooners' most dangerous runner. Immediately, Wilkinson began to reassess the talent he had on hand, which was considerable even with the departure of Andros and Golding. In addition to Burris and Walker, the experienced linemen included John Rapacz, a former Marine who at six-foot-five was an imposing presence at center; Norman McNabb, who had played service football for two years; Homer Paine, who had played one year at Tulsa before going into the army; Stan West, a 230-pound guard whose forte was "playing soft" on defense before cutting down opposing ball carriers; tackle Jim Tyree, one of the few members of the 1945 Oklahoma team good enough to make Tatum's squad; and end Jim Owens, an adept pass receiver and devastating blocker. In the backfield, the Sooners were equally strong with quarterbacks Mitchell and Royal, as well as halfbacks Junior Thomas and George Brewer. With that lineup, Wilkinson believed the Sooners would be at least as good as they were under Tatum, if not better.

One of the decisions Wilkinson made early on was that his teams would fly to away games rather than riding the train. To begin with, there were no convenient rail connections between Norman and the locations of other Big Six schools. In addition, Wilkinson remembered what early aviation supporter Will Rogers said about flying: "If you value your time, you'll fly." Wilkinson believed it. He also understood that aviation was much safer than most Americans realized. As the hangar deck officer of the *Enterprise*, he had seen firsthand how skillful mechanics and attention to detail could keep aircraft flying without mechanical failure, and he had seen skilled pilots land planes that seemed to be falling apart in midair as they reached the carrier deck.

More important, Wilkinson knew from personal experience that the supposed safety of train travel was greatly exaggerated, and faith in that belief could cause monumental life changes. On an August afternoon in 1922 Wilkinson and his family—his brother Bill, his mother, her brother, and assorted cousins—were returning to Minneapolis from an outing in the lakes region of western Minnesota. The Soo Line train had just passed through Annandale with fifty miles to go before they were home. Suddenly, the train smashed into an oil delivery truck. The crash threw the oil truck against a switch that derailed several passenger cars, which then collided with the engine of a freight train. The baggage car was destroyed. The remnants of the smoking car caught fire. Behind the smoking car was the car carrying six-year-old Wilkinson and his family. All around him, the boy saw dying and injured passengers. Some were pinned in the wreckage. Yelling, screaming adults surrounded the boy. Smoke filled his lungs before he was dropped from the car into the arms of a bystander near the train.

In all, thirty-two people were killed in the crash, and the newspapers carried the names of those who were killed or injured. His mother was not listed, but her injuries required her to stay in the hospital for two days. In the following months, Edith Wilkinson became a semi-invalid. A year later, she was dead from heart and liver ailments related to the crash.

The train wreck was the beginning of a tortuous time for the young Wilkinson. A short time later, a child in the neighborhood was killed in a fire a few houses away from the Wilkinsons' home. The combined traumas affected Wilkinson deeply. He became afraid to go to sleep at night, and he drifted off only if his father held him in his arms before putting him in his bed. Wilkinson grieved for the loss of his mother and the family life he enjoyed before she died. Wilkinson expressed this feeling to his father, who tried to encourage his son while preparing him to face that life would not be the same again.

"Never look back. Always look forward," Wilkinson's father told him. It was a lesson Wilkinson would never forget.

For six years, Wilkinson lived as a motherless child, though his father tried to fulfill that role for his son. Then he married a woman named Ethel Grace, who was disciplined and proper, an American Mary Poppins. Shortly thereafter, Wilkinson's father sent him to Shattuck Military Academy, a military boarding school in Faribault, Minnesota. At Shattuck, Wilkinson succeeded academically and starred in five sports, yet he longed for the warm family relationships he knew while his mother was alive, and he missed his friends in south Minneapolis. He cried when he had to return each fall, but his father, a bulwark of discipline, told him to tough it out.

Disciplined. Precise. Demanding in a pleasant, reserved way. The Wilkinson persona was formed.

Wilkinson's first opponents as a head coach were Chuck Baer's Detroit Titans. Highly favored, the Sooners were still unsure of themselves—and Wilkinson shared some of their misgivings. The Titans had been practicing two weeks longer than the Sooners and had already played their first game. Wilkinson saw that as a handicap for the Sooners, but one that was unavoidable. Big Six rules did not allow conference teams to begin fall drills until August 30—and what the Big Six said was law. In the years immediately after World War II, the individual conferences were the most powerful forces in college football. The NCAA, at that time housed in a small room in the offices of the Big Ten, had not reached its elevated status. That would not occur for several more years when the advent of television changed the landscape of college football.

For weeks, the Sooners practiced under the hot September sun in Norman. Now, they were to play their first game for Wilkinson in the chilly Michigan night air. The crowd of twenty-five thousand was the third largest the Titans had ever drawn, and many of the spectators were bunched close to the field eight rows deep in folding chairs. If that were not enough, the game was to be broadcast locally by a Detroit television station. The whole affair took on a carnival atmosphere unlike anything Wilkinson or his players had ever seen.

Those factors were discomforting enough, but what increased the Sooners' uneasiness was taking the field for the first time under a coach they barely knew. Few of the players had gotten to know Wilkinson in 1946. He worked mostly with the quarterbacks and stayed largely in the background. Given Tatum's love of center stage, that was understandable—and unavoidable. The players found Wilkinson more enjoyable to play for than Tatum, whom they called The Dictator behind his back, but they had not seen how Wilkinson reacted under game conditions. Throughout the 1946 season Wilkinson installed himself in the press box high above the field. The Sooners never stood shoulder-to-shoulder with him.

As they prepared mentally for the game, some of the Sooners thought back to Tatum's outrageous behavior, which had been a source of amusement among the players. Tatum knew football, and he was not reluctant to let his players know it. Once, he even saw fit to instruct the team on the proper way to sit on the sidelines. Sometimes, as during the Sooners' season-opening loss to Army the year before, Tatum's behavior bordered on irrational. During the game, the Sooners' Charley Sarratt suffered a sprained ankle and was sitting on the Sooner bench with his foot in a bucket of ice water. Tatum walked by, picked Sarratt's foot up out of the bucket, lifted the bucket to his lips, and took a long drink.

After watching in disbelief, one of the Sooners informed Tatum what he had done.

"It's all right. He's one of ours," Tatum instructed the player.

While the Sooners were glad to be rid of Tatum and his histrionics, right now they would be reassuring. As it was, the Sooners could merely sit quietly in the locker room, waiting on benches along the wall for the game to start. Wilkinson and Jones sat together on a wooden bench on the other side of the dressing room. Almost as unsure as their players, they looked at the floor and said nothing.

As Wilkinson expected, the tension disappeared once the game began. After kicking off to Detroit, the Sooners held the Titans for three plays and forced a punt, which Mitchell returned to the OU 27. On the first two plays, Mitchell handed off to Royal, who gained 22 yards and a first down at the OU 49. Three times later in the drive, Mitchell ran or sneaked for key first downs. Finally, he scored on a quarterback keeper from the 2, and the Sooners took a 7–0 lead.

Five plays later, Detroit's Jack Kurkowski slammed through the middle of the Sooner defense and ran 56 yards to score. The Titan extra point was good, and the Sooners found themselves in a closer game than oddsmakers had anticipated.

Early in the second quarter, the Sooners kicked a 23-yard field goal to take a 10–7 lead, an advantage they held until the final minute of the first half, when

Detroit was forced to punt with thirty-five seconds remaining. The high kick sailed to the OU 40, where Mitchell took the ball. He ran laterally across the field, faked a handoff to Sarratt, and headed upfield. He dodged one Titan tackler and broke free of another. Other Titans, who heard a penalty horn on the play, ran downfield perfunctorily, showing little interest in pursuing Mitchell as he dashed down the sideline to the end zone. The Detroit players were right. There was a penalty, but against the Titans. The Sooners declined it and headed to the locker room with a 17–7 advantage.

Early in the third quarter, Mitchell pitched wildly, and the Titans recovered at the OU 41. They scored on the first play—another touchdown run of more than 50 yards—to cut the Sooners' lead to 4 points. Late in the quarter, the Sooners partially blocked a Detroit punt, took over at the Detroit 29, and scored in four plays to increase their lead to 24–13. Detroit added another touchdown late in the fourth quarter to cut the OU lead to 24–20, but the Sooners intercepted Detroit's last-second desperation pass in the Sooner end zone to preserve Wilkinson's first victory as a head coach.

After a come-from-behind 26–14 victory over Texas A&M, Wilkinson prepared his Sooners for the annual confrontation with Texas in the Cotton Bowl in Dallas. The Longhorns had beaten the Sooners for seven consecutive years, and with strong-armed Bobby Layne at quarterback, they were again considered the superior team. To combat Layne, Wilkinson and his assistants designed a ball-control game plan to keep the ball out of Layne's hands.

As a result, Wilkinson drove the Sooners through a rigorous week of Split T timing drills, especially the quarterback option play. The quarterback option Wilkinson taught his quarterbacks was the same as had been devised by Faurot. The quarterback would call the option play in the huddle. Once at the line of scrimmage, he would look over the defense. If the opponent was in a 6–2 defense with the ends boxed outside, the quarterback would keep the ball at the corner and cut upfield. If the defense was in a 5–3 formation, the quarterback would pitch to the trailing halfback. Technically, the play was an option, but the outcome was ordained before the quarterback ever started calling signals.

That is, until the week of the Texas game. In practice, the OU coaches switched the scout team defense between a six-man line and a five-man line to see how Mitchell and the offensive starters would respond. They never anticipated what took place. On every play—regardless of the defensive alignment—the scout team backed off the line of scrimmage, and each time Mitchell kept the ball and turned upfield.

Finally, Wilkinson stopped the drill.

"Jack, what happened? You're not pitching out when the defense alignment dictates it."

Mitchell's response was as simple as it was revolutionary.

"It's just like basketball, Coach," Mitchell said. "If you have a two-on-one fast break and the defender comes toward you, you pass it. If he doesn't, you keep it."

Immediately, Wilkinson realized Mitchell was right. Using Mitchell's method, the defense could never know whether Mitchell was going to keep or pitch because even he didn't know when the play started. Forget how Faurot originally designed the play. Mitchell had figured out a better way.

Against the Longhorns, Wilkinson's plan seemed to be working as halftime approached. The underdog Sooners were clinging to a 7–7 tie as time on the stadium clock expired with the Longhorns at the OU 3. Jubilantly, the inspired Sooners headed for the dressing room. Before they could leave the field, referee Jack Sisco stopped them. Texas, he said, had called a time out, but the clock operator had not stopped the clock in time. He awarded the Longhorns one more play from the OU 3, a decision that drew immediate ridicule from the Oklahoma section of the Cotton Bowl.

When order was restored, Texas came to the line of scrimmage. Layne handed off to Jim Canady, who was hit hard by the Sooner line and fumbled. The ball bounced backward to the Texas 6. Layne picked it up and lateraled to halfback Randall Clay, who raced through the confused Sooners. Touchdown Texas!

Texas kicked the extra point and headed to the dressing room with a tainted 14–7 lead.

Wilkinson and his assistants charged onto the field, arguing that Layne's knee touched the ground as he picked up the ball. The play should have been down at the 6, they argued. Game films would later show that Wilkinson was right, but Sisco ignored Wilkinson's protests and headed off the field, refusing to discuss the call.

The break seemed to invigorate the Longhorns, who had been outplayed by the Sooners in the first half. Midway through the third period, Texas scored again to take a 21–7 lead. Early in the fourth quarter, the Sooners stopped the Longhorns, and Tom Landry punted into the Sooner end zone. The touchback put the ball at the Sooner 20. On first down, Thomas broke through right tackle and picked up 8 yards before being hit. As Thomas was going down, he lateraled to Mitchell, who was trailing the play. Mitchell dashed past the Texas defenders and ran the remaining 72 yards untouched to score.

After the kickoff, Texas began a drive from its 16. At the Sooner 40, Layne dropped back to pass. Burris broke through the Texas line and hit Layne just as he threw the ball. Downfield, Royal intercepted the pass, and the excited Sooners prepared to go on offense. But Layne jumped up grinning at Burris. Sisco had thrown a flag for roughing the passer. The call enraged many Sooner fans. They sent pop bottles raining onto the field. Even the Sooner players feared for their safety and moved to the center of the field to escape the angry fusillade.

Like the disputed call at the end of the first half, the play was crucial. Instead of having the ball and a chance to tie the game, the Sooners were backed up to their 23. When Texas scored again to make it 28–14, the game was all but decided. Another Texas touchdown in the final minute only served to anger the Sooner fans further. When the game ended, they stormed onto the field to get Sisco. A Texas state highway patrol car came to Sisco's rescue, but it was pelted by pop bottles and stadium cushions as it carried Sisco and the other officials safely from the stadium. The Sisco incident embarrassed Wilkinson and proved to be the first in a series of events that threatened to send him to Minneapolis and the mortgage banking business sooner than he might have expected.

After the favored Sooners were tied, 13–13, by the Kansas Jayhawks, TCU coach Dutch Meyer used a 4–4 defense designed to stop OU's running game to upset the Sooners, 20–7. Wilkinson's Sooners now stood 2–2–1, but more important, they had lost two and tied one in their last three games. For two weeks in a row, they had been tied or beaten by teams that oddsmakers considered inferior to the Sooners. Sportswriters and fans alike began to wonder the same thing Wilkinson had asked himself on the train from Jacksonville. Was he really tough enough to be a head coach? But unlike the winter before, Wilkinson was now sure of the answer. He knew he could do the job. He only needed to make the right moves.

On the Monday following the TCU loss, Wilkinson broke with his normal practice routine. Instead of the light workout usually scheduled, Wilkinson drove the Sooners through a rough two-hour practice, the hardest they had experienced under him. He demoted several starting players and told the squad to elect captains to serve until the end of the season. They chose Tyree and Walker. The Sooners responded to Wilkinson's decisive moves, defeating Iowa State, 27–9, and Kansas State, 27–13, to set up a battle with Missouri. It would be Wilkinson versus Faurot, pupil versus master, for a share of the Big Six championship. On Friday night before the game, Wilkinson knew the future of his coaching career was still very much in doubt. A loss to the Tigers might mean the end.

As always, Missouri was impressive on offense. The running game was the third best in the nation, averaging 285 yards a game. In addition to three strong running backs, Faurot could count on an offensive weapon Wilkinson did not possess. Unlike the Sooners' Mitchell—a superb runner but a mediocre passer at best—Missouri quarterback Bus Entsminger was both a capable runner and a talented passer. To counteract the Tigers' advantage, Wilkinson devised a daring game plan. The Sooners would ignore Entsminger's passing and hope to stop Missouri on the ground by using a seven-man line and stationing linebackers in the handoff holes preferred by Missouri. The plan had one obvious weakness. It required flawless execution by Royal and the others in the defensive secondary.

As the game began, a chilly fog hung over Mizzou's Memorial Stadium. Through a scoreless first quarter, the tenor of the game was established. It would be a punting duel between Royal and Missouri's Bill Day. The Sooners stopped the Tigers on their first series, and Day punted 49 yards into the wind. The Sooners could not move either, and Royal answered with a 67-yard punt that forced Missouri deep into its own territory. The Sooners immediately recovered a wild pitchout by Entsminger but were unable to score and gave the ball up on downs.

The gambling defense arrayed by Wilkinson continued to stifle the Tiger running attack, forcing Day to punt again. The punt was fielded by Brewer at the OU 30, where he dashed laterally across the field, crossed in front of Mitchell, and faked a handoff to him. The Tigers converged on Mitchell, and Brewer raced 70 yards to score. Now trailing and unable to move on the ground, Missouri took to the air. Entsminger threw one touchdown pass and completed another key throw to set up a second Tiger touchdown. Missouri missed both extra points, leaving the Tigers with a 12–7 lead at halftime.

Neither team scored in the third quarter, but on the second play of the final period, Royal dropped a punt out-of-bounds at the Tigers' 1. The Sooners stopped one running play, and Faurot elected to have his team kick out of danger on second down. OU got the ball in MU territory but could not move. Again, Royal lifted a punt high into the leaden gray sky, driving it out-of-bounds on the Tiger 4.

With the Tigers trapped deep in their own territory, the Sooners pressed on defense. On first down, Entsminger handed off to one of his halfbacks, but the Sooners' Frankie Anderson, a substitute guard playing in his first college game, slammed into him, knocked the ball loose, and the Sooners recovered. In two running plays, the Sooners moved to the Missouri 2. In the Sooner huddle on third down, Mitchell called a quarterback sneak. At the line of scrimmage, he saw the Missouri tackle edging toward the center of the line. Mitchell quickly called an audible, changing the play to an end run by Brewer. Brewer swept outside the Tiger defense to score, and OU led, 14–12.

After the kickoff, Entsminger went to the air again, moving the Tigers to the Oklahoma 20 before a jarring tackle by linebacker Myrle Greathouse jarred the ball loose from the Missouri receiver. The Sooners recovered. With time running out, Missouri began to gamble on defense. Shooting the gaps in the Oklahoma line on every play, they tried to destroy the Sooners' timing, but the Sooners moved to two first downs, taking time off the clock as they did so. At midfield, the drive seemed stalled on third-and-8. Mitchell called a 22, a handoff to Brewer over right guard.

At the line of scrimmage, Mitchell saw the Mizzou tackle and linebacker move into the hole where Brewer was to run. In a split second, Mitchell decided he would fake to Brewer and keep the ball himself. Brewer stood no chance of making the first down. Perhaps he might. The ball was snapped. Mitchell moved to his right and extended his left hand to fake to Brewer while keeping the ball tucked carefully behind his right hip. Brewer hit the hole at full speed, and following Split T form, did not look down to see the handoff. He slammed into the line and was covered by the Missouri defense. At the bottom of the pile, Brewer came to a painful realization. He did not have the ball!

As the bodies unpiled, Brewer heard the roar of the crowd and sensed that all the other players were looking downfield. He instinctively followed their gaze and saw Mitchell racing down the right sideline—with the ball. Mitchell was stopped short of the end zone, but two plays later, he scored the third OU touchdown, clinching the Sooners' 21–12 victory.

In years to come, Wilkinson would regard Royal's final two punts and Anderson's tackle as the most critical plays in his coaching career. Without them, it is doubtful he would have spent a second season at OU.

The following week, the Sooners clinched a tie for the Big Six championship by beating Nebraska before preparing to meet Oklahoma A&M in the final game of the season. Aggie coach Jim Lookabaugh was so determined to avenge OU's 73–12 victory the year before that he and four assistants drove to Lincoln to scout the Sooners against Nebraska. What he learned proved insufficient to stop the resurgent Sooners, who beat their cross-state rivals, 21–13, to finish Wilkinson's first season 7–2–1. They were ranked sixteenth in the nation in the final Associated Press poll, but voted not to accept a bowl invitation.

Wilkinson could not know it then, but 1947 would be the last season in which a 7–2–1 record would be considered a good year at Oklahoma.

1948

One year after he became the coach at Oklahoma, Bud Wilkinson came close to leaving. If Oklahoma fans did not appreciate the job he did in 1947—and some did not—then Wilkinson was uncertain whether OU was a place he should plan to stay. He was offered a new contract and a raise by the university, but his ties to Norman were not yet deeply rooted. At the same time, the U.S. Naval Academy was, for the first time in its history, in search of a coach who was not an active duty naval officer. As a result, athletic director Tom Hamilton called Wilkinson in January to talk about Wilkinson's replacing him as the coach of the Midshipmen. Wilkinson was interested.

Wilkinson liked Hamilton, but he knew he could never truly replace him. Hamilton was a Navy legend. As a football player at the Academy, Hamilton led the Midshipmen to the national championship in 1926, when the ten-year-old Wilkinson read about Hamilton's exploits in the *Minneapolis Tribune*. With Hamilton leading the way, the Midshipmen rolled to a 9–0–1 record, the only blemish being a 21–21 tie with Army in which Navy came from behind and Hamilton drop-kicked an extra point to tie the game with thirty seconds left.

That was just the beginning for Hamilton. After being named to the All-America football team, he served two years on navy surface ships, became a navy pilot, and fought with distinction in World War II on the USS *Enterprise*. Hamilton was Frank Merriwell incarnate.

The pinnacle of Hamilton's career arguably came at the start of the war when he developed the navy's Pre-Flight program. The navy had initiated the V-5 pilot training program in the mid-1930s with an average of seven hundred pilots per year earning their wings. After the Japanese attack on Pearl Harbor, however, the training of navy pilots became a priority. Hamilton, then a lieutenant commander, was named the head of the V-5 physical training division.

The situation, as Hamilton saw it, was dire. American males had become soft and undisciplined during the two decades of peace since World War I. Now, with war on the horizon against Germany and Japan, Americans needed to be prepared physically and mentally to face Axis pilots who had been training for war for years.

Hamilton's assignment had nothing to do with actual flight training itself. His Pre-Flight program was twelve weeks of preparation before flight school. The cadets would spend each morning on infantry drill and academic classes. The rest of the day was filled with ninety minutes of running, wood chopping, or calisthenics; ninety minutes of instruction in team sports, boxing, or wrestling; and two hours of intramural or varsity team sports.

To Hamilton and others, "team sports" meant football—an explosive, violent game that requires teamwork, courage, reflex behavior, and the ability to concentrate on an assignment under pressure. Football was also the sport seen as closest to actual warfare, which was a critical component of the equation. The ultimate goal of the Pre-Flight program was to teach cadets that there was no substitute for victory in life-and-death wartime confrontations in which there were no rules. Beyond that, the navy did not want to invest the $250,000 it took to train a combat pilot if he had not demonstrated fierce competitiveness.

There were some in the navy who saw the same need Hamilton had identified, but they were disdainful of Hamilton's belief that a war could be won with games. One of the loudest critics was Gene Tunney (the former world heavyweight champion), a Marine private in World War I and now the navy's director of physical training. Tunney believed the way to develop what he called "the warrior psychology" was individual strength training and calisthenics.

Hamilton and his allies believed Tunney's vision was shortsighted. It would be fine if you are training boxers—or gladiators—but World War II would be a mechanized war in which the need for communication and coordination was pivotal.

The navy's top brass decided there was enough value in Hamilton's plan with its emphasis on developing ruthless, determined combat pilots that it established Pre-Flight facilities at the universities of Iowa, North Carolina, and Georgia, and at St. Mary's College in California. By the end of 1942 the Pre-Flight program had prepared ten thousand cadets for navy flight school, twice as many as the total for the previous eight years. Included in that number were a skinny eighteen-year-old from Connecticut named George Bush and a twenty-year-old from Ohio named John Glenn.

Hamilton's Pre-Flight program proved a success, preparing thousands of American naval pilots who turned the tide of the war in the Pacific. But the navy Pre-Flight program had one unintended consequence. It became the crucible that caused the democratization of football coaching knowledge. Coaching principles that had been the possession of a few successful high priests came into the hands of young coaches throughout the country.

Even as a young coach, Wilkinson realized that his participation in the Pre-Flight program dramatically altered the trajectory of his career. Had he not been part of the Pre-Flight program—or had he been assigned to one of the Pre-Flight locations using a traditional offense and had never learned the Split T from Faurot—he (and Tatum as well) would not have been in such demand after the war. And the experience of conducting highly organized, rigidly timed practices imbued Wilkinson's own coaching style with the traits that would eventually influence his success at Oklahoma.

Yes, Wilkinson believed, he and Hamilton were brothers under the skin, and the two could work together successfully at the Naval Academy. Both had been All-Americans in college. Both had served on the same ship, the USS *Enterprise*. Hamilton was the flight deck officer during the heart of World War II, when the Big E was engaged at the Battle of Saipan and the Battle of Leyte Gulf. Later, Wilkinson was the hangar deck officer at the end of the war during the Iwo Jima invasion when the *Enterprise* had to withstand furious kamikaze attacks. At one point in the conflict, the crew of the *Enterprise* stayed at battle stations for a full week, launching and recovering aircraft for 174 straight hours.

For his part, Hamilton fully appreciated the vagaries of coaching, having served as the Naval Academy's football coach on two occasions. He was the Navy coach when Wilkinson was an undergrad at Minnesota. Over three seasons, Hamilton's teams went 19–8 before he returned to the fleet. Hamilton became the head coach a second time in 1946, when archrival Army was considered the best team in the nation. During that season, Hamilton's team entered the Army-Navy game with a record of 1–7 after losing seven straight games. Army, with Doc Blanchard and Glenn Davis, was 8–0–1. Army led, 21–6, at halftime, but Hamilton's impassioned locker room speech rallied the Midshipmen, who fought back and trailed Army only 21–18 as the game was drawing to a close. With the ball at the Army 3, the Midshipmen tried three times to run for the winning touchdown. Each time, they were stopped short. Then time ran out.

Hamilton could have chosen on any one of those plays to try a potentially game-tying field goal, but he did not. After the game, he was hounded by sportswriters wanting to know why he hadn't gone for the tie against a team that had not lost in three years. Hamilton's answer became the stuff of football legend: "A tie," he said, "is like kissing your sister."

In 1947 the Midshipmen compiled a 1–7–1 record and were outscored by their opponents, 165 to 86. After the season, Hamilton chose to retire from active duty to become the Naval Academy's athletic director. Wilkinson—with a military school and navy background and a successful first season at Oklahoma—was the young coach Hamilton wanted to lead the fortunes of his beloved Midshipmen.

The search for a new coach was a major step for the Academy. In the history of the Naval Academy, the football coach had always been an active duty naval officer, but Hamilton and the Academy had seen the handwriting on the wall. They knew the next football coach had to be a man whose chosen profession was coaching, not a line officer who was serving a three-year tour of duty as part of a military-oriented career. And even Hamilton, perhaps the finest player Navy had yet produced, had not been able to overcome that difficulty.

Wilkinson flew to Annapolis and was given a tour of the Academy. He liked everything he saw. Especially, he liked the atmosphere and the spirit of the Academy. In all of America, Wilkinson believed, perhaps only Notre Dame had team spirit equal to the service academies. Next to discipline, spirit was the quality Wilkinson most prized, and the service academies had both in abundance.

Through his friendly discussions with Hamilton and interviews with the officers in charge of lower levels of administration, Wilkinson sensed that he was creating a favorable impression. He began to consider the idea of coming to Annapolis seriously. When Wilkinson was taken to visit the commandant, there remained only one major issue to be discussed.

Diplomatically, Wilkinson addressed it. At Army, Red Blaik had the privilege of handpicking fifty of the two thousand new cadets each year. Would he have the same freedom at Navy?

No, Wilkinson was told. Such a policy was not possible.

The answer to the question effectively ended Wilkinson's interest in leaving Oklahoma for the Naval Academy. As long as that policy remained in place, he could not see being the coach at Navy as an opportunity—opportunity in the coaching profession, after all, being a question of who is on your schedule and how many games you can win. At Navy, it was a one-game schedule, and the chances of winning were not good.

Back in Norman, Wilkinson turned his attention to the aspect of coaching that attracted him the least—recruiting. If Wilkinson had his way, football teams would be assembled the way they were when he played at Minnesota in the 1930s. Any student who was interested could try out. Those who were good enough—or persistent enough—would stay on, and it was the coaches' job to mold them into a team. However, Wilkinson realized that attitude was not realistic. Other than the dispersion of coaching knowledge that occurred with the navy's Pre-Flight program, the organized recruiting of players was the most important change in college football since Wilkinson's days as an undergrad. Understanding the need to recruit actively, Wilkinson established a plan for obtaining the best athletes from what he considered Oklahoma's natural recruiting area. It was bounded by the Kansas border on the north and Dallas on the south. It covered the state of Oklahoma and those areas of Texas that were closer to Norman than to Austin.

In those areas, Wilkinson relied upon a loose network of former OU players and alumni—as well as OU fans—to send him letters informing him of the best players in the area. If a high school player sounded promising enough, Wilkinson would send one of his assistants to check on the prospect. If a high school player seemed capable of playing football at the major college level and his grades and character were good, he would be offered a scholarship to OU. The system seemed simple enough. The problem was the same as it had always been. There was time enough to coach only a limited number of players. How did you make sure you were getting the best ones?

Actually, Wilkinson knew, separating the wheat from the chaff is easy once all the players are assembled on the same field. The difficulty lay in assessing the ability of a high school player in isolation from the rest, when the caliber of competition a player faced was very much open to question. Then there was the second nagging doubt. Is the player who is a star in high school as good as he is ever going to be—or will he mature into a truly fine college player? The latter was the question that made coaches turn gray. And for better or worse, Wilkinson had to follow in the footsteps of the best judge of talent he ever saw. Jim Tatum. Big Jim never seemed to be wrong.

Wilkinson was blessed with a legacy of talented players he had inherited from Tatum, many of whom had two more years of eligibility left, but then they would be gone. To scout for new talent, Wilkinson selected two men who had been football stars at Oklahoma before he arrived. The first was Bill Jennings. The second was Frank “Pop” Ivy, who had just finished a career in pro football with the Chicago Cardinals (and whose nickname was derived from his prematurely receding hairline). Jennings and Ivy had been teammates on the Oklahoma team that won the Big Six championship in 1938. Unlike Wilkinson, who had a Big Ten background, Jennings and Ivy grew up in Oklahoma and were familiar with the geography and culture of the Southwest. If anyone could find OU’s future stars, it would be Jennings and Ivy.

Already, Jennings had experienced success. In 1947 he came back from Hollis, Oklahoma—Darrell Royal’s hometown—with two exceptional recruits. One was a lineman named J. W. Cole. The other was a big, fast fullback named Leon Heath. By the spring of 1948 Ivy had yet to prove himself. Wilkinson assigned Ivy western Oklahoma and the Texas Panhandle as his recruiting territory and handed him a list of potential prospects and a map. In White Deer, Texas, a small town about forty miles northeast of Amarillo, Ivy uncovered a young six-foot-four giant named Jim Weatherall.

Weatherall grew up near Oklahoma City but played high school football in White Deer. He had wanted to attend Oklahoma A&M, but Aggies coach Jim Lookabaugh never contacted Weatherall after his campus visit. Disheartened, Weatherall decided he would go to Texas. Then, Ivy arrived at his door. New to recruiting, Ivy was straightforward with Weatherall.

“Jim, I’m just as scared as you are,” Ivy told Weatherall. “You’re the first guy I ever tried to recruit.”

Taken by Ivy’s sincerity, Weatherall agreed to visit OU. When he did, Wilkinson and Jones saw the potential that Lookabaugh had missed. Shortly thereafter, they and Ivy paid a return visit to Weatherall’s home in White Deer, and Weatherall chose to cast his lot with the Sooners.

For a young coach, it was an embarrassment of riches. Not only did Wilkinson have Jack Mitchell, a better runner than any other T-formation quarterback in history, he also had Royal, as complete a football player as Wilkinson had ever seen. Yet Wilkinson continually wrestled with what position would be best for each to play. Had he used them most effectively the year before? Was there a way to make them even better?

Mitchell was blessed with such a forceful personality that he had been dubbed “General Jack” by an Oklahoma City sportswriter, and the nickname stuck. At 175 pounds, Mitchell was a marvelous athlete. When he finished high school in Arkansas City, Kansas, he was offered a full basketball scholarship to Kansas State and a half scholarship to play for Phog Allen at Kansas. But Mitchell wanted to play football. At the time, Texas was one of the few schools recruiting nationally, and the Longhorns offered him a scholarship. After a celebrated freshman year with the Longhorns, Mitchell went into the service.

When the war ended, some of Mitchell's relatives told the OU staff about his exploits, and Tatum—never one to miss a recruiting opportunity—was on hand to meet Mitchell's train at the Arkansas City depot when he arrived. Mitchell told Tatum that he intended to return to Texas, but he agreed to attend one of Tatum's tryout camps during the summer of 1946, knowing that if what he saw at Oklahoma didn't please him, he could always keep driving south to Austin. What was critical in Mitchell's mind was the nature of his own football abilities. Although a gifted runner, Mitchell was a poor passer. And the more he saw of Tatum's run-oriented Split T—and the more he thought about trying to compete with Bobby Layne at Texas—the more attractive OU became. Finally, he decided to stay.

Royal, on the other hand, had always wanted to be a Sooner. As a boy, Royal waited expectantly for each autumn Saturday. He would bring the family radio out on the front porch, turn on the OU football game, and play imaginary football games in the front yard. The play-by-play of the actual game was of little interest, but Royal would respond instantly whenever the OU band played Boomer Sooner, leaping fire hydrants and dodging trees with added vigor. During the week, he practiced passing by throwing the *Daily Oklahoman* onto neighbors' porches. He also delivered the coming attractions circular for the local theater, receiving no money but instead a free admission. For Royal, it was just as good as money. Without it, he could not have afforded the dime it cost to go to the movies.

After Royal finished junior high, his father gave up trying to eke out a living in Hollis and moved the family to Porterville, California. Royal went with them, but he soon became homesick for Hollis, especially after he was told by the Porterville football coach that he was too small to play varsity football. At the same time, an assistant coach at Hollis High School wrote Royal a letter inviting him to come back to Hollis to play football. In addition, the coach promised him a job, lunch every day, and a place to stay. With thirteen dollars his father gave him, Royal hitchhiked back to Hollis.

During Royal's senior year in high school, an Oklahoma coach came recruiting for the Sooners, and Royal's childhood dream seemed about to come true. Then World War II intervened. Royal spent three years in the Army Air Corps, where he did not play football at all for two years. Finally, in 1945 he became the only player without college or professional experience to make the Third Air Force squad, where he learned the fine points of playing defensive back from former Tennessee star Bob Andridge.

When the war ended, Royal might have gone to Tennessee, but the Volunteers' coaching staff believed he was too old and did not want to invest time and effort in a twenty-two-year-old with a wife and two children. Tatum and Wilkinson had no such reservations and could not believe the shortsightedness of the Tennessee staff. On offense, Royal was a true triple threat—able to run, pass, and kick with exceptional skill. On defense, he was a superb pass defender, sure tackler, and elusive punt returner.

As successful as Royal was on the football field, his life off of it was far from easy. Although many of the war veterans were married, the Royals were one of the few couples with children, which worked an additional hardship. With Edith Royal needed at home to take care of the children, Royal worked at the campus pool hall racking balls for two dollars a week. Through their first two years in Norman, the Royals managed a meager existence in married student housing.

By 1948 their lot had improved. They moved into a converted garage apartment. Crowded into the small apartment were the Royals, their two children, and a nonpaying roomer named Otto Burgett. Burgett was a friend of Royal's from Hollis, who slept in a double bed with the Royal's oldest child. Burgett taught Royal to play chess, and Royal—fascinated with the strategic complexities of the game—attacked it with the same competitive fervor he brought to bridge games with Wade Walker and his wife or handball matches with Wilkinson. It was a hectic existence, but one that Royal relished as only a young man who has cheated certain death can.

Four days before Christmas in 1946 Royal had left Edith and the children in Norman while he drove back home to Hollis to visit his grandparents before the Sooners left to play in the Gator Bowl. Exhausted and alone, Royal went to sleep driving seventy miles per hour along U.S. 62. His car skidded off the road, flew over an embankment, and crashed head-on into a tree. Miraculously, Royal was thrown from the car and was not seriously hurt, but within hours his bruised muscles were so sore he could barely lift the phone to his face to call Tatum and explain what had happened.

"Well, get on back here for X-rays and treatment," Tatum told him. "You won't be able to play in the game, but you might as well count on making the trip because it may be the only chance you'll ever have to see a bowl game."

At Tatum's insistence, Royal flew with the Sooners to Jacksonville, where he lounged in the sun while the Sooners tried to regain their timing from a month-long layoff. A couple of days before the game, Tatum came to Royal and asked him to punt in the game. Royal said he would. The next day, Tatum came with another request.

"Darrell, we need you to play defense for us," he said. "You don't have to tackle anybody, but we need you for pass defense. You gonna be ready to go?"

Royal could hardly believe it. He thought Tatum must be kidding.

"No, I don't think I'm ready," Royal said.

"Come on, Darrell, you gotta gut it and go!"

The next day, Royal played the entire game, even making one tackle as the Sooners beat the Wolfpack, 34–13. By the end of the game, he felt better than he had since the accident.

As a souvenir of the game, each of the Sooners was given a small, alligator-shaped tie clasp. Royal, unable to afford jewelry for his wife, took the clasp to a jeweler and had it made into a bracelet for her. Edith cherished the gift, not so much because of its intrinsic value, but as a constant reminder of how close she had come to losing Darrell.

In 1947 Mitchell became the first quarterback ever to lead the Big Six in rushing. He was not large, but he had learned from playing basketball how to fake out a defender without losing momentum. In addition, he could cut upfield swiftly on the option play because he dug his heel—not his toe—into the turf, enabling him to cut at nearly a ninety-degree angle. With Mitchell performing superbly at quarterback, Wilkinson had been able to use Royal's talents as a defensive back and at left halfback, where he was a capable runner and accurate passer. By the fall of 1948 Wilkinson was concerned that other teams would begin to defense the Sooners' running attack more successfully. His solution was to move Mitchell to fullback and install Royal as the quarterback, where his superior passing ability might prove critical.

Wilkinson also needed to identify the abilities of the rest of his team, so, as he had during his first season as head coach, he turned to drills he had developed in 1946 to overcome the player assessment problem experienced during Tatum's tryouts. The problem during those tryouts was that there were so many participants and so little time. How could you tell who was really tough enough to play big-time college football? To identify those who could, Wilkinson devised his one-on-one drill (which in years to come would become known as the Oklahoma Drill). In it, a blocker and a tackler would take their positions face-to-face in a narrow space between blocking dummies laid on the ground about three yards apart. On the snap count, a running back carrying a football would try to run through the three-yard "hole." The genius of the drill was its simplicity. Could the blocker successfully move the defender aside, or would the defender shed the blocker and tackle the runner? Unlike a situation where there were seven linemen arrayed across the line of scrimmage, this was hand-to-hand combat where the victor was clear. There was no relying on a teammate. Everyone—coaches and other players—could see who won. It taught toughness, technique, and tenacity. A player's weaknesses were exposed quickly. And those who could not—or would not—hit hard were eliminated from consideration.

The one-on-one drill focused primarily on a player's ability to block or tackle, but Wilkinson devised a second drill to teach proper technique to running backs. In the Split T, the emphasis is on speed and quickness. While a lineman holds a hole open, the running back takes a handoff from the quarterback and slips through the hole quickly. The runner is to charge through the hole with his head up and his eyes on the field ahead of him. He is not to look down at the ball. It is the quarterback's responsibility to lay the ball into hands and arms of the running back. In Wilkinson's drill, the running back was to take a handoff and head straight toward a blocking dummy, where Wilkinson was stationed behind it. Suddenly, Wilkinson would step out on one side of the dummy, and the runner was to cut to the opposite side. As a result, Wilkinson could see how quick his running backs were and which were running with their heads up, as they were supposed to do.

Wilkinson made one other change prior to the 1948 season. With the help of the university building and grounds department, he created a sign that was to be hung above the door where each player could see it as he headed out of the locker room. In red lettering on a white background, the sign read simply:

PLAY LIKE A
CHAMPION
TODAY

Each time a player left the locker room, he was expected to slap the sign. By doing so, he would commit to giving his best in a game—or in practice drills. The sign summarized Wilkinson's belief that championship teams are built one day at a time and that effort expended in practice would translate to excellence during a game.

The Sooners opened the 1948 season against Santa Clara, a formidable football power coached by Len Casanova. With Royal at quarterback, the Sooners jumped to a 10–0 lead, but soon the Broncos cut the lead to 10–7, and the Sooner offense started to falter. Wilkinson quickly moved Mitchell back to quarterback. On the first play, Mitchell called for Junior Thomas to hit the right side of the line behind Buddy Burris. When the Santa Clara linebacker took a step inside, Mitchell checked signals, shifting the play to the spot off tackle that the linebacker had left open. Thomas burst through the open hole and outran the Santa Clara secondary to score. Leading at the half, 17–7, the Sooners seemed in control. One touchdown early in the third quarter was all the Sooners needed to deliver the knockout punch—an ability Wilkinson regarded as the mark of a champion. But the Sooners could not put the Broncos away. Instead, Santa Clara scored twice to win, 20–17.

After the game, Wilkinson sought solace in a corner of the Sooners' locker room. Curt Gowdy, who handled radio broadcasts for the Sooners, came into the locker room to console Wilkinson after the loss. Gowdy found Wilkinson alone at the end of a bench with his head in his hands. Gowdy could see Wilkinson had tears in his eyes, and he placed his arm on the young coach's shoulders.

"That was a tough one," Gowdy said.

"They are a good team, but we should have beaten them," Wilkinson said. "But I'll tell you what. We won't lose another game for three years."

Returning to Norman on the team plane, Wilkinson was perplexed. His players looked great the first ten minutes of the game, and he told them so, but they faded terribly in the second half. In addition, the Sooners' pass defense seemed more vulnerable than he liked. The next day, Wilkinson found solutions to both problems. He approached a slender sophomore named Buddy Jones and asked him to play safety to strengthen the team's porous pass defense. Jones was Wilkinson's type of player. A high school star at Maud and Holdenville, he returned from the service and was offered football scholarships by Tulsa and Oklahoma A&M, but not to OU. Jones wanted to be a petroleum geologist, so he came to OU anyway. Because Wilkinson believed the football team should be open to any student, just as it had been at Minnesota, he allowed Jones to try out as a 155-pound walk-on. That situation did not last long. Jones blocked and tackled with such intensity that Wilkinson gave him a scholarship. The problem was, there was no place for Jones to play on offense. With Thomas, George Brewer, and a talented sophomore named Lindell Pearson (who had transferred from Arkansas), Jones was doomed to the bench.

"Buddy, there's no way you can make our team on offense. I'd appreciate it if you'd concentrate on playing defensive safety," Wilkinson said.

Jones agreed. Wilkinson's first problem was solved.

Later that day, Wade Walker and Homer Paine, the two Sooner co-captains, came to Wilkinson's office in the field house with a solution to the other.

"Coach, if we looked good for ten minutes before we faded, why don't you play us for ten minutes and then put in a fresh line while we come out and rest. Then put us back in and we'll go twice as hard," they suggested.

The plan appealed to Wilkinson. He believed that a football player should be able to play both offense and defense, just as collegians had in his day. He also knew that a good player who is tired is not always a match for an average player who is fresh. He accepted the logic of Walker's and Paine's proposal, and Oklahoma's famed custom of alternating lines was born.

Now, only one decision remained. Who was going to play quarterback, Mitchell or Royal? Wilkinson was disappointed in his experiment with alternating quarterbacks. He realized the selection of one starting quarterback was essential if the Sooners were to become the team he believed they could be.

With the pass defense shored up by Buddy Jones and both alternating lines going full speed, the Sooners were impressive in their 42–14 victory over Texas A&M. However, the game did little to clarify in Wilkinson's mind the proper course regarding Mitchell and Royal. Against the Aggies, both looked sharp. As the annual grudge match with Texas approached, Wilkinson was certain a decision—regardless how painful—had to be made.

The only essential quality for a quarterback, Wilkinson believed, was leadership, and both Mitchell and Royal had the traits Wilkinson desired. Yet the qualities of leadership, Wilkinson knew, were delicate and difficult to maintain. A quarterback must have unquestioned authority without seeming to be dictatorial. If he is able to achieve this and his teammates believe in his ability to select the proper play, they will execute their assignments so well that their efficient execution will more than make up for a quarterback's lack of technical knowledge or athletic ability. That is why Wilkinson never corrected or criticized his quarterbacks in the presence of the rest of the team. Quarterbacks needed to be taught in isolation so their leadership authority would not be jeopardized.

To accomplish that, Wilkinson put in hours of face-to-face work alone with his quarterbacks. He would play an imaginary football game with them using photographic slides of various defensive formations. From his experience in the navy, Wilkinson knew how quickly men could learn to identify the silhouettes of various airplanes through repetitive aircraft recognition drills. Why, Wilkinson reasoned, couldn't the same principle be used to teach a quarterback to recognize various defensive formations, thus enabling him to call plays most likely to be effective against that defense?

With the help of university photographer Ned Hockman, Wilkinson made slides showing various defenses from ground level—as a quarterback would see them during a game. Wilkinson would sit down with a quarterback in his office, put a pad of paper between the two of them to represent a football field and make a mark on the paper at the 20. Then he would flash one of the defensive slides on the screen—for example, a wide-tackle six with three linebackers and two safeties.

The quarterback would then imagine himself standing over center just before he called the snap signals. He would look downfield at the safety and then scan forward toward the line of scrimmage to count the depth of the defense. In this case, the defense would be three layers deep. Next, he would look in front of his own center. If there was a man there, it was an odd-man line. If not, it was even. Then he would look to see if his ends were covered. Finally, he would tell Wilkinson the play he would call in such a situation. At first, it took a quarterback several seconds to analyze all the facets of the defense he needed to know—far too long to do in a game. But as he practiced, his comprehension speed would increase until noting those things became second nature.

Suppose, in this case, the quarterback called the fullback off tackle. Wilkinson would move the ball for a loss of 2 yards because the worst play to call against a wide-tackle six is the fullback off tackle. If the quarterback could not see why, Wilkinson would explain. After a quarterback made that and other mistakes a few times on paper, he was unlikely to make them in a game.

Wilkinson would go through an entire game with each of the varsity quarterbacks four or five times a week. By the time Saturday came around, Mitchell and Royal—and the quarterbacks who would succeed them—knew what play Wilkinson expected them to call under any circumstance. Wilkinson's concentrated drills were the reason OU quarterbacks rarely, if ever, called the wrong play. They might not call the very best play for the situation, but they would never call the wrong one. And if the play called in the huddle would not work against the defense the quarterback encountered at the line of scrimmage, a quick check signal enabled him to "audible" to another play. Soon, it became second nature. By the 1948 season Mitchell and Royal were using audibles more effectively than any other quarterbacks in America, college or pro.

Wilkinson's efforts to school his quarterbacks involved more than a love of gimmickry or a desire to convert a player to his offensive philosophy. He believed that a quarterback—in the game and properly trained—knew more about what was happening on the field than coaches on the sidelines or in the press box.

Wilkinson also knew that football players do not have time to decide intellectually what they are going to do. The time between plays is simply too short. And once the ball is snapped, football is nothing but reaction. However, before a play begins, a quarterback has eight to ten seconds to think ahead. Wilkinson also understood that a quarterback's situation is not like a lawyer or a doctor behind a desk. He is in a situation of high emotion and physical stress. He is breathing hard and may have been hit the play before, but Wilkinson knew the play selection drills would eventually create a semiautomatic reaction that would not fail him on the field.

As Wilkinson saw it, both Mitchell and Royal were intelligent and effective play callers. Royal had the additional advantage of being able to pass. The problem was that Royal simply could not run the quarterback option play. His execution was stiff and mechanical. Mitchell, on the other, seemed to have been born to run the option. He was fluid and decisive. The players had confidence in Mitchell, and he handled the Split T like a master. However, he was an ineffective passer. As Wilkinson and his staff considered the alternatives, the choice became clear. Wilkinson was committed to the Split T—primarily a rushing offense—so the Sooners would stick with Mitchell at quarterback. General Jack was the man who made it all work. They would find ways to use Royal's passing from left halfback as they had in 1947.

As the annual battle for Red River bragging rights drew closer, Wilkinson and his staff were increasingly confident of the Sooners' ability to end Texas's eight-game winning streak. Bobby Layne had graduated, and Wilkinson believed the Longhorns would not be able to withstand the Sooners' prolonged ground assault.

That Saturday, in front of seventy thousand fans in the Cotton Bowl—the largest crowd ever to see a football game in the Southwest—the Sooners sensed they had the upper hand. Led by linebacker Myrle Greathouse, the Sooner defenders swarmed over the Texas ball carriers and allowed only two first downs in the first half. By the third quarter, Mitchell and the Sooner offense had built a 14–0 lead, but Texas retaliated with a touchdown. The ensuing kickoff sailed into the end zone, and the Sooners took the ball at their own 20. On first down, Mitchell gained 6 on a quarterback sneak. Then Heath—starting his first game as a Sooner—broke through the middle of the Texas defense and rambled 68 yards to the Texas 12. On the next play, Thomas charged straight off tackle, then cut back to his left and scored. A missed extra point gave OU a 20–6 advantage.

On the ensuing kickoff, the Longhorns' Perry Samuels, a world-class sprinter, caught the ball at the Texas 15 and ran it back 65 yards before Royal dashed across the field to tackle him from behind at the OU 20. Three plays later, Longhorn fullback Tom Landry scored, and Texas fans sensed a ninth straight victory in the making.

After the Longhorn kickoff, the Sooners were unable to move on offense, and Royal punted. With a minute to play, Wilkinson and his assistants analyzed the situation. Texas was only 58 yards from the Sooner goal, and although Paul Campbell was not in Layne's class as a passer, he was capable. The Longhorns' best hope of victory was easy to see. They would give Campbell three chances to hit Samuels in the open and win the game. Oklahoma refused to let that happen. On first down, the Sooners forced an incompletion. On second down, they sacked Campbell for a 13-yard loss. With one chance left, Campbell threw as far as he could, but his pass was intercepted, cementing the Sooners' 20–14 victory.

The Sooners had finally beaten Texas! Sooner fans raced onto the field, tore down the goalposts, and paraded them around the floor of the Cotton Bowl. A new era had dawned.

The following week, the Sooners manhandled Kansas State, 42–0. The Sooners dominated the Wildcats in the windswept game in which Royal scored two touchdowns, passed for two others, and punted magnificently. The most electrifying play came on a punt return in the first quarter, however. Royal and Mitchell dropped back near the Sooner goal to field the Wildcat punt. While the punt was still in the air, Wilkinson could tell Mitchell was planning to field it rather than letting it bounce, which is what Wilkinson told the Sooners to do inside their own 10. The normally composed Wilkinson ran down the sidelines, waving his arms to get Mitchell's attention.

"Don't catch it! Don't catch it!" he yelled.

Mitchell caught the ball anyway.

After he made the catch, he crisscrossed with Royal and handed the ball to him. Immediately, Royal was open down the sideline with a fleet of blockers in front of him. As Royal dashed along the sideline, Wilkinson raced back upfield alongside him.

"Way to go! Way to go!" he cheered as Royal returned the kick 96 yards for a touchdown.

Because the Texas heat can be overpowering even in early fall, it was the habit of the Southwest Conference to play games at night until November. As a result, the Sooners were always at a disadvantage when they played a Southwest Conference team under artificial lights, as they were scheduled to do against TCU in Fort Worth. To compensate for this disadvantage, Wilkinson assigned Jennings and Hargesheimer to scout TCU diligently, enabling the Sooner coaching staff to develop a plan to counteract Dutch Meyer's 4–4 defense.

Wilkinson's plan was unconventional, but potentially highly effective. He stationed Heath, the Sooners' powerful fullback, outside the end as a flanker, giving the Sooners additional blocking muscle on sweeps. If Meyer responded by moving his linebacker outside, Mitchell could then slice the Horned Frog defense with inside handoffs to his halfbacks. Despite TCU's efforts to stifle the Sooners' running game—and the Sooners' five lost fumbles—the Sooners prevailed, 21–18.

That fall, the Sooner coaches began to hear reports about a remarkable athlete named Billy "Curly" Vessels playing for Cleveland High School. In one game, he scored five touchdowns on runs of 97, 93, 90, 76, and 3 yards while playing with his right wrist in a cast.

Gomer Jones went to Cleveland to scout Vessels firsthand. When he returned to Norman, the Sooner staff was eager to hear what he had learned, but the story Jones told was one Wilkinson and the other coaches could scarcely believe. They knew Jones enjoyed telling jokes, and as he related Vessels's life story, the other coaches kept expecting Jones to come to a punch line, nudge one of them slightly with his elbow, and walk back to his office chuckling to himself.

But there was no punch line. The story Jones related was all true.

Curly Vessels was born in Depression-ridden Cleveland in 1931, one of five children born to a father and mother who did little for him except endow him genetically with a magnificent body. As a young child, he ran unsupervised through the streets, but he was a gregarious, outgoing little boy, and the sound of his laughter was a symbol of hope to Cleveland's 2,500 residents.

With Vessels's family background being less than ideal, the townspeople devised a plan to help the little boy they loved. While he was in grade school, they introduced Vessels to sports. The high school wrestling coach devised a health chart for him to follow. The men who gathered at the barbershop timed him during his daily sprints and took him to see football games at Oklahoma A&M or Tulsa. Throughout grade school, he was the water boy at the Cleveland High games. During the summers, one of the local ministers took him fishing, and in return Vessels went to church on Wednesdays and Sundays. The people of Cleveland liked his boyish charm, but they were equally impressed by his extraordinary desire to rise above the circumstances of his birth.

When Vessels was a sophomore in high school, his parents moved from Cleveland to Oklahoma City, but Vessels wanted to escape the sordid home environment he had known and avoid the influence of his trouble-prone older brother. He chose to stay in the town he loved—and that loved him back. For the next two years, he lived with various families in Cleveland or by himself in his family's old house. Bud Newcum, a Cleveland druggist, gave Vessels a job in his drug store. There, Vessels ate his meals and frequently stayed for extended periods.

By the time he was a senior, Vessels was well known to college football recruiters. Tulane brought him to New Orleans for a week before Mardi Gras. Georgia, Kansas, SMU, Illinois, Baylor, Arkansas, and Oklahoma A&M all courted him. Despite the attention from these schools, Vessels had only one school at the top of his list—Oklahoma A&M. Bob Kurland, the Aggies' seven-foot basketball star, and Bob Fenimore, the football team's star tailback, were Vessels's idols. He routinely hitchhiked forty miles from Cleveland to Stillwater to serve as the Aggies' unofficial ball boy during basketball season, a position that enabled him to occupy a place on the bench next to A&M's revered coach, Henry Iba. Once, Vessels even spent the night in Kurland and Fenimore's dorm room when the weather was too frigid for him to hitchhike back to Cleveland.

That was the story, Jones told his colleagues. If they wanted to get Vessels to Oklahoma, they would have to find a way to persuade him that OU offered him something Oklahoma A&M could not. Otherwise, they would be spending long hours trying to devise ways to stop him on the football field.

After the Sooners defeated Iowa State, 33–6, they faced Missouri, which had stunned the nation by ending the sixteen-game winning streak of Doak Walker-led SMU in a 20–14 upset. The Tigers were not to be taken lightly. As a result, Wilkinson believed it was critical that the Sooners devise a play or formation the opposition would not expect. Coaching, Wilkinson had come to believe, was exactly what Iba had told him shortly after he became the head coach at Oklahoma. Iba's philosophy was as simple in concept as it was complex in execution. Coaching, Iba believed, should be viewed as nothing more than preparing players in practice to meet any conditions they might see during a game—and drilling them until they are able to recognize those conditions immediately and react automatically. Football, Wilkinson also knew, is a game of morale, and if players line up and see the opposition aligned exactly as the coach said they would be, they gain confidence. If, on the other hand, a team lines up and sees an alignment the coach has not prepared them for, confusion sets in. Confidence falters.

At the time, the Sooners had only four basic plays, and Wilkinson never added to that list until a play had been tested in practice in full pads. Just as he had prepared the fullback flanker as a surprise for Meyer, Wilkinson drilled the Sooners on a surprise play for Faurot. The standard Split T had no trap blocking schemes, a fact Faurot knew as well as Wilkinson—if not better—but Wilkinson devised a special trap play for the Missouri game. The play called for Mitchell to fake a handoff to Thomas as the center and right guard double-teamed the Tiger middle guard. The left guard was to pivot to his right and throw a trap block on the Tigers' left tackle. After Mitchell completed the fake, he was to spin around and run up the middle in the hole created by the double team and the trap block. Mitchell and the other Sooners did not think much of Wilkinson's "quarterback spinner," a derivative of an old single wing play. As adept as they were at the Split T, the Sooners thought the play was silly, but they perfected it to please Wilkinson.

Early in the game, Missouri jumped to a 7–0 lead, but late in the first quarter the Sooners drove 55 yards to tie the score. The game remained deadlocked at 7–7 at half. After the Sooners recovered a Missouri fumble at the Tiger 35 early in the third quarter, Wilkinson sent in a substitute with a message for Mitchell. Now was the time for the quarterback spinner.

Reluctantly, Mitchell called the play. It worked to perfection.

Coached by Faurot to respond to the initial point of attack, the Tigers converged on Thomas. When Mitchell completed his spin, the field was wide open before him. He burst through the open hole, outran the defensive halfback, and dashed 35 yards to score. OU now led, 14–7, and the play broke the game open. Three minutes later, the Sooners blocked a Missouri punt inside the Tigers' 20. Thomas scored on a slant from the 4. Later, Mitchell returned a punt 70 yards to give the Sooners a 28–7 lead. The scoring did not stop until OU had completed a 41–14 rout.

At the urging of Bob Breeden, the publisher of the newspaper in Cleveland, Vessels had been attending football games in Norman sporadically for two years. Breeden arranged for Vessels to come to OU for Visitor's Day, which fell on the Saturday of the Missouri game. Vessels sat on the sidelines with the Sooners as they defeated Missouri and spent the night in Jeff House (the Sooners' athletic dorm, originally built as a dormitory for nurses during the war). The next morning, Vessels accompanied Wilkinson to his office. There, the two watched the films of the previous day's game, and Wilkinson explained the theory behind the Split T and how Vessels would fit into his plans.

Vessels was captivated by Wilkinson. Unlike most football coaches Vessels had met, Wilkinson was quiet and polished. Wilkinson convinced Vessels that he would be helping himself, his friends, and the state if he stayed at home to go to college. That made sense to Vessels. More important, however, Wilkinson was the only coach who emphasized education. By the time his day with Wilkinson was finished, Vessels was ready to be fitted for a red Oklahoma jersey.

Two weeks later, the Sooners met Kansas for the Big Seven championship (the name of the conference's name having been changed with the addition of Colorado). Both teams were undefeated in conference play, and the Jayhawks had won seven straight.

The night before the game, Royal and Greathouse retired early. During the night, a phone call to their room awakened them. It was not good news. Greathouse's mother had died of a heart attack in Amarillo. She had watched her son play every game in high school and had even driven to Norman to see him play. For the rest of the night, Greathouse lay in his bed sobbing. The next morning, Greathouse told Wilkinson what had happened.

"We can arrange to fly you back to Amarillo," Wilkinson offered.

Greathouse refused.

"My mother would have wanted me to play," he said.

And play he did. Greathouse intercepted a pass to set up one Sooner touchdown and led the swarming Sooner defense that neutralized the Jayhawk running attack. Royal and Mitchell returned punts for touchdowns of 73 and 67 yards, respectively, as the Sooners trounced the Jayhawks. It was not even close: Oklahoma 60, Kansas 7.

The next week, the Sooners outlasted Oklahoma A&M, 19–13, and they were offered the chance to play in the Sugar Bowl against North Carolina.

The Tarheels were coached by Jim Tatum's mentor, Carl Snavely, and were ranked third in the final AP poll. Oklahoma was fifth, but the season-opening loss to Santa Clara and close calls against TCU and A&M left many observers with the opinion that OU was overrated. Each had played Texas. OU escaped with a 20–14 victory. North Carolina and its All-American tailback, Charlie "Choo Choo" Justice, pounded the Longhorns, 34–7.

The game plan developed by Wilkinson and his staff was aimed at preventing the triple-threat Justice, who ranked second in the nation in total offense, from hurting the Sooners through the air. Justice had fallen ill the week before the game, and it seemed doubtful he would have the strength to run the Tarheels to victory. As a result, the Sooners double-teamed Art Weiner, Justice's favorite receiver, thereby forcing him to run or find another receiver.

At the same time the coaches were developing their game plan, Mitchell spent hours in the film room watching film of North Carolina's games. What he noticed was that the Tarheels went into an eight-man front, goal line defense at about the 12-yard line. When Mitchell saw that, he knew that the Sooners could grind out 2 to 3 yards on every down—an insight that would pay dividends.

On game day, North Carolina took the opening kickoff and drove to the Oklahoma 15. There, Justice tried to throw, but the Sooner pass rush hurried him, and he was forced to throw an outlet pass to the right flat. Greathouse cut in front of the Tarheel receiver, intercepted the pass, and returned the ball to the North Carolina 13 before he was caught from behind.

On first down, Mitchell saw the Tarheels go into their goal line defense. He knew what to do. He carried the ball on four straight plays, making a first down by inches at the Tarheel 3. Mitchell then got to the 2 before OU was penalized 5 yards for illegal motion, leaving the Sooners 7 yards from the end zone. Thomas picked up most of that on two carries. On fourth down with inches to go, Mitchell called the option play, which would give him the greatest chance of finding the Tarheels' defensive weakness. He moved laterally along the line of scrimmage, waiting for a hole to emerge. In an instant, a hole materialized inside the tackle. Mitchell, master of the option, cut upfield and fell across the goal line for a Sooner touchdown.

Late in the first quarter, OU fumbled at its 30. North Carolina scored in five plays, but the conversion was wide, and OU retained a 7–6 lead. In the second half, the Sooners continued to wear down the Tarheel offense, but they had trouble moving the ball against the Tarheels, who had scouted the Sooners thoroughly. It was also the first time all season the Sooners had encountered a foe physical enough to stop them without resorting to special defenses.

Midway through the third quarter, Wilkinson moved Royal to quarterback. From the OU 46, he hit Frankie Anderson with a long pass that Anderson took away from a Tarheel defender at the North Carolina 10. Two plays later, the Sooners scored the touchdown that would provide the final margin of victory.

The 14–6 triumph assured the Sooners of increasing national respect. But equally important, OU cleared $50,000 in bowl receipts (which, at that time, did not have to be shared with conference members). It was a sum that enabled the OU athletic department to achieve a degree of financial stability it had never enjoyed before.

The game also marked Mitchell's final performance in a Sooner uniform. In the years since, most records established in the 1940s have been surpassed. One that has not is Mitchell's record for punt return average. In three years as a Sooner, Mitchell seldom—if ever—called for a fair catch on a punt. Instead, he relied on the substitution habits of the day. The concept of rested specialty teams composed of speedsters had not yet been developed, so Mitchell (who did not play defense for the Sooners) could count on being better rested than the players coming down the field to tackle him. Mitchell was not fast, but he was deceptively elusive and averaged 23.8 yards on each punt return. It is an NCAA record that may never be broken.

1949

Before 1949 OU had never put together two great football seasons in a row. Injuries, stronger opponents, or bad luck always caused one great year to be followed by one of disappointment. That seemed to be the Sooners' fate in 1949 as well. With Buddy Burris, Jack Mitchell, Homer Paine, Pete Tillman, Myrle Greathouse, and others gone, Wilkinson faced the first major rebuilding job of his career.

It was with some trepidation, then, that OU president George Cross picked up the newspaper to read that Wilkinson had gone to visit the University of Wisconsin. One newspaper story said that Wilkinson would be offered the Badger coaching job for a salary of $12,000—a remarkable sum in 1949, when the average income for a family of four was $5,300.

Cross waited nervously in Norman for Wilkinson's return and invited the young coach to his office. What Cross heard was good news. Wilkinson said he was not offered the head coaching job at Wisconsin. Instead, he had only gone as a courtesy to his longtime friend Harry Stuhldreher, who was Wisconsin's athletic director and one of Notre Dame's famed Four Horsemen. Stuhldreher merely wanted Wilkinson's counsel on general coaching problems at Wisconsin.

Cross was grateful for Wilkinson's honesty, and the situation caused him to realize that he was no longer alone in his appreciation for the caliber of man—and football coach—that Wilkinson was. Cross also took the newspaper rumors to heart and offered Wilkinson a new contract. He would be paid $15,000 a year to be

Oklahoma's football coach, athletic director, and professor of physical education. Wilkinson insisted on the latter title because it gave him the security he desired should his coaching success ever fail to satisfy the university or its alumni. Nevertheless, the salary was generous. It was $1,000 more than Cross himself was paid.

With many of the war veterans beginning to graduate, recruiting high school seniors was becoming increasingly important for OU and every other football program. Wilkinson always insisted that his assistants look for boys with speed, scholastic aptitude, and character. Wilkinson preferred speed over brawn for athletic reasons. Football is a game of inches, and speed, Wilkinson understood, is what would get you those inches. He also placed high emphasis on scholastic ability, for he saw football as an adjunct to obtaining a college education, not as an end in itself. Finally, he wanted character because it meant you could count on a player to do what was required regardless of the circumstances.

"Remember," he would tell his assistants, "the majority of the players on a football squad are dissatisfied. Of your fifty-five men, only twenty-two get to play much. Only eleven are completely happy. They're the starters. The rest aren't playing enough to suit themselves, their families, their girlfriends, their fraternity brothers, or their high school coaches. So it is important to get boys who are healthy mentally as well as physically."

There was not time, of course, with such a small staff, to evaluate every prospect who was recommended by fans or alumni. Some invariably were recruited by other schools, and some simply chose not to attend college. One in particular was a halfback from Commerce, in the coal mining area of northeastern Oklahoma. Wilkinson received a postcard advising him of this player's potential, but it came with a mixed recommendation. The halfback was a courageous and dedicated athlete, but might be too slow to play at Oklahoma. The halfback's name was Mickey Mantle.

With Mitchell departed, Wilkinson spent much of the spring attempting to find the right person to play quarterback in the fall. Should it be Darrell Royal, who had been Mitchell's backup in 1947 and 1948? Or should it be one of the reserves, notably Claude Arnold? As it had in 1948, the problem of what to do with Royal vexed Wilkinson. For two years, Royal had competed closely with Mitchell. In fact, Wilkinson would have preferred to use Royal, who was as good a play caller as Mitchell and a better passer. He had one glaring weakness, however. He still had not mastered the quarterback option play.

In running the quarterback option, Oklahoma quarterbacks were taught to move forward as they turned to fake a handoff so that they were gaining yardage even as they paralleled the line of scrimmage. After the fake to a halfback charging forward, the quarterback would continue to the end of the line, where he would either keep the ball or pitch out to the trailing halfback *depending upon the reaction of the defensive end.* If the end moved in to tackle the quarterback, he would pitch back to the halfback, who would follow the fullback around the end. If the end held back to stop the wide play, the quarterback would cut upfield. Wilkinson drilled his quarterbacks to be able to make the pitch to the halfback without looking at him. Wilkinson believed that unless the quarterback was looking upfield directly at the defensive end, the threat of the quarterback's keeping the ball was not real. An OU quarterback had to be able to toss the ball sideways and a little behind without looking to a halfback running as hard as he could.

Time after time, the quarterbacks would practice the play. Fake the handoff. Move to the corner. "Read" the defensive end. Pitch or keep. It was a play tailor-made for Mitchell. It baffled Royal.

"Darrell, you have to look directly at the defensive end, watch what he does, and then either keep it or pitch out," Wilkinson would explain in his precise diction.

Royal understood the play, of course, but he could never quite execute it smoothly. Unlike Mitchell, his movements lacked the split-second fluidity that made Mitchell so devastating. And since the option play was at the heart of the Oklahoma offense, Mitchell had remained the starting quarterback in 1948. In 1949 Royal *had* to learn if he was to be the Sooners' quarterback.

Before the high school spring semester ended, Wilkinson sensed that without any strict recruiting rules, other schools would not respect the decision of Vessels and others to attend OU. A player's verbal commitment was merely an expression of his *intentions.* He could change his mind without penalty, and there was no penalty for another school trying to get an athlete to change his mind (the NCAA's letter of intent would not be instituted until 1964). As a result, Wilkinson arranged summer jobs for Vessels and Eddie Crowder (a talented quarterback from Muskogee) at Camp Lincoln on Lake Hubert, near Brainerd, Minnesota. Wilkinson himself had been a counselor there during his college days, and he was certain the experience would be good for Vessels and Crowder. They both seemed to like children, and it would enable them to spend the summer in active pursuits that would prepare them for the rigors of fall football practice. Spending the summer in the Minnesota woods would also make it difficult for Oklahoma A&M to find them.

Among Vessels's charges at Camp Lincoln were the Rountree boys, Charles and Joseph, who were the sons of a prominent Oklahoma City surgeon. The boys grew fond of Vessels and he of them. In many ways, Billy was as lonely and homesick as they. When Vessels came back to Oklahoma in August to work out for the All-State football game, he called Mrs. Rountree to tell her about her boys. After a few days of practice at Taft Stadium, he called her again, this time to express disappointment that she had not come to see him practice.

It was too much for Kitty Rountree. A former social worker, her humanitarian instincts ran too deep to let Vessels flounder. She was also a rabid OU football fan, and the combination made it imperative for her to help Vessels. She said she would come that afternoon. After practice, Vessels came to her car and asked if he could visit some evening.

"Why not hop in now and have dinner with the doctor and me?" she said.

Kitty and her husband were an unusual couple. A hard-driving blonde perfectionist, Kitty was nearly as tall as her husband and was considerably more vocal. Oklahoma University—and its football team—were her two chief passions in life. Immediately, she went about setting Vessels on the straight and narrow path.

"Never forget that the university is more important than the football team," she lectured Vessels. "And if you're going to represent the university, I don't want your elbows on the table!"

In contrast to his wife, Charles Rountree was a quiet man of medium stature who cared little about football. A prominent orthopedic surgeon, Rountree normally wore a serious expression not uncommon to men in the medical profession who understand that they hold the fate of others in their hands. In Rountree's case, the effect was heightened by his penchant for wearing bow ties, which his remarkably strong fingers tied so tightly that they were soon frayed.

At the Rountrees', Vessels found the type of family environment he had hungered for. The Rountrees' house would become his weekend home for the next four years.

As fall two-a-day practices neared, Wilkinson dreaded the thought of spending more practices trying to teach Royal how to execute the quarterback option. Royal's inability to master the play was doubly frustrating because Royal was so intelligent, so coachable, and so dedicated. Wilkinson had been particularly fond of Royal since his first spring as head coach. One afternoon, Wilkinson had gone into the locker room after practice, showered, and come back out to find Royal practicing punting with one of the student managers. The manager would arrange four blocking dummies in a rectangle about five yards square. Then Royal would toss the ball in the air to simulate a snap and kick the ball into the square that was his target. After several kicks, Royal would have the manager move the dummies to another area of the field, and he would punt to that rectangle. Royal was the most accurate punter Wilkinson had ever seen, and now he knew why. Royal was also the first punter Wilkinson had seen practice kicking *after* the team had finished practice. Most kickers came out early and practiced before the rest of the team arrived.

Curious, Wilkinson walked over to Royal and asked him why.

"Because," Royal began, slightly out of breath, "in a game I'll have to be able to punt when I'm tired. I need to practice that way, too."

Wilkinson could not have expressed it more succinctly himself. He left practice with new respect for Royal.

Shortly after two-a-days began, Wilkinson found himself astounded with Royal again. For a player who had not been able to execute the option play for three years, Royal now seemed to have perfected it. Hoping to inspire further confidence on Royal's part, Wilkinson took him aside during one practice.

"Darrell, you really seem to have perfected the option play this year," Wilkinson told him. "What are you doing differently?"

"It's easy, Coach," Royal said. "All you have to do is watch the defensive end and react to what he does."

By his senior year, Royal was something of a coach on the field. He wanted to make coaching his profession, so he spent hours talking to the coaches, asking questions, and studying films. In addition, he had spent the previous three years talking with Wilkinson during the weekly quarterback meetings. Because of Wilkinson's communications ability and his willingness to explain *why* certain things were done, Royal had absorbed three years of coaching savvy. In the beginning, some of the other Sooners thought Royal's frequent visits to the coaches' offices were to curry favor with Wilkinson and his assistants. But by 1949 they understood that Royal was seriously dedicated to making coaching his career.

Another Sooner who planned to make coaching his career was Wade Walker, who had already acted as a de facto coach when the Split T was first installed at Oklahoma. Walker and Royal often talked about their prospects, which seemed bright. Head coaches across the country were looking for dedicated young assistants to help them switch to the Split T, and Wilkinson's former players ranked high on the list.

Walker and Royal had been close friends since they first arrived in Norman. When Walker was still single, Royal and his wife would invite Walker over for dinner frequently. And once Walker was married, the two couples frequently played cards together. Not only that, Walker and Royal had developed a close bond as teammates. When Royal could find no one to field punts for him, Walker would volunteer. They often engaged in punting contests, in which Walker was given a five-step advantage on each kick. The five steps did him no good. Royal always won. To reciprocate, Royal would shag golf balls for Walker. And many was the hour Royal spent following the arc of Walker's nine-iron shots off the practice tee, an exercise that Royal found invaluable in training himself to track the flight of a punt or pass in the air.

Realizing that they had little time left to spend together at OU, Walker and Royal made a pact during their senior year. Whichever of them became a head coach first would call, and the other would come to assist him.

The Sooners were scheduled to open the season against Boston College on a Friday night, but rain drenched the field. Wilkinson convinced Denny Myers, the Boston College coach, to reschedule the game for Saturday night. And just as in baseball, fans' tickets were stamped with a rain check stamp good for the next night. For Royal, the game was pivotal. The team would rise or fall with his ability to replace Mitchell as the starting quarterback. Gomer Jones could sense Royal's apprehension. As the Sooners left the locker room, Jones slapped Royal on the back.

"Stay loose, kid," he told Royal. It was a ritual Jones would repeat every game that season.

On the opening kickoff, Junior Thomas took the ball at the five and streaked down the right sideline for a touchdown. The Sooners never slowed down, overpowering Boston College, 49–0. The next week, they soundly defeated Texas A&M, 33–13, before preparing to battle unbeaten Texas, which had outscored its first three opponents, 147–7.

A thunderstorm threatened in the distance as Texas took an early 7–0 lead, but after the Texas touchdown, the Sooners fought back, driving 66 yards for a touchdown in pouring rain. At the Texas 40, Royal handed off to Thomas, who zoomed through the line, broke away from a Longhorn linebacker, and headed straight for the goal with a Texas defender right behind. Thomas faked left, cut right, and then left the defender far behind. In all, he evaded eight would-be tacklers in his dash through the mud to tie the game.

Rain fell the rest of the first half, and the teams played cautiously. Royal's punting (especially a 71-yard punt to the Texas 8) kept the Longhorns in their end of the field. By the fourth quarter, the Sooners had added two more touchdowns, including Royal's pass to Jim Owens that sealed the 20–14 victory—only the fourth time in history the Sooners had won two straight from the Longhorns.

By the middle of the 1949 season Wilkinson and Jones had perfected what would later become known as the Oklahoma Defense, but was known to the Sooners as the 72 defense. Until that time, Oklahoma, like most college teams, used a combination of defenses based on a seven-man line (such as the 7-diamond or the 7–2–2). In the 7–2–2 (or seven-box defense) devised by Amos Alonzo Stagg in 1890, the so-called linebackers played opposite the opponent's offensive ends or might drop a yard off the line of scrimmage to create a five-man line with two outside linebackers. The problem, as Wilkinson saw it, was that if linebackers played that far outside, they could not see what was taking place in the interior of the line (i.e., the movements of the center and offensive guards) to anticipate what type of play was developing. They had to hold their ground until the play developed.

Wilkinson considered this a serious weakness and sought ways to realign the defense.

"Let's move the linebackers in opposite the other team's offensive guards and move the defensive tackles out slightly to a spot just outside the outside shoulder of the offensive tackles," Wilkinson suggested to Jones. "There, the linebackers can 'read' the guards, who will pull or double-team or something that will tell us what the play is."

To compensate for a weaker strength on the outside, Wilkinson moved two defensive halfbacks even with the linebackers on the outside corners. This position, which had not existed previously, became known as cornerback. Behind the linebackers and cornerbacks were two defensive safeties. The resulting 5–4–2 Oklahoma Defense proved remarkably versatile, able to cover running plays and passes with equal facility and form the basis of standard defenses in college and pro football to this day.

In its Big Seven opener, OU thrashed Kansas, 48–26, as Thomas scored four times and the Sooners intercepted six passes. In ensuing weeks, the Sooners pounded Nebraska 48–0, Iowa State 34–6, Kansas State 39–0, and Missouri 27–7 to set the stage for the team's first game in the expanded Memorial Stadium. After the 1948 season the regents had approved a $1 million expansion, which would increase the stadium's capacity from 30,000 to 55,000. Room for most of the new seating came by eliminating the cinder track around the football field, thereby allowing the gridiron to be lowered six feet. The solution added thousands of seats to Owen Field, but it also left little room around the football field. Fans in the new seats were virtually next to the field, a fact that would give opponents claustrophobic nightmares.

Those who did not believe the Sooners would ever fill the new stadium were surprised to find the new seats sold out the very first time they were available.

On November 19, an overflow crowd of 61,000—including 6,000 who purchased standing-room-only tickets—came to see the Sooners try to avenge their loss to Santa Clara the year before. The Sooners gave the capacity crowd what it came to see, a 28–21 victory, as Thomas scored three touchdowns and the Sooners extended their winning streak to nineteen games. The following week, the Sooners crushed Oklahoma A&M, 41–0, and received a bid to return to the Sugar Bowl to meet Louisiana State.

Complacency. That was what Wilkinson feared most. Buoyed by a series of easy victories, the Sooners had spent the entire season believing they were better than they truly were. Wilkinson wanted to put them to work scrimmaging before the Sugar Bowl to make sure they did not become overconfident of beating the Tigers, who had overcome a schedule of tougher opponents.

As was his custom, Wilkinson chose to have the Sooners work out away from the distractions of the city and established pregame drills in Biloxi, forty miles east along the Gulf Coast. OU arrived in Biloxi on Tuesday before the game. Practices began on Wednesday with two-a-days and continued until the day before the Sugar Bowl game. The rugged practice schedule was necessary, Wilkinson believed, because he needed to make sure the Sooners had the mental toughness to defeat the Tigers.

Wilkinson wanted his team to practice in secrecy, so when drills on the Biloxi high school field began, workers draped canvas around the chain-link outer fence. After an hour photo session, the press was ushered out, and the Sooner workouts began in earnest. Two days before the game, Wilkinson received a call from a Biloxi resident informing him that Oklahoma's last two workouts had been scouted by three men hiding behind a tarpaulin on the roof of a garage near the Sooners' practice field. Wilkinson, who rarely lost control of his emotions, was furious.

By the next morning at practice, Wilkinson had regained his composure. He gathered the players and told them they had been watched by spies but not to let on that they knew. The Sooners found it hard to act nonchalant. They had been practicing new formations Wilkinson had designed, and they began to find themselves unconsciously looking around in apprehension.

Wilkinson was not content to accept the intrusion. He counterattacked. He sent a scouting party of five (including Oklahoma City dentist Dr. C. B. McDonald, OU photographer Ned Hockman, and a Biloxi policeman) to surprise the spies while they were watching the OU practice. The reconnaissance team moved in on the garage the informer had described and found a man where the informer said he would be. The spy was standing on a five-foot ladder, which gave him a clear view over the canvas fence the Sooners had erected. He was screened from view by a blanket stretched between two garages and was equipped with binoculars and a notepad.

Caught in the act, the spy tried to cover his face with a handkerchief. McDonald grabbed it away, and a Biloxi photographer snapped a picture. The spy broke free and ran into a nearby house, where the owner threatened to prosecute if the raiding party trespassed onto his property. A photograph of the spy was distributed nationwide by the Associated Press. Royal saw the picture in the New Orleans paper.

"That's Piggy Barnes. I played football with him in the army," Royal said.

On Saturday night, the Sugar Bowl held its annual New Year's Eve press party at Antoine's Restaurant. At the party, Wilkinson walked over to LSU athletic director Red Heard and Tiger coach Gaynell Tinsley (a teammate of Wilkinson's on the 1937 College All-Star squad). At first, their conversation was strained but pleasant. Suddenly, Heard began shouting and waving his arms.

"If you're charging that we had anything to do with that or knew anything about it, you're a liar," Heard yelled at Wilkinson.

From inside his suit coat, Wilkinson produced three photographs and showed them to Heard and Tinsley. They showed Barnes, a former LSU player, and two neutral witnesses standing next to him the instant after McDonald removed the white handkerchief.

"All you're doing is trying to manufacture something to arouse your boys," Heard continued. "You know you're gonna get beat, and you're finding an alibi ahead of time."

Tinsley tried to quiet Heard, but Heard would not let up.

"You're the coach of the year. You're smart," Heard said sarcastically. "You're smart enough to come up with something like this. Yes, sir, you're the coach of the year. You're a smart young fellow."

Wilkinson's face was flushed and intense, but he kept his temper as Tinsley tried to assure his former teammate that he had no knowledge of any spying. Preferring to let the matter drop, Wilkinson walked away.

On the morning of the game, Wilkinson publicly challenged Barnes and his accomplice, Elbert Manuel (another former LSU football player and the owner of the house where Barnes had sought shelter), to present themselves before the kickoff of the Sugar Bowl game for identification by the three neutral witnesses who had accompanied the OU expedition. Neither appeared.

The oddsmakers had installed the Sooners as 8-point favorites, but LSU had the benefit of a home field advantage in front of eighty-two thousand fans. In addition, Tinsley had developed a defensive strategy to stop the Sooners' running attack. The Tigers had heard what opponents said about the Sooners' Thomas, who led the nation in scoring with 117 points. If Thomas isn't running with the ball, he's catching it. Either way, he's in the end zone. But Tinsley wasn't distracted by concentrating on Thomas. Tinsley had his team practicing hard to stop Heath, whom Tinsley regarded as the key to the Oklahoma attack. If the Tigers could stop Heath, he believed, they could stop the Sooners.

The Tigers kept the ball in OU territory most of the first quarter with a wide-open passing attack featuring fake handoffs and laterals. Royal saved a touchdown when he broke up a Tiger pass near the Sooner goal. Later, he boomed a 50-yard punt to the LSU 14 to keep LSU far from the Sooner end zone. On defense, the Bengals were so determined to stop the Oklahoma running attack that Tinsley resorted to a modified Oklahoma 5–4–2 defense with the two deep defenders only 5 yards behind the line of scrimmage. The defense worked in the first quarter, when the Sooners were running into a steady south breeze and Royal was probing for weaknesses in the LSU defense.

In the second quarter, the Sooners began to take advantage of the wind at their backs. Royal tried to drop back and throw, but immediately he saw that the LSU spies had done their work well. Each time he dropped back, the receivers were covered perfectly. If the Sooners were to take advantage of LSU's defense loaded to stop the run, it would have to be with halfback option passes, which would force the defense to choose between covering the run or the pass.

The tactic worked. Lindell Pearson rolled to his right and threw a 40-yard strike to Bobby Goad, who was brought down at the LSU 8. Three times, the Sooners slammed into the LSU line, but they could not score. On fourth-and-goal from the LSU 3, Royal's quarterback keeper off left tackle was stopped inches short of the LSU goal.

For a moment, it appeared the unheralded LSU line might be superior to the Sooners'. The impression was fleeting, however. The Sooners kept the Tigers pinned in their end of the field and forced the Tigers to punt. Buddy Jones, whose unique defensive gifts Wilkinson had realized, settled under the LSU punt at the OU 45 and dashed back 18 yards to the LSU 37.

After Heath picked up 3 yards on first down, Royal called another halfback option pass. He pitched to Pearson, who spotted Thomas deep behind the LSU safety. Stretching high above his head, Thomas grabbed Pearson's pass at the LSU 2 and scored. Royal had made his message clear. The Tigers could no longer mass their troops at the line of scrimmage.

The ensuing kickoff was fumbled by the Tigers, and the Sooners quickly converted the LSU turnover into a second touchdown, which Thomas scored on a 5-yard sweep. At halftime, OU led, 14–0.

The Tigers received the second half kickoff and drove to midfield before the drive stalled, and they were forced to punt. On first down at the OU 14, Royal called for a handoff to Heath over right guard. The Tigers were lined up in a 7-diamond defense as the Sooners came to the line of scrimmage. Against such defenses, the center of the OU line was to double-team the opponent's middle guard, but Tinsley had developed a defensive variation that called for the Tigers' middle guard and linebacker to cross charge and disrupt such blocking schemes. Jones, a master of line blocking tactics, had spotted LSU using this technique while reviewing game films and had prepared his linemen for it. When the ball was snapped, the LSU middle guard charged to the right of the Sooners' center Charlie Dowell, but he and the right guard sensed what was happening and used the defender's momentum to carry him out of the play. The Sooners' right guard bypassed his man and blocked the LSU linebacker, clearing the way for Heath. In a fraction of a second, the entire center of the LSU defense was obliterated. Heath exploded through untouched, and his 86-yard touchdown run became the longest in Sugar Bowl history.

Trailing 28–0 in the fourth quarter, LSU was desperate, passing on every play, but a Sooner interception put the ball at the LSU 30. On first down, the Sooners lost 4 yards, but Royal had seen a weakness in the Tigers' defense. On second down, he gave the ball to Heath over right tackle. Strong and fast, Heath broke several tackles near the line of scrimmage and then outran the secondary to the goal. As he neared the end zone, he turned partially around—and in a gesture of open defiance—motioned for the Tigers defenders to come after him.

The Sooners' victory was total. In its sixteen-year history, the Sugar Bowl had never seen anything like it. Oklahoma's 35 points were the most ever scored in the game, and its 35-point margin of victory was likewise a record. Perhaps the only consolation for Tinsley and the Tigers was that their defensive game plan had been right. Stopping Heath was the key to beating Oklahoma. They simply could not do it.

OU fans were proud of the No. 2–ranked Sooners' impressive victory, believing it showed that the Sooners—and not the Fighting Irish of Notre Dame—were the best team in the nation. After one Associated Press story referred to the team as "Okies," the national AP sports editor received a postcard with the clipping glued to it. The word "Okies" was circled. The message on the card was brief, but to the point: "Dear Sir: You sonofabitch."

Part II

THE DYNASTY BEGINS

1950

From August to December each year, Wilkinson had little time for anything but meeting the weekly demands of the football season at hand. Once the season was over, however, he found enjoyment in reading. His favorite subject was military history, not only for its own sake, but also because Red Sanders had convinced him of its applicability to football.

In 1950 Wilkinson's attention was drawn to a volume published first in Germany and later translated into English—*Infantry Attacks*, by Field Marshal Erwin Rommel. The book was a collection of writings by the German tank commander describing his battles in World War I and his strategy for tank warfare. In it, Wilkinson found firsthand accounts describing tanks and men in battle: Brief, swirling confrontations. Decoying tactics. Flanking movements. Power against power.

Wilkinson quickly grasped that Rommel deployed his forces so that the point of attack was never clear, that it could come from anywhere. And more important, the point of attack could actually *change* as the battle went on depending upon the reaction of the opposing forces. A football team must be able to do the same thing, Wilkinson reasoned. Thus, the Split T—as commonly implemented—was only a halfway point. It was fine to spread the offense to force the defense to cover a wider front, but plays that incorporated run-pass options could make the offense even more potent. Reading Rommel's work convinced Wilkinson he had been right in using Darrell Royal and Lindell Pearson to throw halfback option passes, but he decided to work even harder to make every play that the Sooners ran an option that allowed his players to change the point of attack after the ball was snapped. Until then, he would not have created the ultimate offense.

Billy Vessels had to face reality. As much as he professed to like what Wilkinson said about the value of a college education, he had come to school to play football, not to study. As he surveyed his grade reports for the spring semester, it was clear what his priorities were. Athletes had to have only twelve hours of D to remain eligible. Even at that, Vessels did not qualify.

Wilkinson began a series of talks with Vessels—purportedly about football—and tried to emphasize the importance of other things in life. Among them was the bitter truth that unless he took his studies more seriously, he would never get to play the football he loved. It did no good. By midsemester, Vessels's grades had not improved. The matter came to a head shortly before spring practice, when Wilkinson called Vessels to his office.

"Billy, you can't play," Wilkinson told him.

Never in his life of disappointments had Vessels been hurt so deeply. Worst of all, he would have to tell Kitty Rountree, a situation he did not relish. As they normally did, the Rountrees picked him up at Jeff House on Friday afternoon and drove to their home in the fashionable suburb of Nichols Hills. As they did so, Vessels had no inkling that Wilkinson had called Kitty to let her know where her favorite Sooner stood.

Unlike most weekends, the Rountrees were silent as Dr. Rountree drove from Norman to Oklahoma City. Vessels wondered why they had even bothered to invite him to come. When they reached the Rountrees' house, the three did not retreat to the wood-paneled recreation room in the basement, where they normally conversed. Dr. Rountree led the way to the living room, took a seat in his chair, and directed Vessels to the sofa across from him. Kitty sat in a Queen Anne chair to the side.

"Either you start studying or you quit coming to see us," Rountree said sternly. "We're just not going to tolerate your wasting your time and our time trying to make you a better person. This situation concerns us, and we're resolved to do something about it—even if you aren't."

"Do you want to salvage this, Billy? Do you want a future?" Kitty asked him pointedly.

"Yes," Vessels said.

"I'm not kidding, Billy," she told him. "You'll study and study and study some more until you can't look a book in the eye. Think it over carefully. It's going to be all or nothing."

The discouragement on Kitty's face hurt Vessels deeply. He could barely imagine how he would feel if he failed the people back in Cleveland.

During Easter break, the regimen started. Kitty set up a study hall in the guest bedroom reserved for Vessels in the Rountrees' house. At first, Vessels could not stand the confinement, so she let him take walks every thirty minutes to keep him from quitting entirely. Daily, the time devoted to study increased. By the end of the semester, his world consisted of little but his study table and books. But in the end, he passed every course.

Now, all that separated Vessels from continuing his football career was passing six hours in summer school. Vessels's study routine continued, and each day his schedule was the same: Attend class. Study. Vessels, now paying the price for nearly two semesters of slovenly study habits, had virtually no time for the summertime activities normally enjoyed by college students.

During the long summer, the only free time Vessels was granted on a regular basis involved brief workouts with several other Sooners. A couple of days each week, he would meet Leon Heath, quarterback Claude Arnold, and halfback Dick Heatly at the practice field to work on some new plays Wilkinson had designed. Vessels had seen all three in action the previous year and could not believe that he was included in the group for any reason other than availability. After all, he had not even been a starter on the freshman team, playing No. 2 quarterback behind Eddie Crowder. Vessels fully expected to spend his career as a defensive back like Buddy Jones.

What Vessels did not know was how fully he fit into Wilkinson's plans. As good a defender as he was, Vessels ran too well with the ball not to be used on offense. Wilkinson had seen it in practice, and if he needed further convincing, Vessels's twisting, driving return of an interception in a freshman game against Tulsa had been enough. In short, Vessels was the first player Wilkinson had ever seen who was both the fastest player on the field—and the toughest.

Wilkinson had Vessels practicing with the starting backfield because Wilkinson *expected him to be playing with them.* To prevent him from feeling undue pressure, Buddy Jones would continue to be listed as the starting left halfback until Vessels was ready, which Wilkinson expected to be midseason. Until the season started, Wilkinson never gave Vessels any indication of his high expectations for him. The only suggestion Vessels would receive regarding his future would be avuncular hints from Gomer Jones during Vessels's first grueling two-a-days with the varsity.

Except for those workouts—which Wilkinson had cleared with Kitty—Vessels spent his summer studying. One evening, Wade Walker even drove from Norman to Nichols Hills to see if Vessels wanted to go out with his sister-in-law, an attractive girl who had come to visit.

"He can't. He's studying," Kitty told Walker.

It seemed to Vessels that Kitty was, if possible, even more demanding than Wilkinson. But the discipline worked. By fall, Vessels was eligible.

Going into the 1950 season, the Sooners had won twenty-one straight games, but Wilkinson and his staff faced a challenge even greater than the year before, which seemed minor beside their current dilemma. Ten of eleven offensive starters had finished school (including five All-Americans), and so had seven of the team's top reserves. Not only that, the nature of the team had changed. Gone were virtually all of the war veterans, and the coaches had to build a team around nineteen- and twenty-year-olds. This was truly *college* football for the first time since Wilkinson became head coach. With inexperience confronting him at every position, Wilkinson was fully resigned to the end of the winning streak. It might come against Texas A&M, Wilkinson thought. If the Sooners were fortunate enough to beat the Aggies, they seemed certain to fall to Texas. And if the Sooners did not play well, Wilkinson could see them losing both games by as much as three touchdowns.

Amid a team of college freshmen and sophomores, Wilkinson had two bastions of maturity—center Harry Moore and Claude Arnold. When Moore, then a senior, became the Sooners' starting center, he was twenty-seven years old. Ten years earlier, Moore had been forced by death of his father to work in the zinc smelter in Blackwell to care for his mother and two sisters. In 1942 he enlisted in the Marines and eventually became a torpedo plane pilot. After the war, Moore wanted two things for himself—a degree in petroleum engineering and a chance to play college football. Oklahoma was the perfect location.

Of roughly the same vintage was Arnold, who was twenty-five. Originally recruited in 1942, Arnold spent most of the next three years in the service. At the time he was discharged in 1946, Tatum was scouring the state for players. In his travels, he came to Okmulgee to see Arnold, then recovering from an appendectomy. Tatum gave Arnold a scholarship and talked him into coming to summer practice, where Arnold pulled muscles in both legs. Arnold sat on the bench through the 1946 season, and it did not take him long to realize that Tatum did not like to throw to his ends. Discouraged, Arnold gave up his scholarship but stayed at OU. In 1947 Arnold coached and quarterbacked a fraternity intramural team that became the talk of the campus.

Aware of Arnold's achievements and the team's need for a mature quarterback to succeed Mitchell and Royal, Wilkinson began re-recruiting Arnold. Eventually, he persuaded Arnold to return to intercollegiate competition in the spring of 1948 and offered him a scholarship. Arnold quickly emerged as the No. 1 backup behind Mitchell in 1948 and Royal in 1949.

All in all, Wilkinson was pleased with his new starting backfield. Only Heath returned from starting backfield in 1949, but Arnold was a better passer than Mitchell or Royal, and he worked hard to avoid ball-handling errors—a trait that particularly endeared him to Wilkinson. In addition, Vessels and Heatly were talented halfbacks capable of making big plays. Wilkinson's greatest worry was how they—and the rest of the Sooners—would react to the end of OU's twenty-one-game winning streak when it came.

After beating Boston College, 28–0, in the season opener, the Sooners braced for Texas A&M in Norman. The Aggies were strong and experienced with three standouts—fullback Bob Smith and halfbacks Bill Tidwell and Yale Lary. The trio gave the Aggies a running attack the equal of Oklahoma's. The Sooners stumbled through the first quarter handicapped by a Vessels fumble, a clipping penalty, and an 11-yard punt. OU eventually fell behind when Lary scored on a reverse on the final play of the first quarter.

After the A&M kickoff, the Sooners were unable to move against the Aggies' nine-man defensive front, but an exchange of punts gave the Sooners the ball at the A&M 43. For the first time, the Sooners were starting in Aggie territory. After a Sooner first down, Heath burst over left tackle at the A&M 25. Two would-be tacklers charged up to stop him, but the powerful Heath (nicknamed "Mule Train" after a popular song of the time) stiff-armed each of them and stormed into the end zone standing up. Jim Weatherall's conversion tied the game at 7–7.

Less than three minutes later, OU scored again when Arnold flipped a short pass to Heath, who rambled 50 yards to score. On the Aggies' first play after the Sooners' kickoff, Tidwell got outside the right flank of the Sooner defense and outran the secondary to score. Two plays. Twenty-five seconds. Two touchdowns. What had begun as a defensive battle was turning into an offensive merry-go-round, and Wilkinson was worried. The Aggies seemed able to run at will against the Sooners, and he feared the inexperienced reserves might find themselves outmanned at the wrong time.

On the second play of the fourth quarter, the Sooners' outside containment broke down again, and the Aggies took a 28–21 lead. With time running out,

Arnold threw a short pass to Vessels, who was open in the flat. His knees driving like powerful pistons, the electrifying sophomore dashed 32 yards through the broken Aggie defense to score. But when Weatherall's extra point hooked low and left in the fierce wind, the Sooners still trailed, 28–27. Just as Wilkinson had feared, the Sooners now faced the looming prospect of defeat after twenty-two straight victories.

On the sidelines, Wilkinson spurred the defense on.

"You guys gotta stop them!" Wilkinson yelled as the defense went on the field. "If you make them punt, we'll still win this game!"

On the field, the Sooner defense dug in, forcing a Lary punt that sailed out-of-bounds at the Sooner thirty-one. The clock read 1:46 left to play.

"We've got 'em, Coach! We've got 'em!" Arnold yelled, clenching his fists in determination as he ran onto the field.

Wilkinson was not so sure, but he liked the show of enthusiasm. With it, his players might just do what they said they would. In the stands, there was an eerie silence, a sense that destiny would take care of the Sooners and their "middle aged" quarterback, who would be called upon to do what he had wanted to do for three years—throw critical passes in a do-or-die situation.

On first down, Arnold went back to the man who got the previous touchdown. He threw into the left flat to Vessels, who ran 30 yards to the A&M 39. On the next play, Arnold threw a flare pass to Heath, who was open in the right flat, but the setting sun blinded him, and the pass sailed incomplete. Undeterred, Arnold dropped back and hit Tommy Gray on a down-and-out pattern for 11 yards and another first down. Arnold then hit Heath for 14 yards and Gray for 10 yards to move the Sooners to the A&M 4.

With forty-four seconds left, the crowd was in a frenzy. Arnold faked a handoff inside and pitched to Heath on a sweep around the left end. Heath ran around one tackler and hurled himself across the goal line. Memorial Stadium erupted. Hats and stadium cushions sailed through the air. The Sooners had done it! When the siren signaled the end of the game, the joyous Sooners lifted Heath and Arnold to their shoulders in celebration. The young Sooners had come of age.

The Sooners had now won twenty-three straight, but Wilkinson and Jones were concerned about the Sooner defense. To graduation, they had lost the entire starting line, both linebackers, and Royal, their best pass defender. The Sooners had given up 271 yards and four touchdowns against Texas A&M. How could they possibly hold No. 4–ranked Texas? The oddsmakers had the same doubts. They made the No. 3–ranked Sooners 6-point underdogs to the Longhorns, who had a potent passing attack and one of the nation's biggest lines (averaging six-foot-one, 205 pounds per man).

From the opening kickoff, the Sooners seized the initiative. Buck McPhail's short, bounding kickoff was fumbled by the Longhorns, and McPhail recovered at the Texas 33. OU gained only 3 yards in three plays, but Heatly's punt went out-of-bounds on the Texas 3. The center of the OU line stopped three Texas running plays, forcing the Longhorns to punt the ball back to the Sooners.

On first down from the OU 48, Arnold ran a quarterback keeper and made 3 yards. Running the option play to the right, he drew in the defense and pitched to Vessels, who dashed 19 yards for a first down. Arnold then handed off to Heath, who steamed through the Texas defense to the Longhorn 2. Two plays later, Vessels scored on a slant over right tackle. Weatherall's extra point made it 7–0. Early in the second quarter, the green Sooner defenders were fooled by a tackle-eligible pass that gained 20 yards and a trap play that allowed Texas to score on the next play. The Longhorns kicked the extra point, and the game was tied.

In the fourth quarter, the game was still tied, 7–7, when the Sooners got the ball at their own 37. On second down, Arnold called the halfback run-pass option and pitched to Heatly. Heatly ran to his right, jumped, and threw. Heatly's pass was slightly off target, and Bobby Dillon, the Longhorns' All-American defensive back, leaped to catch it. He came down just in bounds and took off along the open sidelines to score. Dillon's 45-yard touchdown run put Texas ahead with thirteen minutes to play. The extra point try was wide, leaving the Longhorns with only a 6-point advantage.

Eight minutes later, the Sooner defense, holding its ground in the sweltering afternoon sun, forced the Longhorns to punt from their 16. The snap was low, and the Texas punter bobbled it. Unable to kick, he tried to run. The Sooners swarmed over him at the Texas 11-yard line.

On first down, Vessels slanted off right tackle, but he was stacked at the line of scrimmage. With the game on the line, Arnold called time out. In the huddle, he called a play that Wilkinson had put in especially for this game—a reverse trap. The play was designed to look like the play the Sooners had just run, but Arnold was to fake a slant handoff to right halfback and then pitch to Vessels coming back in the opposite direction.

When play resumed, Arnold took the snap, turned his back to the line of scrimmage, and faked to Gray, who sliced off left tackle. Then Arnold flipped an inside pitchout to Vessels coming back to the right. The fake caught the Texas lineman flatfooted. As Vessels reached the line of scrimmage, one Longhorn defender reached out in a vain attempt to grab his ankle. Vessels broke the tackle and charged ahead. Four yards in front of him, Vessels saw Moore cut down the cornerback, laying the field wide open to the end zone. At the 5, the Texas linebacker came over hard and hit him high, but Vessels lowered his left shoulder and exploded upward, knocking the Longhorn to the ground. Now, only two Texas defenders separated him from a touchdown. At the goal line, Vessels spun free from the first and blew past the second to score standing up. In his career at Oklahoma, Vessels would make longer runs. None would be more critical or more memorable. Without it—and Weatherall's ensuing extra point—the Sooners' quest for their first national championship would have ended on the floor of the Cotton Bowl. And for the rest of Vessels's career at Oklahoma, Wilkinson never used the reverse trap play again.

After two fourth quarter comebacks in as many weeks, the Sooners and their fans deserved a break. They got it. The Sooners crushed Kansas State, 58–0, and then defeated Iowa State, 20–7, before flying to Boulder to play Colorado, coached by Wilkinson's close friend Dal Ward (who had been the freshman coach at Minnesota during Wilkinson's senior year). At Colorado, Ward doggedly stuck with the single wing offense even though other schools seemed determined to copy Oklahoma's success with the Split T. The main advantage of the single wing, Ward reasoned, was that opponents see it only once a year and have just one week to prepare for it.

Colorado was big and physical with a powerful fullback named Merwin Hodel, who scored early in the game to give Colorado the lead, but the Sooners blocked the extra point attempt. In the second quarter, OU scored twice—on Vessels's 46-yard run and his 8-yard pass to Heatly—to take a 13–6 halftime lead.

In the Colorado dressing room, Ward realized the Buffs had to do something to stop Vessels, who had run virtually unchecked in the first half. From scouting reports, Ward knew Arnold was reluctant to run the ball, and he decided to use that fact to the Buffs' benefit in the second half. With Heath's effectiveness hampered by a shoulder injury, Ward told the Buffs' ends and cornerbacks to concentrate on covering Vessels or Heatly on the option play, forcing Arnold to carry the ball.

The Buffs' scouting reports were right. Arnold seldom ran, and actually preferred not to. Unlike Mitchell, Arnold believed he could not run the ball often and maintain the team's backing. In reality, it made little difference to the Sooners. They valued Arnold's abilities as a passer and play caller and understood that the entire attack worked better if Arnold carried the ball at times.

Ward's strategy represented a direct challenge to Arnold. They would give the Sooners the quarterback keeper any time they wanted it, gambling that Arnold did not have the strength—or toughness—to carry the ball play after play. Ward was wrong. On the Sooners' first possession of the second half, they drove 72 yards in ten plays to score with Arnold, keeping the ball the last five plays and scoring the touchdown from the Colorado 4.

Midway through the fourth quarter, Vessels intercepted a Colorado pass and returned it 29 yards to the Colorado 49. On every play but one, Arnold carried the ball and stumbled into the end zone for the winning touchdown with seven minutes to play. By the time the game was over, Arnold had carried twenty-four times for 132 yards—more than Mitchell (arguably the best runner of Wilkinson's quarterbacks) ever gained in a single game at Oklahoma.

OU's 27–18 victory set a modern collegiate record of twenty-seven straight victories, and Arnold's willingness to take the brutal pounding from the Buffaloes was one of the major factors in the triumph. Yet on the airplane headed back to Norman, Arnold walked along the aisle of the airplane apologizing to his teammates for running the ball so many times.

When the Sooners played KU the next week in Lawrence, the weather had turned bitter cold. Recalling his playing days at Minnesota, Wilkinson dispatched athletic business manager Ken Farris to find straw to put around the Sooner bench a foot deep to keep the players' feet warm. Trainer Joe Glander found chemically treated hand warmers at a sporting goods store in Kansas City.

From the beginning, Sooners moved the ball on the outmanned Jayhawk defenders. In the first quarter, Heath alone gained 71 yards. However, fumbled pitchouts stopped the first two Sooner drives. When a third fumble killed a 74-yard OU drive at the KU 5, Wilkinson knew it would take more than straw and hand warmers to beat Kansas.

The Jayhawks, 5–2 on the strength of a high-powered offense centered around the running of Wade Stinson and the multiple talents of sophomore Charlie Hoag, were averaging 31 points per game. Fired by the opportunity to break the Sooners' winning streak, the Jayhawks were playing inspired defense as well. Just before halftime, KU scored to take a 7–0 lead. For the first time since adopting the Split T in 1946, the Sooners were scoreless at intermission.

The second half did not start much better. On KU's first play from scrimmage, Stinson cut off left tackle and burst into the open. With no one near him, it was a footrace between Stinson and Vessels to the goal line. The fleet Vessels could not make up the difference. Stinson went 71 yards to give the Jayhawks a two-touchdown lead.

When, Wilkinson kept asking himself, would the Sooners shake their malaise and realize that every drive did not have to end in a fumble? If it did not happen soon, he was certain the Sooners' winning streak was in its final moments. The answer was quick in coming. Methodically, the Sooners moved from their own 20 to the KU 44 on faultless Split T execution. Three plays later, Arnold went to the air and hit Kay Keller on a crossing route across the middle. Tackled at the goal line, Keller lunged forward into the end zone. Weatherall's conversion cut KU's advantage to 13–7.

On the last play of the quarter, misfortune struck the Sooners again. At the OU 40, Vessels took an inside pitch from Arnold, cut inside the right end, and found running room. After crossing the KU 45, he tried to cut back to the open field, but bumped into one of his blockers. The collision jarred the ball loose, and KU recovered. Another opportunity lost.

With such good field position, the Jayhawks sensed that one more touchdown would clinch their upset, but KU gained only a yard on two plays. On third-and-9, Hoag took a pitchout and faded to throw a halfback pass. From his position in the OU secondary, Vessels broke his defensive assignment. Instead of holding his ground as Hoag looked downfield to find a receiver, Vessels charged in high to block Hoag's pass. He crashed into Hoag, but not in time. Hoag's pass was complete for a first down. But quickly, the cheering of the KU fans faded. Twenty yards back upfield, Hoag lay on the ground in pain. Hoag was carried off the field on a stretcher, his jaw dislocated and a gash in his cheek where the force of Vessels's blow had driven his teeth through the skin. The Jayhawks' spirit left the field with him.

Five minutes later, Arnold threw a 32-yard touchdown pass to Jack Lockett to tie the game. For the third time in the season, Weatherall was faced with a critical extra point. And as he had against Texas A&M, Weatherall missed. The game remained tied, 13–13.

The OU defense forced the Jayhawks to punt, and the Sooners took over at midfield. On first down, Arnold flipped a 15-yard buttonhook pass to Vessels, who was open at the KU 35. Vessels hesitated for a moment for blockers to arrive, and then he raced down the sidelines to score.

In a matter of moments, the Sooners scored two more touchdowns on a 19-yard interception return by linebacker Tom Catlin and on Arnold's fourth touchdown pass of the game.

The Sooners' offensive statistics in the 33–13 victory were unbelievable. Nearly 300 yards rushing and 200 yards passing. But the seven lost fumbles had almost cost the No. 3–ranked Sooners dearly.

The following week, the Sooners defeated Missouri easily, 41–7. Combined with Ohio State's upset loss to Illinois, the victory moved the Sooners to No. 1 in the polls for the first time in the school's history. But the Sooners would have to defend that position against Nebraska in a battle for the Big Seven title in Norman. Leading the Cornhuskers was Bobby Reynolds, the third—and many considered the best—of the brilliant sophomores to begin their college careers in 1950. At five-foot-eleven, 175 pounds, Reynolds was smaller than either Hoag or Vessels, but he was remarkably talented. Coming into the showdown with Oklahoma, Reynolds was leading the nation in scoring with 134 points in eight games and was averaging nearly 160 yards a game rushing. In addition, Reynolds was the Huskers' punter and was as dangerous as Vessels when used as a passer or pass receiver.

On November 25, a Big Seven record crowd of fifty-four thousand—including five thousand from Nebraska—jammed into Memorial Stadium to see the confrontation of two exciting teams and two exceptional football players. From the opening kickoff, the Sooners' offense was flawless. The Sooners drove to the Nebraska 16, where Arnold went to his right on the option play, faked the pitchout to Vessels, and cut upfield to score. The Ruf-Nek blunderbusses boomed their approval. A national championship was at hand.

It was now Reynolds's turn. On first down from the Nebraska 23, Reynolds tried to sweep around right end, but Jones charged in and cut Reynolds down for no gain. On second down, Reynolds sliced off left guard, but Jones was there to meet him again, limiting him to a gain of 3 yards. On third down, Reynolds took a pitchout and dropped back to pass, but was dropped for a 10-yard loss. Kicking with the wind, Reynolds punted 52 yards to Jones at the OU 33. Jones bobbled the kick, but fell on it.

The Sooners kept charging. After two handoffs to Merrill Green made only 2 yards, Arnold gained 20 on an option keeper around right end. On third-and-1 at the Nebraska 23, Arnold gambled. Instead of taking the easy yardage, he dropped a short pass in the flat to Heath, who sped down the sidelines to score. With 5:18 left in the first quarter, the Sooners were threatening to turn the Big Seven's game of the year into a runaway.

After the Sooners forced Reynolds to punt again, Vessels was hit hard and fumbled as he twisted off left tackle. Nebraska recovered at the OU 20. On first down, Reynolds sliced off right guard. He pulled away from one tackler, stiff-armed another, and darted through the Sooner secondary to score standing up with twenty-three seconds left in the first quarter.

Late in the second quarter, Nebraska tied the game with 4:27 left in the half when Reynolds scooted untouched into the end zone to score from the OU 22. The Sooners did not keep the ball for long. When Heatly was hit hard on a sweep around right end, he fumbled, and the Cornhuskers recovered at the OU 16. On the second play, Reynolds came dashing to his right again. Now here, now there, shifting speeds and bouncing off tacklers, Reynolds evaded virtually the entire Sooner defense to score. Reynolds was proving as good as advertised. Bang. Bang. Bang. Three touchdowns in four possessions, and Nebraska led, 21–14.

Remarkably, the Sooners roared right back with offensive fireworks of their own. Vessels returned the Nebraska kickoff 28 yards. On second-and-3, Arnold caught the Cornhuskers playing deep and dropped another short pass to Heath. Heath rambled down the sideline to the Nebraska 10 before the Cornhusker safety stopped him. Two plays later, Vessels scored from the seven, and Weatherall tied the game at 21–21.

In the third quarter, the Sooners took command. On the opening drive of the half, they drove 75 yards in eight plays and scored on Arnold's sneak. Less than a minute later, the Sooners got the ball back when Reynolds was hit hard and fumbled at the Nebraska 9. On the first play, Vessels burst through a hole at left tackle to score. OU had a 35–21 lead with less than five minutes gone in the third quarter.

The Cornhuskers tried to rally, and fortune seemed to be siding with them, when Jones, who had shadowed Reynolds so well all afternoon, injured his knee and left the game. Wilkinson believed that might unleash Reynolds to do more of his open field magic, but the Sooners intercepted a Nebraska pass at the OU 17.

The Sooners pressed the offensive quickly. Green dashed up the middle for 14 yards and a first down. On the next play, Arnold pitched to Vessels, who headed around right end. Leading the way for Vessels, Heath cut down the defensive end. Finding no running room, Vessels reversed his field and came back to the left. Heath, who had doubled back in front of Vessels, brush blocked the Cornhusker cornerback. Vessels slipped from the grip of one tackler, dodged another, and raced downfield. The Cornhusker safety had the angle on Vessels and was converging rapidly, but Heath dove in front of the defender, and Vessels cut behind the block. Nearing the goal, he cut behind another key block by Lockett to complete the 69-yard run.

Players and fans besieged Vessels at the end of his magnificent run that put the Sooners ahead by three touchdowns. Wilkinson, too, was in awe, but not of Vessels. He was dazzled by Heath. The fullback's individual effort in throwing three blocks on one play—one 50 yards from the line of scrimmage—was the greatest individual effort Wilkinson had ever seen!

Despite a 21-point lead, the Sooners were uncertain. Reynolds had scored that much in the first half. As the third quarter ended, Nebraska scored on a quarterback sneak, and Reynolds's extra point cut the OU lead to 42–28. Three possessions later, OU drove 55 yards to score again when Vessels threw a 24-yard pass to John Reddell to increase the Sooners' lead to three touchdowns.

Time was now the Sooners' ally. Nebraska scored once more, but there were only fifty-three seconds left, and the Sooners ran out the clock to preserve the victory.

In Vessels's individual confrontation with Reynolds, the Sooner star emerged the victor, just as he had with Hoag. Reynolds scored 23 points, but was held to 89 yards in 25 carries. Vessels, on the other hand, scored three times, threw one touchdown pass, and set an OU record with 208 yards on 18 carries—an average of 11.5 yards per carry.

On Sunday night, the Sooners gathered on the top floor of Jeff House to watch the game film with the coaches. The game looked as impressive on film as it had on the field. Reynolds working his magic, and Vessels, Heath, and the other Sooners executing their assignments flawlessly. When the film came to Vessels's touchdown run on which Heath had made three blocks, Wilkinson showed the play three times, praising Heath's all-out effort—but neglecting to say anything about the run itself.

When the review session was over, the Sooners filed out of the room. Wilkinson called Vessels over to him. Vessels, certain Wilkinson wanted to save his praise for a private conversation rather than making the other Sooners jealous, complied.

"Billy, I want to talk to you about that long run you made," Wilkinson said.

"Yes. sir," Vessels said.

"Don't ever do that again. That is not the way we run that play. From now on, run the plays as they're designed."

While the Sooners were securing their right to be No. 1, the No. 2–ranked Kentucky Wildcats were watching their hopes of an undefeated season crumble in eight-degree cold and four inches of snow in Knoxville, Tennessee. The blizzard, so bad that a train of Kentucky fans did not arrive at the stadium until halftime, crippled the Wildcats' finely tuned passing game.

The Sugar Bowl selection committee, on hand to invite Bear Bryant and his team to the New Year's Day game, decided to reconsider after the Wildcats were upset by Tennessee, 7–0. Earlier, the Orange and Cotton Bowls had discussed invitations with Bryant, but he had refused to consider them until the season was over. He wanted to play in New Orleans. By the afternoon of the loss to Tennessee, the other major bowls were filled, and the Sugar Bowl was Bryant's only chance.

After the game, Bryant went to a room in the Andrew Johnson Hotel in Knoxville to meet with the president of the Sugar Bowl and the commissioner of the Southeastern Conference. A telephone line to New Orleans was kept open as the discussions of Kentucky's fate proceeded. Bryant, at his persuasive best, tried to convince Sugar Bowl president Charles Zatarain that his Wildcats were still worth inviting. After his discussion with Bryant, Zatarain went to the telephone and talked briefly with the members of the selection committee.

"Kentucky is a great team," Zatarain told his colleagues back in New Orleans. "They still have my vote."

There was silence in the Knoxville hotel room as the members of the committee conferred. Finally, they asked Zatarain to extend an invitation to Bryant and his Wildcats. Just as Zatarain turned to make the formal invitation, Bryant grabbed the phone.

"If you invite me, I'll beat Oklahoma," he said.

Bryant's bravado was premature. Oklahoma had not been officially invited. Wilkinson and Cross were not sure the school should participate in a third straight bowl game, and Wilkinson said there would be no discussion of a bowl bid until after the regular season ended.

All OU had to do to win its first national championship was defeat Oklahoma A&M. The Sooners knew an impressive victory would clinch the title and went to work. Despite a cold northwest wind whipping through Lewis Field, Arnold threw four touchdown passes in the first half (three to Lockett to set an OU record), and the Sooners coasted to a 41–14 victory. After the game, they voted unanimously to meet Kentucky in the Sugar Bowl.

The national championship victory secured Wilkinson the respect he had previously not been accorded. Never again would there be talk at Oklahoma about getting a "big name coach" to replace him.

Convinced that Oklahoma would be Kentucky's opponent in the Sugar Bowl, Bryant traveled to Stillwater to scout the Sooners against the Aggies. He returned to Oklahoma City the following Friday for a special Sugar Bowl luncheon with the Oklahoma City Quarterback Club. Wilkinson and Bryant were acquaintances of long standing, having met during their navy Pre-Flight coaching days during World War II. Privately, Bryant shared his concerns with Wilkinson about trying to coach football at the same school where Adolph Rupp had made basketball a virtual religion. The week prior to the Wildcats' crucial game with Tennessee, inclement weather prevented the football team from practicing outside. Bryant assumed his team would be able to use the gymnasium, but he was informed otherwise. The basketball team began its preseason workouts that week, and Mr. Rupp would have the gym occupied.

For the Touchdown Club luncheon audience, Bryant embellished the story, however.

"We had a big banquet last week, and Adolph Rupp, our basketball coach, was given a big, beautiful four-door Cadillac. I got this cigarette lighter," he told them.

Despite such good-natured camaraderie, Wilkinson and Bryant were fierce competitors. Both were intent on winning the Sugar Bowl, and each went about the work of strengthening his team for the game, which was three weeks away. Bryant, a marvelous defensive strategist, was nearly paranoid about Oklahoma's Split T offense, and he developed a plan to contain the Sooners' superior speed. He would try to out-muscle Oklahoma by putting his biggest players on defense. He would use four tackles in the defensive line—Bob Gain, Pat James, Jim Mackenzie, and Walt Yowarsky (who weighed 208 pounds but had played only one game on defense in his entire football career). Yowarsky had one assignment. He was to line up opposite Weatherall and do nothing but try to break through, harass Arnold, and shut down the Oklahoma option play. Bryant planned one further gamble. He would use an unprotected punter and instruct his linemen to do little blocking on punts. Their job was to get downfield as quickly as possible to make sure Vessels did not get free in an open field.

Wilkinson's job was no less formidable. Kentucky had one of the finest passers in the nation in Babe Parilli, and Jones's knee injury suffered against Nebraska was so serious he would not be ready for the game. Wilkinson liked to have his best players on the field at all times—regardless of the position they normally played—and finally settled on a replacement for Jones, who had earned All-America recognition for his pass defense and punt returning ability. He would move Lockett, an end who normally played cornerback on defense, to Jones's spot at safety and play the intimidating Vessels on defense as well as offense.

As Wilkinson was preparing the Sooners for the Sugar Bowl, his name became embroiled in rumors regarding a coaching vacancy that stunned seasoned football fans perhaps more than any other. Bernie Bierman, Wilkinson's own mentor and a legend among college football coaches, was being forced out at Minnesota. The taciturn Bierman, aloof and solitary, had created a coaching record among the greatest in college football. For much of his coaching career, the selection of a national champion had been a matter of informal consensus. Still, his teams had been accorded three straight national championships from 1934 to 1936 (the years Wilkinson played for the Gophers), a feat never equaled before or since. In 1937 the wire service polls formalized the ranking procedure, and Bierman succeeded in winning two more titles (1940 and 1941). Based upon these performances, Bierman ranked with the greatest coaches of his time and might have stood alone at the top of his profession had it not been for the fiery Knute Rockne, whose exploits at Notre Dame became legend.

In the days before systematic recruiting, when college football teams consisted of a random assortment of students who tried out for the team, state universities had an inherent advantage. And Minnesota, being one of the largest, gave Bierman a mathematical probability of coming up with more good athletes than a coach at a smaller school. Given this complement of good athletes, Bierman's coaching methods—far advanced for the time—were enough to produce the finest college teams in America in the decade before World War II. And when the war did come, Bierman joined the navy and became the head football coach at Iowa Pre-Flight in 1942, where again he produced a team that would dominate opponents.

After the war, Bierman returned to Minnesota, but the secrets of organization and training, which Bierman and a few others once kept closely guarded, had become common knowledge. With that knowledge—and the opportunity to recruit the best veterans returning from the war—young, capable coaches like Wilkinson, Tatum, and Bryant enjoyed immediate success. Their rise, and Bierman's downfall, roughly coincided with an intensified need to *lure* the best players to your school. If you did not, they would go elsewhere. Organizing and teaching, the disciplines at which Bierman excelled, were no longer sufficient.

As a result, Bierman's postwar teams did not win as they had before. Minnesota alumni, accustomed by Bierman to unparalleled success, became dissatisfied. A decade after his last national championship, Bierman was hounded from his job. As Wilkinson watched events unfold, helpless to assist his former coach, he could only recall his father's chilling words: "No matter how able or successful he may be, every coach eventually reaches a point where a lot of people want somebody else."

It had happened even to Bierman. If he, a molder of five national championship teams in eight years, was not immune to that curse, could *any* coach hope to be?

Rumors persisted throughout the season that Wilkinson would leave Oklahoma to take a job at another university. At that time, Oklahoma was not a *destination*, a job that a young coach would regard as the culmination of a career. If anything, it was regarded as only a stepping stone to a true coaching plum—somewhere in the East or upper Midwest. The idea that Wilkinson would *stay* at Oklahoma, the most nouveau of the *nouveau riche* of college football, if he had an opportunity to go elsewhere, was inconceivable to many.

As the Sooners kept winning, the rumors kept swirling. Finally, Cross called Wilkinson to verify his intentions. Wilkinson made it clear that he would not follow Bierman at Minnesota out of respect for his former coach.

"If Bierman couldn't make it there, I don't think I could either," Wilkinson confided to Cross.

In early December, however, Ike Armstrong, the athletic director at Minnesota, came to Norman in an attempt to persuade Wilkinson to consider the Minnesota job. After a brief visit, he returned to Minneapolis and asked J. L. Morrill, the university president, to call Cross and ask for permission to make an offer to Wilkinson.

Cross, whose sense of propriety was offended by the lateness of the gesture, nevertheless gave his permission, partly out of courtesy to a colleague and partly to determine if Wilkinson was just another contract-jumping coach or if he truly was different. Cross also understood he could not prevent Minnesota from making an offer to Wilkinson, nor would he truly know Wilkinson's character unless he gave Wilkinson an opportunity to make his own decision. Without temptation, Cross believed, there is no virtue.

Wilkinson's public statements regarding the matter were brief: "I appreciate being contacted relative to the Minnesota job, but in view of the fact that my contract at Oklahoma still has three years to run, it is impossible for me to consider any other coaching situation. I am very happy at Oklahoma."

Almost immediately, there were rumors that Bryant was discontented playing second-fiddle to Rupp and would come to Minnesota. Those rumors, too, were still smoldering by the middle of December, when Frank Leahy, the head coach at Notre Dame, came to Oklahoma City to present the O'Donnell Memorial Trophy, symbolic of the national championship, to the Sooners. But Leahy carried a sobering message to those giddy enough to believe the Sooners' invincibility, now extended to thirty-one games, could last forever.

"Last year, they carried me off the field at the end of a perfect season," he said. "This year, we lost four and they almost *ran* me off."

The Minnesota matter seemed to die, but then Wes Fesler was named the new coach at Minnesota. Soon, a Minneapolis sportswriter began questioning why Fesler, who had recently resigned as head coach at Ohio State, citing poor health, would agree to take on coaching responsibilities at Minnesota, a team his Buckeyes had beaten, 48–0. When it was learned that his contract was for three years, the suggestion was ominous. It coincided with the end of Wilkinson's current contract with Oklahoma. Fesler, it seemed, was to serve as an interim coach until Wilkinson, the now-storied son of Minnesota, could return to claim his rightful inheritance.

In the midst of all this media speculation, New Year's Day in New Orleans finally arrived. The day was cloudy but warm, and the long-awaited Oklahoma-Kentucky contest could easily hinge upon which team's endurance gave out first—a situation Bryant understood instinctively. Before the opening kickoff, Bryant cleared the Kentucky locker room of underclassmen and spoke to his seniors.

"I want you to give it your absolute all," he told them. "Play till you drop on the field."

Kentucky won the toss and chose to receive. On the Wildcats' first series, the Sooners threw the Wildcats for losses twice and forced Dom Fucci to punt. Standing without protection, he got the kick away, and it rolled dead 50 yards downfield at the OU 26.

On OU's first play, Arnold took the snap and turned to hand off to Vessels, but the Wildcat tackles all tried to shoot through the Sooner line. One was successful and grabbed at the ball, which slipped from Arnold's hand and rolled back to the 21, where Yowarsky then fell on it.

On first down, Kentucky went for the jugular. Parilli faked a handoff, dropped back, and then faked a short jump pass. Recovering his balance, he lofted a long, arching pass toward the Sooner end zone. The ball sailed over Lockett, and the Wildcats' Wilbur Jamerson wrested it from the grasp of Gray. Only moments into the game, the Sooners found themselves trailing, 7–0.

After an exchange of punts, OU got the ball back deep in its own territory at the 8. On first down, Vessels picked up 4 around right end. Arnold went to his left on the option and kept the ball for 3 yards. On third down, Arnold pitched to Heath, who stormed through the Kentucky line for 8 yards and a first down. With momentum now in the Sooners' favor, Arnold went wide again. He pitched to Vessels, who shook free around right end. Charlie McClendon, the Wildcat cornerback, took a futile dive at Vessels's feet and missed, the cleats on Vessels's shoes cutting a deep gash along McClendon's face. Vessels was finally stopped at the Kentucky 14, but the officials called a holding penalty against the Sooners, which moved the ball back to the OU 20.

On the next play, the Sooners fumbled again.

For the rest of the first quarter and much of the second, the two defenses held firm, but late in the second quarter, Kentucky started to move. Jamerson broke clear to the Wildcat 36, where he was stopped hard and fumbled, but Mackenzie fell on the ball to retain possession for the Wildcats. On first down, Parilli threw a 16-yard strike to Jamerson. After an incomplete pass, Parilli went deep again, this time to the speedy Al Bruno. Bruno took Parilli's pass on the run at the 15, and Lockett finally dragged him down at the OU 1. On the next play, Jamerson slammed over right guard to score, but the extra point try was no good. Kentucky led, 13–0.

OU received the second half kickoff and seemed to have new life. On fourth-and-1 at the OU 39, Arnold gambled. Expecting the Wildcats to be braced for Vessels or Heath, Arnold handed off to Gray over left tackle, and he made the first down by inches. From there, the Sooners drove to a first-and-goal at the Kentucky 4. Shifting his alignment to get more power in the lineup, Wilkinson sent McPhail in to play fullback and moved Heath to right halfback. On first down, Heath gained 2. On second down, the Wildcats stopped Vessels cold. On third down, the Sooners went to the right, but Yowarsky shot through, dove, and grabbed Vessels's heel, spilling him for a 6-yard loss. On fourth down, Arnold threw to Frankie Anderson in the end zone, but the pass bounced off his fingertips. Oklahoma's best drive of the game had been stymied.

Fearful of turnovers that would threaten Kentucky's lead, Bryant kept the Wildcat offense conservative. On two possessions in a succession, the Wildcats punted without making a first down. Then, early in the fourth quarter, the Sooners got the ball at the OU 20 after a missed field goal attempt by the Wildcats. On the first play, Vessels took a lateral from Arnold and raced 20 yards to the OU 40. After Arnold kept for 2, Vessels got 12 more around right end. At the Kentucky 39, Arnold faced another critical fourth-down situation, but instead of inches, the Sooners needed 3 yards. Arnold gave it to Heath, and the right side of the Sooner line cleared the way for Heath to make 6.

Moments later, the Sooners were faced with fourth-and-1 at the 23. Arnold's decision was the same. Heath carried off right tackle and got 6 again. From the 17, Arnold pitched to Vessels, who started around right end, but stopped and rifled a perfect pass to Green in the end zone. Weatherall kicked the extra point. Suddenly, the never-say-die Sooners were in position to create another fourth-quarter miracle.

With seven minutes to play, there was more than enough time for the Sooners to score again if they could get the ball back. When three Kentucky running plays gained only 2 yards, it seemed the Sooners' miracle of New Orleans was about to take place. Fucci punted short across the OU 40, but the Sooners fumbled on the return, giving the ball back to Kentucky. Try as they might, the Sooners could not stop the Wildcats, who milked the clock on every play, draining with it the life from the Sooners' thirty-one-game winning streak.

Back at the hotel after the game, Gomer Jones took off the brown suit he had worn every Saturday since 1948. It had been lucky all right, but its luck had run out. When the Sooners departed from New Orleans the next day, Jones left it in the closet at the hotel for someone else who might need good fortune. Much to Jones's dismay, the suit arrived at his home in Norman a week later, along with a polite note from the hotel manager, who assumed the suit had been left at the hotel by mistake.

1951

One of the pivotal moments in the history of college football took place not in any stadium, but in a small library on the first floor of the large white house at the corner of University and Boyd in Norman. At the time, rumors of Wilkinson's impending departure to Minnesota to succeed Bernie Bierman were still rampant, and George Cross was besieged by callers wanting to know what he intended to do about it. He told each caller that he had talked to Wilkinson, and Wilkinson had assured him that he was not interested in accepting the Minnesota position.

Just as the clamor was subsiding, Wilkinson came to Cross's office one day in March and told Cross he intended to resign as the football coach at Oklahoma.

Cross was exasperated.

"What school is it now, Bud?" Cross asked his astonishingly popular football coach.

"None," Wilkinson said.

What lured Wilkinson was not another coaching job but a position in public relations with the Western Company, an oil field service company operated by OU alum Eddie Chiles. Chiles had been active in OU's recruiting program and had come to know Wilkinson well. It did not take Chiles long to see that a man who could become the hero of an entire state would be invaluable to his business. And so Wilkinson, the son of a businessman, was attracted to the stability and financial opportunities offered by the oil industry. For four years, he had lectured his players about majoring in fields that could offer them secure futures after football. It was little wonder that he, too, was influenced by his own logic, especially after seeing what happened to Bierman.

The thought of leaving football was now more palatable to Wilkinson than it had been in 1946, the last time he had faced a similar decision. He could now look back and see that he had accomplished everything he could have hoped for in coaching. As he had asked, he had been given the opportunity to recruit a class of freshmen and coach them until they ripened four years later. As seniors, those players won a national championship. What more could there be? He could not exceed what he had already accomplished. He could only repeat it.

Cross reluctantly accepted Wilkinson's decision and asked him to send a formal letter of resignation. A few days later it arrived, pointing out—as Wilkinson had in person—that leaving OU to take a job outside of coaching was not in violation of his contract. Wilkinson's letter said that his resignation would be effective at the convenience of the university, but no later than the end of the 1951 football season.

For Cross, Wilkinson's resignation was the last straw. The previous six months had not been easy for Cross. First, there were the rumors about Wilkinson's departure for Minnesota. Then came the clamor over the Sooners' national championship and heartbreaking loss in the Sugar Bowl. These distractions kept him from confronting the real crisis at the university—a decline in enrollment spawned by the Korean War. Finally, there had been his own problems with the Oklahoma legislature.

Student enrollment at the university was down over 20 percent from the prior year, a chilling statistic that did not bode well for funding in the year ahead. In February, Cross appeared before an appropriations committee to explain the university's need for more money. Cross's request was far from modest—an increase of over 50 percent to make up the shortfall from reduced tuition revenue. Cross's thirty-minute presentation—carefully rehearsed and minutely detailed—spelled out the need for funds. After his presentation, he collected his notes and prepared to answer any questions. One state senator, who seemed to have been asleep throughout Cross's presentation, raised his hand.

"I'd like to ask the good doctor why he thinks he needs so much money to run the University of Oklahoma," he said.

Cross, normally restrained and patient, lost his composure. The legislator had not paid attention to a thing he had said! Cross seized the only words he could think of to convey his message: "I would like to build a university of which the football team could be proud."

The words, spoken in frustration, were repeated in newspapers around the country and the *Reader's Digest*. Lost, of course, were the circumstances under which he made the statement or the irony he was trying to convey. Instead, he was taken to task for overemphasizing athletics. Why, Cross wondered, had he not stayed the simple botany professor he started out to be?

After receiving Wilkinson's letter of resignation, Cross invited Wilkinson to come to the president's residence at the corner of University and Boyd to discuss finding a successor. When Wilkinson arrived, Cross invited him into the small library behind the mansion's main staircase.

Cross sat in the upholstered chair he routinely used when he read in the library. He offered Wilkinson a similar chair on the other side of a small fireplace. A couple of logs glowed in the fireplace, providing just enough warmth to ease the early spring chill. As the two men talked, Cross sensed that Wilkinson was, in truth, reluctant to leave the university. Cross wanted to keep him at Oklahoma, so he began trying to talk Wilkinson out of his decision to resign.

"Bud, after working with young men and having a significant impact on their lives, could you really find fulfillment as an employee of a business, where your sole responsibility would be to improve the profits of the corporation?" Cross asked.

Wilkinson said he could.

The longer the conversation lasted, the less sure Cross became that Wilkinson really meant what he said—and the less certain Wilkinson became that he really was ready to leave coaching. After nearly five years, Cross knew Wilkinson well, and one of the traits he noticed was that while Wilkinson could make *football* decisions rapidly, others took far longer. Cross could see that Wilkinson, who worried over everyday decisions more than most people because he wanted to analyze every side of a question, was troubled. It was clear to Cross that Wilkinson could be dissuaded from leaving OU if they talked long enough!

Cross kept talking and kept asking Wilkinson thoughtful questions. After two hours, Cross succeeded. Wilkinson changed his mind. He would stay at Oklahoma.

At the same time Cross was experiencing his trials as president of the university, Wilkinson and Kitty Rountree had new worries about Billy Vessels. Vessels's grades were no longer a problem, but the Rountrees, in particular, were constantly trying to get Vessels to think seriously about what he would do with his life. The Rountrees understood that there was only a limited number of games that his strong, speedy legs could play before they would give out. When that day came—and come it would—he needed to be prepared to face life after football. There would be no more touchdowns. No more cheering crowds. No more daily fanfare. Just living day to day and doing a job, the same as everybody else. Vessels appreciated their concern and thanked them for it.

"Don't worry," Vessels told them. "I'm not. Everything always falls in place for me. It will again."

At about the same time, Wilkinson was facing a problem with another of his star players—Jim Weatherall. Quick and strong, Weatherall was the prototype of a new type of defensive tackle who was capable of charging straight ahead to rush a passer or pursuing laterally to tackle a ball carrier. Weatherall's defensive prowess had first brought him to the attention of Jones and Wilkinson as a sophomore. As a junior, he had been a consensus All-American, but those honors were based primarily on his defensive ability. On offense, his blocking ability was no better than average.

Weatherall was one of the few starters returning in 1951, and he had to play exceptionally well for the Sooners to continue the level of play they had established in 1950. During spring practice, Weatherall seemed to be falling into sloppy blocking habits on offense.

One morning, Wilkinson began the staff meeting by asking, as he customarily did, "Are there any players who should be moved up or down?"

"Jim Weatherall," Jones said with a pained look on his face. "He's great on defense, but he's only average on offense. And he won't listen when I try to teach him."

"He needs to learn," Wilkinson said matter-of-factly.

Wilkinson routinely used the Sooner depth chart as an instrument of discipline. If a player loafed or practiced poorly, Wilkinson would never berate him in front of his teammates or other coaches. If he mentioned it at all, chances are he would merely take the player to one side, put his arm around the player's shoulders, and ask him if everything was going all right.

The Sooners quickly learned this was Wilkinson's way of saying, "If there's nothing wrong, why in heaven's name aren't you trying harder?"

If a player did not respond, he could count on being moved down on the depth chart, which Wilkinson and his staff updated each Tuesday. Being an All-American was no guarantee of protection from Wilkinson's depth chart discipline, as Weatherall soon discovered. That afternoon, Jim Weatherall, All-American, found himself on the fifth team holding blocking dummies for the other Sooners.

Weatherall was devastated by his demotion because he was a man of two personalities. On the football field, he was a brutal competitor who hit opposing linemen and ball carriers with remorseless fury. Even among his teammates, he was known for his violent hitting. He was reputed to have the boniest, sharpest elbows on the team. Off the field, Weatherall was remarkably pleasant, even shy. He was also naive. So complete was Weatherall's faith in Wilkinson and the other coaches that when he saw his name listed on the fifth team, he was actually convinced he might not make the team.

The demotion increased Weatherall's intensity and caused him to pay greater attention to Jones's instruction regarding the fundamentals of blocking. After a particularly good practice, Weatherall moved up to the third team. In two more days, he was practicing with the starters. Without fanfare, Wilkinson had achieved his goal, but the quiet, proud Weatherall never asked why he had been demoted in the first place.

Because of the Korean War, freshmen were eligible for varsity competition in 1951, and Oklahoma recruited several with considerable potential. Carl Allison, a fullback from McAlester, was not blessed with as much speed as Wilkinson preferred, but Wilkinson was impressed with his intelligence and competitive drive. There was Gene Calame, a quarterback from Sulphur, whose father coached the Oklahoma School for the Deaf football team and was deaf himself. Gene's mother was also deaf, and living with his parents gave Calame determination to overcome adversity and an ability to sense things that other players could not.

Each freshman class contains an athlete who inspires the awe of his teammates and coaches. Some never improve because, as Wilkinson knew, they are as good as high school seniors as they will ever be. Other potential stars are only beginning to fulfill their promise and will mature into excellent college players, but even as freshmen, their level of ability is an increment above the others. In 1949 Vessels had been such a player. In 1951 it was Buddy Leake.

Leake came from Memphis, where he was recruited by Dr. Phil White, an Oklahoma City physician and OU All-America halfback in 1920, who had played football with Leake's father while in medical school. On a visit to Memphis, White saw Leake play and mentioned him to the OU staff. When Leake was chosen to play in the All-American high school game in Memphis, Wilkinson assigned Bill Jennings to evaluate Leake. Jennings saw Leake play quarterback and halfback, then switch to defensive back and run back an interception 65 yards for a touchdown. When it started to rain at halftime, Jennings decided to leave. He had seen what he came to see.

When the freshman reported for the first day of fall practice, Leake—a true triple-threat player—quickly demonstrated his ability to run, pass, and kick with astonishing skill. Calame, also a quarterback but far less gifted, watched in dismay. He went back to his room in Jeff House certain that with Leake at OU, he would never play.

In the season opener, the Sooners met overmatched William & Mary. On the Indians' first play, the Sooners stripped the ball from the quarterback's hands and recovered. Five plays later, the Sooners scored. On the next series, the William & Mary center snapped the ball over the punter's head, and OU recovered again. Once on offense, Eddie Crowder tossed a short pass to halfback Frank Silva. Breaking free of the William & Mary defense, Silva headed toward the goal with only Indians' safety Pat Reeves in his path. Streaking downfield, Vessels dashed over to block Reeves. Vessels came in low in front of Reeves and then exploded upward with his shoulder and forearm, his elbow glancing across Reeves's face. The force of the blow broke Reeves's nose so badly he had to be taken to the hospital.

After the Sooners' convincing 49–7 victory, the William & Mary team returned to Virginia, but Reeves was forced to stay behind in the hospital in Norman. Each day until Reeves recovered, Wilkinson went to visit him—and insisted that Vessels go, too. During one visit, Wilkinson and Vessels were asked to wait before they could see Reeves. With characteristic politeness, Wilkinson broached the subject of the block Vessels had thrown.

"Billy, where did you learn that block?" Wilkinson asked. "You certainly didn't learn it here."

"No, sir," Vessels said. "When I was in high school, I used to hitchhike to Tulsa to watch the University of Tulsa play. On those trips, I saw Hardy Brown deliver his 'hump block' like this."

Vessels started to demonstrate.

"No, thank you, Billy," Wilkinson said. "I've already seen how you do it."

Wilkinson was certain that Vessels had not meant to injure Reeves and that he was sorry he had done so, but because Vessels had never been hurt seriously in a football game, he did not understand how thin is the line between "star" and "has been" due to injury. Instead, the ferocious block only added to the growing Vessels legend.

The victory over William & Mary gave the team—short on returning starters—the type of easy victory it needed to gain its bearings before playing Texas A&M in College Station for the first time since 1907. A cold evening rain, glistening in wind-blown sheets under the stadium lights, made playing conditions less than perfect. Spurred by a home crowd of thirty thousand—including the seven thousand cadets who stood throughout the entire game—the Aggies took a 7–0 lead in the second quarter. With ten seconds remaining in the first half, OU still trailed and was mired at its own 26. Everyone was expecting a pass, but Crowder—thoroughly tutored by Wilkinson in play selection—knew the situation called for something other than the obvious. Taking the snap from center Tom Catlin, he faked a handoff and retreated as if to pass. Vessels stayed in place to block. Suddenly, Crowder tossed a short shovel pass to Vessels and continued to retreat.

The Cadets took the fake. Intently watching Crowder, the A&M defenders did not see the low shovel pass and backed up to protect against a long pass. Vessels darted through the gaping hole created by the Sooner line. As Vessels crossed the A&M 30, the halftime gun sounded. Vessels kept running and completed a 74-yard touchdown run, giving the Sooners a 7–7 tie at halftime.

The Sooners ran into the locker room, shouting boisterously and slapping each other on the back. Wilkinson walked into the dressing room slowly to spoil their reverie.

"Look at you!" he said with disgust. "You're in here celebrating when you ought to be quiet and thinking how poorly you've played. You haven't played at all well, and you're lucky to be hanging on!"

The third quarter proved Wilkinson correct. The Aggies scored again to take a 14–7 lead, and the OU offense remained ineffective. The Sooners tried to come back on the wet, slippery field, but the determined Aggies controlled the ball the remainder of the game.

Wilkinson was not pleased. During the entire fourth quarter, when victory was there to be seized, the Aggies ran twenty-eight plays to the Sooners' five—and two of those had been punts. This was not the kind of fourth quarter performance Wilkinson had grown accustomed to during the two previous years. Nor was the loss to Texas A&M the kind of game Wilkinson would enjoy discussing with the members of the Touchdown Club. Wilkinson knew from experience that a coach doesn't have to explain victory, but he also knew that a coach *can't* explain defeat sufficiently to please some fans. As a result, Wilkinson had learned it was best not to make excuses when the Sooners lost or to brag too much when they won.

Wilkinson was also certain that the kind of lackluster effort the Sooners displayed against the Aggies would not be sufficient to defeat Texas, which was 3–0 after switching to the Split T under new head coach Ed Price.

Texas stung the inexperienced Sooners early, taking a 9–0 lead. In the second quarter, Texas intercepted a Crowder pass and drove inside the OU 10 again, but the drive stalled at the OU 6. Now deep in their own territory, the Sooners had to drive or they would be forced to punt from their end zone. On first down,

Buck McPhail (now the starting fullback after Leon Heath's graduation) slammed into the middle of the Texas line and exploded for 12 yards. A delayed handoff to Vessels got another first down at the OU 35. Two more first downs moved the ball to the Texas 40.

Then, Crowder handed off to McPhail, who hit the center of the line and broke into the secondary. Stopped but not downed, McPhail looked for someone to lateral to. In a fraction of a second, McPhail spotted a red jersey and pitched the ball. The unsuspecting recipient was left tackle Art Janes, who grabbed the ball as tightly as he could and started running. The surprised Janes caught the equally surprised Longhorns flatfooted. He dashed to the Texas 9 before being stopped.

Three handoffs moved the ball to the Texas 2 on fourth down, where the Longhorns would be stacked in an eight-man line with the linebackers close up behind them, forming a nearly impregnable wall. In the huddle, Crowder surveyed the faces of the Sooner linemen. Catlin, now the starting center after a brilliant year as a sophomore on defense, could do it, Crowder decided.

Crowder called the play, a short-yardage variation of the quarterback spinner Mitchell had run to beat Missouri four years before. The game—and the Sooners' consecutive scoring streak—lay in the balance. Catlin snapped the ball to Crowder and charged forward into the Texas line. Crowder took the ball and faked a pitchout. Then he whirled toward the goal line through the spot where Catlin had been. There were no defenders there! Crowder fell across the goal line before being smothered by the Texas defense. Weatherall's extra point made the score 9–7 just before the half.

In the third quarter, the Sooners made only two first downs, but Heatly's punts kept Texas bottled up until early in the fourth quarter. Then, the Longhorns began a seventeen-play drive that carried to the OU 3 before Weatherall and the rest of the OU line stopped the advance. The Sooners now faced a long march to score. As Crowder got ready to head onto the field, Wilkinson leaned toward him.

"Why don't you run that screen pass?" Wilkinson said.

Crowder could scarcely believe his ears. A screen pass? The Sooners seldom threw screen passes at all, much less from their own 3-yard line. Once in the huddle, he followed Wilkinson's instructions. Crowder took the snap and retreated quickly. As they had been instructed, the Sooner linemen brush blocked their opponents for an instant and let them slip by. The Texas linemen came charging toward Crowder, but he flipped a short pass to Vessels in the flat. No sooner had Crowder released the ball than he was smashed by two Texas defenders. They drove him back out of the end zone and slammed him into the wooden goalpost with so much force that it broke the upright and left Crowder unconscious on the floor of the Cotton Bowl.

Taking Crowder's pass in the end zone, Vessels was immediately surrounded. Determined to prevent a safety, Vessels dodged one Texas defender and fought his way forward out of the end zone. As he reached the Sooner 1, he was grabbed by a Texas defender. Vessels planted his foot to pull away, but he was hit again. The tackle, hard but clean, caught Vessels squarely. With Vessels's cleats planted in the turf, something had to give. As Vessels went to the ground, the force of the tackle twisted the ligaments in Vessels's right knee.

Moments later, the previously unconscious Crowder was aroused by the sound of nearby hammering. He looked up and saw the Cotton Bowl groundskeepers nailing a piece of wood to the broken upright to hold it in place. Expecting to see the trainers bending over him, Crowder was startled by the lack of activity in his vicinity. Sitting up groggily, he looked to his left, where two dozen people were huddled. At first, the Cotton Bowl crowd was silent. Then there was a low humming sound as spectators talked among themselves. In a matter of moments, Crowder understood why he awakened to find himself alone. Curly Vessels, the man no one could stop, was being carried off the field on a stretcher.

With his team demoralized and trapped deep in its own territory, Wilkinson ordered Heatly to punt the ball out of danger and walked to his accustomed spot in front of the Sooner bench. Then he went over to Leake and put his arm around the freshman's shoulders.

"Buddy, the next time we get the ball, I'm going to put you in," he said. "Don't get nervous."

Leake went in with the ball on the Sooner 6. On the first play, Leake faked right as McPhail gained 2, then watched McPhail limp off the field. First Vessels, now McPhail. Never had Leake seen football played with such intensity!

Two plays later, Crowder called a play that would give Leake the ball for the first time. As the Sooners broke the huddle, Leake saw the orange jerseys arrayed in front of him. This was his chance. He would hit them as hard as he could. On the snap count, Leake charged forward, and Crowder gave him the ball. The Sooner line created a gaping hole. Crossing the line of scrimmage, Leake could see only one defensive back and acres of green. Leake's mind was spinning. What should he do now? Leake tried to fake the Longhorn halfback, but he grabbed Leake's leg and brought him down. Leake's run made 11 yards and gave the Sooners a first down. The Sooner fans roared their approval of Vessels's young replacement, but it would be the Sooners' last hurrah in a 9–7 defeat.

On the sidelines behind the OU bench, far removed from the spotlight he was accustomed to, Vessels took the most valiant steps of his career. Gamely, he tried to run on his weakened, throbbing knee, but it would not support his weight. He slumped to the ground in frustration. Vessels's charmed athletic life—so different from his life off the football field—had come to an end. He was hurt. And hurt badly.

After the game, Vessels was transported to the student infirmary on the SMU campus near the Cotton Bowl, where Dr. Donald O'Donoghue, the Sooners' orthopedic specialist, examined Vessels's injury. O'Donoghue found no damage to the bone or cartilage in Vessels's knee, but the ligament damage was severe, probably torn. O'Donoghue wanted to operate that night. Vessels, who now trusted Charles Rountree implicitly, refused. He would not let any doctor, no matter how capable, cut on his knee without hearing Rountree's opinion. And if surgery was necessary, he wanted Rountree to do it.

Vessels spent the night in the SMU infirmary and flew back to Oklahoma City the next day. On Monday, he went to Rountree's office. Vessels had never seen Rountree in a professional setting before, and he was amazed how different he was. He was pleasant, of course, but there was a cold, dispassionate precision with which Rountree's strong fingers carefully probed the ligaments around Vessels's knee. As Vessels watched, his emotions swirled inside him. On one hand, he had complete confidence. On the other, he felt a sickening fear that Rountree would reach the same conclusion as O'Donoghue.

At last, Rountree looked up at Vessels, whose athletic career—and very likely his future—lay in the hands of the quiet man who had taken him into his home.

"Let's put a cast on it for eight weeks and see what happens," Rountree said.

Vessels felt a rush of relief. For the moment, at least, no one would be cutting on his leg.

Vessels's right leg was placed in a long cast that stretched from his foot to his hip, but he remained undaunted. He had overcome adversity many times before. But what, he wondered, would his teammates do without him? How could they possibly beat KU, Missouri, and Nebraska?

The following week, the Sooner practices increased in duration and intensity. For the first time in his coaching career, Wilkinson had lost two in a row. This was a start even worse than 1947. Injuries had played a part in the Sooners' early-season difficulties, but Wilkinson believed this team—his first without any mature war veterans to provide leadership—lacked the mental discipline required to win with consistency. They were physically talented and played hard on Saturday, but they did not practice hard during the week, when football games are truly won or lost. What they lacked was the will to prepare.

"You've all heard about the will to win," Wilkinson told the Sooners. They nodded. "Well, I want you to know that I think the will to win is greatly overrated. On Saturday, when the stands are full and the band is playing, *everyone* has the will to win. What separates great players and great teams is the will to *prepare*. That means working as hard as you can to get better Monday through Thursday, when there's no cheering crowd in the stands. Great teams have the will to prepare, and from what we've shown so far this season, we don't have it. If you want to be a great team, you have to develop the will to prepare. I can't do it for you. You have to do it for yourselves."

Uncertain when—or if—the Sooners would develop the will to prepare, Wilkinson and his staff decided they would help them develop it. Practices the week before the Kansas game started in the afternoon and finished under the stadium lights. Wilkinson drove his young players to give their best, but they did not fully understand his seriousness until they heard him raise his voice in anger. During one drill, McPhail, who was emerging as an equal to Heath at fullback, did not concentrate and fumbled.

"McPhail!" Wilkinson shouted, "Get out of here until you learn to hold on to the ball!"

McPhail, used to Wilkinson's encouragement, was shocked. In disbelief, he went to the nearby practice field and started jogging around the field.

Three plays later, Crowder called a pass to right end John Reddell.

Reddell, a member of Jack Baer's national champion baseball team, had remarkable hands and caught virtually every pass thrown to him. Crowder's pass to Reddell was perfect, but he dropped it. Wilkinson exploded.

"Reddell, get out of here! Go over with McPhail until you learn how to catch the ball!"

Reddell was shocked. So were the rest of the Sooners. But it got their attention.

On the way to the locker room, Wilkinson came up to Reddell, patted him on the shoulder pads, and smiled.

"It'll get better tomorrow, John," Wilkinson told him.

Wilkinson was a master of organization, and his coaches and players knew they could count on a reassuring regularity in each week's schedule. Each Sunday afternoon, the coaches would gather at the field house and watch film of the game the Sooners had played the day before. Then, they would go over the scouting report of the next team to be played. On Sunday evening, the players would see film of Saturday's game, and each player was given a graded report of his performance, as well as a copy of the scouting report.

On Monday, each of the assistants was responsible for presenting to the rest of the staff his game plan for the upcoming game *in writing*. Each coach would take his turn, and the coaches would then formulate a single, unified game plan. When new assistants first arrived at Oklahoma, they were taken aback by Wilkinson's insistence that game plans be submitted in writing. It meant a great deal more work, and they could not see the necessity for it. Gradually, they came to understand Wilkinson's reasoning. People pay greater attention to something they write than what they speak verbally. And if aspects of an assistant's game plan were accepted and failed to be successful, there was no disavowing his recommendation.

By Tuesday noon, the coaches had to complete the defensive game plan so the players could be given their individual defensive assignments by position. Almost always, a player was given only information concerning how he was to respond to certain situations. That way, a copy of the team's overall defensive strategy could not be stolen by an opposing team. By Wednesday noon, the offensive game plan had to be in place so that Wilkinson could meet with quarterbacks to teach them what plays to call in various circumstances during the upcoming game. From Tuesday through Thursday, coaches watched film of the upcoming opponent to try to discern anything that the scouting report or game plan preparation had overlooked.

By Thursday night, there was little that could be done to affect the course of the game.

"The hay's in the barn," Wilkinson would tell his assistants as they gathered at his house for Old Fashioned Night, an opportunity to sip cocktails and talk about topics unrelated to football.

If the Sooners were to play a weak opponent on Saturday, Wilkinson would work the Sooners hard in practice and dwell on the strengths of the opponent. By game time, the Sooner players would be scared they might lose if they did not play their best. Wilkinson even psyched himself into believing it because he knew that letting down and relaxing was exactly how good teams generally lose to poorer ones. Against a good opponent, on the other hand, Wilkinson would reduce to a minimum the number of plays the Sooners would use, so his players wouldn't make mistakes. In a big game, Wilkinson knew, the winner is usually the team that makes the fewest mistakes, and players do familiar things best.

Kansas came into Owen Field with a 3–1 record, having lost only to Colorado two weeks before. Spurred by Wilkinson's intense practices, the Sooners took the opening kickoff and drove 74 yards to score on Leake's 4-yard run. Late in the first quarter, a KU punt gave the Sooners the ball at their own 17. On first down, Crowder handed off to McPhail charging off left tackle, and McPhail was off to the races for a 66-yard gain before he was hauled down. On the next play, Crowder came back with essentially the same play to the right side with Leake, who cut through the opening and dashed 16 yards to score. The first quarter was not yet over, and the revitalized Sooners did not seem to miss Vessels at all.

Early in the second quarter, McPhail exploded through the middle of the line from the KU 10 to give the Sooners a 20–7 lead. Already, the chastened McPhail had redeemed himself with 142 yards. Leake, starting for the first time, had 60. Midway through the third quarter, the Sooners held a 20–14 lead when McPhail fumbled at the 50 after a 10-yard gain. When the Jayhawks converted the fumble into a touchdown and a 21–20 lead, the Sooners seemed to have lost their invincibility.

With the KU defense now wary of McPhail and Leake, Crowder began going to the underrated Heatly. Starting at the OU 36, Crowder threw a short pass to Heatly, who gained a first down at the 48. Heatly powered off right tackle for another first down at the KU 41, then caught two passes that carried the Sooners to the KU 6. Finally, Heatly followed right guard J. D. Roberts into the end zone to give the Sooners the lead. Weatherall missed the extra point try, and OU clung to a precarious 5-point lead, 26–21. The Sooners could not breathe easy until a late interception by Larry Grigg set up Leake's fourth touchdown to give the Sooners their final 33–21 margin of victory.

It was like the days of old. The Sooners gained 425 yards rushing and proved they could come from behind to win. McPhail set a new single-game rushing record with 215 yards. Leake had 121. Heatly had 70 and an additional 56 in pass receptions. Grigg, always capable but seldom appreciated, had two fourth-quarter interceptions. And for the first time in his life, Vessels had to be content sitting in the shadows, watching others take center stage.

The following Saturday, nearly forty-seven thousand fans jammed Memorial Stadium for the showdown with Colorado. The balmy Indian summer weather of the week before had vanished. Cold, wind-blown rains drenched Norman on Friday and Saturday morning. It was the second clash between Wilkinson and Ward, and both teams were undefeated in Big Seven games. Wilkinson expected a wide-open attack from the Buffaloes, and his greatest concern was reverses to the weak side by Colorado wingback Woody Shelton.

Wilkinson's answer to this threat was as fortuitous as it was unorthodox. Instead of stationing a large, powerful player at defensive end, find a smaller, faster, more maneuverable player who was aggressive and smart enough to cut down a wingback reverse behind the line of scrimmage. Wilkinson and his assistants reviewed the players at their disposal. Finally, they agreed on Calame, the freshman quarterback from Sulphur. It did not matter that he had never played the position before. Wilkinson wanted his best players in the game, and Calame had continually distinguished himself in practice.

Wilkinson also installed a new offensive weapon for the game, too. It was called the counter option pass. The play was not overly complex on paper, but it required several players to fake convincingly for it to succeed. After taking the snap, Crowder faked a handoff to the right halfback. Then he would pivot to his right so that his back was to the line of scrimmage. As he did, the fullback would run past, and Crowder would fake a handoff to him, all the while keeping the ball tucked against his body. Then came the most difficult fake of all. Crowder had to drop back nonchalantly and watch the defensive safety over his shoulder. If the safety charged up to stop the fullback, Crowder would throw long to the right end. If the safety stayed deep, Crowder would throw a short pass to one of the halfbacks in the flat.

As the teams took the field, Wilkinson was eager to see how the new changes would work. He found out on the game's first play. McPhail booted the kickoff deep to Carroll Hardy, the Buffalo's tailback and the Big Seven's leading rusher. Hardy started upfield at full speed. At the 20, he was hit by a determined Calame. Calame's fierce tackle stopped Hardy in his tracks. It also knocked Calame unconscious, and he was carried from the field on a stretcher.

The Sooners' new offensive play proved even more successful. Early in the game, Crowder used it to hit Heatly with a 27-yard touchdown pass. The next time Crowder called the play, McPhail faked so well that Tom Brookshier, Colorado's superb safety, charged in to tackle him. That left Reddell wide open for a 67-yard touchdown pass. Later, Crowder hit Leake with a 38-yard scoring pass and Jack Lockett with a 28-yard touchdown. The game was barely into the second quarter, and already the Colorado defense was in shambles. The Sooners led, 34–0, and Crowder was five-for-five for 167 yards and four touchdown passes. His fakes so confused the Buffalo defense that on one play, the Buffs' middle guard had his arms wrapped around Crowder and let him go to chase McPhail.

At that point, Pop Ivy called down from the press box to inform Wilkinson that Crowder was one touchdown pass from tying the national record set by Kentucky's Babe Parilli the year before. But Wilkinson, who did not believe in consciously trying to set records or embarrassing an opponent, pulled Crowder out of the game to give experience to younger Sooner quarterbacks.

Oklahoma's 55–14 victory shocked the other Big Seven schools, who had watched with anticipation as the Sooners lost to Texas A&M and Texas. With Vessels out, they had hoped this might be the year the Sooners would stumble. It was not to be. Vessels, languishing on the sidelines, seemed scarcely to be missed. Leake played flawlessly, and at times sensationally, in Vessels's place. At the same time, McPhail continued to live up to Leon Heath's legacy. Heatly played with his characteristic consistency. And Crowder proved to be a field general in the tradition of Mitchell, Royal, and Arnold. Victories fell in place for the '51 Sooners as they had for their predecessors. Kansas State succumbed, 33–0. Missouri tried passing on nearly every down, but was overcome, 34–20. Iowa State was dispatched with ease, 35–6.

As the season wore on, the offensive line, such a question mark at the beginning of the season, began to exert its superiority. Central to the success was Catlin, who each week seemed to set new standards by which all other Split T centers would be judged. Catlin's play was critical, for center is one of the most demanding positions in the Split T. Unlike most formations—including the single wing—in which the center concentrates on getting the ball to the hands of the quarterback or tailback and is helped in blocking by a guard, the Split T center must be able to snap the ball and make his block alone. His ability to handle a defender one-on-one frequently determines his team's chances of winning. Catlin's size allowed him to handle defenders single-handedly with remarkable regularity, thereby releasing one of the Sooner guards to take out an opposing linebacker downfield. Jones taught Catlin the subtleties, too. How to head fake an opponent into believing a play is going one way, then hit him with a reverse body block to take him out of the play. How to protect himself on deep snaps by taking a step backward as he snapped the ball, thus giving him a precious split second to ready himself for the defensive charge. How to brush block on wide plays, move laterally with the sweep, and then ambush his man when he tried to cover the play.

Jones's ability to teach every lineman such nuances of blocking was central to Wilkinson's football philosophy. Taking a key from Rommel, Wilkinson believed in giving his linemen freedom to make decisions on the field. How far to split. Whether to take an opponent inside or outside. When to release one block and head downfield to throw another. These were choices best made by a player on the field rather than preordained by a coach.

As a result, Wilkinson and Jones developed a system that gave each lineman an objective—clear the hole for the ball carrier—but did not dictate how it was to be done. To be sure, there was a preferred way for it to be done, and Jones spent hours teaching his charges how to perfect their technique. And there were general rules to follow (start low, never leave your feet), but within those guidelines, each lineman became a highly mobile blocking machine, a human tank on a grassy battlefield.

"Find your opponent's weakness. Every player has one," Jones would repeat time and again. Soon the Sooner linemen began to believe him, and the belief that a player could use his brain to defeat a physically stronger opponent paid tremendous dividends for the often out-sized Sooners.

In the conquest of brain over brawn, speed over size was pivotal. Wilkinson realized that the majority of boys play football because of an inner pride and love of the game. They have to. A lineman starts each play lined up eighteen inches from a man who weighs 200 to 220 pounds, is well conditioned, and is equally aggressive. If that lineman is successful in moving his opponent, somebody else is going to carry thirteen ounces of air surrounded by a pigskin through the hole he made. And the fans and sports pages are going to sing the praises of the guy who happened to carry the air. There simply are not enough heroic positions on a football team to have people play football for glory alone. On each play, there are eleven individual confrontations, and although they may go unappreciated by most fans, a team must win at least seven of those struggles to be successful. Superbly conditioned and alternated to keep fresh players in the game at all times, Sooner linemen became the most dangerous blockers in college football.

In the last two games of the season, the Sooners went on to manhandle Nebraska, 27–0, and Oklahoma A&M, 41–6, to end the season with seven straight victories and extend their mastery of conference opponents to twenty-six consecutive victories.

The Sooners finished tenth in the final AP poll and won the Big Seven, but despite feelers from the Orange Bowl about an invitation to play Georgia Tech, the regents voted not to allow the Sooners to participate in a fourth consecutive bowl game.

Within days, another bombshell hit. On December 12, 1951, the Big Seven announced shocking new regulations to curb recruiting abuses and ensure that student athletes were indeed students first and athletes second. On the positive side, the new rules standardized the types of financial aid athletes could receive. The new regulations also banned all postseason athletic events—including bowl games and NCAA tournaments. Even the Olympics. The rules also prohibited recruiting visits with athletes away from campus and prohibited schools from paying athletes' expenses for campus visits. In addition, spring football was limited to twenty days, and redshirting (the practice of extending a player's eligibility over five years by letting him practice but not play in games) was outlawed.

Wilkinson was disturbed by these changes because the neighboring Southwest Conference had none of these restrictions. The rest of the members of the Big Seven were not as disturbed as Wilkinson because their greatest complaint was the success of Oklahoma since World War II. Unable to compete at Oklahoma's level athletically, they conspired to rein in the Sooners administratively. Not for another five years would they understand that the secret to competing successfully was to build their own programs rather than trying to cripple Oklahoma's.

1952

The injury Billy Vessels suffered against Texas was the turning point in his life. Separated for the first time from the sports he loved, Vessels was forced to find meaning in life beyond football. With Leake playing brilliantly at left halfback and the Sooners winning week after week, more and more of Curly Vessels, son of Cleveland, Oklahoma, began to give way to a new person. Blessed with extraordinary athletic gifts not of his own making, Vessels had never been forced to learn humility until the fall of 1951. He was always the center of attention, the person everyone wanted to meet. But in watching himself being replaced by a freshman, Vessels grew to understand the transitory nature of athletic stardom. On Saturday afternoons, he was just another guy in the stands wearing a bow tie, and he finally realized that was the way he must be prepared to live most of his life.

When Vessels's cast was finally removed, he found a new commitment that pleased Wilkinson. He began soaking his knee daily in the training room whirlpool. To strengthen the knee, he began running distances with the Sooner cross-country team. In the spring of 1952 Vessels joined the OU track team. During spring football practice, Vessels threw himself into every drill. He played in all five of the intrasquad games and almost all of the scrimmages. Finally, in the Varsity-Alumni game, he ran back the opening kickoff 85 yards. In the summer, he ran barefooted in the sandy bed of the Arkansas River near Cleveland. Each day he drove himself to run. With each stride, his knee became stronger and better able to endure the burdens his legs were made to carry.

Deep inside, Vessels felt a new sense of responsibility. To his teammates. To the Rountrees. To Wilkinson. To the people of Cleveland. To himself. He would let none of them down.

Vessels was not the only Sooner to come to understand what Wilkinson meant when he talked about competing with yourself and developing self-discipline. J. D. Roberts was learning lessons of his own. After the 1951 season Jones took Roberts to the film room and showed him games in which he was just one step from making a tackle.

"If you weren't so heavy, you would be fast enough to make those plays," Jones told him. "You need to be down to two hundred pounds to be as good as you can be."

After that, Roberts played handball and was careful about what he ate. He dropped from a pudgy 240 pounds to two hundred, as Jones had asked. And Jones was right. He was faster.

In addition to his appetite, Roberts also found it difficult to control his temper. Near the end of the spring semester of 1951 his car became embroiled in a traffic tie-up in front of a fraternity house. Angry words were exchanged, and Roberts charged out of the car. In the fight that ensued, no one was injured seriously, but Roberts had developed a reputation for such behavior, so he was suspended from the university.

That summer, Roberts worked at a construction job in his hometown of Dallas. When it came time to report for fall practice, Roberts defiantly refused to take the steps necessary to be reinstated at OU. He would not make the first move. The university would have to ask *him* to come back. One day at work, the construction superintendent came to Roberts and told him he had a visitor. As Roberts walked toward the gate, he could see that the visitor was his father. Their conversation was brief but pointed. Roberts's father, a day laborer all his life, told Roberts that OU and football were his tickets to a better life. Petty, childish pride had no place. He should be in Norman, where his future lay. Roberts was ashamed. Taking time off from work had cost his father money, and Roberts knew it. What's more, he knew his father was right.

Humbly, Roberts returned to Norman to seek an appointment with George Cross and asked Wilkinson to attend as well to assume responsibility for his behavior. Roberts took a seat at one end of a long conference table. Cross seated himself at the other end with Wilkinson between them. The meeting was brief. Cross came directly to the point.

"We don't have any name for probation, but whatever the name is, you're on it," Cross told Roberts. "In the future, if you even see a fight on campus, I want you to go two blocks around it."

The 1952 football season came just in time to ease the sorrows of a parched state suffering through one of its longest droughts since the Dust Bowl of the 1930s. With September came an excuse to talk about Crowder, Vessels, McPhail, and company. Anything but the weather. At the same time, there is no record of anyone paying particular attention to a strapping, suntanned young man from North Dakota arriving at the bus station in Norman. Roger Maras had left his home in Fargo the day before and, after a journey of more than nine hundred miles, finally arrived in Norman the week before the start of Oklahoma's two-a-day workouts.

There were other schools interested in Maras, most of them in the upper Midwest, but Maras wanted to see how good he really was. He had read about the Sooners, their thirty-one-game winning streak, and their national championship in 1950, so he wrote Wilkinson to inquire about the possibility of obtaining a scholarship. Wilkinson received dozens of such letters each year, and he couldn't see why a great prospect would want to play college football so far from home. He suspected that if a player from Bishop Shanley High School were really talented, Notre Dame would already be after him. Unknown to Wilkinson, Notre Dame was.

Still, the newspaper clippings Maras sent to OU were impressive enough that Wilkinson had his assistants learn more about Maras. What they found made Maras seem even more intriguing. He was exactly the type of player Wilkinson was looking for—a slashing running back who could play defense. In one game, Maras had scored four touchdowns on returns—two kickoff returns, one punt return, and one interception return. For good measure, he had also scored a fifth touchdown from scrimmage.

As the OU staff learned more, Maras sounded better and better. He was six feet, 190 pounds (the same as Vessels). In addition to playing football, Maras was on the basketball team and the track team. In track he ran the one-hundred-yard dash in ten seconds flat (the same as Vessels) and finished second in the one-hundred-yard dash and third in the shot put in the North Dakota state track meet. Beyond that, he played in the outfield on Fargo's American Legion baseball team, which he led to the state championship in 1950.

Wilkinson and his staff never expected to consider a player from so far away as North Dakota, and Maras's inquiry seemed to have come out of the blue. As a result, Wilkinson traveled to Fargo to meet Maras and his family.

While in Fargo, Wilkinson also visited with Maras's coach, Sid Cichy. Cichy told him that Maras was the most highly regarded football player in the state and had been chosen for the all-state team for the past two years. Cichy said that as good as Maras was at carrying the ball or receiving passes, he was a complete football player. He was a devastating blocker and so capable on defense that he could charge the line of scrimmage to stop an opposing ball carrier or drop back into pass coverage.

Even though Maras's background would be decidedly different from the rest of the Sooners, Maras had the kind of character Wilkinson wanted. That night, he went to the Maras home and talked to him and his parents about what he could expect playing football at Oklahoma. Maras was honest with Wilkinson about being torn between going to college and playing football or signing a professional baseball contract. Wilkinson told Maras he understood and offered Maras a scholarship anyway. Maras accepted.

That summer, Maras played baseball on a city league team to maintain his amateur status and promised to be in Norman before two-a-days began. When the time came, Maras said goodbye to his parents and to his older brother (who had been stricken with polio the year before) and boarded the bus to Oklahoma.

Once in Norman, Maras called the football office to let them know he had arrived. He was picked up at the bus station and taken to see Wilkinson. Once Maras explained about his long bus ride, Wilkinson realized how tired his new recruit must be and arranged for him to go to Jeff House, where he could shower and relax.

"Put him in the room with Vessels," Wilkinson told his staff.

Maras could not have realized what a compliment he had been given. It was Wilkinson's habit to put players who played the same position in the same room, thereby making it easy for them to learn from each other. It was also his habit to put a promising player in the same room with an established star so the new Sooner could learn how to conduct himself should he achieve stardom. Vessels, a senior, would be gone for the 1953 season, and if Maras was as good as advertised, Wilkinson could foresee Maras being his starting left halfback for the next three seasons.

For two days, Maras received further indoctrination into the OU program, was assigned his space in the Sooner locker room, and got to know many of the other Sooner players. On the third day, it was time for the one event Maras had to complete before he would be officially enrolled at Oklahoma. He had to take the university's entrance exam. Wilkinson personally escorted Maras to the building where the exam was being given and wished him luck.

Midway through the exam, Maras came to a life-changing realization. He had been a B student at Bishop Shanley and was liked by his teachers, but he didn't really enjoy school. He preferred physical challenges to mental ones. And he needed to be up and moving. Sitting in lecture halls and reading books was not how he wanted to live the next four years of his life. He perfunctorily filled out answers to the remaining questions on the exam and left.

That night, he called his father and told him he was going to play baseball.

Maras's father knew it was the right choice. His son missed his recuperating older brother. He missed his friends in Fargo. And the elder Maras realized his son was not one to sit in a classroom if there was a baseball game going on.

The next day, Maras informed Wilkinson of his decision and boarded the bus that would take him back to North Dakota. The following spring he signed a contract to play baseball for the Cleveland Indians. Eventually, he changed the spelling of his last name. He replaced the second "a" in "Maras" with an "i" so that the spelling of his last name would not lend fuel to hecklers prone to calling him "mare ass" from the stands. Within a decade, he would make baseball history.

That fall, OU faced one of the most difficult schedules in the nation. In the first four weeks of the season, the Sooners would play four highly rated teams—Colorado, Pittsburgh, Texas, and Kansas. Then in November, they would go to South Bend to play Notre Dame in a game that had been sold out since May.

As the opener approached, offense was not Wilkinson's primary concern. With Crowder and McPhail returning, he had perhaps the best quarterback and fullback in the nation. Certainly, the best for what he wanted his team to do. And in Vessels and Leake, whom Wilkinson moved to right halfback, the Sooners had the best tandem of halfbacks in America. Some said the OU backfield was better than Notre Dame's legendary Four Horsemen. But Wilkinson knew that defense, not offense, was the key to winning, and even the team's offensive stars were greeted with the same words of wisdom with which Wilkinson started fall practice every year:

"Anyone can play offense. It takes a man to play defense," Wilkinson would tell the Sooners.

Unlike other coaches, who took advantage of the liberal substitution rules to play offensive and defensive platoons, Wilkinson insisted that his players be able to play both ways. This caused no shortage of concern among bystanders in Norman, who stood during that fall's sun-scorched two-a-day workouts and watched the best offensive backfield in America tackling and playing pass defense like the rest of the Sooner squad.

Much of this training that fall came from detailed technique drills Jones had developed, but part came from drills Wilkinson added to the OU regimen to improve quickness. During the summer, the OU staff had occupied itself, as it did annually, watching game films exchanged with other schools. This education process allowed Wilkinson and his staff to keep current with tactics being used by teams throughout the country, including many the Sooners would never play. Not the least of these films were those obtained from Wilkinson's friend Red Sanders, now the head coach at UCLA. As the OU coaches watched the films, they noticed the fluidity of the UCLA players, which was noticeably better than other teams. In secondary blocking and defensive pursuit, the Bruins were smoother and more efficient in their movements than other players. Immediately, Wilkinson called Sanders to find out how he had accomplished it.

Just as Wilkinson's coaching reputation had grown since he first met Sanders, Sanders himself had become one of the nation's premier coaches since moving from Vanderbilt to UCLA. In addition, Sanders's southern directness with words had made him one of the most quotable coaches in America, an ability made more visible by West Coast sportswriters.

"Winning isn't everything. It's the only thing," Sanders told a sportswriter with the *Los Angeles Herald* after losing to USC in 1949. Later, Sanders explained the importance of the crosstown rivalry with the Trojans in unmistakable terms. "Beating SC is not a matter of life or death. It's more important than that," Sanders said.

Sanders also continued the innovative coaching style he had established at Vanderbilt. One of the most noticeable of his innovations was changing the UCLA uniforms. Sanders replaced the navy blue jerseys (which had been in use when Jackie Robinson played for the Bruins) with a color that Sanders called "powder keg blue" and added a shoulder stripe to give the impression of motion. The changes gave the Bruins a recognizable look that was unlike any other school in America, which had been Sanders's intention all along.

"Changing the uniforms made it easier to tell our players in black-and-white game films," Sanders told Wilkinson.

Now, Wilkinson had a more serious question to ask his innovative friend. How did Sanders get his players to move so fluidly anywhere on the field? Sanders told Wilkinson it was due to a set of drills he and his staff had developed, which were known collectively as "wave drills." In them, a coach would stand on a platform and wave his hands left, right, forward, or backward. The players, facing him, would run at full speed and change direction as the coach signaled. Immediately, Wilkinson and his staff installed the drills as a part of the OU practice regimen. The new drills were so effective that a marked difference in the reaction, agility, and poise of the Sooners was readily apparent.

The last weekend in September, the Sooners opened the season against Colorado. The Sooners were riding a five-year, twenty-six-game Big Seven winning streak that began the week after a 13–13 tie with Kansas in 1947. But Wilkinson could see that the Sooners' streak might end because of the unique challenges presented by Colorado. In Colorado, Oklahoma faced a team with offensive explosiveness to match its own. The Buffaloes had two talented tailbacks—senior Zack Jordan and sophomore Carroll Hardy (with Leake, the cream of the previous year's freshman crop), who was equally talented as a defensive back.

The Sooners were two-touchdown favorites, but Wilkinson understood that any game in Boulder would be difficult because of the altitude. The Sooners were used to Norman, which was 1,170 feet above sea level. Boulder was at 5,430 feet, and the difficulty in breathing was a factor Wilkinson did not want to leave to chance. He flew the Sooners to Boulder on Thursday, giving his players two full days to acclimate to the rarified air of the Rockies. Good athletes, the single wing, and the altitude were factors Wilkinson never took lightly against Colorado.

The first six minutes of the game contained moments of frustration for both teams. Vessels, playing against a real opponent for the first time in eleven months, bobbled the opening kickoff but recovered. On the first play from scrimmage, Vessels fumbled again. This time, Colorado recovered. In a comedy of errors, the Sooner defense managed to hold the Buffs without a first down through the first quarter even though the offense lost three more fumbles. Twice, Colorado fumbled the ball back to Oklahoma. Late in the first quarter, the Sooners completed a 66-yard march with Vessels circling right end to score from the Colorado 2. After the OU kickoff, Colorado completed a touchdown drive of its own to tie the score at 7–7, but the Sooners came back to take the lead on a short run by Leake.

Midway through the third quarter, the Buffs scored to tie the game. When Colorado forced the Sooners to punt, the Buffs came back to score another touchdown to take a 21–14 lead. With five minutes to play, the Sooners stopped another Colorado drive when sophomore linebacker Kurt Burris intercepted a pass at the OU 22. The Sooners drove through the Colorado line for a series of short gains but faced a fourth down at the Colorado 49.

Crowder looked to Wilkinson on the sideline. Wilkinson's answer was unequivocal. He nodded. With the game on the line, Wilkinson chose to gamble on fourth down. There simply was not time to punt and hope the Sooners would get the ball back. Crowder went with his best, and Vessels knifed through the Colorado line for 17 yards. With two minutes to play, Vessels scored from the 1.

Those OU fans who had seen the miracle victory over Texas A&M in 1950 believed the Sooners could win any game in the final seconds, but this time, there would be no miracle finish. The game ended in a 21–21 tie.

Braced by the difficult opener, the Sooners had less trouble with Pittsburgh than anticipated, stopping the Panthers, 49–20, in a game that demonstrated clearly how vulnerable the Sooners were on defense. As the Sooners entered their annual Red River battle with Texas, Wilkinson knew there were no tricks to shore up the suspect Sooner defense, but he sensed that some offensive changes might surprise the Longhorns, who had already beaten LSU and North Carolina and barely lost to Notre Dame.

Aware that football teams lapse into habit patterns, Wilkinson had his coaches "scout" the Sooners as if they were an opponent to see if OU was tipping off its plays in any way. This practice alerted Wilkinson to something Texas could key on. OU's pass routes always sent the ends long and the halfbacks to the flat. For the Longhorns, Wilkinson reversed the patterns. Against Texas, the halfbacks would fake to the sidelines and then go deep. The ends would run short, square-out patterns to the sidelines.

Unlike some coaches, Wilkinson seldom relied on hunches, but while the Sooners were eating breakfast in the Worth Hotel on the morning of the game, Wilkinson's intuition came to the fore. He walked over to the table where Crowder was sitting.

"Come by my room thirty minutes before we catch the bus to the stadium," he told Crowder and then went upstairs to pack.

At the appointed time, Crowder arrived.

"Ed," Wilkinson said, "I have a premonition that if we use the counter option pass today, as we did against Colorado last year, we'll have the same success."

With the game only twenty seconds old, the Longhorns fumbled on the first play from scrimmage. In five plays, the Sooners drove to the Texas 2. The Sooners lined up in their Split T for a play they had run hundreds of times in practice. Crowder would fake a handoff to Vessels, then follow him through the line. Crowder called signals. Catlin snapped the ball. Crowder moved to his left. Vessels charged forward in the classic manner of a T-formation halfback, his arms parallel in front of his body so that he could keep his eyes on the hole in front of him—not the ball—on the handoff.

Crowder faked to Vessels, who slammed forward into the Texas line. Crowder followed right behind him. Within seconds, Crowder and Vessels found themselves under a pileup in the Texas end zone. To Vessels's amazement, he found the ball in *his* arms! The deft Crowder had placed it there so that Vessels would get credit for the touchdown.

Later in the first quarter, the Sooners got the ball back at their own 25. After a first down at the OU 35, Crowder called the counter option pass. Running the play to perfection, Crowder faked to Leake through the line, then dropped back to make his fake to McPhail. McPhail slammed into the line hard, drawing the center of the Texas defense to him. Crowder rolled to his right and threw a 27-yard bullet to Leake, who was open at the Texas 38. Five Longhorn defenders converged, but Leake quickly spun to his left, evaded all of them, and dashed in to score.

On the ensuing kickoff, the Longhorns fumbled, and the Sooners recovered at the Texas 29. Crowder called the counter option pass again, this time hitting end Max Boydston for a touchdown. The Sooners were penalized for holding, however, and Crowder had to find another way to get the Sooners in the end zone. It proved as easy as the Sooner fans hoped.

Crowder called a reverse to Vessels, who cruised 29 yards to the Texas 12. On the next play, Vessels got the ball again, slashing over left tackle. He gained 5 yards before being hit, but as he was falling, he pitched back to McPhail, who was trailing the play. McPhail ran the remaining 7 yards to score.

The OU defense held Texas on downs in its next series to force a punt, which the Sooners returned 37 yards to the Texas 29. On first down, Crowder put the Sooners in the end zone again. The counter option pass, so deceptive that even the officials had difficulty following the play, worked its magic. Crowder hit end John Reddell, who was wide open over the middle and waving one arm to get Crowder's attention. The touchdown put the Sooners ahead, 28–0, with four minutes left in the first quarter. In the final three quarters, Texas scored three times but could get no closer than three touchdowns to the Sooners. The Sooners' 49–20 drubbing of the Longhorns was the most one-sided OU victory over Texas since 1908.

The following week, the Sooners traveled to Lawrence to play Kansas in a game that worried Wilkinson far more than it did the Sooner faithful. OU fans could see only a Sooners team that was undefeated with perhaps the most exciting backfield in the history of college football. The Sooners could score on anyone at any time—and with uncanny quickness. What Wilkinson saw was a team that had played three tough games in a row and would be playing for the third time on the road. Besides that, Wilkinson knew the Jayhawks had an exceptional offense and a defense that was better than the Texas defense. The Jayhawks had won nine straight games since falling to the Sooners the year before. Cheered on by a standing-room-only crowd of thirty-eight thousand, the Jayhawks might be more than the Sooners could handle.

Early in the game, Wilkinson's worst fears seemed about to come true. Vessels fumbled at the OU 8, and the Jayhawks recovered. Charlie Hoag carried the ball four straight times, finally scoring from the 1 with nine minutes left in the first quarter. Two minutes later, however, Hoag fumbled, and the Sooners recovered at the KU 16. On third down, Leake took a pitchout from Crowder and skirted left end for 10 yards and the tying touchdown.

Late in the quarter, KU's Gil Reich tried to throw long, and Larry Grigg intercepted, giving the Sooners the ball at their 42. Everyone in the stands should have known what was coming next.

The Sooners' success with the counter option pass rested on Wilkinson's understanding of deception—a product of his playing days at Minnesota and his reading of Sun Tzu, Rommel, and other military strategists. In no less measure was it a product of Crowder's ability as a ballhandler, which few quarterbacks at Oklahoma—or anywhere—have surpassed. Blessed with large, quick hands, Crowder practiced hours on moving the ball as deceptively as possible. This ability came into play on numerous plays from the Oklahoma Split T, but reached its zenith in the counter option pass, which required not only clever ball handling, but also courage and superb body control. For the play to be successful, Crowder had to be absolutely relaxed in the seconds between his fake to McPhail and the instant he cocked his arm to throw.

The appearance Crowder had to create is one any football fan has seen scores of times in photographs of T-formation quarterbacks. Not the ones that focus on the quarterback, but the photographs in which the quarterback has handed off to one of the other backs and is but a small, fuzzy figure in the background. The look is unmistakable—the casual, over-the-shoulder gaze and the relaxed, slump-shouldered posture. It is a portrait of an athlete in repose. He is no longer a part of the play. He is just an observer. That posture comes naturally to a quarterback once the ball has left his hands, but Crowder was remarkably able to recreate the same pose with his back to the line of scrimmage and the ball in his right hand tucked neatly next to his body.

It takes courage for a football player to stand with his back to tacklers, unbraced against the possibility of a vicious blindside tackle, especially when he knows all the while that is *exactly the treatment he deserves*. It also takes practice, and Wilkinson drilled and drilled Crowder to perfect his natural technique.

At the same time, the other key to the success of the play was McPhail. For the play to work, the defense *must* converge on McPhail with a vengeance, and the better McPhail faked, the harder and more often he would be hit. That unselfishness, Wilkinson believed, was McPhail's greatest trait. Yes, he could run. Yes, he could block. But it was his faking that made him so exceptional.

Wilkinson knew there was no shortage of players with the courage to be tackled—often savagely—if they are carrying the ball, but the courage to take that kind of punishment when someone else would get the ball—and the glory—is rare. Without complaint, McPhail performed his assignment. Driving into tacklers. Twisting. Leaping. McPhail did everything great ball carriers do when they have the ball. Few have ever done them without the ball as convincingly or as well as McPhail.

Crowder took the snap, faked a handoff to Leake, and then faked another handoff to McPhail. McPhail charged forward. Crowder rolled to the right. Max Boydston, the fastest player on the OU squad, found himself wide open, and Crowder hit him at the KU 30. No one stood a chance of catching him.

On KU's next possession, Carl Allison intercepted a Jayhawk pass at the OU 36. Keyed by a 13-yard pass from Leake to Boydston and Vessels's 13-yard run to the KU 1, the Sooners drove in to score on Vessels's short dive. The Sooners seemed to have the game under control, but their momentum quickly vanished. The Jayhawks answered with two touchdowns and would have tied the Sooners except for an errant extra point attempt. As it was, OU clung to a 21–20 lead.

Later in the third quarter, KU drove to the Sooner 5 before being repulsed. In response, the Sooners drove the length of the field to score. In the fourth quarter, the Sooners scored two more touchdowns. Each drive was highlighted by a Vessels pass, the first a 43-yard strike to Boydston that carried to the KU 2 and the second a 34-yard pass to Reddell that moved the ball to the KU 6.

The 42–20 final score and the headlines in the Sunday morning papers did not tell the full story of how hard the Sooners worked to win the game. Nor did they convey a subtle shift in the minds of sportswriters from the East and Midwest, many of whom had taken notice of OU's victories over Pittsburgh and Texas and had gone to Lawrence, Kansas, to see the Sooners play.

Before the season, sportswriters in the East considered Jack Scarbath, the quarterback of Jim Tatum's Maryland Terrapins, the leading candidate for the Heisman Trophy. The Sooners' victory over KU showed these writers two things. Crowder, of whom they had only read before, was perhaps a better quarterback than Scarbath. And in Vessels and Catlin, the Sooners possessed two players more valuable than either Scarbath or UCLA's highly publicized tandem of linebacker Donn Moomaw and tailback Paul Cameron.

In the next two weeks, OU defeated Kansas State, 49–6, and Iowa State, 41–0. Neither game seemed particularly noteworthy for the Sooners, but the victory over K-State remained etched in Wilkinson's mind by the play of Veryl Switzer, the Wildcats' peerless black defensive back.

In 1950 Kansas State's Hoyt Givens and Harold Robinson had become the first black athletes to play at Memorial Stadium, but neither influenced the outcome of the game. But in 1951 at Manhattan the Sooners received a thorough introduction to Switzer. Playing safety on defense, the fierce-tackling Switzer led a Wildcat defense that forced five OU fumbles. As Wilkinson and his assistants prepared their game plan in 1952, neutralizing Switzer was one of the key elements. As a sophomore, the five-foot-ten, 180-pound Switzer had been voted All-Big Seven and second team All-America. Faced with lack of offensive firepower, Kansas State coach Bill Meek started playing Switzer at offensive halfback as well. Never before had the Sooners faced a team on which a black athlete was the central figure, and Wilkinson wondered how his players would react. Would they, like some players on other teams, take racially motivated cheap shots at Switzer? Or would they accept him as a tough, talented equal?

In the week before the game, Wilkinson sensed a tenseness among his players and fans in Norman that he suspected would not be there if the Sooners were playing an all-white team with a 1–4 record. Having played with black players at Minnesota, Wilkinson himself felt no such apprehension or prejudice, but Wilkinson was not blind. In a state where public restrooms were marked "Colored Only" and a university community like Norman could still have a sundown law, Wilkinson understood that others might have feelings different from his own.

On Saturday the Sooners began to steamroll the Wildcats as expected, and most of the tension seemed to disappear. Wilkinson was pleased with the demeanor of his players, considering that they had to contend with Switzer on virtually every play. Meek had installed Switzer as a roving middle linebacker in the Wildcats' 5–2 defense. Ranging from sideline to sideline, Switzer made eighteen unassisted tackles, but it was a play in which he failed to make a tackle that impressed

Wilkinson most. With the Sooners at the Kansas State 1, Crowder called an end run by Vessels. As Vessels swept to his right, Switzer came in to make the tackle, but McPhail dropped him with a rolling block. Vessels scored standing up. After the play, McPhail and Switzer found themselves on the ground facing each other. As both started to get up, the gregarious McPhail—who was in the habit of shaking hands with his teammates wherever he saw them on campus—extended his right hand to Switzer. Switzer extended his right hand, and the two shook hands warmly.

Switzer's grace and self-control under such trying circumstances impressed Wilkinson. Someday, he thought, if he could find a black player with the same type of talent and character, he would recruit him to play for the Sooners, thereby integrating the OU athletic program. That, Wilkinson decided, would be the most important thing he could ever do for Oklahoma.

While the Sooners were dispatching their lackluster Big Seven opponents, the encounter with Notre Dame on November 8 continued to grow in importance. As the day of the game approached, a sellout crowd of 57,500 was expected. Sooner fans with tickets got to South Bend any way they could. Some flew. Others drove. Many bought tickets on one of the thirteen special trains—containing 104 Pullman cars—chartered to make the journey to Indiana.

After winning his fourth national championship in 1949, Notre Dame coach Frank Leahy had suffered through two mediocre seasons, but he had managed to restore the Fighting Irish to national prominence. Now, they were a team of considerable talent. Quarterback Ralph Guglielmi, halfbacks Johnny Lattner and Joe Heap, fullback Neil Worden, and tackle Frank Varrichione all were considered top professional prospects.

As always before Notre Dame plays a big game, the pro-Irish sportswriters in Chicago began to write about the game as if the 14-point underdog Irish should not be on the same field with the No. 4–ranked Sooners. Wilkinson knew better. The Sooners were 5–0–1. The tenth-ranked Irish 4–1–1. Both had beaten Texas, and the only difference in their records was that OU had beaten Pittsburgh. Notre Dame had lost, 22–19.

As badly as Wilkinson wanted to win the game, he could not help but admire the Notre Dame spirit, which had allowed a tiny all-male school to be a football power for three decades. If there was a school that embodied the zest for the game that Wilkinson admired, it was Notre Dame. And it was that admiration, and a desire to establish Oklahoma's football program as one of national stature, that prompted Wilkinson to schedule the game in the first place. Win or lose, Oklahoma was playing in a game of national significance, perhaps the game of the year. Win or lose, it would establish OU's claim as a national football power. The game, which would be one of the first ever broadcast on television nationwide, was expected to draw more than twenty million viewers—an audience of unheard-of proportions.

What continued to bother Wilkinson most was his team's inadequacy on defense. As the Sooners had rolled along averaging more than 40 points a game and the Crowder-Vessels-McPhail-Leake backfield was getting all the attention, some people forgot that OU had given up 20 or more points on three occasions. Wilkinson had not forgotten, and he knew Leahy would try to find a way to exploit those deficiencies. The Irish were big and quick on defense. They were also deep. Too many of OU's best players were forced to play both offense and defense. If they tired—or were injured—there would be weaknesses the Irish could exploit.

The pregame workout proved what Wilkinson feared. Leake could kick, but he could not run at full speed after an injury suffered against Kansas had been reinjured in practice. Still, Leake wanted to play, and there seemed no other choice but to start him at right halfback. Merrill Green, the alternate right halfback, was also injured, and Larry Grigg, one of Wilkinson's defensive specialists, had played little on offense all season.

The Sooners received the opening kickoff and put themselves in a difficult situation immediately. On the Sooners' first play from scrimmage, Crowder pitched out to McPhail, who fumbled. Notre Dame's Dan Shannon recovered the ball in the air and ran to the OU 34. After Lattner gained 14 yards for a first down at the OU 13, the Sooner defense stiffened. The Irish tried a fourth-down field goal, but a stiff south wind curled the kick wide left.

In the second quarter, the Sooners took over at the Notre Dame 28 after a short Irish punt. From there, Crowder went to work. The counter option pass, deadly against lesser opponents, fooled the Irish as well. McPhail's fake was so perfect that even Lattner charged up from his safety position to make the tackle. Crowder rolled to his right, then calmly looked back to his left and hit Vessels where Lattner should have been. Vessels dashed in to score untouched.

The Irish came back and scored a touchdown to tie the game with four minutes to play in the half. Two minutes later, the Sooners recovered an Irish fumble at the OU 31. On first down, McPhail drove into the Irish line for 7 yards. The Sooners desperately needed a first down, and Crowder gave the ball to Vessels over the left side. A huge hole opened up, and Vessels shot through. As the Irish middle linebacker closed in, Vessels slowed for an instant, then took off. He glided fluidly away from the Irish linebacker and headed for the sideline with Notre Dame safety Dave Flood, a 9.8 sprinter, a yard behind. Step for step they ran, Vessels and Flood in a one-on-one contest of speed and endurance. The competitive Vessels would not let himself be beaten. The farther they ran, the farther Vessels moved ahead. By the time he crossed the goal line 62 yards later, Flood was 10 yards behind. Leake kicked the extra point, and OU was on top, 14–7.

The Irish tried to rally behind Guglielmi's passing, but the OU defense kept pouring in. In an effort to stop Roberts, Menil Mavraides clipped him from behind. Furious, Roberts turned and swung an elbow at Mavraides's midsection. The officials did not see Mavraides hit Roberts from behind, but they saw Roberts swing at Mavraides and ejected him from the game.

It was perhaps the most important play of an immortal game.

The Irish drove nearer the Sooner goal. With only seconds remaining before the half, Guglielmi saw a receiver open in the Sooner end zone and threw, but Vessels, forced into service on defense along with Crowder, intercepted the pass to end the threat.

At halftime, Wilkinson worked with Crowder to stop the harassment he was receiving from the Irish defense when he tried to change plays at the line of scrimmage. Notre Dame had scouted the Sooners well. They knew that Crowder was so comfortable calling audibles that he changed plays at the line of scrimmage as much as 75 percent of the time. When he did so, he would follow the system Wilkinson developed. If the play he called in the huddle was "24"—a handoff to the right halfback off tackle—and he saw the play would not work, Crowder might shout, "Add three," meaning that the play would become "27," a sweep to the left side by the right halfback.

To counter the Sooners' audible ability, Leahy instructed his defensive captain to shout a defensive shift in response, such as "left one" or "right one-half." This signaled the Irish line to shift accordingly (i.e., moving one position to the left or half a position to the right). All through the first half, Notre Dame's "jamming" of OU's audibles seemed to confuse the Sooners and forced Crowder to call another audible. The new audible was met with a response from the Irish defense. As a result, the potent OU offense ran far fewer plays than normal in the first half, which is exactly what Leahy wanted to accomplish. The Irish also knew that Crowder seldom threw short, and so Leahy stacked a 5–3–3 defense to stop the Sooner running game and cover the deep pass routes.

Early in the third quarter, Lattner intercepted an errant Crowder pass and sped 27 yards to the OU 7. Wilkinson tried to send in fresh substitutes, but in the confusion on the sidelines, the Sooners took too much time. They were penalized 5 yards for delay of game. Three plays later, the Irish scored, and the extra point tied the game, 14–14.

The Irish kickoff bounded short and was recovered by the Sooners at the OU 43. In two plays, the Sooners gained 9 yards to the Notre Dame 47. The Irish jammed eight men near the line of scrimmage, bracing for a handoff to McPhail. The Sooners came to the line of scrimmage. The Irish defenders jumped from spot to spot trying to confuse Crowder. Instead of the handoff to Vessels he had called in the huddle, Crowder yelled "Gap," a concealed check signal Wilkinson had devised that would not tip off the Irish to a changed play.

The audible play was Vessels around right end. Notre Dame stayed in its 8–3 defense. Catlin snapped the ball, and Crowder pitched to Vessels. When McPhail cut down the end, Vessels turned upfield and was free down the sideline again. At the 15, Flood came up to make the tackle, but Vessels suddenly cut back to his left, leaving Flood behind. Leake's extra point made it 21–14 with four minutes left in the third quarter.

After the OU kickoff, OU's lack of depth became apparent. With Roberts banished from the game, the Irish began to attack the middle of the Sooner line and moved inside the OU 20. On the next six plays, Worden got the ball, slowly grinding closer to the Sooner goal. Finally, two minutes into the fourth quarter, Worden scored to tie the game.

On the ensuing kickoff, Grigg took the ball and headed upfield toward a sea of converging green jerseys. Grigg lowered his head to plow through the Irish defenders. As he did, Shannon launched himself airborne and slammed head-on into Grigg. The force of Shannon's tackle staggered Grigg, causing a fumble that the Irish recovered at the OU 24.

The collision dazed Grigg, who was barely able to walk to the Sooners' huddle. It knocked Shannon unconscious, and he was carried off the field on a stretcher. As he lay on the sidelines, Leahy hurried over to him and lifted one eyelid with his thumb.

"God bless you, Danny Boy," he said.

Again, the Irish attacked the center of the OU defense, but this time the ball went to Lattner. On a trap play over right guard, Lattner broke free to the OU 8. The Sooners dug in, poised to charge the instant the Irish centered the ball. Suddenly, the Irish quarterback stepped back from center. The Sooner line charged. But the Irish had not snapped the ball! The entire Notre Dame backfield had shifted into the single wing formation.

Penalty flags flew, but to Wilkinson's amazement, they were against Oklahoma! The normally composed Wilkinson stormed onto the field to protest. The Sooners had not been offside, Wilkinson yelled. They'd been drawn offside by a trick shift. In the T formation, the quarterback does not move until the ball is snapped, Wilkinson shouted. The Irish had run a trick shift! That's against the rules! But the more Wilkinson protested, the louder the Notre Dame fans yelled.

After the penalty was assessed against the Sooners, Worden banged to within a foot of the goal. On the next play, the Irish scored, but the Sooners broke through and blocked the extra point try. The Sooners, now trailing 27–21, could still win if Vessels and Crowder could work their magic one more time.

The Notre Dame kickoff was deep, and Vessels took it at the Sooner 4. Late on the overcast afternoon, the turf had become trampled, and Vessels—driven by his desire to win—started too fast. He lost his balance and slipped to the ground at the 6. Still, the Sooners did not quit. Vessels broke loose for 14 yards on a pitchout to get the Sooners out of a hole. Then, when Notre Dame was penalized 15 yards, OU had a first down at the 44.

Crowder returned to the huddle to see who had strength enough to carry the ball. With no experienced right halfback to share the load, McPhail and Vessels had been carrying the ball on virtually every down. Grigg, the best right halfback available, remained shaken up by his collision with Shannon. On each play, Crowder had to decide whether to give the ball to a back who was tired or one who was slightly groggy. Nevertheless, the Sooners drove gamely forward. In 11 plays, the Sooners reached the Notre Dame 35. Crowder went to the counter option pass one more time. McPhail did his job and froze the Irish linebackers and secondary. Crowder saw Boydston open and threw, but the ball sailed long. Two more running plays lost 5 yards, and the Sooners were forced to punt.

With six minutes to play, OU got the ball back at its 34. Vessels sliced through left tackle for 10 yards and, as the defenders surrounded him, pitched back to McPhail. The determined McPhail got 19 more yards to the Notre Dame 37. On first down, Crowder gave the ball to Vessels, and he plowed forward 9 yards to the Irish 28. Crowder gave the ball to Vessels one more time, and he slammed through the hole over the left side, breaking into the Irish secondary. Hit at the 21, Vessels twisted for more yardage. An Irish defender grabbed his arm, and the ball popped free. Lattner dove on it to end what seemed to be the final Sooner threat.

The Sooners got one more chance, however. After the defense held and forced Lattner to punt, the Sooners regained possession at their 45. On first down, Vessels picked up 4. Twice Vessels tried to throw, but both passes fell incomplete. Finally, on fourth down, the Sooners had to gamble. Crowder attacked where the Irish were not ready—a sweep to the left. Grigg gained 11 for a first down.

By now, the throng was screaming, Notre Dame and Oklahoma partisans giving as much of themselves as the players. Crowder pitched to Vessels, who swung to the right side looking for a receiver. No one was open. Vessels pulled the ball down and ran. Cutting quickly through the Irish, Vessels dashed to the Irish 27.

The din grew louder. Crowder called a 26-screen pass to Boydston, but Boydston did not hear Crowder say "screen." He ran a normal 26 pattern, which carried him deep downfield. Rushed hard, Crowder looked for Boydston in the flat. But he was not there! Crowder did the only thing he could and threw low toward the sidelines, the ball bouncing before it reached anyone.

With two seconds left, the Sooners came to the line of scrimmage for their last chance. Amid the tumult, Crowder called signals, turned, and pitched to Vessels again. Vessels rolled to his right and pegged a throw for Boydston in the end zone. Notre Dame's Paul Reynolds batted the ball to the ground.

The stadium erupted. Notre Dame students stormed the field, lifting the victorious Irish to their shoulders, and even tried to tear down their own goalposts. Wilkinson hurried to the center of the field to congratulate Leahy. In the midst of the pandemonium, they shook hands.

"Just the luck of the Irish, Bud," Leahy said.

"I disagree," Wilkinson told his friend. "You have a great team."

Half an hour later, the stadium lay quiet, and the Sooners began to replay in their minds a game that would become legend. As Wilkinson had told them, you remember the games you lose. Not a player dressed in red would ever forget.

One lone Sooner made his way to the Notre Dame dressing room. Stopped by the guard, Roberts asked to go inside. There he found Leahy.

"Coach, I want to apologize for what I did," Roberts said.

Leahy patted Roberts on the shoulder and comforted him, then watched as Roberts walked across the dressing room to apologize to the player who had fouled him.

As damaging as the game was for the Sooners' hopes of another national championship, it propelled Vessels to national stardom. Before, he had been known by name only. Now, twenty million people had *seen* him, and the impact was overpowering. In one of the biggest games in college football history, Vessels had been remarkable, gaining 195 yards rushing in seventeen attempts and another 28 pass receiving. He scored all three Sooner touchdowns. On virtually every important play the Sooners made, Vessels was involved. When the game was on the line in the final minutes, Vessels got the ball on nearly every down.

The men who would vote for the Heisman Trophy found a new player worthy of the honor. They could see, as Wilkinson had, that Vessels was the fastest and toughest man on the field. He was clearly the finest football player in America.

In the days following the Sooners' loss, there was talk that the Sooners had made too many mistakes, that the interception by Lattner and the five fumbles had doomed the Sooners. Wilkinson knew better. Of the five fumbles OU lost, only one was a mechanical failure. The rest occurred because the Irish hit—and hit hard—because they wanted to win. And that, Wilkinson believed, is one of the great lessons of football.

As Vessels and Wilkinson were flying to New York for the Heisman Trophy presentation, Wilkinson turned to the young man who would win the trophy.

"Billy, when you get to New York, they will make a big deal of you," Wilkinson told him. "Just remember that what's important is not what you've done at Oklahoma, but what you'll be doing in twenty-five years. Life is more important than football."

Despite the emotional letdown of the loss to Notre Dame, the Sooners ended the season with crushing victories over Missouri, Nebraska, and Oklahoma A&M. The Sooners would have been an attractive bowl candidate, but the Big Seven rules laid out in December 1951 did not allow postseason athletic events—the only conference in the nation with a rule so drastic. Disdainful of the Big Seven ruling, the OU regents decided that if the team and coaches wanted to play in a bowl, they should be allowed to do so. Seldom was a football team so besieged by academic politics.

Less than a week later, rumors raced across the OU campus that the Sooners could receive an invitation to play in the Orange Bowl in Miami. Gathering on the lawn of the president's residence, they chanted, "Let's go south! Let's go south!"

In response, Cross said he would allow it if the players voted to accept a bowl bid, but warned that if they did go, it might result in OU being expelled from the conference. Cross asked Wilkinson to poll the squad. Gathering the team together, Wilkinson explained the difficult situation. Then he left the players to discuss the matter. Crowder and Catlin, the team captains, came back with the team's answer. The Sooners wanted to go if the conference rules could be changed. They could not, Wilkinson explained. The regents, left with little choice after the Sooners took such an unselfish stand, also thought better of their previous defiance and voted to follow the Big Seven rules.

Bud Wilkinson walks past Memorial Stadium on the OU campus on January 19, 1947, the day he was named head football coach at the University of Oklahoma. Earlier that day, the University of Maryland announced that Jim Tatum had been named the head coach of the Terrapins, clearing the way for Wilkinson to be named the coach of the Sooners. He was three months shy of his thirty-first birthday.
Photograph courtesy the Oklahoma Historical Society (2012.201.oVZ001.8099)

Gomer Jones (*left*) patrolled the Sooner sidelines with Bud Wilkinson for seventeen seasons. The two had played against each other in the 1930s—Jones at Ohio State and Wilkinson at Minnesota. Both were All-Americans.
Photograph courtesy the Oklahoma Historical Society (2012.201.B1370.0769)

OU president Dr. George Cross and his wife, Cleo, were avid Sooner football fans. Cross played briefly at South Dakota State before giving up the game to concentrate on his studies. Cross came to the university in 1934 and was named president in 1943. Over the years Cross became Wilkinson's chief supporter and believed Wilkinson was of such benefit to the university—and the state—that in order to keep him at OU, Cross arranged for Wilkinson to be paid more than he was as president.
Photograph courtesy the Oklahoma Historical Society (2012.201.B0149.0232)

Jack Mitchell (*left*), Wilkinson's first All-American quarterback, was a master at running the Split T quarterback option play and led the Sooners to eighteen victories in Wilkinson's (*right*) first two years at OU. He was an All-American in 1948 and started the Sooners on a thirty-one-game winning streak.
Photograph courtesy the Oklahoma Historical Society (2012.201.B1370.0786)

Darrell Royal (No. 21 with the ball) prepares to follow Wade Walker (No. 60) and Dee Andros (No. 70). All three leveraged their playing experiences at OU into head coaching opportunities. Royal coached at Mississippi State and Washington briefly before winning three national championships at Texas. Walker coached Mississippi State for six years, and Andros coached for fourteen years (three at Idaho and eleven at Oregon State).
Photograph courtesy the Oklahoma Historical Society (2012.201.B0162.0584)

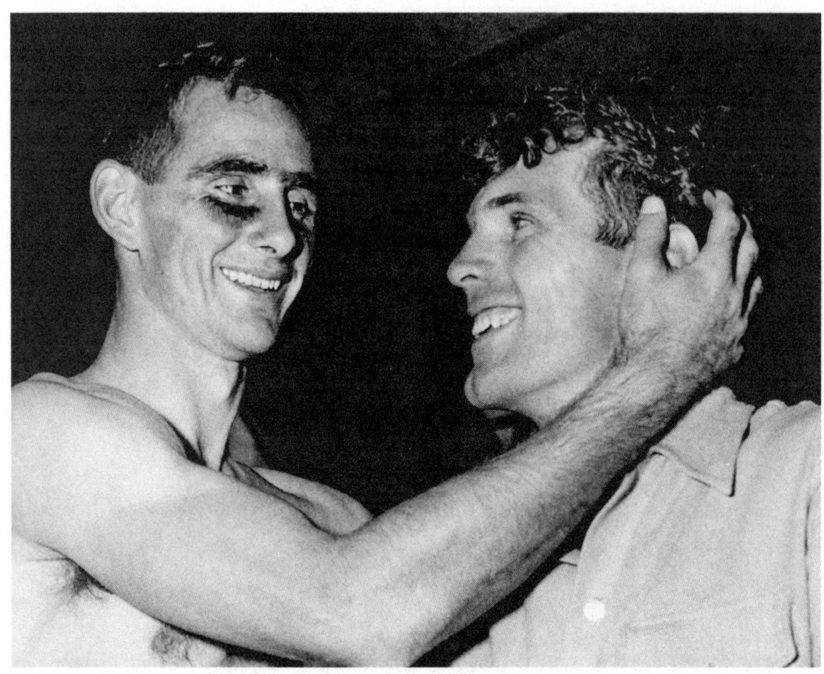

Defensive safety Buddy Jones (*left*), who began playing at OU as a walk-on, and fullback Leon Heath celebrate Oklahoma's 35–0 Sugar Bowl victory over Louisiana State. Heath was voted the MVP of the game after gaining 170 yards in fifteen carries, including touchdown runs of 86 and 34 yards. Both Jones and Heath were All-Americans in 1949.
Photograph courtesy the Oklahoma Historical Society (2012.201.B0314B.0109)

Claude Arnold (*left*) was nearly twenty-six years old when he became Bud Wilkinson's starting quarterback in 1950. The addition of a true passing threat made OU's offense even more formidable, as Arnold's passing yardage was twice Darrell Royal's in 1949. Arnold carried the Sooners to a 10–0 regular season that helped OU earn its first national championship and extend its streak of consecutive victories to thirty-one games. That streak was ended by Kentucky in the 1951 Sugar Bowl.
Photograph courtesy the Oklahoma Historical Society (2012.201.B1370.1019)

After the 1951 Sooners lost two of their first three games and Billy Vessels to injury, the situation looked dire. However, Bud Wilkinson's reconfigured backfield of (*left to right*) fullback Buck McPhail, quarterback Eddie Crowder, right halfback Dick Heatly, and left halfback Buddy Leake helped carry the Sooners to seven straight wins and a top ten national ranking.

Photograph courtesy the Oklahoma Historical Society (2012.201.B0149.0664)

Bud Wilkinson and Frank Leahy (*right*) shake hands before the nationally televised Oklahoma–Notre Dame game in 1952. Wilkinson endeavored to schedule nationally renowned teams in order to place the OU football program among the nation's elite. The impetus for the game with the Fighting Irish came when Leahy ate dinner at Wilkinson's house in early 1951.

Photograph courtesy the Oklahoma Historical Society (2012.201.B1370.1017)

By the early 1950s these three coaches were emerging as the most successful of their generation. They are (*left to right*) Bud Wilkinson, Jim Tatum, and Bear Bryant. Both Tatum and Bryant were three years older than Wilkinson. Before World War II, Tatum had already been a head coach at North Carolina, and Bryant was being considered for the head coaching position at Arkansas. Wilkinson would not become a head coach until 1947.
Photograph courtesy the Oklahoma Historical Society (2012.201.B1370.0885)

OU's Billy Vessels won the Heisman Memorial Trophy in 1952, the first for a Sooner player. During the year, Vessels ran for 1,072 yards and accounted for another 374 yards passing and pass receiving, but it was his performance against Notre Dame—seen on national television—that convinced many Heisman voters that Vessels was indeed the best player in the nation. Wilkinson had reached that conclusion two years before. He said that Vessels was the first player he ever saw who was both the fastest player on the field—and the toughest.
Photograph courtesy the Oklahoma Historical Society (2012.201.B1329.0649)

Bud Wilkinson met Red Sanders (*left*) in 1945 when they were assigned to the navy's flight training center in Pensacola, Florida. With World War II nearly over, there was no naval air training, so Sanders (in peacetime, the head football coach at Vanderbilt) and Wilkinson spent their days playing golf and talking football. Eleven years older than Wilkinson, Sanders served as a mentor to the young Wilkinson and remained a confidant until his death in 1959. Sanders's 1954 UCLA Bruins were co–national champions.
Photograph courtesy the Oklahoma Historical Society (2012.201.B1370.0917)

Bud Wilkinson and two Oklahoma All-Americans—Bo Bolinger (*left*) and Tommy McDonald—show off the 1955 national championship trophy. Bolinger was the fifth and last of Sooner All-Americans from Muskogee. Others included guard Buddy Burris, quarterback Eddie Crowder, center Kurt Burris, and end Max Boydston.
Photograph courtesy the Oklahoma Historical Society (2012.201.B1370.0872)

Central to the success of Bud Wilkinson's teams in the mid-1950s were assistant coaches Port Robertson (*left*) and Ted Youngling (*center*). Robertson was also the OU wrestling coach and the athletic department's academic advisor. It was his job to deliver each class of freshmen football players mentally disciplined and academically eligible for Wilkinson. Because he kept the academic records for OU athletes, he was in the habit of calling players by their first and middle names. Some thoughtful Sooners regarded Robertson as the noblest man they ever knew.

Photograph courtesy the Oklahoma Historical Society (2012.201.B1370.0946)

Bud Wilkinson and quarterback Jimmy Harris discuss the nuances of the Oklahoma quarterback option play. Wilkinson was the first coach to understand fully the potentially devastating effectiveness of the option play and made it a primary weapon in the Sooners' Split T attack.
Photograph courtesy the Oklahoma Historical Society (2012.201.B1370.1025)

In Clendon Thomas (*left*) and Tommy McDonald, Bud Wilkinson had arguably the best pair of halfbacks in the nation in 1956. The year before, Thomas agreed to play left halfback with the Sooners' alternate unit to balance the capability of the starters and the alternates. In 1956 Thomas became the starting right halfback and led the nation in scoring. McDonald was second.

Photograph courtesy the Oklahoma Historical Society (2012.201.B0390.0545)

Bud Wilkinson's teams played Notre Dame six times in the decade from 1952 to 1962. The Sooners came out the victors only once—the 1956 game played at Notre Dame. The Sooners realized how much the victory meant to Wilkinson and carried him off the field at the end of the 40–0 triumph.
Photograph courtesy the Oklahoma Historical Society

Talking with Bud Wilkinson are Bobby Boyd (*left*) and David Baker, the alternate quarterback and starting quarterback for the 1958 Sooners, the last of eleven consecutive OU teams to finish the season in the top ten. Unlike many other coaches, Wilkinson welcomed one-platoon football because it meant a player had to play offense and defense, as was the case when he played in college. Boyd and Baker were prime examples of Wilkinson's ability to recruit and train backs to play defense. Boyd was named to the NFL's 1960s All-Decade team. Baker was the fifth player selected in the 1959 NFL draft and was regarded by coaches and teammates as the hardest-hitting tackler they ever saw.
Photograph courtesy the Oklahoma Historical Society (2012.201.B1370.0776)

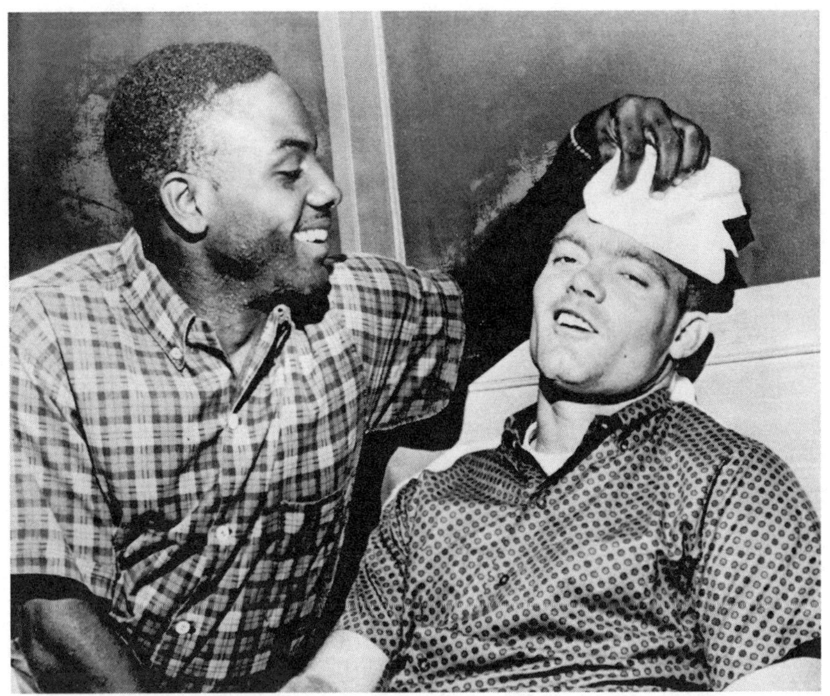

Prentice Gautt (*left*) pretends to comfort Brewster Hobby, one of twelve victims of the food poisoning incident at the Chez Paree before the 1959 season opener against Northwestern. Gautt was one of only two Sooners who did not attend the dinner. The 45–13 loss was the worst of Wilkinson's coaching career and shattered the Sooners' aura of invincibility.
Photograph courtesy the Oklahoma Historical Society (2012.201.B0553.0186)

In the second game of the 1963 season, the Sooners met defending national champions USC, then ranked No. 1. Wilkinson and his staff developed a game plan to control the ball on offense and harass USC's receivers on defense. It worked. With the temperature on the field hovering at 118 degrees, OU ran nearly twice as many plays as USC and shut down the Trojans' vaunted I-formation attack. The Sooners won, 17–12. The following week, they were ranked No. 1 in the nation for the first time in five years.
Photograph courtesy the Oklahoma Historical Society (2012.201.0VZ001.8092)

Part III
THE GLORY YEARS

1953

September 26, 1953, was the day America invaded Norman.

Oklahoma was getting used to playing in big games, perhaps the biggest of which had been played in South Bend the preceding fall. But never before had the most important game in college football taken place in Norman. Anyone involved with OU was besieged by requests for tickets. So great was the demand that seats normally reserved for the OU band, which customarily sat in the middle of the stands near the OU student section, were secretly apportioned to others.

All other Sooner rivalries now seemed to pale beside this new one with Notre Dame. Even the coaches were sometimes portrayed as bitter rivals, but in truth, Wilkinson and Leahy were good friends. Both were superb coaches who believed in the value of hard, competitive football. The differences were largely related to style. Wilkinson had come to Oklahoma with a distinctly Big Ten background. Leahy *was* Notre Dame.

Leahy played for Knute Rockne in 1928 and 1929, but suffered a preseason knee injury in 1930. He spent the season assisting Rockne, and when Rockne checked into the Mayo Clinic for two weeks of medical treatment after the season, he asked Leahy to come along for an operation and to keep him company. For two weeks, Leahy lay in the same room with Rockne, where the conversation centered around football hour upon hour. After his graduation, Leahy was hired as a coach at Georgetown by Jim Crowley, one of Notre Dame's Four Horsemen.

When Crowley moved to Fordham in 1933, Leahy went with him and helped create "The Seven Blocks of Granite," a line that included an undersized, overachieving guard named Vince Lombardi.

In 1939 Leahy became head coach at Boston College at thirty-one, the same age at which Wilkinson became the head coach at OU. In 1941 Elmer Layden—another of the Four Horsemen—resigned as the head coach and athletic director at Notre Dame. Leahy, the man who had shared a hospital room with the master, was chosen to replace Layden.

Leahy coached remarkable Fighting Irish teams for three years, the last two winning national championships, before he entered the navy in 1944. In 1946 he returned to Notre Dame and took over his former position from caretaker Hugh Devore. From 1946 through 1949 Leahy's teams went undefeated in thirty-eight games (but were tied twice, 0–0 by Army in 1946 and 14–14 by USC in 1948). Leahy won his third national championship in 1946 and another in 1949.

Notre Dame's football fortunes had waned since then, and Leahy's winning percentage, which had fallen from .952 to .883, now ranked behind Wilkinson's .885. But Notre Dame's victory over OU in 1952 signaled to Irish faithful the return to the top of the mountain. The Irish had played the toughest schedule in the nation in 1952, defeating three other conference champions besides Oklahoma. Virtually the entire team—Guglielmi, Lattner, Heap, Worden, and others—returned to challenge OU's string of twenty-five straight home victories in Memorial Stadium.

Never had the Sooners seemed so overmatched on paper. If the Sooners had looked inexperienced at the start of Wilkinson's rebuilding year in 1950, his 1953 team was even less seasoned. Nearly half of the players were sophomores, and they seemed incapable of staying on the same field with the Irish. The offense was decimated. Gone were Crowder, Vessels, McPhail, and the entire right side of the starting line. The defense remained no better than a year before. Wilkinson could not believe people thought the Sooners might beat Notre Dame. He had to hope the home field advantage and the searing late summer heat of Norman, to which the Irish would be unaccustomed, might make a difference. Otherwise, desire and spirit were the only things the Sooners possessed in equal measure to the Irish.

The biggest change from 1952 came as the result of new NCAA rules, however. First, freshmen—no matter how talented (think Buddy Leake)—were not eligible to play in NCAA games. They played only in limited games against other freshmen. This rule had little effect, Wilkinson realized, unless you were blessed with a player who possessed remarkable football gifts. Those cases were rare, he knew.

More important were the limitations on substitution. Now a player who started a quarter could leave the game and return only once during the quarter. The NCAA's goal had been to neutralize the effect of players with specialized talents and emphasize more well-rounded abilities. The rule had Wilkinson's unwavering support. He liked the new rule because it brought college football more in line with the game he had played as an undergraduate. Still, that did not prevent Wilkinson and his assistants from spending much of spring practice revamping the starting lineup to address college football's new realities.

Wilkinson understood instinctively that the new rules placed a premium on defensive ability. If a player—regardless of his offensive potential—was a defensive liability, his usefulness to the team was limited. As a result, Wilkinson reasoned, you had to find all-around players, but defensive ability came first, so he chose the players for his starting and alternate teams on the basis of their defensive ability, not their offensive potential. He would then fit their talents as best he could to some offensive position.

Because of the new rules, Leake would become the quarterback. Jack Ging would alternate at left half with Gene Calame. Co-captain Larry Grigg would start at right halfback ahead of Merrill Green because of Grigg's defensive ability. And Max Boydston would be moved to fullback, the position he played in high school.

This change in substitution rules also caused Wilkinson to spend most of the spring practice drilling the squad on defense rather than offense, as he usually did. OU linemen had been taught to go both ways for years. Backs, on the other hand, needed to be groomed to play defense. The Sooner staff had only twenty days in the spring to teach them. Thus, with this revamped lineup, which had never been tested under fire, Wilkinson and his staff prepared to take on the strongest team they had ever faced.

Out-of-town visitors for the Notre Dame game were legion. The Skirvin, which was considered the top hotel in Oklahoma City (and the one where the Sooners stayed the night before games in Norman), was booked full. Harold Keith, OU's sports publicist for nearly a quarter century, had never seen anything to match it.

Four months before the game, requests for press credentials and hotel rooms flooded Keith and the hotels in the area. In May, Dan James, the president of the Skirvin, sent a short letter to Keith:

> Dear Harold:
>
> We have just about reached the end of our rope in connection with the Notre Dame game and I think it would be wise to get right down to some

serious thinking about handling these people and would appreciate your letting me know what the requirements will be from your office.

I would suggest that everything be held to a minimum and would also appreciate it if you would use all the facilities that you can obtain in other places and relieve us to take care of only those big shots which you consider a must.

P. S. If we live through this deal and keep a few friends, we will be fortunate.

Finally, game day arrived. On a sweltering Oklahoma afternoon with the temperature approaching one hundred degrees, the Sooners won the toss, and Wilkinson chose to take the benefit of a twelve-mile-per-hour south wind.

The Sooners' kickoff was low and twisting. The ball landed at Lattner's feet, squirted between his legs, and rolled out-of-bounds at the Notre Dame 4. In three plays, the Irish moved to a first down at the 23. On the next play, the Irish fumbled, and the Sooners recovered.

The Sooners picked up 9 yards in three plays and faced a fourth down at the 14. Leake kept the ball on a quarterback sneak and made 6. On first down from the 8, Ging hit off left tackle and cut to the outside for 5. Leake sneaked for 2, then tried the same play again, but was stopped inches short of the goal. Faced with another fourth down, Leake pitched back to Grigg, who cut inside to score. Leake's extra point put the Sooners in front, 7–0.

On OU's next possession, Boydston was hit hard at the OU 42 and fumbled. The Irish evened the score quickly. Guglielmi and Lattner teamed on a 29-yard pass play to the OU 12. Four plays later, Guglielmi connected with Heap in the end zone. The Notre Dame extra point tied the game with six minutes to play in the quarter.

Early in the second quarter, the Sooner and Irish defenses held sway. Then, on first down at the OU 20, Leake chose to go long as he had seen Crowder do so many times. He faked to Boydston, hid the ball on his hip, rolled out, and threw. His pass hit Carl Allison perfectly, and Allison raced to the Notre Dame 18 before he was caught from behind. Five plays later, Ging sliced over left tackle for the touchdown. The Sooners were back in the lead, 14–7.

After only three plays, the Irish were again forced to punt as the OU defense continued to hold the powerful Irish offense in check. How long, Wilkinson wondered, could the Sooners' good fortune last? In twenty minutes against the team expected to be the national champions, the Sooners had given up a mere 37 yards rushing and 67 yards passing. The Sooners' spirit, it seemed, was exceeding even that of the Irish.

Soon, Wilkinson got the answer to his question. On the Sooners' next possession, Leake called for a quick kick on third-and-10 at the OU 33. This time, disaster struck. One Sooner lineman missed his blocking assignment, and Irish linebacker Don Penza charged through, blocking Boydston's kick and recovering it at the Sooner 9. Four plays later, Guglielmi scored on a quarterback keeper.

At the half, the 14–14 game was tighter than anyone could have imagined. What's more, the Sooners *should* have been leading! They would have been ahead comfortably, but turnovers deep in Sooner territory had taken their toll. Unlike the fumbles caused by the fierce Irish defense the previous season, these errors were mechanical. They had to stop.

Early in the second half, Guglielmi threw long to Heap, who was well covered by the Sooner secondary, but he made a phenomenal catch and scored, and the Irish moved into the lead for the first time. After the ensuing kickoff, Leake and center Kurt Burris did not connect on the snap, and the ball slipped free. Penza recovered again. Seven running plays later, the Irish slammed home another touchdown to take a commanding 28–14 lead.

Wilkinson was now concerned. The big Irish line was dominating the line of scrimmage, but more important, the Sooner offense was simply not gelling. Three fumbles and a blocked kick led to all of the Irish touchdowns, and they had driven no farther than 42 yards for any of them.

Finally, the Sooners got a break. Midway through the fourth quarter, the Sooners recovered an Irish fumble at the OU 38. If the Sooners were to make a comeback, this might be their only opportunity. Relying on Grigg and Boydston, Leake drove the Sooners to a first down at the Irish 31. Two plays later, a defensive holding penalty moved the ball to the Notre Dame 16. Suddenly, the Irish defense rallied. Three running plays gained only 2 yards, and then the Irish stormed Leake on fourth down and threw him for a 9-yard loss. Even worse, Grigg limped off the field with an injured ankle. Green hurried into the game to replace him.

Immediately, the Irish decided to test Green, who did not possess Grigg's extraordinary defensive ability. Lattner swept the left side toward Green, but Green charged the play and threw Lattner for a 3-yard loss. Two plays later, the Irish were forced to punt.

Lattner drilled a 47-yard kick deep to Green at the OU 40. Cutting quickly, Green evaded several Irish tacklers and suddenly broke into the clear, faked out Lattner at the Notre Dame 10, and scored standing up. Leake's extra point put the Sooners back in a position to tie, 28–21, with five minutes to play.

After the OU kickoff, the Irish got one first down, but when they tried to fool the Sooners with a halfback pass, Green stepped in front of the intended receiver and leaped to intercept the pass. The Sooners now had one more chance.

With 3:08 to play, the Sooners could still tie the game. Wilkinson saw that the Irish line was overpowering the smaller Sooners, so he instructed Leake to throw a screen pass on first down. It was a play the Sooners seldom used, which, in Wilkinson's mind, made it perfect for the situation. What's more, Wilkinson knew that *Leahy knew* the Sooners did not throw screen passes, and Wilkinson was willing to bet the Irish had not been coached to be wary of it. Notre Dame's relentless charge suggested to Wilkinson that the Irish had been coached to rush Leake with reckless abandon, thereby making them vulnerable to the screen pass.

The play worked as diagrammed. When Leake dropped back to pass, the OU line let the Irish linemen filter through. Leake gave ground, and the Irish lineman stormed toward him. The screen pass was open! Leake dropped the ball in the flat to Allison, who headed downfield with two blockers in front of him and only one Notre Dame defender between him and the goal. Unfortunately, the defender was Lattner, and he defended the play perfectly. He knifed between Allison's blockers and tripped him up at the Notre Dame 43. Two plays later, Leake tried to challenge Lattner again, but Lattner—who would eventually win the Heisman Trophy at the end of the 1953 season—again showed why. He intercepted Leake's pass to end the final Sooner threat.

Wilkinson walked to the middle of the field to congratulate Leahy, then hurried to the Sooner locker room. On the way, he counted the Sooners' turnovers. Eight of them. Five fumbles. Two interceptions. One blocked kick. Never again would he let his team give away a game like that.

Wilkinson was not the only person who realized the Sooners had lost a game they should have won. As the stadium was clearing, broadcaster Harry Wismer rode down the elevator from the press box and encountered the Rev. Theodore Hesburgh, the highly respected president of Notre Dame.

"Father," Wismer said, "you bastards were lucky."

As he did after almost every home game, Wilkinson invited a number of people to an open house at his home. Many of the guests had already arrived when Leahy finally came in the front door.

"Bud, can I borrow one of your shirts? Mine is soaked," Leahy explained.

Wilkinson took Leahy to his bedroom, where he complied with his friend's request. Refreshed, Leahy came into the living room, and Wilkinson introduced Leahy to the other guests, most of whom were loyal OU supporters. Wilkinson watched in amazement as Leahy conversed with them, always remembering their names perfectly.

How did he do it? Wilkinson had never seen anyone as good as Leahy, who had a politician's gift for recalling people's names months—even years—after he had met them. How Wilkinson wished he had the same ability! He was good at remembering names, but only if he encountered someone in the surroundings where he had met them before. If he met someone at the golf course, he could remember the new acquaintance's name perfectly there. But if he were to meet the same man at a business meeting, he might find his memory totally blank.

At last, the crowd at the open house began to dwindle, and Leahy left to join his team. He never bothered to return the shirt he borrowed, which enabled Wilkinson to regale friends with the story of how he once lost a football game—and his shirt—to Frank Leahy on the very same day.

The defeat would become a watershed game in Wilkinson's coaching career. Wilkinson knew that most big games are lost, not won. And the Sooners had certainly *lost* to the Irish. The inexperienced Sooners had moved the ball well on offense and held the No. 1 team in the nation to 224 total yards, but the eight mistakes had cost them a momentous victory. Professionally, Wilkinson valued defense and kicking, but personally he *loved* a daring, innovative offense. The loss to Notre Dame reinforced for him the risks of such an offense. By the time he met with his assistants on Sunday, he had determined that never again would the Sooners take such chances inside their own 30.

Graduate assistant Jack Santee watched as the freshmen under his tutelage ran through their drills. He was pleased. They were good athletes and seemed to possess a drive that was unusual even for freshmen at OU. After the drills were completed, he divided the players into teams so he could see them perform under competitive conditions. The No. 2 team ran a pitchout to the left halfback, who swung to the right. Suddenly, he cocked his arm and fired a pass to the right end. The pass was on target, but high. The end jumped to catch it, but the defensive back—a small, half-scholarship halfback from New Mexico—leaped at the same time and tipped the ball away from the receiver's hands. The ball popped upward, and for a lingering second, seem to hang suspended in the air. Both players hit the ground standing, but the small halfback immediately spun around the end, caught the ball as it came down, and raced toward the opposition's goal.

Santee was amazed. He could never remember seeing such a display of sheer athletic ability and football sense. This Tommy McDonald kid was going to be good, even if he was small. But that didn't matter at OU. Heart was what mattered, as Jack Ging and Buddy Jones had proved.

Santee rushed to the coaches' locker room, ebullient with his new discovery. Excitedly, he described the play McDonald had made to the other assistants.

"McDonald can be even better than Vessels!" he said excitedly.

From in front of his locker, Wilkinson turned with a look of skepticism.

"Careful, Old Man," Wilkinson said firmly.

The odyssey that brought McDonald to Norman had begun innocently enough several months before. Bruce Drake, the OU basketball coach, had just returned from a coaching clinic in Albuquerque, New Mexico, where he happened to attend a football all-star game that McDonald played in. When Drake returned to Norman, he stopped to visit with the Sooner football coaches.

"Check on that McDonald kid from Albuquerque Highland," Drake said. "I saw him play in a postseason football game, and I heard some awfully good things about him."

At the time, Wilkinson generally did not recruit beyond Oklahoma and West Texas. He believed that any player worth having would want to attend the college closest to his home, especially if it had a good football team and was the state university. Because Drake's enthusiastic report, however, Wilkinson sent Pop Ivy to Albuquerque to have a look. McDonald's high school coach met Ivy at the airport. With him were two players, one of whom was McDonald. McDonald was about Ging's size and had some of the same cockiness, but he seemed friendly and talkative.

Ivy accompanied the coach and the two players to the coach's home, where he had set up a projector. Together, they looked at game films from the preceding season. What Ivy saw amazed him. This McDonald kid did everything. He ran inside. He ran outside. He threw passes. He made jarring tackles. He dominated the game.

Next, they went to McDonald's house so Ivy could meet his parents and see the scrapbook his mother had kept. Mrs. McDonald had sent the same scrapbook to Leahy and his staff at Notre Dame. Leahy's reply was polite but discouraging: "Your son is too small and would sit on the bench at Notre Dame. He should look for a smaller school where he could play more." As a result, McDonald assumed he would go to New Mexico or Southern Methodist, the only two schools to recruit him.

Ivy returned to Norman and told Wilkinson to offer McDonald a scholarship. The athletic budget was tight, however, and Wilkinson had heard enough about supposed stars from small high schools to be wary. He suggested that McDonald be given a half scholarship.

A short time later, McDonald and his parents drove to Norman, and McDonald was given a chance to meet with Wilkinson. As they talked, McDonald began thinking that at five-foot-six, 143 pounds, he might be too small to play at Oklahoma.

"I know my size is against me," McDonald said. "I don't want to sit on the bench."

"Why, Tommy," Wilkinson said, "if that's what you think you're going to do here, then that's what you'll do. But if you make up your mind that you are going to play for Oklahoma, you'll do it. You will have to decide."

After meeting with McDonald, Wilkinson decided he was worth a half scholarship. McDonald accepted, and shortly thereafter, his parents sold some cattle to make the down payment on a car for McDonald to drive to and from Norman. At the time, McDonald was one of the few freshmen to have a car, and it quickly became a subject of dispute. New Mexico and SMU realized what they were losing and called for an NCAA investigation into what OU had offered McDonald. In the end, he and OU were cleared, but McDonald was not able to enjoy life at OU in peace.

For much of McDonald's freshman year, recruiters from other schools came to Norman hoping to entice him with offers of a full scholarship, but once McDonald saw the caliber of the other freshmen, he vowed to stay at Oklahoma even if he was never offered a full scholarship there. The Oklahoma coaches, not blind to McDonald's ability, took no chances. They arranged for him to receive a full scholarship as soon as the money became available.

Technically, Port Robertson's job at OU was wrestling coach. As such, he was the best in the nation, guiding Oklahoma's wrestlers to back-to-back national championships in 1950 and 1951. As a student at OU, Robertson had been a skilled wrestler himself, but an unfortunate injury kept him from achieving his own personal goal—becoming a national collegiate champion. That failure made him an exceptional coach. He was determined to make every athlete at OU live up to his potential.

When World War II interrupted Robertson's coaching career, he rose to the rank of captain in the field artillery and was decorated for gallantry in action during the invasion of Normandy. Besides a Purple Heart, he carried one other remnant of his wartime experience. Trapped in a foxhole, he—like many GI's—found himself face-to-face with the specter of death as a young man. A German hand grenade rolled into the foxhole next to him. Alone, he prayed: "Dear Lord, if you let me live through this, I will never take your name in vain again." Robertson was far from the only soldier to offer such a prayer. But when Robertson's prayer was answered, it was not in the makeup of Port G. Robertson to go back on his word.

For a generation, OU athletes would be mesmerized by the hard-working, self-effacing Robertson, who was able to outwrestle young men half his age yet seldom raised his voice and—except in moments of extreme frustration—never uttered anything resembling profanity.

As athletic director, Wilkinson recognized Robertson's extraordinary integrity and asked him to serve as academic advisor to all of OU's athletes. Robertson, a moral force capable of taming even the strongest and most recalcitrant of students, was to deliver each year's crop of incoming freshmen—mentally prepared and academically eligible—for Wilkinson and Jones the following spring. Robertson was the perfect man for the job. Despite his outward contrast to the urbane Wilkinson, their philosophies were strikingly similar. Both were driven by a desire to excel and believed discipline was essential to do so.

"There are two things you should never have to worry about," Robertson would tell his wrestlers. "One is whether you have your technique down. The second is whether you're physically conditioned to meet the challenge. That just leaves one other thing—whether you're good enough to beat your opponent. But if you have your technique down and are physically conditioned, you can count on the fingers of one hand the number of people on the face of the earth who can beat you."

As the rock of discipline at OU, Robertson was unwavering. If a freshman skipped study hall or committed some other infraction, Robertson had one surefire punishment—running the steps of Memorial Stadium, which were seventy-two rows high at the time. He would routinely assemble the offending Sooners at 6 A.M. with his stopwatch. Raised on a farm, Robertson rose before sunrise as a matter of course, so meting out such punishment—which neither Wilkinson nor Jones found enjoyable—was simply all in a day's work for Robertson.

"Hit the ramparts!" he would yell and keep count as the offending Sooners paid penance for their misdeeds.

In one other respect, Robertson was indispensable. Like Wilkinson, his love of athletics had led him into a career in coaching. Yet, unlike Wilkinson, who reaped the financial rewards accorded a head football coach, Robertson labored in anonymity—head wrestling coach, freshman football coach, academic advisor,

Jeff House proctor—for a pittance of what he might have earned if his ability had been applied in the business world.

Like a father who wants only the best for his sons, Robertson—who shared Wilkinson's belief that athletes should aspire to careers that would allow them to make a comfortable living in later life—unselfishly steered scores of young Sooners into careers that would enable them to enjoy a measure of financial success Robertson himself could never hope to achieve. Only the crassest of young men—despite their willful struggles with his iron hand—failed to understand that Robertson was a friend. And the noblest man most of them would ever know.

The week following the loss to Notre Dame, Wilkinson instituted his new conservative offensive discipline against Pittsburgh. The Sooners dramatically reduced their errors, but OU was held to 63 yards rushing—a new low for a Wilkinson team—and had to settle for a 7–7 tie with the emotionally charged Panthers. The Sooners' plane ride home was quiet and subdued. The Sooners were 0–1–1 when they easily could have been undefeated, but they were inexperienced and struggling. Wilkinson could sense that players were not comfortable in their positions. Changes had to be made immediately. With most major college teams, Wilkinson realized, talent was nearly equal. So were methods of preparing a team for a game. That made up perhaps 96 percent of the game. It was the remaining 4 percent—the intangibles—that spelled the difference between victory and defeat. And that was where the Sooners were struggling.

Wilkinson knew there was also depth chart housekeeping to do. The most urgent need was to find a replacement at left halfback for Ging, who had suffered a separated shoulder. Wilkinson and the Sooners were disheartened by Ging's injury, for they all knew that of any of the Sooners, the 157-pound Ging least deserved misfortune. Few players brought such toughness and desire to the game. Now, Ging was out for the season. And because he was a senior, it seemed he would never play football again.

Boydston, an end of All-America caliber but clearly less capable at fullback, was moved permanently back to right end, where his speed and ability could be fully utilized. Bob Burris, who had played left halfback against Notre Dame and installed as a fullback against Pitt, was put at fullback to stay. But the most important change needed to be made at quarterback. As talented as he was, Leake suffered from the same malady that had afflicted Darrell Royal. Leake simply could not master the option play, and his failure to do so meant he could not move the Sooners consistently. Continuing to play him at quarterback cost the

Sooners doubly. He was ineffective as a quarterback, and it meant he was not available to play halfback, where he was, like Boydston, of All-America caliber. Wilkinson did not blame Leake, who had tried as hard as Royal to master the position. But as coach, Wilkinson knew it was his job to put the right players in the right positions, and he had failed. In Leake's place, Wilkinson put Gene Calame.

Against Texas, the changes seemed to make a difference. In the first quarter, halfback Tom Carroll charged up from his spot in the secondary to disrupt a Texas sweep to the outside. With one hand, he reached out and intercepted the pitchout. A Texas player hit Carroll's arm and knocked the ball loose, but Carroll fell on it at the Texas 25. Six plays later, Grigg scored.

In the second quarter, the Longhorns drove a 42-yard punt to Green at the OU 20. Green faked a handoff to Leake and turned upfield. After getting a couple of blocks, Green was loose down the sidelines.

"Get out the kicking tee!" Green yelled to Wilkinson as he dashed past the Oklahoma bench.

The 19–14 victory over Texas on national television seemed to lift the Sooners, who pounded Kansas, 45–0, the following week with a school record 537 yards rushing. One week later in Norman, the fledgling Sooners faced Colorado, the Sooners' fourth major test in five games. Twice in the first three quarters they had to come from behind to tie the Buffaloes. Finally, they took a 20–13 lead with seven minutes left in the game, but the struggling Sooners could not deliver the defensive coup de grâce. The Buffaloes drove 80 yards to tie the score 20–20 with 1:30 left to play, twice fooling the Sooners with trick plays on fourth down. Some Sooner fans, discouraged that the current team had little of the offensive magic of a year before, began to file out of the stands certain that they had seen the young Sooners let victory slip through their grasp yet another time.

Calame took the ensuing Colorado kickoff at the OU 15 and ran it back to the 30. On first down, Leake attempted a long halfback pass that fell incomplete. On second down, Calame ran the option to the left and was stopped for no gain, but some of the Sooners' home field magic remained intact. The Buffaloes were penalized for holding, moving the ball to the OU 49.

With forty-four seconds left, Calame called a rollout trap, a play devised by Wilkinson that the Sooners seldom used. As Calame started to his left as if to pass, he pitched to Green heading in the opposite direction. Green sped through an open hole and cut to the sidelines, where he outran the Colorado secondary. When Green crossed the goal with thirty-six seconds left, the fans in the aisles and the Colorado players were awestruck. The Sooners were becoming as invincible as their predecessors.

In succeeding weeks, the Sooners kept winning. They defeated Kansas State, Iowa State, Nebraska, and Oklahoma A&M in convincing fashion. The only close call came against Missouri. Late in the fourth quarter, Grigg dove headlong to knock down a certain touchdown pass before Calame led a flawless 80-yard march to score the winning touchdown in a 14–7 triumph.

At the end of the regular season, the Sooners were ranked No. 4 in the nation and earned the right to play Maryland in the Orange Bowl. The Big Seven had rescinded its unpopular rule against bowl participation, and so for the first time since the narrow loss to Kentucky, Wilkinson had to prepare his team for a bowl, this time against a team coached by Jim Tatum.

Tatum's Terrapins were big and fast. They shut out six opponents and held three others to a single touchdown. No one played them close.

"This is the greatest team I've ever coached," Tatum said when he came to Norman to scout Oklahoma during the season finale with Oklahoma A&M.

The Sooners, on the other hand, were not the greatest team Wilkinson had ever coached. In fact, the Sooners always had to earn victories the hard way. Other than Green, they had no breakaway running threat. They lacked the poise and finesse of earlier Sooner teams. And they did not pass well. That the Sooners led the nation in rushing was not so much a credit to the running ability of the backs, but an indication of how poorly the Sooners passed.

Given one-platoon rules that limited the use of offensive specialists, Wilkinson simply did not believe a college team could be consistently good at passing. The reasons, he thought, were self-evident. Without any kind of interference from a defense, a pro passer will hit five of five passes. The average college quarterback, on the other hand, will misthrow two. Beyond that, a receiver might drop one, and the defense would break up one. So for the average college quarterback, passing was a 20 percent proposition. And by that yardstick, the determined but athletically limited Calame was the walking definition of average.

The Sooners had succeeded because they had courage and desire. And armed with those qualities—and superb training from Jones and Wilkinson's other assistants—they played as well as they could. That, Wilkinson believed, is what the game of football is really about, but to stand a chance against Maryland, the Sooners would have to play well *and* get some breaks. Otherwise, the larger Terrapins, who allowed an average of only 84 yards per game rushing, would overpower the Oklahoma running game.

The Terrapins entered the game without Bernie Faloney, their starting quarterback, who was injured at midseason. It seemed he might be able to play in the Orange Bowl, but two days before the game, he reinjured his knee. At a bowl press conference, Tatum explained what that meant to the Terrapins.

"There goes our ball game. Faloney is the heart and stomach of our team," said the earthy and impulsive Tatum, who was technically correct but did not seem to consider the effect such a statement might have on his team's morale.

OU won the opening coin toss and chose to receive, giving Maryland the benefit of a strong wind at its back. Early in the first quarter, the Terrapins took advantage of that wind and punted out-of-bounds at the OU 1-foot line. Rather than risk the type of fumble that had doomed the Sooners against Notre Dame, Calame sneaked twice out to the 5, and then Leake punted to the Sooner 37.

Charlie Boxold, the replacement for Faloney, quickly moved the Terrapins to three first downs to put the ball at the OU 4. There seemed to be no stopping the massive Maryland offense, but the Sooners braced for the onslaught. On first down, the Terrapins went straight ahead for 2. Then they tried to go wide, but Grigg charged up and stopped the ball carrier for no gain. On third down, the Terrapins gained another yard. The ball game had barely begun, and already the Sooners had their backs to the wall. Now, on fourth-and-goal from the 1, the next play might tell the story.

Maryland came to the line of scrimmage. Ralph Felton, the Terrapin fullback, drove straight ahead. The center of the OU line charged forward to meet him. Slowly, the players unpiled. Suddenly, the referee placed the ball on the ground and signaled first down in the opposite direction. The Sooners had held!

Twice more in the first quarter, the Sooners withstood Maryland thrusts deep into OU territory. Finally, early in the second quarter, the Sooners went on offense from their own 20. After two first downs, the Sooners reached the Maryland 39. On first down, Burris ran over right tackle, picking up 3 and causing Maryland to call a time out.

In the huddle, Calame reviewed his play sequence. In each series, he had called two inside running plays before passing or running wide on third down. This time, he would go wide on second down with the quarterback option.

Calame took the snap and faked a handoff to the miraculously recovered Ging hitting off left tackle. Then Calame moved along the line of scrimmage and turned upfield at the corner, where the Terrapin defense converged to stop him. At the last instant, he pitched to Grigg. There, at the left corner, where the defensively sound Faloney normally would have been playing, Grigg broke into the open. He got outside Boxold and cruised down the sideline to score. Leake kicked the extra point, and OU found itself ahead of the national champions, 7–0.

Late in the first half, the Terrapins seemed to be driving again. But Grigg and Calame broke up long passes by Boxold before the Sooners dropped Boxold for a 5-yard loss. Another Maryland thrust had been blunted. The OU bench erupted in cheers until the Sooners saw Calame hobble from the field, his left hand clutching his right arm in pain. With Calame out and alternate quarterback Pat O'Neal previously injured, the Sooners had only one quarterback left—third-string senior Jack Van Pool, who had not even lettered as a junior. Hurriedly, Wilkinson sent in Van Pool for the last three plays of the first half.

In the locker room at halftime, Van Pool was hesitant. He had spent hours in quarterback meetings with Wilkinson over four years, but had seldom been called upon to utilize those lessons under game conditions, much less against the No. 1 team in America.

"What shall I call this half?" Van Pool asked Wilkinson.

"It's your ball game," Wilkinson told him. "You call it."

Through much of the second half, Maryland monopolized the ball, but OU's defense held firm. When Oklahoma had the ball, there were eleven Sooners on the field, but each play became a test of Van Pool. Would this be the down when he makes The Big Mistake? But with every play, Van Pool held his own. He and the other Sooner defensive backs stifled Maryland's limited passing game. And when the Terrapins tried to run, the Sooner linemen kept the plays contained at the line of scrimmage.

Finally, late in the fourth quarter, the Sooners knew victory could be theirs if they could control the ball for just four minutes longer. For those final minutes, Van Pool would wear the mantel of Mitchell, Royal, Arnold, and Crowder. With each play, the Sooners killed time on the clock and moved closer to a victory no one—perhaps not even the Sooners themselves—had thought possible.

First to the left. Then to the right. On each play, the Sooner line drove the Terrapins aside. Inside. Outside. With the wisdom of three years at Wilkinson's side, Van Pool mixed his plays brilliantly, driving the Sooners to three first downs to secure Oklahoma's 7–0 victory.

One-third talent. One-third conditioning. One-third spirit. One-platoon football was a delicate balance of qualities that Wilkinson loved. Certainly, he knew, the Sooners' talent did not carry them, but the Sooners' conditioning and spirit, as Wilkinson knew they could, enabled the Sooners to emerge victorious.

1954

In 1952 both Wilkinson and Jones had moved into new houses on a quiet suburban street called Brookside Drive, just south of the OU campus. Through the years, the Wilkinson and Jones families became close, and because Jones and his wife had no children, the Joneses always spent Christmas with Wilkinson and his family.

By 1954 the proximity of the two houses caused Wilkinson and Jones to develop a daily ritual that would continue each football season for the next ten years. Wilkinson believed the late-night staff meetings favored by many head coaches accomplished little because everyone was tired. As a result, he insisted that the Sooner coaching staff begin its days with 6 A.M. meetings. Each morning, Wilkinson would awaken at 5 A.M. He would walk to Jones's house, where he and Jones would have coffee and briefly discuss the day ahead. Shortly before six, they would leave for the football offices to join the rest of the Sooner staff.

When Wilkinson first arrived at OU, the football offices were located in the field house. In the early 1950s they were moved to the north end of Memorial Stadium next to the architecture department on the second floor. The offices—designed with the help of architecture student Eddie Crowder—were far from lavish. In fact, only Wilkinson's office was large enough to accommodate more than a desk and a couple of chairs. The offices were modest at Wilkinson's insistence. Always of the belief that the football program must fit within the framework of the university, Wilkinson dictated that the coaches' salaries and offices would be in line with members of the OU faculty in equivalent positions. Despite the fact that he was paid more than the university president, Wilkinson saw himself as a department head with an office the same size as the heads of the academic departments.

The football offices had a small conference room, where most of the staff meetings occurred. The day would begin with such a meeting, during which the coaches would discuss personnel, injuries, or changes in the depth chart. The morning meeting would last until approximately nine o'clock, when the coaches would adjourn for breakfast. Usually, they would go to the OU student union or to a nearby café to continue their discussion. Jones seldom joined the other coaches, however. For Jones, his home was truly his castle, and he would retreat there for breakfast and lunch.

In the afternoons, the coaches would watch films of an upcoming opponent or prepare for the afternoon's practice. Each practice was meticulously timed so that every player was given equal opportunity for drill. With practices usually limited to two hours, the number of players the coaches could effectively handle was sixty-six. And to do that, Wilkinson and his assistants would spend four hours in preparation for each hour of time on the practice field.

The atmosphere Wilkinson created at Oklahoma during that time was unlike any other football program in the country. This came as a shock to Sam Lyle (a former LSU end who played against the Sooners in the 1950 Sugar Bowl) when he joined the Sooners staff after three years on Bobby Dodd's staff at Georgia Tech. Lyle was uncertain what to think of Wilkinson. He was not like any other football coach Lyle had seen before. Wilkinson never raised his voice, on or off the field. He never berated his players regardless of what kind of mistakes they made. He would sit quietly and talk about things like moral fitness or bits of philosophical wisdom, such as competing with yourself to be the best football player you could be.

After his previous experiences at LSU and Georgia Tech, Lyle understood the importance of getting total effort from players, but he was used to much more direct orders, often spoken in a threatening tone. That the Sooners understood and responded to Wilkinson's instructions amazed Lyle. Even more confusing were statements Wilkinson might make in staff meetings.

"Perfection," Wilkinson would say, "is not attained at the point at which nothing else can be added, but at that point at which nothing else can be taken away."

For weeks, Lyle lay awake nights analyzing such statements. Finally, he could stand it no longer. He went to see Jones, who had now been with Wilkinson for eight years.

"Gomer," Lyle said tentatively. "Is the Old Man a phony or what?"

Jones stood up from his chair, so agitated that Lyle thought Jones might be going to hit him.

"Bud Wilkinson is a gentleman and the finest gentleman you will ever meet in your life," Jones said, ending the discussion.

Wilkinson did not believe in basing his team's preparation on emotional speeches before a game. He believed that how a squad prepares Monday through Thursday is more important than any pep talk a coach may give. Players are either ready to play or they are not. It is as simple as black and white—and there are no shades of gray. If a player is ready, he will be willing to give what it takes to win, and it is easy to see who is giving his all and who is not. Yet despite his avowed belief that *emotional* pregame speeches were unimportant, Wilkinson always addressed *motivational* subjects with the Sooners before they took the field. And he did so with remarkable effect.

"Don't lie to yourself," Wilkinson would tell the Sooners. "Don't tell yourself you did the best you could, if you didn't. Only a fool lies to himself."

Wilkinson believed it was imperative for each player to give his all as his responsibility to his teammates. From that came trust and team unity. Yet as much as Wilkinson preached team unity, he understood there would be conflicts among his players. Young men, brimming with testosterone and rewarded throughout their young lives for being physically aggressive, could not be expected to be models of polite behavior. Add to that the competitiveness they displayed—and Wilkinson recruited for—and you had a formula for confrontation.

This came as no surprise to Wilkinson. As a young man, he had excelled in this realm. As a young coach, he understood that the Pre-Flight program was designed to identify men who possessed that competitive streak before the nation invested in their pilot training. As a result, Wilkinson viewed courage—both physical and mental—as one of the chief developmental aspects of football. It was not like boxing, where the *intent* of the sport is to deliver a physical beating to an opponent, but the need to hit—and hit hard and hit repeatedly—was one of the requirements for playing college football.

The problem became acute with the arrival of the recruiting class of 1953, which included a number of players who possessed greater physical gifts than many of the upperclassmen. Each year, Wilkinson regarded the top twenty-two players (that is, the starters and alternates) as The Team. He believed that if a player would ever make a significant contribution at OU, he would be good enough to make The Team as a sophomore. To upperclassmen, that meant a sophomore would contribute by playing with the alternates (that is, the second unit). A position on the starting team was the province of juniors and seniors.

As the Sooners began the 1954 season, Wilkinson expected great things of his new sophomore class, which might be good enough, he believed, to win a national championship. He even told them so, not to build up their confidence—they had no shortage of that—but to prepare them for the disciplined sacrifices necessary to achieve that goal.

Still, Wilkinson could sense there was trouble among his players, much of it swirling around two of his most talented and cocky players, Tommy McDonald and Jimmy Harris. They were among the lightest players on the team at 170 pounds. McDonald was shorter at five-foot-nine. Harris was four inches taller. McDonald had been overcoming athletic obstacles and bigger athletes all his life. So had Harris.

A single wing tailback, Harris led Terrell to the 2A Texas state championship. He originally committed to Texas A&M, where the coach got him a summer job pouring concrete in College Station. Wilkinson arranged for Harris to get a job in the oil fields, which was hard work but paid much better. Because Harris's father died when he was ten, he had been working since then to help his mother make the eighteen-dollar-a-month mortgage payment.

Harris had all the right tools. He was fast, intelligent, and played excellent defense. Wilkinson could always find a place for such a player. As a freshman, Harris started his career at OU competing with McDonald for the No. 1 left halfback spot, but the Sooners were short on quarterbacks, and so a quarterback is what Harris became. In less than a year, he went from being the No. 6 freshman quarterback to directing the Sooner starters.

Yes, they were cocky. Yes, Wilkinson, Port Robertson, and the other coaches were tired of it, but they realized that the cockiness brought a sense of bravado that enabled them to accomplish things athletically that others would not even attempt. They had the courage and toughness to pull it off. Wilkinson had seen it in Jack Mitchell. He'd seen it in Darrell Royal. He'd seen it in Billy Vessels. And that kind of cocky confidence is what produces national championships.

Another who was tired of their cockiness was senior center Kurt Burris, and he intended to do something about it. McDonald was not so bad. He was irritating, but he was playing with the alternates—where he was supposed to be. Harris was a different matter. Calame, the starting quarterback, had played in the season-opening victory over California with his ribs heavily taped. If his condition became worse or he suffered other injuries, Harris was in line to become the starting quarterback as a sophomore. And, Burris believed, there's a price to be paid for such hubris.

In special team drills before the TCU game, Harris was lined up in the backfield for punt protection. Rather than going through the drill half speed, Burris burst through the line, cocked his right arm, and drove it into Harris's face. The Sooners' helmets at that time did not have face guards, so the full brunt of Burris's blow crashed into Harris's jaw, breaking two of his front teeth. With his mission accomplished, Burris turned and ran back upfield to block for the punt return.

What Burris did not realize was that Harris was right behind him. He jumped on Burris's back and began pounding the sides of Burris's helmet with his fists as blood gushed out of his mouth. Other Sooners separated them, but Burris turned and glared at Harris.

"Remember what I'm telling you, boy" he said to Harris. "No sophomore should be starting for this football team."

Harris turned and walked away. Burris's cheap shot meant Harris was winning. And Harris knew it.

From the beginning, the Sooners' second game of the season against the TCU Horned Frogs did not go well. Early in the game, the Sooners fell behind, 2–0, when a deep snap on a punt rolled out of the end zone. Then, just before halftime with the score unchanged, Calame suffered a shoulder injury. The situation Burris had railed against was imminent.

At the start of the second half, Harris went in to quarterback the Sooner starters. It took only minutes for Harris to prove himself. Early in the quarter, he caught a TCU punt at the OU 31 and dashed 69 yards to score the Sooners' first touchdown. The Horned Frogs rallied to score on two 80-yard drives to take a 16–7 lead. At the start of the fourth quarter, OU marched 75 yards to score on Harris's 2-yard keeper. Leake kicked the extra point to cut TCU's lead to 16–14.

Late in the game, TCU punted deep to Leake, who took the line drive kick 15 yards beyond the TCU coverage. Leake cut to the right sideline toward the Sooner bench. Hemmed in, he swerved back to his left and brought the punt back 50 yards to the TCU 10, where the last TCU defender brought him down. On the next play, the Sooners scored to give the Sooners a scant 20–16 victory, but one that lifted OU to No. 1 in the polls.

Eight hundred miles from Norman in Starkville, Mississippi, two former Sooners were attempting to follow the same course that Wilkinson and Jones had established seven years before. In 1954, barely five years after he left Oklahoma,

Darrell Royal had been named the head coach at Mississippi State when Murray Warmath left to take the head coaching position at Minnesota (a turn of events that George Cross viewed with considerable relief). As Royal had promised, the first call he made when putting together a staff was to Wade Walker, then an assistant at Texas Tech.

"I'm afraid it doesn't pay very much," Royal said to Walker.

Walker interrupted him.

"It doesn't matter," said Walker. "I'll be there."

The two Sooner teammates would remain together for two years before Royal moved on to Washington. After that, Walker succeeded Royal as the Bulldogs' head coach, and stayed at the helm of Mississippi State through the 1961 season. His best year would be 1957, when the Bulldogs would go 6–2–1 and end the year ranked fourteenth in the country. It would be another seventeen years before Mississippi State would have another nationally ranked team.

People tended to think of Ed Gray in compound adjectives. Easy-going. Devil-may-care. Happy-go-lucky. Because of his outward flippancy, only a few saw his serious dedication to football. In a class of exceptional sophomores, Gray was the only one to begin the 1954 season as a starter. Gray walked around the OU campus with a perennially stiff neck and a scab on his nose, both the result of his own particular blocking style. The sore neck came from his habit of butting his head into the stomach of opposing linemen as he blocked them. The scab sprang from the same cause. Every time Gray hit a defender especially hard, the force of the blow would force the front of his helmet down over his prominent nose. For obvious reasons, his teammates began calling him Beaky Buzzard.

If nothing else, Gray was not afraid to be himself. He enjoyed tropical fish and kept an aquarium in his room in Jeff House. When it was time to clean the bowl, Gray simply plugged the shower drain in Jeff House, turned on the water, and dumped the fish onto the tile floor. The procedure often irritated other Sooners and once led to the demise of Gray's entire collection. One of Gray's teammates put a piranha in Gray's aquarium, and it ate all his fish. Gray spent the next year trying to find out who did it so he could exact revenge.

Another of the stallions in the 1953 recruiting class was Jerry Tubbs. In the early 1950s a near constant state of war existed among the Southwest Conference schools—and Oklahoma—to recruit players like Tubbs. When it came to recruiting the very best high school football players, the state of Texas could become a small universe. Often, there was bad blood between SWC schools over past recruiting confrontations. As a result, the SWC letter of intent became a matter of course. A boy who signed it committed himself to that school in the SWC, although he could choose to attend another school outside the conference. The problem was that SWC schools began to believe that a conference letter of intent meant the player was signed, sealed, and delivered—which, of course, he was not. Sometimes, players would sign with a Southwest Conference school and then choose to go to Oklahoma, a situation that never seemed to end amicably.

Tubbs understood the heated arguments that could develop and, remarkably mature for his age, wanted no such complications surrounding him. He signed a conference letter of intent with Baylor, but he added a handwritten note: "I believe I'm going to go to school at Oklahoma. But if I don't, I'll come here."

Tubbs had thought through his decision carefully. The product of a deeply religious family, he was encouraged to go to Baylor by his parents. Others in Breckenridge wanted him to go to Texas. No one wanted him, a Texas schoolboy star, to go to Oklahoma. In the end, that was the reason Tubbs chose Oklahoma. If he went to Baylor or Texas and it did not work out, Tubbs knew he could always say it was somebody else's fault, that he was pressured into going there. But if he came to Oklahoma and something went wrong, he couldn't blame his family. He couldn't blame his friends. The responsibility would be on his shoulders alone. That was the way Tubbs wanted it. And he wanted to play for Bud Wilkinson.

In keeping with his religious beliefs, Tubbs did not care much what other people thought of him. While other students wore slacks and sport shirts to class, Tubbs wore jeans and a T-shirt, much as he might have at home in Breckenridge, a farming, ranching, and oil center in north-central Texas. Tubbs was interested in only two things—making good grades and playing good football. And the Sooners knew they could count on seeing the study light on Tubbs's desk shining through his window as they left Jeff House to go out on dates on Saturday night.

Tubbs's one concession to personal vanity was concern over his hairline, which began to recede during his freshman year. Once, he went to a beauty salon in Oklahoma City and came back with a lotion that was supposed to make hair grow. He would stand in front of the mirror in the bathroom for hours, massaging the lotion into his scalp.

One day, Gray could stand it no longer. As he opened the bathroom door to go back to his room, Gray turned back in Tubbs's direction.

"Eggs, Jerry," Gray said. "Try eggs."

Another of the sophomores whose persona belied his ability was Billy Pricer, a short but powerful fullback from the wrestling hotbed of Perry, Oklahoma, where

Pricer had been both an All-State football player and state champion wrestler. Pricer quickly proved himself a devastating blocker on offense, but his progress on defense was less rapid.

One afternoon during two-a-days, Pricer was crouched low at his linebacker spot, his hands on his knees and his weight balanced. He was ready to spring in any direction to make a tackle. The ball was snapped. The halfback came charging into the line. Pricer lowered his shoulder and prepared to plow into the halfback and slam him to the ground. Suddenly, Pricer felt a sense of isolation. The halfback was faking! Quickly, he looked around to locate the flow of the play. As he did, Burris slammed into him.

"Pricer!" came a shout. He recognized the voice of Gomer Jones.

Pricer stood up and faced the short, round coach, who was the same height but thirty pounds heavier.

"Pricer, what in the world happened? Didn't you check your key?"

"What's a key, Coach?" Pricer said.

There was no talk of keys at Perry High School. You just chased the guy with the ball and tackled him.

"A key," explained Jones, "is something that tells you where the play is going *before* it happens. If a halfback leans his weight to one side before the snap, that's a key. If the tackle looks to his right or his left, that's a key. If a guard pulls to his right or left rather than charging straight ahead, that's a key. Do you understand?"

Pricer still looked confused.

"I'll show you," Jones said.

The Sooner offense huddled to call another play. The defense set itself. Pricer assumed his position. Jones stood behind Pricer and grabbed the belt on Pricer's pants. The offense came to the line of scrimmage and snapped the ball. Before the play could develop, Jones yanked Pricer to the left.

"See the guard!" he said. "He stepped to his right, not straight ahead. It's going to the right. See?"

Sure enough, the play went to the right—Pricer's left—just as Jones had said.

"But you know the plays!" Pricer protested.

"That has nothing to do with it. I just watched the key. That's all you have to do."

On the next play, Jones yanked Pricer to the right, putting him in position to stop a sweep to that side.

"Did you see the guard's eyes?" Jones asked. "Just before the snap, he looked to the side. That's your key!"

After several plays, Pricer began to understand. Jones was pleased. He and Wilkinson expected to make Pricer the alternate fullback, and that meant he would be playing linebacker in critical situations.

Even though the Sooners played well in the hard-fought victory over TCU, Wilkinson was concerned about the effect of injuries on his lineup. The Sooners were dangerously thin at quarterback and fullback. And none of the fullbacks, who became linebackers in OU's defensive scheme, was good enough to please Wilkinson and Jones. At the same time, they had Tubbs—perhaps the greatest natural linebacker they had ever seen—languishing with the alternates. Something clearly had to be done.

It had not taken Wilkinson long to learn that Tubbs was an extraordinary football player with a temperament similar to Jim Weatherall's. That is, he was quiet and reserved off the field, a terror on it. Tubbs was the center for the alternate unit and would see considerable playing time behind Burris. But as a linebacker, Tubbs was already capable of starting and clearly superior to any of the fullbacks who would play linebacker beside Burris in the Sooner defense. The solution was as simple as it was daring. Tubbs would become the starting fullback. Wilkinson was not worried about Tubbs's ability to carry the ball. He knew that virtually any player can be taught how to carry the ball, but the innate ability to follow the ball on defense could not be taught, and that is what Tubbs possessed.

The Sooners had a week off to prepare for Texas, and Tubbs's concentrated instruction in playing fullback began the Tuesday after the victory over TCU. As Wilkinson expected, ball carrying did come easy to Tubbs. What came hardest was teaching him how to block the defensive cornerback. After spending years blocking from a crouched position at center, Tubbs's transition to the running block at the corner did not come smoothly, especially on the Sooners' muddy practice field.

As with all elements of the game, Wilkinson decided to simplify instruction by breaking down the block into identifiable steps for Tubbs to master. Unlike some head coaches, Wilkinson did not oversee Sooner practices from a tall tower. Instead, he preferred to be on the ground alongside his players, where he could interact with them face-to-face, a preference he expressed whenever an acquaintance would try to discuss the intricacies of coaching football with him.

"I don't coach Xs and Os," Wilkinson would say. "I coach people."

To give Tubbs the practice he needed, Wilkinson had the Sooners run the halfback sweep to the left and then to the right repeatedly. Each time, Tubbs would hit the blocking dummy held by one of the freshmen, but each time, his execution of the block left something to be desired.

"Let's run it again, gentlemen," Wilkinson would say quietly. Each time, he puffed out his cheeks and exhaled slowly through his lips, his characteristic expression of frustration.

Finally, Wilkinson had reached the limit of his patience. He took Tubbs's place as the Sooners ran the play one more time. Wilkinson lined up at the fullback position, ran ahead of the trailing halfback, and blocked the dummy as he wanted Tubbs to do it. Then, he walked back to the corner and began to show Tubbs in slow motion. As Wilkinson did so, his foot slipped, and he fell face down on the muddy field. But just as he taught his players, Wilkinson kept his feet churning, driving ever forward to move the dummy out of the play.

Tubbs was mortified. Because of his failure to learn, Wilkinson—the kind but distant "Great White Father" (so nicknamed by the Sooners because of his prematurely graying hair)—was on his hands and knees in the mud. Tubbs's heart ached. He would make any sacrifice—do anything within his power—to get the coach he loved out of the mud. With determined effort, Tubbs reached a level of execution that satisfied Wilkinson.

Just as Wilkinson prepared his quarterbacks to call the offense plays, he thoroughly drilled his linebackers in calling defenses to prepare them for formations and plays they might see in a game. Burris was perhaps the best lineman Wilkinson had yet coached. In addition to being physically dominating, Burris was generally regarded as the Sooner with the greatest football savvy, a trait that worked in tandem with his keen eyesight to enable him to see nearly everything that took place on a football field.

These gifts—and an intensity level that ranked among the highest Wilkinson had coached—made Burris the natural choice to be the Sooners' defensive quarterback. Before each play, Burris would weigh the down, distance, score, wind, time left in the game, and the details of the OU scouting report (which outlined the types of plays an opponent was most likely to run in a given situation). With this information, Burris would, in a matter of seconds, decide the best formation in which to array the OU defense. While the opponents huddled offensively, Burris would turn his back to the line of scrimmage and, through a series of hand signals, relay the defensive formation to his teammates.

Sixty to eighty times each game, the Sooners' ability to defend against an opponent's offense rested, in large measure, on Burris's ability to make the right choice of defensive formation. To prepare Burris and his other defensive signal callers to make those decisions, Wilkinson had instituted a system to scout an opponent and develop offensive and defensive game plans to overcome that foe. The system, thorough and unchanging from week to week and season to season, left little to chance in the Sooners' preparation.

Each week, one of the assistants was selected to scout the next opponent on the Sooners' schedule. By Sunday evening, the scout had returned to Norman and prepared a written report for Wilkinson and the other assistants. Unlike many coaches, Wilkinson insisted that the scout's report—and the prospective game plans prepared by each assistant the following day—*be in writing*. That way, there was no chance of miscommunication, and it was clear in black and white what each coach had recommended. There was no room for backpedaling later.

After the final defensive game plan was decided on Tuesdays, Wilkinson would walk to Jones's house on Tuesday evening, and the two would sit at Jones's kitchen table with scissors and glue, cutting apart the mimeographed defensive instruction sheets so they could give each player only those keys he would use in his position. The ends would receive their assignments. So would the tackles, linebackers, and defensive secondary. None of the players would know exactly what the other members of the team were doing in the same situation, a practice that prevented an entire defensive game plan from falling into the hands of an opponent.

A summary of the defensive game plan was given only to the defensive "quarterback," who had to learn it quickly and thoroughly. The defensive plan Burris received for the Texas game looked like this:

I. GENERAL

The Texas offense is built to sustain the ball with an extremely powerful straight ahead attack. If this general plan is successful, they are usually content to stay with it and get their scores through long, sustained drives. They do not run wide or throw too often if they can make their normal attack move the ball.

If they are unable to move the ball with the driving offense, they will go to their wide attack and will also use flankers and throw the ball. However, during the past two years, they have seldom mixed these two types of attack. They seem to play one or the other, and it is usually apparent which one they are using.

Late in the first half or late in the game or when a penalty or a yardage loss has put them in an extremely unfavorable down and yardage position, they have always gone to a flanker pass attack. You can anticipate this almost 100%. In addition to their passes, they use the draw and screen when employing this offense in these game situations. The draw and screen will be used almost immediately if we are successful in rushing them. LOOK FOR THESE PLAYS IN THESE SITUATIONS.

II. OKLAHOMA DEFENSES

In setting our defenses for this game, we have used alignments which put us in an extremely strong position against particular plays in the Texas attack. They will probably move the ball at times against us, but the percentage will be in our favor in being in the right defense at the right time if we can keep them from breaking long gains. It is vitally important that you remember this. You must keep our team reminded of the fact that even though they are moving the ball, we will stop them since we will be in the strongest possible defense against particular plays they might try to run many times during any sustained drive.

1. Defense 62
   This should be our soundest all-around defense for this game. It has no particular strengths against particular plays with the exception of the ability to stop short passes and plays up the middle from 60 Tight. You should use 62 any time you are in doubt as to what defense to call.
2. Defense 72
   Do not plan on using regular 72 unless we appear defensively superior (which is extremely unlikely) or our other defenses are not successful. Use 72 Right or 72 Left. Call these defenses to the side you expect a play to be run. BREWER HAS A TENDENCY TO BASE HIS ATTACK RUNNING TO EITHER THE WIDE FIELD OR SIDELINES. HE WILL CONTINUE TO DIRECT HIS ATTACK AT THE AREA WHICH IS SUCCESSFUL.
3. Defense 60 Left–60 Right
   We will use these defenses to stop 26–27, 28 Lead and 29 Lead. Try to guess with them and be in these defenses when you expect these plays to be run.
4. 60 Left Rush–60 Right Rush
   These defenses should make it almost impossible for them to have time to throw the ball. They also will be good alignments to use to try to force an error for a loss or a fumble.

Once the game started, all the Sooners' meticulous preparation for Texas seemed for naught when Leake fumbled the opening kickoff and the Longhorns recovered at the OU 29. Texas moved to a first down at the OU 18 and then gained 8 on the first play of the next series. The Longhorns tried to pound over right tackle, but the Sooners stopped them for a yard gain. On the next play, the Longhorns went to the opposite side, but the Sooners stopped the play again. Then Burris took over. He stopped a dive for 2 yards, then recovered a fumble to stop the Longhorn drive at the OU 5.

A motion penalty against the Sooners moved the ball back to the 1, where Harris knew he should take no chances. He called on Leake to punt, and Leake booted the ball out to the OU 35. The Longhorns tried two long passes that fell incomplete, but completed a halfback pass that moved the Longhorns to the OU 6. Two plays later, the Longhorns scored. With eight minutes left in the first quarter, Texas led, 7–0.

Late in the first quarter, the Sooners scored after a 73-yard drive as Leake sliced over left tackle from the Texas 1. Immediately, Wilkinson sent in the entire alternate unit, which included six sophomores who had seen little playing time. Still, they stopped the Longhorns and forced a punt that was killed at the OU 42.

On third-and-7 in OU territory, alternate quarterback Pat O'Neal went to the air. He called a pass to right end John Bell. Recently converted from guard to end, Bell ran the wrong pattern, but as O'Neal's pass hung in the air, Bell hustled to overcome his mistake. Finally, he reached the ball, caught it, and raced 40 yards to the Texas 15. Sensing the kill, Wilkinson sent in the starters. In five plays, OU scored on a keeper by Harris.

For the rest of the game, the Sooners' defensive prowess stopped the Texas attack. Only once in the final three quarters of the 14–7 victory did the Longhorns move inside the OU 20.

Freshman Clendon Thomas considered himself lucky to be at the University of Oklahoma. A star on a lackluster Oklahoma City Southeast team that won only two games his senior year, Thomas was one of the last players given a scholarship by OU in 1954. Once he arrived at OU, Thomas had no intention of being run off, even though he spent the first several weeks of his freshman season on the fifth team. Actually, there was not a full team—only eight or nine players—and they were always listed as All Others on the depth chart. Those on the All Others list were known to themselves and the rest of the squad as the AOs, and they were coached by Adam Esslinger, a former Oklahoma A&M player who owned a dairy store near the stadium.

One afternoon, the freshman team scrimmaged against the varsity, and all of the freshmen were given a chance to play—even the AOs. Thomas punted well on several occasions and was on defense when the varsity sent sophomore halfback Bill Brown off tackle. Thomas hit Brown squarely, stopping him cold with a hard but clean tackle.

Leon Manley, a member of the 1949 Sooners who was in Norman recuperating from a pro football injury, walked over to Thomas.

"Nice tackle, kid. Are you Carl Dodd?" Manley asked.

"No. Clendon Thomas," he said, gesturing toward the grass-stained piece of athletic tape on the front of his helmet where his name, now faded, had been written during the first day of practice. The next day Thomas moved up to the fourth team. Within two weeks, Thomas was on the starting freshman team. His days as an unknown at OU were over.

The narrow but convincing victory over Texas moved the Sooners back into the No. 1 spot in the Associated Press football poll as the Sooners found themselves safely within the confines of the Big Seven. They pummeled Kansas, 65–0, and then shut out Kansas State, 21–0. In late October, the Sooners traveled to Boulder to face Colorado, which again posed the toughest test in the conference for Oklahoma. As always, Wilkinson took the Sooners to Colorado a day early so they could adjust to the thin air of the Rockies.

Against the Buffaloes, Calame was at half speed because of his shoulder injury, and Harris was weakened by the flu, so Wilkinson sent O'Neal in to quarterback the first team after a scoreless first quarter. O'Neal was quarterbacking the OU starters for the first time and wanted to look good, but the three running plays O'Neal called gained only 6 yards. The Sooners faced fourth-and-4 on their own 44. A punt was clearly in order, but O'Neal did not call for Boydston to punt. Instead, he called a quarterback keeper.

As O'Neal brought the Sooners to the line of scrimmage, Wilkinson watched on the sideline in disbelief. He grabbed Calame by the shoulders.

"Quick! Go in for Pat! Stop the play!" Wilkinson shouted, as he pushed Calame on the field.

Wilkinson hoped the officials would see Calame come onto the field, stop the play, and penalize OU 5 yards for having twelve men on the field. But at least the

Sooners would get a chance to punt! On the OU bench, O'Neal's brother Jay, the fourth-string quarterback, watched in mixed bewilderment and horror as his audacious sibling called signals on fourth down. It was the wrong thing to do, a stupid thing to do. Jay pulled his sideline coat over his head.

Calame was too late. O'Neal took the snap from Burris and moved to his right. At the corner, he shunned a pitchout to Leake and turned upfield. The Buffaloes piled into him, stopping him 2 yards short of the first down. When O'Neal got to the sideline, Wilkinson met him.

"Don't you know we kick on fourth down?" he asked.

"Yes, sir," O'Neal answered and said no more.

The Buffaloes took advantage of O'Neal's blunder and drove to score on a 19-yard screen pass. The Sooners blocked the extra point attempt to hold Colorado's lead at 6–0.

Just before halftime, the Sooners drove 76 yards, but time ran out with the ball on the Buffs' 1. Disheartened, the Sooners trotted off the field to sit on bales of hay in the Colorado gymnasium. In the gym, Wilkinson was still baffled by O'Neal's fourth-down call.

"I'll bet you thought it was third down," said Wilkinson, hoping that lapse, rather than the failure of his hours of counseling, was the reason for O'Neal's unusual behavior.

"No, sir," O'Neal replied. "It was fourth down. I knew exactly what down it was. I made a mistake. I'm sorry. I thought we could make the yardage."

O'Neal's honesty, if not his football savvy, impressed Wilkinson.

Early in the third quarter, Colorado drove across midfield. All the while, Calame, who hadn't played since the season-opening victory over California, had been sent in to quarterback the starters. Wilkinson kept him in the game on defense, too, and Calame attacked the Buffs' offense plays aggressively. He challenged end runs. He batted down passes. Finally, the Sooners stopped the Buffaloes at the OU 13, but Calame had no more to give. His shoulder and ribs were throbbing with pain. Wilkinson took him out of the game.

Now, Wilkinson was left with only one healthy quarterback who had game experience—O'Neal. With the third quarter nearly over and a touchdown 87 yards away, Wilkinson decided to give O'Neal another chance.

"Run the fullback off tackle on the first play, but don't give it to him. Keep it yourself," Wilkinson told O'Neal as he headed onto the field with the alternates.

The play worked. O'Neal gained 7 to the OU 20. Bob Burris got 8 over right guard. McDonald gained 5 on an inside trap. Burris got 5 more and another first down at the Oklahoma 38. Now, O'Neal had the Sooners rolling. In six plays, they drove to the Colorado 26 before the quarter ended and Wilkinson sent the starting unit back in. O'Neal directed the starters to a touchdown in only four plays. Leake kicked the extra point to give OU a 7–6 lead.

The Buffs rallied and drove across the 50, but Leake intercepted a long Carroll Hardy pass at the OU 29. The Sooners could not move, and on third down, Boydston quick kicked 59 yards to the Colorado 15. Wilkinson sent the alternates back into the game, and again they came through. Holding the Buffs for three plays, they forced Hardy to punt, and McDonald ran the punt back to the OU 48.

After the Sooners moved to a first down, O'Neal's bravado returned. He called a double reverse pass option by McDonald. The play worked to perfection. O'Neal pitched to Burris, who handed off to McDonald and headed downfield. McDonald ran to his right, stopped, and threw back to Burris. Burris was wide open. He dashed to the Colorado 1 before being stopped. On the next play, O'Neal sneaked in to ensure OU's 13–6 victory.

The close margins of victory the Sooners registered over K-State and Colorado caused OU to drop to No. 3 in the polls, but the Sooners rolled on to defeat Iowa State, Missouri, Nebraska, and Oklahoma A&M soundly and win their eighth straight Big Seven title.

After the victory over Iowa State in the seventh game of the season, Wilkinson came to Harold Keith's office to talk about a matter he seldom discussed—individual honors. Usually, Wilkinson preached team play and sacrifice, which he believed were two of the essential elements of football. But this year, Wilkinson thought Kurt Burris was having an exceptional season and was probably the best player in the nation.

Two years before, Vessels had proved that a player from the Big Seven could win the Heisman Trophy, which was awarded by New York's Downtown Athletic Club to the most outstanding football player in the nation. Traditionally, the trophy went to a back. In fact, the trophy itself—showing a ball carrier with one arm outstretched to stiff-arm a potential tackler—seemed a mute symbol of prejudice against linemen. The winner was selected each year by the nation's sportswriters, and they voted for players whose names they knew. Understandably, an interior lineman had never won the Heisman Trophy. Two ends had won the trophy—Larry Kelley of Yale in 1936 and Leon Hart of Notre Dame in 1949. Only in 1948, when Pennsylvania's Chuck Bednarik was the dominant player in the East, did a lineman come close. Bednarik finished a distant third behind SMU's Doak Walker and North Carolina's Charlie Justice (the Sooners' Jack Mitchell finished eighth).

Wilkinson and Keith knew Burris stood little chance of winning the award, but decided to bring attention to Burris—and interior linemen everywhere—with a publicity campaign. The two decided to write a short letter to every sports editor in the nation—approximately 3,500 of them—making a case for Burris as the finest player in the nation. Keith had a directory with names and addresses, but there was less than a week before the Heisman voting was to be completed. How could they possibly get the job done?

Keith developed an inspired solution. He explained the problem to his friend Raymond White, who was chairman of OU's Department of Office Administration. White called in two classes of secretarial students. With one hundred typewriters in two rooms, the students went to work. They typed all 3,500 letters. Keith signed them and put them in the mail.

The campaign was remarkably successful. Burris didn't win. Alan Ameche, a fullback from Wisconsin, did. But Burris finished second and garnered more votes than any lineman before him—and more than such well-known backs as Ohio State's Hopalong Cassady, Notre Dame's Ralph Guglielmi, and California's Paul Larson.

Thanks to Burris's ability and Keith's diligence, Burris cleared the way for a series of Sooner linemen who would—despite the built-in prejudices of the Heisman selection process—become serious candidates for the trophy in years to come.

1955

To Bud Wilkinson, college football was never an end in itself. It was only a stage in a person's life and was secondary to obtaining a college education, which would prepare a young man for his life's work. As a result, Wilkinson would call each of the Sooners to his office in May after spring practice was completed. Together, they would discuss the player's performance the year before, his prospects for the coming year, and his goals in life.

In these brief talks, Wilkinson was positive and encouraging, yet he was always straightforward about a player's chances of becoming a regular at OU. Hardest for him were visits with players who simply lacked the physical ability to play at Oklahoma. Without exception, Wilkinson encouraged these players to stay at OU and graduate. Many could have been stars at other schools, but Wilkinson explained that in the long run, transferring would be a mistake.

"The people you meet and the education you get at OU will have a great impact on your life," he would tell those whose time would be better spent studying than trying to play football. All the while, Wilkinson knew that the lure of being recognized as an athlete, which can sometimes overshadow everything else in a young man's life, would cause some to leave Oklahoma. Whenever it happened, Wilkinson was saddened.

So intent was Wilkinson on his players finishing their educations that he sometimes helped them find jobs even after their four years of eligibility were completed.

Several married players with families might not have been able to afford to finish school had it not been for Wilkinson's assistance, but the humanitarian nature of Wilkinson's actions was disregarded by the NCAA during an investigation of the OU football program.

In April 1955 the NCAA found OU guilty of offering athletes cost-free education beyond their normal period of eligibility, paying emergency medical expenses for wives and children of athletes, and permitting "university patrons" to provide OU players with "fringe benefits" of nominal value.

The Sooners were placed on probation from April 26, 1955, to April 26, 1957. No ban was placed on bowl participation, but most Oklahomans thought the penalty too stiff for the minor nature of the findings. Privately, Wilkinson thought the NCAA's allegations petty, but did not criticize the decision publicly out of belief that some form of national organization like the NCAA was needed.

Enforcement of rules for college athletics on a nationwide basis had not begun seriously until 1951, when the NCAA moved from the Big Ten offices in Chicago to its own office in Kansas City. Until that time, the NCAA and its executive director, Walter Byers (who had been a newspaperman with the United Press), had been relatively powerless. Then came the advent of television. And the NCAA, the only organization operating across conference lines, became the beneficiary of the millions of dollars in revenue generated by televised college football games. The landscape of college athletics would never be the same.

By the beginning of fall practice in 1955 it was clear to Wilkinson that depth chart discipline was needed to teach talented but free-spirited Tommy McDonald a lesson. One morning McDonald found himself demoted to the second team. He went to Gene Calame, now a graduate assistant coach while in law school, to find out why. Calame said he was blocking low instead of high, as Wilkinson taught.

"You're going to have to start working on that block," Calame told McDonald.

McDonald responded. At the next practice, he hit anyone who moved—and hit him high. The next day, he was back with the starters.

A more subtle lesson about team spirit came from Ed Gray. Among his other nicknames, Gray was known by the Sooners as "Shane" because he had seen the movie more than a dozen times. One day in practice, Gray decided to enforce his own form of Shane morality. Although Wilkinson insisted that only quarterbacks were to talk in the huddle, McDonald continually pestered Harris to let him carry the ball. Finally, Harris called a play that would send McDonald through the line behind Gray. Gray took his stance and whispered to Doyle Jennings, a 220-pound tackle across the line of scrimmage:

“Here he comes on two.”

When the ball was snapped, Gray rolled to the side, and McDonald was knocked to the ground full force by Jennings.

Gray rose to his feet and looked down at the incensed McDonald.

“You see, Mac,” Gray said. “You’re not gonna go anywhere without our help.”

Wilkinson phrased his request as diplomatically as he could. In his nine years as a head coach, he had never asked a player to do what he was about to ask Clendon Thomas to do. The rangy sophomore sat in a chair in front of Wilkinson’s gray, metal desk and listened intently to what Wilkinson was saying.

“Clendon, you have earned the right to start at right halfback,” Wilkinson said, “but I want you to play with the alternates to give us better balance.”

Thomas did not hesitate or complain. Yes, he said, he would be glad to play with the alternates if that is what the coaches wanted. It was the answer Wilkinson expected. He had never coached a player quite like Thomas before. Remarkably humble given his ability, he was genuinely happy to play anywhere it would help the team. Lots of players *say* that, Wilkinson knew, but few truly mean it. Thomas was one of the rare ones who did.

The Sooners were to open the season at North Carolina with a starting backfield that had been rebuilt, although the task was less imposing than it first appeared. Harris, who had started some games in 1954 when Calame was injured, became the starting quarterback to stay. The entire alternate backfield of McDonald, Burris, and Pricer—with whom Harris had played much of the previous season—moved up to the starting unit with him. Jerry Tubbs, the starting fullback the year before, was now able to return to center with the departure of Kurt Burris.

Actually, Wilkinson was less concerned about the starters than about the ability of the alternates and the third team. The game was the Sooners’ first regular season game in the South, and Wilkinson was concerned about his players’ ability to take eighty-five-degree temperatures and 90 percent humidity. All might have to play against the Tarheels.

The Sooners took the opening kickoff and drove to the North Carolina 31, where the Tarheels held on fourth down. The Tarheels were unable to move and punted. On first down, the Sooners were penalized for clipping on the return, and the ball was moved back to the OU 1. On first down, Wilkinson sent in Ken Northcutt to give Tubbs a rest at center. Instantly, Wilkinson realized he had made a mistake. Harris had practiced taking snaps almost exclusively from Tubbs. When Harris tried to take the snap from Northcutt, the ball glanced off his hands and rolled into the end zone, where the Tarheels recovered. The Tarheels' extra point try was no good, but the Sooners found themselves suddenly behind a big, fired up North Carolina team.

Misfortune plagued the Sooners during the rest of the first half. They fumbled into the end zone for a touchback. They were stopped on downs at the North Carolina 13. Just before the half, McDonald swept around right end from the Tarheel 8. Surrounded by a gang of Tarheel tacklers, he dove for the end zone flag, but came up a yard short. The Sooners went to the locker room trailing a team they believed they should be beating easily. As Wilkinson knew, spirit—the quality that could make a team play beyond its outward physical capabilities—did not belong solely to the Sooners.

In the second half, the Sooners' fortunes improved. With an excellent line and Thomas playing on the alternate unit, Wilkinson knew he could change units at will with little or no drop-off in talent. No other team in the nation, even those with more players on their squads than the Sooners, could match the Sooner alternates. As a result, Wilkinson did not hesitate to let his starters rest. He knew that if Tarheel coach George Barclay substituted his second unit, the Sooner alternates would quickly dominate them. If Barclay left his starters in as the steamy afternoon wore on, they would begin to falter. Eventually, the rested Sooners—either the starters or the alternates—would strike.

The break came more quickly than Wilkinson expected. On their first possession of the second half, the Sooners started driving from the OU 26. Harris got 11 on a quarterback keeper. Then Burris cut through the right side of the line for 15. On the next play, the Sooners had an ineligible receiver downfield and were penalized 15 yards. With the Sooners facing second-and-25, Burris got all the yardage needed for the first down on a trap play, rambling 25 yards to the Tarheel 34. After the Sooners got another first down on McDonald's running pass to Bell, the Sooners scored on Burris's end run. Pricer's extra point put the Sooners in front, 7–6.

Through the rest of the third quarter, the Sooners continued to roll up yardage, but the North Carolina defense refused to break. In the middle of the fourth quarter, the Sooners were still clinging to their 1-point lead, still waiting for an opportunity to put the game out of reach. Finally, they got it. Back to punt for the alternates, Thomas got a low snap that skidded along the ground. Amazingly, he fielded it cleanly and then punted out-of-bounds to the Tarheel 14.

Thomas's play changed the momentum of the game. When North Carolina had to punt the ball back, OU took possession at the Tarheel 39. In five plays, the

Sooners delivered the knockout punch, scoring on McDonald's sweep from the 2 to assure OU's twentieth straight victory.

The following week, undefeated Pittsburgh came to Norman. Led by quarterback Corny Salvaterra and end Joe Walton, the Panthers were big and physical. They played the kind of rugged defense that had held the Sooners to only 67 yards rushing two years before. Although Pitt ran from the Split T, Lyle's scouting report revealed that the Panthers marshaled power off tackle like a single wing team. The standard Oklahoma 72 defense could not hold the Pitt offense.

Working unusually long hours between Sunday and Tuesday night, Wilkinson and Jones devised a special defense. With the Sooners in a six-man line, the ends were to charge in diagonally. The tackles were to play head-on against the Pitt ends and charge straight ahead. And the guards, lined up in front of the Pitt guards, were to slant to the outside between the guard and tackle. This plan concentrated the Sooners' defensive manpower behind the Pittsburgh tackles—where the Panthers would be concentrating their offensive forces—and would prevent the Sooner line from being breached.

The specially designed defense left two openings—one apparent, one real. There appeared to be a weakness with no Sooner playing head-to-head on the Pitt center, offering a perfect place for Salvaterra to run a quarterback sneak. To prevent that possibility, Wilkinson and Jones moved linebackers Tubbs and Pricer tighter than normal. If there was a weakness, it was to the outside. Only the ability of the Oklahoma ends to react quickly to contain to an end sweep would keep the Oklahoma defense from being flanked.

Lyle's report also suggested that Pitt's defense would be vulnerable to inside reverses. Wilkinson believed the Sooners needed a special play, and he had found one that was likely to work during the previous summer while reviewing films of the Wichita Wheatshockers, a team coached by former Sooner Pete Tillman.

The play called for Harris to drop back diagonally to his left, faking first to Pricer and then to McDonald, who would sweep around the right side to get the Pitt defense moving in that direction. Right halfback Bob Burris would take a delayed handoff from Harris and speed around the left side.

As Tillman designed the play, the left guard would pull to his left to lead interference, but Wilkinson believed that would tip off the Pitt linebacker that something was coming. Instead, Wilkinson decided to pull the *right* guard to take out Pitt's defensive end. The linebacker on that side would see the guard pull, but would have a hard time getting to the opposite side of the field in time to stop the play. The play worked to perfection twice. McDonald scored the Sooners' first touchdown on a 43-yard run. In the second quarter, Thomas raced 32 yards to score as OU won, 26–14.

Two weeks later, the OU locker room was quiet as Wilkinson spoke to the Sooners before they took the field against Texas. Except for the distant music from the midway on the Texas State Fairgrounds, all the Sooners could hear was Wilkinson's quiet, articulate voice:

"There once was an old man who was known far and wide for his wisdom, for if someone asked him a question, his answer was always correct. A young boy heard about the wise, old man and tried to find a way to trick him. At last, the boy devised a plan. He went to see the old man carrying a tiny sparrow in his hands.

"He showed the wise, old man the bird in his hands.

"'Is the bird alive or dead?' the boy asked.

"The old man saw through the trick. He knew that if he said the bird was alive, the youth would crush the bird with his hands. If he said it was dead, the boy would let the bird fly away.

"Finally, the wise, old man answered. 'As you will, my son. As you will.'"

The Sooners' game with Texas was the same, Wilkinson told the Sooners. If they willed it, they could win. The decision was theirs.

The key to a Sooner victory would be defending against Joe Clements, the Longhorns' skillful quarterback, who was among the nation's leading passers. Jones, Pete Elliott, and new staff member Ted Youngling took Lyle's scouting report and drilled the Sooners defensively to handle Clements's aerial threat. Lyle's scouting report contained one other vital piece of information. The Sooners might be able to spring a fake trap play against the Longhorns. OU had tried such plays before against Texas, and they had seldom been successful. As a result, Wilkinson was against adding a new play for the game. Jones would not hear of it.

"Sam's right. The play will work," he insisted.

Finally, Wilkinson acceded, believing there was no reason to have good assistant coaches if you refused to listen to them.

On the Longhorns' first possession, Clements threw over the middle on first down. Tubbs grabbed the ball out of the air and ran it back to the Texas 33. Six plays later, Harris called the fake trap play. He faked a handoff to Burris through the middle and then lateraled to McDonald coming to the right. The Longhorns were not fooled, but the swift McDonald outran most of the Texas defenders, faked out the rest, and went 28 yards to score.

Just before halftime, McDonald intercepted another Clements pass and returned it to the Texas 7 (all told, the Sooners would make five interceptions, three of them by Tubbs). On the first play, Harris called a reverse to McDonald. McDonald scored untouched.

In the second half, OU found the offensive going more difficult, but four quick kicks by Pricer and Thomas that averaged over 50 yards each allowed the Sooners to maintain a decided field position advantage and win, 20–0.

By midseason, the undefeated Sooners were becoming renowned for the speed with which they were running plays. No one could remember anything like it. As soon as one play was over, the Sooners would hurry back to the huddle as quickly as they had run the play before. The feisty McDonald, who loved nothing more than to take an opponent's best shot and then hop up as if he felt nothing, was the leader. His energy seemed to galvanize the Sooners and spur them on. Wilkinson sensed it, too. He always kept the Sooners' offensive plays simple to make play selection easy for the quarterback, but no team he had coached got into the huddle and back out of it as fast as this team.

Weighing the value of the hurry-up huddle, Wilkinson decided it was a plus. It gave the quarterback less time to consider the next play, but it also gave the defense even less time to react and did not give them time to see the Sooners' line splits. Besides, it was all natural. Wilkinson could not slow McDonald down, so he just accepted it and started planning a way to use the "fast recovery" tempo to its maximum advantage.

The opportunity came against Colorado, which, like OU, was 4–0. After a scoreless first quarter, the Buffs recovered two OU fumbles and drove to two touchdowns. With the Buffs taking control of the game, 14–0, the Sooners had to do something to destroy Colorado's momentum. After Oklahoma ran back the Colorado kickoff to the OU 46, the Sooners started running plays in hurry-up fashion. As soon as a play was over, the Sooners ran back to the huddle, Harris or Jay O'Neal called the next play, and the Sooners surged forward again. In a matter of moments, OU scored twice. With less than three minutes to play in the half, the Sooners got the ball back again. It seemed impossible to score, but OU started down the field. McDonald threw to John Bell for 8 and to Joe Mobra for 16. Robert Derrick went 34 yards on a handoff, putting the ball on the Buff 2. On first down, McDonald leaped over the goal line, and OU took a 21–14 halftime lead.

The onslaught continued into the second half. From deep in Colorado territory, the Buffs quick kicked. The ball bounced lazily, and it seemed about to roll dead at midfield, but Burris did not wait. He drove into an oncoming Colorado defender, blocking him off his feet. The blow triggered McDonald. He picked up the ball and ran. McDonald darted to the Colorado 13 before he was stopped. Burris scored his third touchdown four plays later. Before the contest ended, Wilkinson cleared the bench as OU won, 56–21.

Over the next five weeks, Oklahoma dominated its remaining Big Seven opponents, outscoring them 206–7. The Sooners completed the season 10–0, the season-ending 53–0 lashing of Oklahoma A&M marking the Sooners' twenty-ninth consecutive victory and 105th straight game in which they had scored. During the eighth week of the season, the Sooners moved into the No. 1 spot in the AP poll, 51 points ahead of Jim Tatum's Maryland team, and stayed there the remainder of the season. The final AP poll accorded the national championship to OU, with Michigan State second, Maryland third, and UCLA fourth.

With the regular season completed, Wilkinson and his staff began to prepare for Tatum and Maryland, the Atlantic Coast Conference champion, in the Orange Bowl. In the final weeks of the season, Wilkinson made it a point not to spend time worrying about the Terrapins, but he had heard plenty. When Maryland beat UCLA, 7–0, and held the Bruins to -21 yards rushing on a muddy field, Wilkinson called his friend Red Sanders.

"Bud, they're the greatest team of the era," Sanders said.

After studying four game films he received from Tatum, Wilkinson and his assistants compiled a game plan. Wilkinson's summary was direct:

> Maryland is a strong, sound football team in every phase of the game. Their squad is big, tough and well-conditioned. They have no weaknesses at any position.
>
> Defensively, they have been a great team. They have been particularly good against running plays. Their team, fans and many competent football writers do not believe we can score against them.
>
> Their offense is based on a powerful, quick-hitting, inside running attack. The most dangerous part of their offense has been their passing. They will punch out three or four first downs. Then, draw up the defensive secondary with a running fake and get their deep receivers open for a touchdown.
>
> Maryland is bigger, stronger and just as fast as we are. Our only chance to defeat them will be to HIT HARDER and play with greater sustained effort through the 60 minutes of the game. They will, no doubt, be ahead of us at the end of the first half and probably at the start of the 4th Quarter. However, if we make them pay a tremendous physical price through the

first 45 minutes of the game, we can defeat them in the last quarter if we have a greater WILL TO WIN.

Our greatest single problem in preparing for the game will be mental discipline on the part of each player. Maryland uses a variety of defensive alignments. You must study your offensive sheet and know exactly what to do on each play against each defense. This takes *real mental courage*. The same thing is true of our defense. Only through mental effort and discipline, by studying OFF THE PRACTICE FIELD, can we prepare adequately for this game.

The No. 1 team in the AP Poll seldom wins a bowl game. You have a great opportunity. By defeating Maryland, you can prove your right to be the National Champions. You can go down in the record book as one of the *TRULY GREAT TEAMS* in the history of football.

BE PREPARED TO MAKE THE GREATEST EFFORT OF YOUR LIFE IN THIS GAME.

The demands Wilkinson placed on defense were substantial. To win, the Sooners had to stop all long passes, the inside running game, and the wide running game. That promised to be a difficult task considering that Tubbs, the Sooners' premier linebacker, had not practiced since injuring his knee in the last game of the season. And the rest of the linemen, as good as they were, would be outweighed forty pounds per man by the Maryland line.

Wilkinson and Jones decided that the key to stopping the Maryland ground game was to keep Ed Vereb, the Terrapins' star halfback, from getting outside. They installed a special defense to prevent the sweep from developing. When Vereb got the ball and went wide toward the Sooner left side, left cornerback Delbert Long was to attack the play aggressively, and the rest of the Sooner secondary was to shift to the left to compensate.

On offense, the Sooners had no less to contend with. Because of Maryland's size and speed, they could hold their ground, wait for a play to develop, and then stop it. Schooled in the same philosophy as Wilkinson, Tatum kept his secondary deep to prevent the long touchdown pass. There would be no easy touchdowns against Maryland.

Early in the game, the Sooners played inspired defense, keeping Maryland in its own territory. Yet the Sooners found themselves stifled on offense. After two unsuccessful possessions, Pricer punted out-of-bounds to the Maryland 24, and Wilkinson sent in the alternates. On the first play, Vereb broke through on a quick slant off right tackle. Mike Sandusky, the Terrapins' 240-pound All-American, cleared a hole over the Sooners' Wayne Greenlee, who was outweighed by fifty pounds. O'Neal charged up from his safety spot to meet Vereb, but Vereb sidestepped him, cut toward the left sidelines, and broke into the clear. Ten yards. Twenty. Thirty. Vereb raced toward the Sooner goal.

After missing the tackle, O'Neal came racing back in an attempt to catch the speedy Vereb. Running diagonally to cut Vereb off, O'Neal gave it everything he had. Driven by Wilkinson's training, it never occurred to him that chasing Vereb was pointless. And because he did not, he accomplished the seemingly impossible. O'Neal dove at Vereb's feet and knocked him down at the OU 10, saving a certain touchdown. Throughout Wilkinson's remaining years as a coach, he would point to O'Neal's play as the greatest example of what a player can accomplish if he gives everything he has.

On first down, Terrapin quarterback Frank Tamburello kept the ball behind Sandusky's block, rolling over Greenlee again for a 6-yard gain. Victimized two plays in a row, Greenlee dug in, remembering what Jones said to do in goal line situations. Dive under the other guy and drive him back into the play.

Greenlee crouched low, determined to undercut Sandusky if the Terrapins came at him again. Sandusky, considered by the Sooner coaches the finest lineman the Sooners had faced in years, saw what Greenlee was planning to do and fired out low from his stance, but the duel made no difference on the play. The play went to the opposite side, where the Sooners stopped it for no gain.

On third-and-4, Greenlee braced for another Maryland charge, trying desperately to think of a way to outmaneuver the powerful Sandusky. Instantly, he remembered something his high school coach in Breckenridge, Joe Kerbel, had taught him in high school. Sometimes, you don't do what seems normal. You have to do something different.

In a matter of seconds, Greenlee chose his course of action. Sandusky came to the line of scrimmage and took his stance. Greenlee dug in low as he had on the play before. The ball was snapped, and Sandusky drove in low to submarine Greenlee, but Greenlee only faked low. He placed his hands on Sandusky's back and leapfrogged over Sandusky into the Maryland backfield as Tamburello started around the end. Greenlee's ambush caught Tamburello unprepared. When Greenlee hit him, the ball bounced loose, and the Sooners recovered.

Through much of the first half, the Sooners continued to struggle on offense, relying on punts and quick kicks to maintain field position. Late in the second quarter, one quick kick was not long enough, and Maryland got the ball at the

OU 39. After the Terrapins got a first down at the OU 29 on a fourth-down gamble, Vereb got loose again. He sliced off left guard for 10 yards to the OU 15, then scored on the next play by faking a halfback pass to the right and cutting back to the left. Maryland's extra point attempt was blocked by Tubbs, and the Terrapins had to settle for a 6–0 halftime lead.

In the Sooner locker room, Wilkinson was disgusted.

"Sit down!" he told the Sooners. "I've never seen anything like this in all my life. They're not doing one thing we haven't worked on. Our line isn't blocking. Our backs are running backward. If you guys don't get busy and start playing football, you're going to get the hell beat out of you."

Wilkinson walked out. The minutes passed slowly as the Sooners waited. They could hear the Orange Bowl halftime extravaganza taking place outside on the field. Finally, the officials came in to inform the Sooners the second half was to begin, and Wilkinson followed them in.

"Let's go out and play football!" he said.

Before the second half started, Wilkinson took Harris aside.

"Start using the 'hurry-up' offense this half and stick to the basic running plays," Wilkinson told him. "The passes we threw in the first half were just to give the Maryland coaching staff something to think about at halftime."

The Sooners quickly took control. The Terrapins got only one first down before they were forced to punt from their 43. Vereb kicked to McDonald at the OU 21, and the bantam All-American took off. Darting away from an armada of Maryland tacklers, McDonald broke free for 33 yards to the Maryland 46.

Harris, calling his plays at a rapid clip, as Wilkinson instructed, started the Sooners moving. Four off-tackle plays moved the ball to the Maryland 26, where McDonald rolled to his right and hit Burris with a halfback pass that Burris carried to the Maryland 7. On the next play, McDonald burst over left tackle for 3 yards. The tiring Terrapins tried to tangle their arms and legs around McDonald to keep him on the ground—anything to keep him from leaping up and running back to the huddle.

"Keep him down," the Maryland players shouted to each other.

"Let me up! Let me up! Let me up!" McDonald yelled.

On second down, Harris ran the option to the right and pitched to McDonald, who scored easily from the 4. Pricer's extra point put the Sooners in the lead, 7–6, and Wilkinson sent in his thoroughly rested alternates.

Already, the Terrapins were shaken by the sudden shift in the tempo of the game. When Wilkinson sent in the alternates for the kickoff, Tatum hesitated.

Rather than substituting at the same time, Tatum waited until after the first play of the drive, a move that required him to use his team's second time out of the half. The Sooner alternates—superior to the Terrapins' second team—forced Maryland to punt. Starting from the OU 49, O'Neal and the alternates continued the assault begun by the starters. In rapid succession, the Sooners ran five plays and moved to a first down at the Maryland 30. On one play, the Sooners got to the line of scrimmage so fast they hit Bob Pellegrini, Maryland's All-American center, in the back. He was still facing away from the ball, trying to set the Maryland defense, when the Sooner horde ran over him.

"Out of the way, you fat pig," one of the Sooner linemen yelled as they stormed over Pellegrini and the other Maryland defenders.

O'Neal moved the Sooners in a determined drive for the Maryland goal line. Twice in the drive, at the 18 and again at the 8, the Sooners needed a fourth-down play to earn a first down. But each time, the Sooners' line moved Sandusky out of the way to get the needed yardage. By now, the massive Sandusky could hardly keep going. His shirttail was out. His shoes were untied. And he was panting like a Saint Bernard.

Pellegrini tried to help him up into position.

"Get out of the way!" Sandusky shouted. "Here they come again!"

The Sooners were just as tired, but they would not give up. Finally, nearly seven minutes after the drive began, O'Neal sneaked into the end zone for the Sooners' second touchdown. Wilkinson sent in Pricer to kick the extra point, and Pricer did his job, giving the Sooners an 8-point lead with less than two minutes left in the third quarter.

Early in the fourth quarter, OU got the ball back at its own 8. Harris gained 7, Burris lost 1, and then Harris tried to catch the Maryland defense off guard with a short pass to Burris. The pass was high, and Burris jumped to snare it. He came down on one leg, and just as he did, a Maryland defender slammed into his knee. The ball slipped from Burris's hands, and he slumped to the ground, his hands covering his face to fight the pain. Carried from the field on a stretcher, Burris would miss the final fifteen minutes of his career at OU.

As Burris lay on the Orange Bowl turf, Paul Burris, patriarch of the family that had produced three OU stars and two more players on the current freshman team, hurried to the field as quickly as his 250-pound frame allowed. For him, the action was unusual. After watching hundreds of his sons' games, Burris knew that most football injuries are minor. But when Bob was hit, Burris knew instinctively that his son was hurt seriously.

Early in the fourth quarter, Tatum pulled Tamburello and sent in Lynn Beightol, Maryland's alternate quarterback, who was a better passer. Twice he led the Terrapins toward the Sooner goal, but each time the Sooners stopped the threat with an interception. The first time, it was Tubbs. The second time it was Carl Dodd, who stepped in front of Vereb at the OU 18 and raced down the sideline 82 yards for a third and clinching OU touchdown.

The Sooners had beaten the bowl jinx. By playing the game of their lives, as Wilkinson had asked, the Sooners had eliminated any doubts that they were the finest football team in America.

After the game, Burris followed as his son was carried to the Sooners' dressing room. By now, he was well known to the OU coaches and players—as well as the guards outside the Sooner locker room—and they let him in immediately. Moments later, the Sooner team physicians confirmed their earlier, on-the-field diagnosis. The injury to Burris's knee was serious but not debilitating. In time, it would heal completely.

As the Sooners celebrated their national championship inside the dressing room, a well-dressed man with a pipe came to the door seeking admittance. The guard rebuffed him, refusing to grant him admission. Rather than argue, the slender, mild-mannered man said he would wait until the Sooners came out.

The elder Burris saw the incident and hurried to the open door. He confronted the guard and beckoned for the man to enter the locker room. In terms the guard could not fail to understand, Burris let him know that the man he did not recognize and had banned from the Sooners' locker room was none other than George Cross, the president of the university.

Far from the headlines, the most important drama of Wilkinson's life was taking place. His goal—nothing short of the integration of the OU athletic program—would require Wilkinson's consummate political skill to accomplish.

During the 1955 season the preeminent high school football player in Oklahoma was a muscular fullback for Oklahoma City Douglass named Prentice Gautt. Not only did he possess strength and speed, he carried himself with a dignity that attracted Wilkinson.

Gautt had begun playing football three years earlier at Douglass Junior High. His hero, the quarterback of the Douglass High School team, was also a musician. The young Gautt vowed to be like his hero. He joined the football team *and* the band, but his days of organized football ended almost before they started. At fourteen, he was too small to be among the Douglass stars and was relegated to the punt return team. During his second day of practice, two former Douglass students, who had returned to school to get their diplomas after serving during the Korean War, hit Gautt hard just as he fielded a punt.

In this confrontation between men and an inexperienced boy, Gautt could not win. Intimidated by the size and strength of his teammates, he quit football to concentrate on the tuba and the drums. Mose Miller, the Douglass coach, could see Gautt's potential and prevailed upon the freshman.

"You'll never get a college scholarship playing in the band," he told Gautt. "You're big and muscular. Come out for football and beat up on some of these people instead of those drums."

Gautt was not hard to convince. As a grade schooler, he and several black friends had ridden the interurban to Norman, walked to Memorial Stadium, climbed over the chain-link fence, and acted out their dreams of glory on the turf of Owen Field. As they were walking back to the interurban station to return to Oklahoma City, they were accosted by a Norman resident.

"Better be out of town by six o'clock," he told them.

Although a university community, Norman was still rooted deeply enough in the Old South to have a sundown law that prohibited blacks from living in Norman or being on the streets after dark.

Undaunted by the segregation laws of the time or larger teammates, Gautt persevered, eventually becoming the star of a Douglass team that won thirty-one straight games and traveled to play black high schools in Texas, Kansas, Missouri, and Arkansas.

"You can rule the mountain if you have that old desire," preached Miller, a stern disciplinarian who got the attention of his players by striking the fence with a board he always carried.

As a senior, Gautt played in the first integrated high school game in Oklahoma between Douglass and Oklahoma City Capitol Hill. The two schools had practiced against each other for years, but they had never played a game. When it finally occurred in 1955, the game drew ten thousand spectators and was televised locally in Oklahoma City. Still recovering from an injury, Gautt scored Douglass's lone touchdown on a 30-yard run, but Capitol Hill won, 13–6.

As he matured, Gautt yearned for more than football glory. He wanted respect as a man. Football was just one means to that end. He also became president of the senior class and a member of the National Honor Society. But that was at Douglass, and Gautt knew there was a larger world to be confronted. The odious signs that read "White Only" over water fountains and restroom doors made him feel as if he were an animal.

Gautt, haunted by his desire to succeed beyond the circumscribed black world, turned a deaf ear to the advice of Miller. Aware of the struggles faced by the first black students to attend OU, Miller advised Gautt not to go to OU. From Miller's standpoint, there was no need for Gautt to endure the trials he would face to become the first black player to wear a Sooner uniform. There were other major universities where Gautt could play football and be readily accepted. Already, Wilkinson's friend Duffy Daugherty—whose Michigan State team was built around black fullback Clarence Peaks—had offered Gautt a scholarship. At Wichita State, Merrill Green—who had successfully recruited a black running back from Pennsylvania named Ted Dean—tried to get Gautt to play for the Shockers. However, he made the mistake of implying to Gautt that he should go somewhere other than Oklahoma because he might not be good enough to play there. The ploy backfired, as it generally does when coaches try to recruit any great player using such an appeal. It only intensified Gautt's desire to be a Sooner.

Technically, Gautt would not be the first black player to try to play football at OU. In 1954 three players from Oklahoma City Dunjee High School—Charles Parker, George Farmer, and Sylvester Norwood—enrolled at OU and joined the freshman squad. Norwood and Farmer tried to commute to school. Struggling to keep up academically and financially, both had to drop out of the university. Parker stayed eligible academically through the first semester, but suffered a concussion in practice when his head struck the steel frame of a blocking sled. Eventually, he, too, left OU.

Wilkinson watched Gautt's high school performances with tremendous interest. In Gautt, Wilkinson saw perhaps the finest high school player in the state. But more important, Gautt's intelligence and character were above reproach, and he seemed to possess the courage necessary to overcome the insults the Sooners' first black player was certain to face. Was Gautt good enough to make the Sooner team? Without question. Could he withstand the pressures off the field? Wilkinson could not be sure, but he believed he had found his Jackie Robinson—or more particularly, his Veryl Switzer.

For Wilkinson, the issue was not *if* Gautt could play football at Oklahoma. The question that haunted Wilkinson was *how* could it be done? Wilkinson feared he could not offer Gautt a football scholarship without the risk of physical or psychological injury to the young player. But if Gautt could *earn* his scholarship, success seemed possible. For Wilkinson, the solution was a matter of politics. He had played football with blacks at Minnesota, so he knew perfectly well the world would not end if the Sooners ceased to be an all-white team.

Others, Wilkinson could be sure, did not share his beliefs. They would be out in force to prevent Gautt from succeeding, and Wilkinson could not be certain what vengeance might be visited upon Gautt—or even Wilkinson's own family—if the situation was improperly handled. But Wilkinson was equally certain that if Gautt came to OU and made the team on his own merits, he could be granted a scholarship without difficulty.

Privately, Wilkinson discussed a solution with the members of the Med-De-Phar Association, a group of black physicians, dentists, and pharmacists in Oklahoma City, who saw in Gautt the same potential he did. Yet they had even more than Wilkinson riding on the shoulders of the young fullback. With or without Gautt, the Sooners would continue to win. But if Gautt left the state to play college football, when would there be another with the ability and character to break the color line?

Wilkinson proposed a plan that could accomplish their mutual objective. If the Med-De-Phar Association could raise enough money for Gautt to enter school on his own, Gautt would have a chance to prove himself and earn a scholarship. The members of the association liked Wilkinson's strategy and set about to make it work. They were successful beyond their dreams, raising $4,000, more than enough to allow Gautt to attend OU for four years regardless of whether he obtained a scholarship or not.

Gautt's boyhood dream of playing football for OU was at hand. So, too, were the obstacles he could not imagine. For comfort in the months ahead, he would turn often to the advice given him by Minerva Sloss, his English teacher at Douglass: "Prentice, nobody can make you feel inferior without your consent."

1956

The following spring, anticipation in Norman ran high. Almost all of the Sooner starters returned, as did most of the alternate team, which some people believed was the second-best team in America the season before. Wilkinson and his staff were not without problems, however. The entire left side of the line was gone, as was right halfback Bob Burris. At center and quarterback, the top two positions were filled by seniors. New talent had to be developed.

In addition, Pete Elliott, one of Wilkinson's key assistants, had left OU to become the coach at Nebraska. The previous Cornhusker coach, Bill Glassford (a teammate of Wilkinson's on the 1937 College All-Star team), had resigned before the Oklahoma game in 1955. Only months after representing the Big Seven in the Orange Bowl, Glassford's team lost four of its first five games of the 1955 season. The Cornhusker fans were unforgiving. Glassford and his family were so besieged by harassing callers they had to disconnect the phone at night to be able to sleep.

Wilkinson knew that the loss of Elliott would hurt, but Wilkinson understood that was one of the risks a coach takes when he seeks assistants of the highest caliber. It was a price Wilkinson was willing to pay. He did not want career assistants. He wanted young men with fresh ideas who were good enough at their chosen profession to become head coaches someday. He would teach them, just as he had been taught, and he would give them the opportunity to learn. All he asked in return was loyalty, and his definition was quite encompassing. Wilkinson fully expected his staff to disagree, and he gave them freedom to do so. But when he reached a decision—or the staff as a whole reached a consensus—he expected every member of the staff to defend it. For an assistant to attend a party where a decision made by Wilkinson was criticized and to say nothing to defend it was considered disloyalty of the highest order.

Otherwise, Wilkinson believed firmly that if a coach was not capable of being a head coach, he was not good enough to coach at Oklahoma. And in return, Wilkinson offered a form of loyalty of his own. Never in the years Wilkinson coached at Oklahoma would the Sooners hear him criticize an assistant.

Not content to maintain the same offense the Sooners used the previous season, Wilkinson and his assistants worked on new variations to the Split T attack. In one formation, remarkably bold for its time, the Sooners sent out two wide flankers—one to the left and one to the right—in an effort to spread opposing defenses across an ever-widening front.

Experimenting with players at different positions continued as well. Despite the success Harris had enjoyed at quarterback, Wilkinson tried moving him to left halfback (the position he had played as a freshman) and inserting Carl Dodd at quarterback to groom Dodd for leadership during the 1957 season, when the Sooners would otherwise find themselves without an experienced senior at that position.

As he did each year, Wilkinson used spring practices as a time for testing new ideas and formations. In the fall, time was far too precious to spend on anything but disciplined preparation for the season at hand. Two-a-days were devoted to concentrated conditioning drills and evaluation of players at each position, and practice time during the season was so limited that it had to be devoted exclusively to preparing for the next Saturday's game.

But spring was a time of learning, for both players and coaches. This experimentation became more necessary every year, as defenses became increasingly able to defend against the basic Split T offense. Only by modifying the offense—and by further incorporating option plays into the Sooner scheme—could the Sooners continue to stay one step ahead of the defense. Driven by his desire to design an offense that could, on every play, change the point of attack after the ball was snapped—as Rommel had done with his tank corps—Wilkinson continued to experiment with new option alternatives.

Not the least of these experiments was a concept that had captivated Wilkinson for some time—giving the quarterback a series of *three* options on the quarterback option play, rather than the two options the conventional Split T afforded him. The extension to a "triple option" maneuver made sense. If the traditional keep-or-pitch option at the corner could put pressure on a defense, a third option would make the Split T even more devastating, especially in the hands of a player like Harris (whose talents, Wilkinson believed, were vastly underappreciated).

The Sooner option play, as it currently existed, called for the quarterback to make a predetermined fake to one of the halfbacks before he proceeded along the line of scrimmage to a spot just outside the end, where he would keep the ball or pitch to the trailing halfback. The play, marvelously simple on the blackboard, was a weapon of immense complexity, for the quarterback as well as the opposing defense, and Wilkinson kept adding nuances to make it more effective. For example, he coached his quarterbacks to take one jab step to the inside at the corner—causing the defensive end to move in that direction—before accelerating around him to the outside. Mastering the nuances of making the keep-or-pitch decision in a fraction of a second had proved difficult for such gifted athletes as Darrell Royal and Buddy Leake, just as defending the play had presented enormous problems for opposing defenses for more than a decade.

Just think, Wilkinson would discuss with his assistants, how devastating the play could be if the fake handoff to the halfback could be made into a bona fide third option. The quarterback could watch defense as he moved along the line of scrimmage. If the handoff was not covered, he would give the ball to the halfback through the hole in the line. If the handoff hole was closed off, the quarterback could move to the corner, where he would make the current keep-or-pitch option.

For days, Wilkinson took his customary place behind the Sooner backfield and watched the Sooners try again and again to execute a triple option sequence, but regardless of how well Harris and the rest of the Sooner backs completed their assignments, the timing never seemed right. By the time Harris reached the handoff spot, the defense had started to close in. Harris had no time to gauge the reaction of defense and make the right choice on the option without being smothered by the defense. As in previous years, Wilkinson was forced to abandon his experiments with a triple option play. At the time, Wilkinson could not know that it would be a decade before Spud Cason, the coach at Monnig Junior High in Fort Worth, would stumble upon the key to the triple option—a realignment of traditional Split T backfield spacing (putting the fullback closer to the line of scrimmage than the halfbacks) in order to accommodate a slow fullback.

By the end of two-a-days the following fall, the Sooners' problem spots had been filled. Ken Northcutt, the alternate center in 1955, was moved to left guard to make room for Bob Harrison, a 215-pound sophomore who displayed the type of promise Tubbs had demonstrated as a sophomore two years before. Wayne

Greenlee and Don Stiller, capable as members of the alternate team in 1955, moved up to become the starting left tackle and left end, respectively.

The choice of Clendon Thomas to replace Burris at right halfback was clear. Thomas, a standout on the alternate unit the season before, had trouble learning to throw the halfback option pass running to his left and mastering cornerback, the defensive position assigned to the right halfback in Wilkinson's one-platoon scheme. But Thomas's all-around abilities, which Wilkinson now believed were in the same class as those of Royal and Billy Vessels, enabled him to adjust quickly.

In a program blessed with dozens of gifted players, disappointment was destined to await some, not the least being Ed Gray. After two years as a starter, Gray found himself beaten out by Tom Emerson as the starting right tackle. Unlike Weatherall and others, who had been demoted momentarily by Wilkinson to rekindle their efforts, Gray's demotion was real. He knew it, and so did his teammates. How would he and the Sooners react to a situation in which a team captain was not a starter? To the pleasure of Wilkinson and Jones, Gray's enthusiasm never waned. Even after his demotion, Gray remained jovial and eager to play. And to the shock and delight of the other Sooners, Gray continued to call Wilkinson "Bud."

Wilkinson knew he had great players—Harris, McDonald, Tubbs, and Thomas, in particular—and he knew that Harris and McDonald did not get along. To Wilkinson, the challenge of making a football team a unit, despite the players' differing backgrounds and temperaments, was one of the great joys of coaching. And he loved the challenge! He also knew that in such a competitive environment, the potential sources of conflict were so great that a team needed a player who was capable of relieving that tension. Wilkinson knew he had two—Gray and Billy Pricer. And in Pricer, Wilkinson had the fullback he would choose over any other in America. He realized the accolades would go to Jim Brown at Syracuse, a six-foot-two, 230-pound fullback with sprinter's speed, but he also knew the even-tempered Pricer was exactly what he needed to make Oklahoma the best *team* in America.

During the summer of 1956 Prentice Gautt became the first black player to participate in the Oklahoma High School All-State game. The North division squad lost both its fullbacks to injuries during practice, and the North coaches asked the state coaches association for permission to use Gautt in the game. It was granted. Two days before the game, Gautt joined the North squad. He shocked the state by scoring three touchdowns—including a 90-yard kickoff return—in leading the North to a 33–9 victory.

Only days after he established his credentials in the All-State game, Gautt stepped out of a car at the main gate of the university. Soon, Gautt found that the coaches and most of his teammates accepted him as he was. Still, it seemed he was walking on eggshells. Feeling that he was constantly being judged, Gautt tried never to offend anyone, always striving to put his best foot forward, to be the perfect representative for his people (or, in the parlance of the time, "a credit to his race").

Gautt's journey to OU had not been easy. Gautt was born a child of the Deep Deuce area of Oklahoma City. A black section centered around the 300 block of Second Street, Deep Deuce was legendary for its cultural climate that flourished in the 1920s and 1930s, the same time as the Harlem Renaissance in New York. By the time Gautt was a teenager in the 1950s, the romance of Deep Deuce was in decline, but it remained the center of black nightlife and was the largest black housing area in Oklahoma City.

If those circumstances were not enough, Gautt's mother died when he was a small boy. Gautt was sent to an orphanage, where he remained until his alcoholic father remarried. Gautt's stepmother turned out to be a remarkable woman. She nurtured Gautt and helped him develop into a thoughtful student, which—combined with his athletic ability—put him in position to step out of his former life and walk onto the OU campus. As broad as his shoulders were, there remained the question of whether they were capable of carrying the burdens that he and Wilkinson had chosen.

As Wilkinson expected, Gautt was a success on the football field, where his natural ability could not be denied. In October, Wilkinson contacted the members of the Med-De-Phar Association again. His message was a joyful one. Gautt would not need the money they had raised. He had earned an athletic scholarship. Wilkinson did not tell them, just as he did not tell Gautt, about the hate mail he had received or the hostility of some alumni. For his part, Wilkinson was not concerned with what they thought. Through the course of the 1956 season and the three years Gautt would play on the OU varsity, Wilkinson would disarm his critics with the sentiments expressed by his friend Red Sanders: "I am only prejudiced against individuals who cannot block or tackle."

Through the fall, Gautt demonstrated exceptional ability just as Wilkinson knew he would. Quickly, he rose to become the No. 2 left halfback on the freshman team and helped lead the Boomers to a 33–12 victory over the freshman team from the University of Tulsa. After the game, the team went to one of Tulsa's better-known restaurants. There, as the team was seated, his presence was conspicuous—the only black face in the restaurant. The manager of the restaurant tried to explain. Of course, he said, the white coaches and players would understand. *They* were welcome, but Gautt simply could not be allowed to stay. The OU coaches and players did *not* understand. Immediately, they rose from their seats. If one of them was unwelcome, none would stay. They left to find a restaurant where they could celebrate their victory as a team.

The Baltimore Colts were going to be good someday. Billy Vessels could sense it. Already they had some great players: Alan Ameche, the fullback from Wisconsin who had beaten out Kurt Burris for the Heisman Trophy, and Jim Mutscheller and Dick Szymanski, who had played for Notre Dame against Vessels in 1952. Astutely, coach Weeb Ewbank had drafted Lenny Moore, a remarkable halfback from Penn State, and Raymond Berry, an end from Southern Methodist who was not particularly fast or strong but could catch anything. There was George Shaw, a great passer developed by Len Casanova and John McKay at Oregon. And the Colts had also signed a kid named Johnny Unitas, who had played in a ragtag sandlot league in Pittsburgh for six dollars a game before signing with the Colts.

Yes, the Colts had the makings of a great team, but Ewbank was so high on Ameche that he cut Buck McPhail. For the first time in Vessels's life, he was not relishing the start of a new football season. Something inside was telling him that Wilkinson had been right. Every fall, when the Sooners first gathered in August, Wilkinson would greet them with the same sobering message: "When football ceases to be fun, quit."

Vessels knew that time had come for him. He had played football seriously for fifteen years, and although his legs were still strong, his heart was no longer in the game. He had scored three touchdowns in his last game with the Colts, and now he would be able to leave the game on top. For him, there would be no broken bones that did not heal properly. No huffing and puffing to get weak, aching muscles prepared to play in Varsity-Alumni games. He would go where he could get away from his past and start a new life. He would go to Miami, where the city was booming, people moving out into the suburbs, and fortunes were being made in real estate.

Billy Vessels walked away from football, never to look back.

The Sooners' opener with North Carolina stood as a landmark game. Jim Tatum had moved from Maryland to his alma mater after the 1955 season, and the confrontation with the Tarheels would be the third time in four years that teams coached by Wilkinson and Tatum would clash. In addition, a Sooner victory would tie the thirty-one-game winning streak established by the Sooners of 1948–50.

Remembering the fierceness with which the Tarheels had played the year before, Wilkinson was prepared for a difficult game, especially with his two top left halfbacks unable to play at full speed. McDonald had suffered a hyperextended knee, and sophomore Jakie Sandefer was out with a twisted ankle. Other than the effect of injuries and the possibility of first-game jitters, Wilkinson felt confident. These Sooners were an exceptional group. Normally, he knew, athletic ability and motivation are inversely related. The more natural ability a player has, the less willing he is to work hard to perfect his skills. He does not have to discipline himself. His talent alone carries him. That was not true of the Sooners. Across the board, they defied the rule. They were highly talented and highly motivated.

On a day hotter even than they had faced in Chapel Hill the year before, the Sooners took the field as preseason favorites to repeat as national champions. For all of the first quarter and half of the second, the Sooners found themselves locked in a scoreless duel with the underrated Tarheels. Despite displaying a wide variety of formations, the Sooners could not score offensively. At the same time, the Sooners thoroughly dominated North Carolina defensively.

Midway through the second quarter, the Sooner alternates—led by the determined Gray—drove 52 yards to score. From the North Carolina 17, O'Neal handed off to David Baker, a sophomore quarterback from Bartlesville, Oklahoma, who had been converted to left half to fill the gap caused by Sandefer's injury. Baker knifed through the Carolina defense to the 7, where he was stopped. As Baker was falling to the ground, he alertly pitched to the trailing O'Neal, who ran the remaining 7 yards to score.

Four minutes later, the Sooners roared back again. After a Tarheel punt, a fumble left the Sooners mired at their own 18. In one play, the course of the game changed. Pricer quick kicked 78 yards to the North Carolina 4. When the Sooners stopped the Tarheels once more, McDonald returned the short North Carolina punt 11 yards to the North Carolina 37. In four plays, completed in an incredible fifty-nine seconds, the blitz was accomplished. McDonald ran for 2. Thomas for 13. Pricer for 10. Thomas for 12. Touchdown!

With only seconds remaining in the half, the Sooners struck again. Thomas intercepted a Tarheel pass at the OU 40 and returned it 10 yards before being cornered. Like Baker, he lateraled before being brought down. McDonald took

Thomas's pitch and dashed 40 more yards to the Tarheel 10. On first down, Harris wheeled around left end for 7. Then he pegged a 3-yard scoring pass to McDonald, who was surrounded by Tarheel defenders in the end zone.

The Sooners' 36–0 victory was as hard-earned as it was total. But it was also costly. In the first half, the Sooners lost Greenlee and Northcutt to identical ankle injuries. Both would require surgery, and their injuries would require Jones to make changes in his starting line. He promoted Joe Oujesky, the alternate left guard, and Gray to the starting lineup.

The following week, the Sooners made football history. In a game that otherwise would have escaped attention, the Sooners pounded Kansas State, 66–0. The difference between this one-sided victory and so many others the Sooners enjoyed at the hands of Kansas State and Iowa State lay not in the game itself. Rather, its significance lay in sequence. It was the Sooners' thirty-second straight victory, breaking the unbeaten, untied record established by the Sooners six years earlier. No team in the history of modern college football had come so far. There was no longer a record to break. Week to week, they would be competing with themselves, trying to extend a streak with no end in sight.

Although it might seem like reverse logic, Wilkinson believed that great teams are built from the bottom up. Although Wilkinson regarded The Team as the top twenty-two players on the squad, he seldom missed an opportunity to emphasize the need for every player—regardless of his place on the depth chart—to give his best every day. It was essential if the team was to improve, and particularly so when the Sooners had to keep sharp to play inspired teams of inferior talent.

To reaffirm the identity of the players who were not regulars, each of the teams behind the starters and alternates had a name of its own. The third team was the Tigers. The fourth team was called the Twilighters because it was generally late in the afternoon by the time they got to play. The fifth team was called the Hoot Owls for obvious reasons. When they took the field, the rest of the team would stand on the sidelines and hoot derisively.

Even in practice, the reserves provided much of the comic relief for the Sooners, even if unwittingly. For example, one of the things that peeved Wilkinson was for any player to say "my fault." Wilkinson believed that if a player did that, he would feel excused of his transgression and tend to forget his mistake. Besides, the rest of the players already knew whose fault it was.

One day, starting right guard Bill Krisher had to make up a lab and could not be at practice. Rather than promote the players behind him for an afternoon,

Wilkinson decided to have third-team guard Dick Gwinn practice with the starters. The Sooners were practicing "touchdown drills," in which they had to start at their 10 and run ten consecutive plays without a mistake. Gwinn, a roly-poly sophomore with an easy smile, was as confident of his own abilities as the other Sooners but was understandably nervous playing between Tubbs and Emerson.

The starters came to the line of scrimmage with the ball to be snapped, as always during touchdown drills, on the second count. When Harris called the first count, Gwinn fired across the line and blocked the man opposite him. The play was ruined.

"My fault!" Gwinn said apologetically.

Realizing what he had done, Gwinn quickly jumped back into his stance.

"No, it's not!" he shouted. "No, it's not!"

Wilkinson, sympathetic to Gwinn's plight, turned away from the players. Immediately, his shoulders began to shake, and his laughter became audible. It was five minutes before practice was back to normal.

On the flight to Fort Worth the following Thursday prior to the Texas game, the Sooners were unusually unruly. Rather than studying their assignments or visiting quietly as they normally did, they laughed and joked all during the short flight. It was clear to Wilkinson that two years of uninterrupted success and two easy victories had made the players overconfident. A team so filled with bravado was a team ripe for a fall, especially when every team on the Sooners' schedule could make its season by beating Oklahoma. That afternoon, Wilkinson called off the Sooners' normal pregame practice. Instead, he called a team meeting. When the players filed into the meeting room, they found him somber.

"You haven't practiced at all well this week," Wilkinson told the Sooners, "but it's no disgrace to be beaten by a team as strong as Texas. Even when they beat you tomorrow, remember that you're still Oklahoma. Be sure to hold your heads up high."

After the brief meeting with Wilkinson, the team held a short meeting of its own. The Sooners voted to stay at the hotel that night and study their game assignments. There would be no movie, no cutting up, on this Friday evening. At dinner, the most emotional of the Sooners—Tubbs, Pricer, and Thomas—left their food uneaten.

At breakfast the next morning, Wilkinson was still somber.

"Keep your heads high," he told the Sooners again. "It's no disgrace to be beaten by a team as strong as Texas."

The Sooners were uncomfortable about talk of defeat, especially from Wilkinson, who was characteristically pessimistic but never before so fatalistic. Now, they were not about to let Texas win.

In the OU locker room, the Sooners were dressed and ready, but Wilkinson still had not come in to lead them down the ramp of the Cotton Bowl. Lying on the concrete floor and trying to prepare himself for his first OU-Texas game, Baker felt an awesome feeling of responsibility. Outside, seventy-five thousand football fans—half dressed in red, half in orange—were waiting for twenty-year-old gladiators to emerge onto the field. Through an open window, the cacophony of the Texas State Fair intruded upon the silent Sooner dressing room. Baker could hear a carnival barker imploring fairgoers to pay twenty-five cents to see his trained penguins. Deep inside, Baker longed to be free to stop and gaze at trained penguins, anything to be delivered from the pressure. Baker was certain he was not the only player who felt that way, but that thought was one that could not be shared, merely endured in silence.

Even the ebullient Gray could sense the building tension. Reclining on the floor with the rest of the Sooners, he raised himself on one elbow.

"I wish the Old Man would come in and tell us that bird story so we can go out and kick the hell out of them!" he said.

When Wilkinson finally came into the locker room to lead the Sooners down the ramp, it was as if he unleashed a pack of greyhounds onto the floor of the Cotton Bowl.

McDonald returned the opening kickoff 54 yards to the Texas 44, and OU scored in seven plays as Thomas knifed into the end zone from the Texas 2. But if the Sooners had not understood the wisdom of Wilkinson's actions before the game, they quickly learned. Texas came out attacking with flanker sets and a spread formation they had never used before. They moved to three first downs before the Sooners stopped the drive with an interception at the OU 25.

On defense, the Longhorns were no less aggressive. In the second quarter, the Longhorns rushed so savagely they disrupted a developing Sooner pass play and caused a fumble that the Sooners finally recovered 29 yards behind the line of scrimmage. In the Sooner huddle, Harris prepared to call the next play. Following the semi-automatic reflexes instilled by hours with Wilkinson, he sensed the time was right for a trick play. He called for the Statue of Liberty handoff to Thomas on a fake quick kick.

Just as the Sooners were about to break from the huddle, Wilkinson sent in a substitution.

"Coach says this is a good time for the fake quick kick," the substitute said breathlessly.

The play worked to perfection. Pricer got the ball, took two quick steps back, and swung his right leg high in the air, at the same time hiding the ball behind his back. Thomas took it on the run and raced 44 yards before he was stopped by the dazed Longhorns. Five plays later, McDonald scored on a 4-yard sweep.

With less than a minute to play in the half, the Sooners had the ball at the Texas 47. Harris faked a handoff to Thomas and dropped straight back. Remarkably accurate at distances of up to 40 yards, Harris hit McDonald sprinting across the middle of the field. Without breaking stride, McDonald reached up, caught the point of the ball on his fingertips at the Texas 20, and streaked into the end zone. In his exuberance, McDonald raced back upfield and jumped like a small boy into Harris's arms.

In the second half, the Longhorns had no resistance left. The Sooners displayed a multitude of new formations, including the single wing and an unbalanced T, and moved the ball almost at will. They scored 26 second-half points, including a touchdown by the fourth teamers, to beat the Longhorns, 45–0, the worst defeat OU had handed Texas since 1908.

Throughout the emotional roller coaster that is a football season, players and coaches become much like a family, one that must endure more intense pressures than most families ever face. The team captains, Tubbs and Gray, provided the day-to-day leadership on and off the field, but the spirited McDonald, the Sooners' winged Mercury, was rapidly emerging as the most visible football player in America.

McDonald was the essence of speed, the asset Wilkinson valued above all others, but McDonald's sprinter-caliber quickness was not nearly so dominant in practice as it became on game day. As Wilkinson made clear to his assistants, track speed and football speed are two entirely different attributes. A football player carries thirteen pounds of equipment and must run a play every twenty-five seconds. He must run as fast as a lightly garbed sprinter who runs in a lane of his own and has twenty to twenty-five minutes to recuperate between events. That's why Wilkinson believed that running is the most overlooked fundamental of football—an attitude he had inherited from Bernie Bierman.

McDonald was the epitome of Wilkinson's beliefs. Wearing gym shorts, Tubbs could come close to outrunning McDonald in a fifty-yard race, but on the football field, there was virtually no comparison. If anything, McDonald seemed faster, quicker, and more agile wearing a helmet and pads than without them. Few players in the history of college football have carried a uniform better than McDonald.

Off the field, the talkative, wise-cracking McDonald had changed little, even as a senior. His exuberance and competitiveness had not waned. As he had as a sophomore, he relished taking the hardest tackle an opponent could administer, then jumping up and returning to the huddle, much as he jumped out of bed each Sunday morning to check his game statistics from the day before to see how his prime competitors for the Heisman Trophy—Southern Cal's Jon Arnett, Tennessee's Johnny Majors, and Notre Dame's Paul Hornung—had performed.

His off-the-field antics—putting shaving cream in the hand of a sleeping teammate or a dead fish under someone's sheets—still held their fascination, but the bantam comedian did not limit his antics to Jeff House. He had lost the top third of his left thumb in a motorcycle accident, and he found that it, too, presented possibilities for merriment. His favorite tricks were to draw faces on it with a ballpoint pen or stick it up to his nose, a practice he occasionally found enjoyable when double-dating with teammates.

He would save his finest performance for movie theaters, however. When he went to a movie, he would routinely buy a bag of popcorn before he went to sit down. As he was walking down the aisle, he would look for someone whose foot was in the aisle. When he found one, he would pretend to trip and toss his popcorn all over the audience. The fellow who had his foot in the aisle would start apologizing, and the whole theater would go into a state of confusion.

On the field, as well as off, McDonald hungered to be the center of attention, and as much as Wilkinson valued McDonald as a football player, he worked diligently throughout the 1956 season to keep McDonald's desire for center stage from destroying the team composed of more modest Sooners.

At the same time, a few Sooners understood that McDonald's antics were designed to disguise his inner insecurities. One who did was lineman Byron Searcy. In a quiet moment shared between teammates, McDonald, the All-American halfback who sought the spotlight on the football field and off (such as squiring his fiancé, Miss Oklahoma Ann Campbell, around the OU campus), admitted to Searcy that he was not a good student and feared that he could not make it in a world outside of football.

After beating Kansas, 34–12, Wilkinson and the Sooners began preparing for Notre Dame. The Irish possessed some excellent athletes—including the triple-threat Hornung—but they were not the caliber of the teams that had beaten the Sooners in 1952 and 1953. In fact, they were burdened with inexperienced sophomores and hobbled by injuries. Hornung had suffered a sprained thumb in Notre Dame's 47–14 loss to Michigan State the week before, and Aubrey Lewis, a world-class sprinter when healthy, was recovering from a severely sprained ankle.

Only 1–3, the Irish were playing so poorly under twenty-eight-year-old coach Terry Brennan (himself a former halfback for Frank Leahy) that the director of Notre Dame's board of athletics was continually having to deny that Notre Dame had deemphasized football. The Irish seemed little match for the Sooners, who were 21-point favorites.

Yet Wilkinson worried that the Sooners were prime candidates for an upset. In newspaper stories, OU's one-touchdown output in the second half of the 34–12 victory over KU the week before—caused by a heroic effort by the Jayhawks rather than a letdown by the Sooners—made the Sooners seem so ineffectual that Michigan State had replaced Oklahoma as the nation's No. 1 team. But Wilkinson needed no special incentive to prepare for the Irish. As much as he admired the Notre Dame spirit, he wanted a victory badly. Notre Dame was the only regular season opponent his Sooners had never beaten.

If Wilkinson wanted victory, Gomer Jones wanted it even more. At Ohio State, he had played against the Irish in 1935 in a game that many considered one of college football's greatest. As the Buckeye center, Jones had spearheaded the Buckeyes' offensive and defensive surges. On defense, he so dominated the Notre Dame offense that the Irish had to devise special signals to let the Notre Dame linemen know whether Jones was playing inside on the line or at a linebacker spot.

With each play, the Notre Dame tailback would look over the defense, note Jones's position, and then shout either "Blubber in" or "Blubber out" before beginning his snap count. Despite Jones's heroics, Notre Dame rallied in the final seconds to win, 18–13, in a game that became immortalized as the greatest victory in the history of Notre Dame football.

For twenty-one years, Jones tried to forget the game, but he had to suffer silently as acquaintances reminded him of it. Once Wilkinson learned of Jones's sensitivity about the game, he, too, developed a perverse enjoyment in bringing the game up. Rather than needle Jones directly, Wilkinson would generally bring it up as an aside.

"You know, Gomer, I was reading a magazine the other day, and this writer was recalling the greatest game he ever saw," Wilkinson might say. "Guess which game it was."

"I know. I know," Jones would mutter and leave the room.

From experience, Wilkinson knew that players would get tight if they flew too long a distance the day before a game, so the Sooners flew east on Thursday and worked out briefly on Friday in nearby Michigan City, Indiana. That night, the Sooners' Friday evening meal was late, and Wilkinson did not schedule the normal Friday evening movie. Instead, he instructed them to go to their rooms and rest. The Sooners, understanding the challenge that awaited them the next morning, complied.

All except Gray, that is. He wrote his nightly letter to his girlfriend back in Odessa, Texas, and turned on the television. Leaning back and munching on the apple he brought from dinner, Gray settled back to indulge his greatest passion—Western movies. Michigan City was within range of the Chicago television stations, and Gray blithely stayed awake until early in the morning watching Westerns and reading comic books.

The next morning, the Sooners were primed. At breakfast, there were few words spoken, and those only softly as the Sooners contemplated what waited for them that afternoon. As always, Wilkinson called the quarterbacks to his room for a brief meeting before the game. When Harris, O'Neal, and Dale Sherrod arrived, they found Wilkinson in a mood they did not recognize. Across his face flashed a curiously restrained smile they had never seen before. It was not the smile of a coldly analytical forty-year-old coach. It was a smile Wilkinson had not worn in years. It sprang from deep inside, hidden away for nearly two decades. It was the confident, swaggering smile of a twenty-year-old guard girding himself to take the field for the Golden Gophers.

"Just relax," said Wilkinson. "We're going to kick the hell out of these guys."

The Sooners, of course, were anything but relaxed. Even those who would not take the field were shaking with nervous excitement. Calame, the assistant coach who would man the headphones in the press box, tried to light a cigarette, but his hands were shaking so badly, he could not get a match to the tip to light it.

"Let me help you," offered Northcutt, one of the Sooners injured during the first thirty minutes of the season. But he, too, was shaking so uncontrollably he could not light the cigarette either.

October 29 proved to be a classic football Saturday. Sunny. Warm. The Notre Dame stadium was filled to overflowing with a record crowd of sixty thousand fans (the largest in stadium history), nearly eight thousand of them from Oklahoma. The game, to be nationally televised as well, was the essence of Americana. The Sooners dressed quietly, went out onto the field, and arrayed themselves in a large circle to loosen up with calisthenics. Minutes later, the Irish came onto the field and ran through the OU circle growling, trying to intimidate the highly favored Sooners. Wilkinson moved the Sooners to another area of the field to warm up.

As soon as he was certain they were loose, he sent them into the locker room to avoid further harassment.

On their first play from scrimmage, the Sooners unveiled the formation they had practiced in the spring but had never used in game. Two flankers were stationed at the edges of the Sooner Split T, Stiller wide to the left and Thomas to the right. The Irish defense, spread thin across the width of the field, could not hope to contend with the Sooners' speed.

Harris pitched to McDonald. The Sooner blockers cut down the Irish with striking precision, and McDonald gained 18 yards. On the next play, the Sooners ran the same play to the left. Thomas gained 9. Eight plays later, Harris hit Bell in the end zone with a 14-yard pass, and the Sooners were rolling. Wilkinson was right. This day would belong to the Sooners.

On Notre Dame's first play from scrimmage, Hornung swung right. The Sooners cross-charged through the middle, and the Irish guard and tackle both blocked Oujesky. Unblocked, Tubbs stormed through the open hole. He slammed into Hornung at full speed, lifting Hornung off the ground and driving him back into his own backfield. At first stunned by the fierceness of the Sooners' charge, the Irish quickly recovered their poise and drove to the OU 26 before Tubbs ranged to the outside on a crucial fourth-down play and stopped Lewis for no gain.

Wilkinson sent in the alternates, who regained field position for the Sooners on Baker's 60-yard quick kick. On fourth down from their 22, the Irish were forced to punt. A bad snap prevented the Irish punter from getting his kick off quickly, and the Sooners flooded through the left side of the Irish line to block the kick. One Sooner grabbed the ball out of the air and ran to the Notre Dame 3. Two plays later, O'Neal wedged into the end zone. Dodd kicked the extra point, and the Sooners led, 13–0. The first quarter was not yet over.

In the second quarter, the Sooner starters returned to the game. At the OU 11, Harris called for a dive off right tackle by Thomas. As the Sooners went to the line of scrimmage, Krisher widened his split away from Tubbs to within a foot of Emerson. The Irish defender widened with him.

Tubbs snapped the ball, and Harris handed it to Thomas. With his man now out of position, Krisher drove straight ahead, leaving a massive hole for Thomas. Tubbs cut down the Notre Dame linebacker, and Thomas cruised 89 yards to score easily. Back in the huddle before the extra point try, Thomas slapped the helmet of each player on the right side of the line in a gesture of appreciation.

Just before halftime, Irish halfback Jim Morse tried to throw on the run. McDonald leaped in front of the Irish receiver, twisted in midair, and came down running. The elusive McDonald streaked into the end zone to give the Sooners a 26–0 halftime lead.

In the second half, the Sooners continued to dominate the Irish, mostly with their swarming aggressive defense. McDonald intercepted another pass to end a Notre Dame drive and then passed to Thomas for a 49-yard gain. Five plays later, Harris sneaked in and then kicked the extra point for a 33–0 lead.

Early in the fourth quarter, Thomas intercepted another Hornung pass and dashed 36 yards to score the final OU touchdown in the 40–0 victory. As the Indiana shadows lengthened across the field, even the Sooners' harshest critics had to admit that the Sooners, although competing in a conference of lackluster teams, were nevertheless the stuff of legend.

As the Sooners celebrated joyfully, the public address announcer read a brief but telling message: "Here is a final score. Illinois 20, Michigan State 13."

For a moment, the stadium was silent as the meaning of the message was absorbed. Then a tremendous roar arose from the Sooners fans. The Sooners threw their helmets in the air in celebration over the meaning of the news. With Notre Dame humbled and Michigan State removed from the ranks of the unbeaten, a second straight national championship seemed assured.

Wilkinson and Jones, wiser in the fortunes of football than their players, exchanged knowing smiles but did not join in the celebration. The season, they knew, was not yet completed. Unexpectedly, a pop bottle sailed out of the stands and smashed onto the ramp where the Sooners would leave the field.

"There may be more of them," Wilkinson told his players with a smile that did not mask the seriousness of the message. "Better wear your helmets to the dressing room, men."

In the Sooner locker room, Jones embraced his beloved linemen. Tubbs. Krisher. Gray. Especially Gray, who had never faltered in his devotion or commitment, even when demoted. Gray and Tubbs quieted the celebration and asked visitors, sportswriters, and photographers to leave the locker room. Wilkinson, who did not really believe in postgame speeches, indulged himself this time. And behind the closed doors, the Sooners reversed tradition. *They* awarded the game ball to Wilkinson.

When Wilkinson finally opened the locker room doors, dozens of sportswriters and well-wishers pressed in upon the Sooners to offer their congratulations. One was a congenial priest who came to pay his respects to the Sooners, his clerical collar causing him to stand out amid the profusion of red and white. At last, he stopped to congratulate McDonald, who told the priest how he had been turned down by Leahy and his staff four years before. The priest shook his head and smiled.

"I'm afraid the Good Lord was not with us that day," he said.

Seldom has there been a football game in which statistics were more misleading. Notre Dame had the ball for thirty-two more plays than Oklahoma, had more first downs, and gained nearly as many yards. Yet seldom has a defeat been more total. It was the worst defeat the Irish had suffered in their own stadium and the worst since defeats at the hands of Army during World War II. So swift, so sure were Wilkinson's Sooners that they scored virtually at will—on defense as well as offense.

How do you tell a team that has just beaten Notre Dame that it will have to play its best game of the year against Colorado the following week? That was the problem, and Wilkinson had known it even as the Sooners were celebrating in the locker room in South Bend. The Sooners were carefree in practice, even though Wilkinson kept telling them they were not practicing well. They were invincible. They had proved it the Saturday before. Tubbs could sense trouble and called a team meeting after asking Wilkinson and the other coaches to leave the locker room. In vain, he and Gray tried to alert the Sooners to the need for more determined effort, but the victory in South Bend was still foremost in most Sooners' minds.

As they had the week before, the Sooners left Norman on Thursday and spent Friday becoming acclimated to the thin Colorado air, but still the approaching game did not concern the Sooners. At dinner in their Denver hotel on Friday night, they laughed gleefully as a Quaker Oats commercial featuring Wilkinson came on the television.

In the commercial, Wilkinson was holding a small boy in his lap.

"I don't like Quaker Oats. It's sissy food," the boy complained.

"If it's sissy food, then I have sixty sissies who eat it every morning as part of their training schedule," Bud said.

The next morning at breakfast in the hotel dining room Harris, McDonald, and Pricer sat together at one table. Wilkinson and Jones were seated at a small table in the corner. Harris looked around the dining room and saw that on none of the Sooners' tables was there a bowl of oatmeal.

Harris caught the waitress's attention, and she came to his table.

"Ask the white-haired gentleman when his boys can have their oatmeal," he said, gesturing toward Wilkinson.

Uncertain why, she nevertheless complied. She walked to the table where the coaches were seated as Jones was taking a sip of coffee.

"Your boys want to know when they can have their oatmeal," she said to Wilkinson.

Jones, trying to hold back a laugh, spewed coffee all over Wilkinson.

That afternoon, a sellout crowd of more than forty-six thousand filled Colorado's new Folsom Field despite a gray, overcast sky and subfreezing temperature. The Sooners, wearing the thirty-six pairs of long underwear Farris had purchased for the game, blew on their hands and stomped their feet trying to keep warm. McDonald, weak from a cold and sore throat he had kept secret from everyone, pestered trainer Ken Rawlinson for throat lozenges.

Five inches of snow had fallen during the night, but the grounds crew cleared almost all of it by game time. Colorado, confident of its offensive firepower, won the coin toss and chose to receive. The Buffaloes drove to the OU 33 before the Sooners stopped the advance and forced a punt. Boyd Dowler, the Buffs' sophomore quarterback, aimed a hard low kick toward the sidelines, and it sailed out-of-bounds at the OU 10.

Colorado stopped the first two Sooner plays for no gain, and Harris called a quick kick to get the Sooners better field position. Pricer's kick was blocked by the Buffs' massive John Wooten, and John Bayuk, the Buffs' big fullback, grabbed the ball in the end zone. The Sooners found themselves trailing for the first time all season.

Late in the first quarter, the Sooners got the ball at the Colorado 45 after a short punt by Dowler. On the sixth play of the drive, McDonald got deep behind the Buff secondary, and Harris hit him with a perfect pass down the middle. The lonely sprinkling of Sooners fans cheered in anticipation of another runaway victory until Harris's extra point try was no good. The Sooners still trailed, 7–6.

Moments later, the tenor of the game changed. Colorado tailback Howard Cook quick kicked, and McDonald hurried back to field the punt. With the Colorado defenders spread out across the field, McDonald picked up the ball and headed upfield. Darting through the scattered defense, McDonald broke into the clear and scored easily. Turning around after the run, McDonald was horrified to see a red flag on the field near the original line of scrimmage. His worst fears were realized. The Sooners were penalized 15 yards, and the Buffaloes kept the ball. Two minutes into the second quarter, Colorado scored on a double reverse and extended its lead to 13–6.

With five minutes left in the half, the Sooners were driving at the Colorado 34. On a third-down keeper, Harris gained 5 but was hit hard and lost the ball. Colorado recovered. The Buffaloes, displaying the power of their single wing and Split T multiple offense, launched a scoring drive, which ended on a wide sweep with thirty-six seconds left in the half. Furious with the course of the game so far, McDonald broke through to block the extra point try. Still the scoreboard carried a sobering message: Colorado 19, Oklahoma 6.

Bud Wilkinson earned sports immortality sometime between 2:30 and 3:00 P.M. Mountain Standard Time that afternoon. At the end of the first half, he did not come immediately to the Sooner dressing room as he normally did. Instead, he waited outside, leaving the Sooners—winners of thirty-five straight games and defending national champions—to pace in disbelief inside the prefabricated metal shed that functioned as the visitors' locker room at Folsom Field.

"Sit down!" Tubbs yelled, his forcefulness calming the beleaguered Sooners.

With heads bowed, the Sooners sat silently on the concrete floor in the cold, tin building. Some pulled their sideline jackets further around their heads to hide their eyes from the glances of their teammates. No one spoke.

At last, Wilkinson opened the door and stepped inside. Carefully surveying his players, he outlined their first half offensive failings and explained what had to be done.

"Put the first half out of your minds," he told the Sooners. "Don't worry about catching up. The second half is a new game, a game you are capable of winning by three touchdowns if you put your minds to it."

Wilkinson paused momentarily to make sure the Sooners understood what he was saying.

"You know, Billy Vessels came all the way from Florida to see you fellows play this game," Wilkinson said. "I don't mind letting you know that right now I'm ashamed of all of you. You aren't worthy of wearing those Oklahoma jerseys. Take them off!"

As soon as he had finished, Wilkinson walked out the door, leaving Jones to discuss the defensive adjustments that would be necessary.

As Jones talked, the Sooners listened and waited for the second half to start, but their hearts pounded the words that lips could not speak: "I am worthy. I am. I am! I AM!"

Outside, the uniformed gate guard came up to Wilkinson.

"You guys are five minutes late," the guard said. "Everybody's waiting. Aren't you ready to come out?"

"No," Wilkinson told him.

Seconds later, Wilkinson opened the door and stepped inside.

"There are forty-six thousand people out there who don't think you can win this football game. There's one guy who thinks you can. And that's me!"

The Sooners charged through the small doorway back onto the field, Pricer so intent that he knocked the door off its hinges.

As the Sooners prepared to take the field for the second half, Wilkinson called Pricer to him. Alternate fullback Dennit Morris, hurt during the first half, would not be able to play again, Wilkinson told him. Pricer would have to keep going as long as he could.

"If you're tired, tell us. We'll send somebody else in," Wilkinson said.

The game turned on the fourth play of the half. Colorado kicked off into the OU end zone, and three OU running plays picked up only 8 yards. The Sooners faced fourth-and-2 at their own 28. Harris decided to gamble. In McDonald and Thomas, Harris had the most talented pair of halfbacks in the nation, either of whom was capable of breaking a long gain at any moment. But the Sooners did not need a long gain. They needed 2 yards. And Harris went with the runner he *knew* would get it. Thomas.

"Let's block," Harris said, as the Sooners prepared to break the huddle. "This might be the ball game."

Driving behind Krisher, Emerson, and Bell, Thomas got 3 yards and the first down. After Harris and Pricer carried the Sooners to another first down, McDonald took over. He swept around right end for 12 yards to move the Sooners across midfield. Moments later, he gained 22 more to the Buff 15 by taking Harris's short pass in the flat.

Three plays later, it was fourth-and-1 at the Colorado 6. Tubbs came to the huddle and told Harris that Colorado was loaded in a goal line defense. Again, Harris chose to go with the best the Sooners had and dare the Buffaloes to stop them. Harris called the halfback option pass to the right with McDonald to get the ball. Harris made the pitchout and rolled to his right to block. McDonald sped toward the corner. The Colorado defense charged to engulf him, blocking his view of Thomas in the end zone. But McDonald had seen all he needed. Thomas was open. McDonald threw. Touchdown Oklahoma!

Harris kicked the extra point, and Wilkinson sent in his emotionally charged alternates.

The Sooner alternates held the Colorado starters on downs and forced a punt. When a holding penalty stalled the alternates on offense, Baker drilled a 47-yard punt that put the Buffs deep in their own territory. The alternates stopped Colorado again, and Wilkinson sent in his starters to receive Dowler's punt. Harris took the ball at the OU 18, and darted upfield to the OU 36. A personal foul penalty against Colorado moved the ball 15 more yards farther upfield.

The Sooners were now in high gear. In seven plays, they drove to the Colorado 11. There, McDonald took a pitchout from Harris and rolled to his right. He faked a pass, then brought the ball down and ran. Just inside the 5, he saw the goal line ahead and dove for the end zone. He made it! Harris kicked the extra point, and the Sooners were back in the lead, 20–19. The Colorado fans, seeing victory taken from them again by the hated Sooners, got even the only way they could. They started bombarding the Sooner bench with snowballs.

With the lead now regained, the Sooners could feel their adrenaline fading and began to sense how tired they really were. Pricer trotted to the sideline, unable to go any longer.

"Coach, I'm pooped," Pricer admitted.

Wilkinson smiled at his eager but unsung fullback. There was no one on the Sooner bench—perhaps no fullback in the country—who could replace Pricer at that moment.

"Go ahead and kick off and go down and make the tackle," Wilkinson told Pricer, giving him an encouraging pat on the rump and sending him back onto the field.

Buoyed by Wilkinson's confidence in him, Pricer drilled the kickoff deep and raced down the field. At the Colorado 36, Pricer and Gray stopped Cook in his tracks.

From scrimmage, Cook twice tried to go wide on the Sooners, but Tubbs and Pricer cut him down for short gains. After Dowler's punt put the Sooners back inside their own 10, the Sooners drove 58 yards before Thomas was hit hard on an end run and fumbled at the Colorado 35. The Sooner alternates came in and stopped Colorado, then moved the ball 54 yards to the Colorado 16. All the while, the frustrated Colorado fans continued to rain snowballs onto the field.

With five minutes to play, Wilkinson sent in the starters. With cobra-like quickness, they struck again. Harris rolled to his left and pegged a touchdown pass to Thomas in the end zone. His successful extra point try ended any hope of a Colorado victory.

After the close call against Colorado, the Sooners again found themselves dropped out of the top spot in the AP poll, replaced by Johnny Majors–led Tennessee. But a 44–0 victory over Iowa State was followed by a 67–14 trouncing of

Missouri in Don Faurot's last season as head coach. Against the Tigers, McDonald was brilliant, gaining 136 yards rushing and averaging 12 yards a carry. He scored on runs of 58 and 23 yards, threw a touchdown pass to Thomas, and intercepted two passes.

Combined with Tennessee's comparatively narrow 27–7 win over Ole Miss, the Sooners' victory enabled Oklahoma to regain its lead in the AP poll with two games left in the season.

Against Nebraska, OU gained 650 yards in total offense, humbling Elliott's Cornhuskers 54–6 as Tennessee struggled to beat Kentucky, 20–7. The Sooners extended their lead in the polls and prepared for the season finale against Oklahoma A&M.

Against the Aggies, the Sooners were at their best. They drove with the opening kickoff to score, with Pricer scoring on a 37-yard run. Later, O'Neal made a shoe-string interception and returned it 63 yards for a touchdown. In the final moments of the game, Wilkinson put in an all-senior team. With the ball on the Aggie 2, Gray turned to Harris in the huddle and broke the rules.

"I've never scored," Gray said. "It's my turn."

With Wilkinson bewildered on the sidelines, the Sooners lined up with Thomas at tackle and No. 73 in Thomas's place at halfback. Gray took the handoff from Harris and scored, clutching the ball around the middle with both ends exposed. After he scored, Gray refused to give the ball to the referee. Instead, he trotted to the sidelines with the ball and confronted a thoroughly mortified Wilkinson.

"Coach, I want to tell you one thing," Gray said. "You've been playing me at the wrong position for four years."

With the 53–0 win, the Sooners earned their third national championship in six years under Wilkinson and marked their fortieth straight victory, breaking the previous all-time record of thirty-nine set by Washington from 1908 to 1914.

Statistically, the Sooners were as impressive as they had been on the field, leading the nation in total offense, rushing, and scoring. Thomas led the nation in scoring with 108 points. McDonald was second with 102. And McDonald, Tubbs, Krisher, and Gray became consensus All-Americans.

McDonald, who won the Maxwell Award, finished third to Hornung in voting for the Heisman and might have won had some voters—impressed by the Sooners' achievements as a team—not placed their support behind Tubbs, who finished fourth. Tubbs was later voted the winner of the Walter Camp Award as the outstanding player in the nation, the first interior lineman to be accorded the honor. Tubbs's selection pleased Wilkinson because he had come to believe that Tubbs was the best "pure football player" he had ever coached.

Despite the passing of time, the decades have not tarnished the achievements of this, the finest team of the Wilkinson era and arguably the best college football team ever assembled.

Part IV

THE TORCH IS PASSED

1957

A harsh winter mist hovered over New York as the *Look* magazine All-America weekend neared its end. The weather, combined with a flood of speculation regarding his future, gave Wilkinson little opportunity to enjoy the city or savor the Sooners' second straight national championship. For two days, Wilkinson's name had been swept up in swirling rumors about who might become the next head coach at Texas now that Ed Price had resigned after three straight less-than-successful seasons.

At the beginning of the weekend, much of the talk centered around Bobby Dodd, the likable and well-respected coach at Georgia Tech, whose belly series offense had carried the Yellowjackets to unprecedented success. When Texas contacted Dodd, he raised eyebrows by admitting he would be seriously tempted if he were a younger man. If he were going to coach ten more years, Dodd told his friends, he would take the job in a minute, but Dodd wanted to coach only a couple more years, then retire. Anyone taking the Texas job would have to spend at least two years setting up an organization and resurrecting alumni support. That would take tremendous effort. Thousands of miles traveling. Hundreds of speeches. Dodd was not prepared to do that. His wife was from Georgia, and he had started several successful business ventures in Atlanta. Besides, the people there appreciated his achievements at Georgia Tech. He could stay forever without pressure.

That was not true of Michigan State's Duffy Daugherty or Iowa's Forest Evashevski, two young but successful Big Ten coaches rumored to be dissatisfied with their current jobs. Daugherty, in particular, was uncomfortable living in the shadow of Biggie Munn, the Spartans' legendary former head coach, who had become athletic director. Daugherty (who had been coached by Wilkinson when he was an assistant at Syracuse) remained one of Wilkinson's closest friends. Daugherty, a garrulous man blessed with a pointed, self-deprecating wit, had once crystallized the difficulty of being a head coach by quoting a fictitious telegram from the Michigan State booster club before a big game: "We're with you all the way—win or tie."

All the attention focused upon Daugherty and others came to a halt after one sportswriter, noting the widespread interest in the Texas job, cornered Wilkinson.

"Bud, would you be interested?" he asked.

"Yes, I would," Wilkinson said.

Within hours, the nation's teletype machines were clacking the news, and the telephone at George Cross's home was ringing repeatedly.

The next day, the speculation intensified. What did Wilkinson mean? Was he *really* interested in the Texas job? Or was he merely playing another of his hypothetical games—just as he had when the coaching vacancy at Minnesota had been open in 1950 and 1953?

In reality, the truth did not seem to matter. Never mind that the Minnesota job had never been a serious possibility. Never mind that no one at Texas had even talked with Wilkinson. Never mind that he had a ten-year contract with Oklahoma. Wilkinson had said "yes," and that was news—regardless of how short-lived it might be.

Publicly, Wilkinson spent much of the next two days politely explaining that his answer had indeed been strictly hypothetical. Privately, he was impatient with the whole affair. No one seemed to understand that a football coach is *always* interested when someone talks about one of the best coaching jobs in the country—particularly if it means significantly greater financial rewards. What made the matter more tiring for Wilkinson was all the talk about the oil wells he had been given to keep him at Oklahoma. That was ridiculous. All he had was his job—a good living, to be sure—a generous expense account, and a TV show, which had been the first of its kind in the nation. But other coaches had those things, too. There were jobs that paid more than Oklahoma, and Texas was one of them.

In signing his ten-year contract at Oklahoma, Wilkinson had agreed that he would not leave to coach anywhere else. He intended to live up to that contract, but when would everyone learn that a football coach does not have a job in the same sense most people do? If his team does not win—or even if it does win, but not enough—a coach may be on the streets again looking for a new job. Who would take care of his family then?

No, a coach must keep his name popping up in such circumstances, just as Wilkinson's had. When a coach's name ceased to be mentioned, it was a sure sign that the value of his stock was dwindling. Wilkinson was happy at Oklahoma. He had no plans to leave. He was not looking for another job, but neither was he saying he would *never* leave.

Even for Wilkinson, Texas would offer new challenges. It was, without a doubt, one of the great coaching jobs in the country, steeped in the aura of Dana X. Bible. And it was the program Wilkinson used to gauge his own success at Oklahoma. In a decade, he had come to understand that coaching at Oklahoma could be reduced to three simple parameters. Each year, your primary goal was to win the conference championship, which he had done for ten straight years. The next goal was to beat Texas. If you could do that, you were good enough to contend for the national championship. Finally, come what may, you must never lose to Oklahoma A&M.

The situation at Texas would be remarkably similar. Texas's goal each year was to win the Southwest Conference championship and play in the Cotton Bowl. With the rise in Oklahoma's fortunes since World War II, a victory over the Sooners meant the Longhorns were capable of competing for the national championship. But, come what may, the coach at Texas must never lose to Texas A&M.

In the preceding season, Price had failed to achieve those objectives to a greater extent than any coach who preceded him at the Forty Acres. Not only had the Longhorns suffered through a 1–9 season, the worst in the school's history, but they had also been soundly defeated by Bear Bryant's Aggies and Wilkinson's Sooners—the fifth straight game they had lost to Oklahoma. Texas had never experienced such an extended drought against the Sooners before.

Since defeating Oklahoma, 28–2, in the first meeting between the schools in 1900, Texas had become accustomed to winning the interstate battle in the Cotton Bowl. In the years before World War I, Texas won ten times. Since the rivalry had been rekindled in 1929, Texas had been even more dominant. Through 1947 Texas had a 15–3–1 record against the Sooners, including eight straight victories beginning in 1940.

Then in 1948 the Wilkinson miracle had begun. The Sooners won three straight, lost by only 2 points in 1951, and then won five straight. It was a string of good fortune Wilkinson knew could not continue. Because of its resources and vast population base, Texas held a considerable advantage over Oklahoma. Wilkinson believed that—assuming competent coaching at Texas—Oklahoma could expect to beat the Longhorns only one year in six.

Back in his office in Norman, Wilkinson was busy reviewing the athletic department's budget for the coming year when he received a telephone call from Darrell Royal. Royal had guided the University of Washington to a 5–5 record in his first year as the Huskies' head coach, but was dissatisfied.

"I'm not happy here," said Royal, not yet thirty-three and already a head coach for four seasons. "It's too wet and too far from home."

Wilkinson could understand Royal's discouragement. To anyone raised in the sunny, arid Southwest, the perpetual rain of Seattle would seem dismal, but if ever there was a tribute to bonds of home, it surely must be Royal's affection for Hollis. The small hamlet, nestled amid the sand flats along the Red River, seemed to Wilkinson a poor substitute for the green fields and forests of his boyhood home in Minnesota. Yet Hollis was home to Royal, as it had been to Leon Heath, Leon Manley, and J. W. Cole. In moments of reflection, Wilkinson had considered the sheer improbability of three starters on his 1949 team—in some ways the best he ever coached—coming from such a place. Even more improbable was that two—Royal and Heath—would become All-Americans. The odds were astronomical. The chances of it happening again were incalculable.

Yet virtually the same thing had happened a few years later. Buddy Burris had been a three-time All-American (1946, 1947, and 1948). Burris was followed by Eddie Crowder, who was an All-American in 1952. Kurt Burris and Max Boydston were All-Americans in 1954. They were followed by Bo Bolinger in 1955. All five were from Muskogee, Oklahoma, population 30,000.

Wilkinson knew these circumstances were attributable to more than happenstance. Each could be traced to that unsung hero of athletics—the dedicated high school coach. Joe B. Metcalf in Hollis and Paul Young in Muskogee were but two of the legions of men who toiled in anonymity to mold more lives than he—or any other college coach—could ever hope to influence.

That was one of the reasons why Wilkinson discouraged his former players from trying to coach at the college level. The other was lack of opportunity. As Wilkinson knew, the coaching fraternity was so small that personal contacts weighed far too heavily in selection decisions. And, if one were truthful, the chances of lasting success were far too limited.

College football was dominated by a comparative handful of schools with such an overwhelming advantage in tradition and recruiting that there were simply not enough colleges where you could find out how good a coach you really were.

And any coach—regardless of his knowledge, ability, and dedication—was at the mercy of the caliber of players at his disposal. One need only look at Tatum, who had gone from an undefeated season at Maryland to a 2–7–1 season at North Carolina, to understand why Tatum pursued recruiting with such fervor.

Wilkinson suspected that realization was finally becoming clear to Royal, and his dissatisfaction at Washington was, at least in part, born of a sense of vagaries of the profession to which Royal felt called. It is a realization every coach must face at some point in his career.

"What can I do to help you?" Wilkinson asked.

"I want the Texas job," Royal said bluntly. "If I can get an interview with the board of regents, I know I can convince them I'm the right man for the job. Can you help me?"

"I don't know, Darrell, but I'll see what I can do."

Wilkinson hung up the phone, knowing that he now faced one of the most difficult decisions of his life.

The dilemma before Wilkinson was real. The fortunes of the Oklahoma football program *and his own livelihood* depended upon beating Texas with regularity. Surely, Royal understood that. Of all the favors he could have asked, why this one? To help Royal, Wilkinson would have gladly called, written—even visited in person—almost any school in the nation. There were only two schools Royal could have chosen that would present such a difficulty for Wilkinson. One was Oklahoma A&M. The other was Texas.

As the coach at Oklahoma, Wilkinson could do nothing directly, but he knew a lawyer for Eddie Chiles's Western Company who was a Texas alum and might be able to arrange an interview for Royal. If he did so and Royal were selected, Wilkinson knew the Sooners would never again dominate Texas as they had for the past nine years. Yet of all the traits Wilkinson valued, loyalty ranked at the top of the list. In the decade Wilkinson had known Royal, he had passed that test: Royal had been loyal to him. Loyal to his wife. Loyal to his children. Loyal to his teammates. Loyal to his calling.

Wilkinson could not deny Royal the dream of his lifetime. He picked up the phone.

"Operator," he said. "I'd like to place a long-distance call to Fort Worth, please."

The hot August sun bore down on the Sooners with a vengeance. Their bodies ached from the strenuous schedule of two-a-day workouts. Their muscles, not used to being hit, hurt with each movement. Except for the large cottonwood tree, far away at the south end of the practice field, there was no respite from the summer heat. As each player waited his turn in the demanding drills, he could not help it if his eyes drifted to that tall, green oasis where Wilkinson would gather the Sooners around him and talk football. Any minute now, it would be over. Any minute, Wilkinson or one of his assistants would blow a whistle, and they would be able to prop the blocking dummies against each other and collapse in the cooling shade of the big cottonwood.

In August 1957, two-a-days were more intense than at any previous time during Wilkinson's tenure at Oklahoma. Gone were the exceptional players who had made the Sooners so formidable over the past two years. Wilkinson and his assistants had to find replacements for players they knew were irreplaceable—players a man might be lucky enough to coach once during his lifetime. They were departed, but the demands of a new season—and the expectations of Oklahoma fans—remained. And, yes, there was the winning streak, now extended to forty games, which gnawed unceasingly at all of them. And only the numbing routine of two-a-days could drive it from their minds.

For two weeks before fall classes began, the Sooners followed the same wearying schedule. Each morning, they were awakened in three shifts at 5:30, 5:40, and 5:50 A.M. Clad in pajamas or jeans, they would troop sleepily across the street to the stadium locker room. While their ankles were taped, they drank a mixture of two parts frozen grape juice to one part lime juice. From experience, trainer Ken Rawlinson knew they were less likely to vomit that drink than anything else during the strenuous workouts.

Practice in the morning lasted from 6:30 to 8:30, ending just before the August sun would begin its path high into the Oklahoma sky, raising the temperature to nearly ninety degrees. Each practice was timed to precision, and the coaches regularly checked their watches and sheaths of paper describing what was to be accomplished. Wilkinson permitted no deviation from the schedule. He believed the habits developed during these two weeks would win more games in November than anything else the coaching staff could do during the rest of the season.

After practice, the Sooners would shower and walk back to the Jeff House cafeteria for breakfast. Then came a two-hour nap followed by instructional meetings with coaches in the field house. After lunch, some players slept. Others studied their assignments. Others played chess or wrote letters home. Then came more meetings and the brutal two-hour workout from 4 until 6 P.M. It was then, when the sun seemed to stand still in the sky, that the old cottonwood looked most inviting. At five o'clock, the student managers brought out cartons of frozen oranges, but there was no water on the field, and woe to the Sooner who did not heed Rawlinson's advice about taking salt tablets.

By seven o'clock, the Sooners were so tired they could not eat or sleep. All they wanted was something to drink. Every day, the players would get half gallon tomato cans from the Jeff House dining hall and fill them with liquid. Some players wanted milk or lemonade. Others chose water or orange juice. They filled the cans with crushed ice and sipped from them like sailors who had been adrift at sea for days.

At night, some went to the movies, not so much to see the movie as to luxuriate in the air conditioning, which Wilkinson did not allow in the dorm because he believed the players should become accustomed to the heat. After the movie, they might cruise the streets of Norman until 10 P.M. to relax. But the next morning, they would be up again before the sun.

Two-a-days were an ordeal for coaches as well. Their days began like the players' at 5 A.M., but they seldom went to bed before 11 and did not get to take naps. By the fourth day, the players could see the grind taking its toll on the coaches. Gomer Jones would begin to lose his voice. Sam Lyle, known for animated use of his hands while talking, became too tired to gesture. And Ted Youngling, who led the calisthenics sessions the Sooners called "grass and gorilla drills," would give out more rapidly on the pushups.

Just when it seemed the heat would overcome them all, Wilkinson would yell, "It's going to be hot in Dallas!" Then, players and coaches alike would find the inner reserve to keep going. Finally, after the end of the first week, the Sooners had become accustomed to the temperature and the drills. They, and the coaches, emerged from the ordeal ready for another season.

As the 1957 season approached, the Sooners were expected by many to win a third consecutive national championship—a feat never before accomplished since wire service polls had been established. But the people with such high expectations did not fully appreciate the degree to which Wilkinson and his assistants would have to rebuild the Sooner team after two years of unparalleled success. Throughout the lineup, the Sooners simply did not possess the speed that had been their calling card for two years. And without Harris and McDonald, the Sooners had no one who could pass effectively.

Only four starters returned—Bill Krisher, Joe Oujesky, Don Stiller, and Clendon Thomas. Bob Harrison, though technically not a starter the previous season, could be counted as one. The alternate center behind Tubbs in 1956, Harrison was an All-American in the making who would have been a starter on any other team. The rest of the Sooner squad was comprised of good, but not extraordinary, football players.

As he had in 1951 and 1953, Wilkinson and his assistants set about reshaping the team in the same way they had before, with a firm faith in the necessity of a sound defense. However, there was one significant difference between the 1957 Sooners and their predecessors in 1951 and 1953. In those years, Wilkinson's players did not have to face the relentless pressure of a forty-game winning streak. The streak itself did not concern Wilkinson. It was not something he and the other coaches had sought consciously. They prepared the Sooners to win each game as it came. The winning streak was simply the result of doing a good job forty weeks in a row. Besides, Wilkinson knew, the real pressure comes not when you win, but when you lose.

Still, the level of performance Wilkinson demanded of himself was staggering. Through the years, several of the Sooner quarterbacks, who knew him better than the rest of the Sooners, believed he had powers bordering on the superhuman. His analysis of games was so uncanny, he seemed to be able to foretell the future. And during conversations, he never seemed to make mistakes. He would never say "now, turn left" when he meant to say "turn right." These traits, which seemed the product of supernatural powers to college students, were nothing more than innate intelligence aided by hard work through enforced sixteen-hour days.

When sleep came for Wilkinson, it came grudgingly. At first, he might play his electric chord organ and the selection of tunes he had mastered—mostly dirges and blues, his friends would tease him. If music did not work, he would read in bed, often poring over a chapter from Will and Ariel Durant's *The Story of Civilization*, which he found sobering compared to the highly charged arena of football. If he still could not sleep, he would dress and then drive to the athletic training room. There he would take a steam bath and lie down on Rawlinson's automatic massage table. When the mechanism went off, even Wilkinson found sleep hard to resist. Often, he would spend the night there, and his car became a familiar sight to the OU night watchman.

Wilkinson's lack of concern regarding the victory streak was likewise influenced by his belief that in football, as in life, the real contest was between each player and himself. Play up to your potential! That was the challenge Wilkinson issued to every Sooner. It was independent of the scoreboard, but Wilkinson knew that if every player gave his best effort, victory was almost always the result. If a player failed to give his best, he could lose even in victory—and defeat for the team was a much more likely outcome.

But what everyone else wanted to talk about was the winning streak, so Wilkinson thought about it, too. He did not know *when* it would end, but he felt sure he knew *how*. Certainly, the Sooners would not be stopped by some new defensive alignment. If you think a defense is going to stop you, all you need to do is change your offense. That was what the Sooners did against Maryland in the 1956 Orange Bowl. Maryland crowded the line of scrimmage with players who outweighed the Sooners forty pounds per man, so OU ran rapid-fire plays every fifteen seconds and wore Maryland down.

To Wilkinson, the answer seemed elementary. In a football game, each team gets the ball about thirteen times, and it must use them well. Suppose a team gets four 15-yard penalties, fumbles the ball and loses it twice, throws three passes that are intercepted, and is stopped by the defense four times. All its chances are gone. The game is over. Wilkinson was certain that is how defeat would finally come for the Sooners.

At the same time, winds of change were sweeping across the landscape the Sooners had dominated with such ease for a decade, and Wilkinson could sense them. A new coaching order was emerging in the Big Seven, as the other schools in the conference finally realized that wailing about the Sooners' football success solved nothing. One by one, the other schools had begun to upgrade their own football programs and hire young, ambitious coaches spoiling to make their mark by tumbling the Sooners.

Missouri brought in Frank Broyles, a former star for Bobby Dodd at Georgia Tech, to install the Georgia Tech belly series. Iowa State, noting the success Colorado enjoyed each year with the single wing, hired UCLA line coach Jim Myers to install the single wing used by Red Sanders's Bruins. Nebraska, eager for a Wilkinson disciple to rebuild the Cornhuskers' football fortunes, hired Bill Jennings, another of Wilkinson's protégés, to replace Pete Elliott (who had left to become the head coach at California). But from Wilkinson's perspective, the most important coaching change took place 270 miles south of the Red River at the edge of the Texas Hill Country. In Austin, Darrell Royal had been selected as the new head coach of the Texas Longhorns.

In his first fall practice with the OU varsity, Prentice Gautt was not playing well. He wasn't hitting with intensity, seemingly fearful of blocking or tackling his white teammates too hard.

Wilkinson called him aside.

"The way you're playing, Prentice, you're not even going to make our traveling squad," Wilkinson told him.

That would have been fine with some of the Sooners, who did not want to play with Gautt. In fact, the year before, one freshman player transferred because of Gautt. But most of the Sooners, regardless of their personal convictions about race, accepted Gautt personally on his own terms as an athlete. Slowly, Gautt began to understand that he, too, would have to ignore color and just play football. When he did, his fears about offending his teammates disappeared.

By the beginning of the season, Gautt was the third team left halfback and had earned his spot on the traveling squad, a fact that caused OU business manager Ken Farris some difficulty as he was completing arrangements for the Sooners' trip to Pittsburgh. Farris had been assured there would be no problem with Gautt's staying in the same hotel as the rest of the Sooners, but he had no roommate.

Shortly before the team was to leave on the trip, Jefferson Davis "Jakie" Sandefer III, the son of an oil man and a halfback who had followed Jerry Tubbs from Breckenridge, Texas, to Norman, went to Farris's office and asked what arrangements had been made for Gautt.

"I'm putting him in a single," Farris said.

"That won't be necessary," Sandefer said. "He can room with me."

Nearly fifty-nine thousand people were packed into Pitt stadium, and thousands more were watching the game from the bluff overlooking the south goalpost. All could see what Wilkinson and his assistants knew. The Sooners were noticeably smaller than John Micheloson's Panthers, but they were leaner and faster. By alternating units every seven minutes as was his habit, Wilkinson knew the Sooners could keep the pressure on the Pitt starters.

After a scoreless first quarter, the Sooners seemed poised to score, but faced a fourth-and-4 at the Panther 12. Quarterback Carl Dodd pitched back to Sandefer, who headed around right end on the halfback option. He saw right end Joe Rector in the end zone and threw. Rector leaped and came down with the ball. The Sooners were rolling again.

For the rest of the afternoon, the Sooners dominated the game, even if they could not move consistently on offense. By the third quarter, the Panther starters were fatigued from playing with no rest. Once, as the Sooners' Byron Searcy blocked Charlie Brueckman, Pittsburgh's All-American center, to the ground, Brueckman fell in a heap on top of Searcy.

"I wish you guys would call a time out," Brueckman gasped. "We've used up all of ours."

Relying on its swarming defense—which intercepted two passes and recovered three fumbles—the Sooners scored 19 points in the third quarter to earn a 26–0 win and remain the nation's No. 1–ranked team.

Through the next three games, the Sooners continued to rely on the one thing they seemed to have inherited from the year before—a steady, opportunistic defense. Instead of leading to lightning-fast strikes by the offense like the year before, this year's Sooners were limited to a methodical, grinding offense. First Iowa State. Then Texas. Then Kansas. All fell victim to the superbly trained Sooners.

All the while, Wilkinson continued to profess to friends that he was not superstitious about the Sooners' winning streak. But one who knew Wilkinson well was not so sure. Howard Neumann was an advertising executive in Oklahoma City who had approached Wilkinson about the idea of a television show four years before. Wilkinson liked the idea. When the show first came on the air on September 8, 1953 (two weeks before the game with Notre Dame in Norman), it was the first coach's show in America. At first, Neumann was simply the producer. Later, he became cohost, and his job was to ask everyman-type questions that would lead into Wilkinson's explanation.

Neumann thought little of the fact that Wilkinson wore the same gray suit and burgundy tie for every game. He had been doing that since he became head coach ten years earlier. When appropriate, Wilkinson wore the same gray fedora, but that didn't strike Neumann as anything special since men who came of age in the 1930s regarded a hat as part of being well dressed. But when Neumann learned that Wilkinson was careful not to step on the sidelines, he thought it unusual. And when Wilkinson insisted they meet for lunch at Strick's restaurant *every* Thursday to discuss that week's television show—and ordered beef barbecue, coffee, and a hot fudge sundae every time—Neumann began to have doubts that Wilkinson was being fully truthful about not being superstitious.

The Sooners already had four games under their belts when Wilkinson received a telephone call from a high school coach named Al Woolard, whom Wilkinson knew from the Coach-of-the-Year clinics he ran with Daugherty. Woolard had enjoyed considerable success coaching in Oklahoma at Commerce and Nowata before moving to Kansas to become coach of the Lawrence Lions.

Woolard's Lawrence teams won state championships in 1952 and 1956, but he was most famous among fellow coaches for having been the coach of a player whose football career ended with high school. The boy's name was Mickey Charles Mantle. During the fall of 1946 Mantle was kicked in the lower leg by a teammate, and within a few hours his ankle had swollen to three times its normal size. His temperature shot up to 104 degrees. At the local hospital, the doctors told Mantle's parents that the boy had osteomyelitis, a potentially fatal bone disease. They said they would have to amputate the leg to save the boy's life.

"Like hell you are!" Mantle's mother said.

After several abortive attempts at the local hospital to defeat the infection with small amounts of penicillin, the Mantles took their son to the Crippled Children's Hospital in Oklahoma City, where an orthopedic surgeon named Charles Rountree had a different idea. Instead, he would give the boy *massive* doses of penicillin. Within a week, the swelling and infection had dissipated.

Wilkinson also knew of Woolard's personal reputation as a coach. He was a perfectionist who never raised his voice in practice and was in the habit of referring to the players as "the kids." He was also quoted regarding his football philosophy: "Building character gets tossed around quite a bit in the coaching business. I don't think you build character by losing."

In other words, he was Wilkinson's kind of coach.

"Bud, I've got a kid who's capable of playing college ball at the highest level," Woolard told Wilkinson. "He can run, pass, and play defense. Beyond that, he's the best high school punter I've ever seen. I've talked to him about coming to Oklahoma."

Wilkinson listened intently, but had questions.

"Doesn't he want to play at KU? Most kids want to play close to home where their parents and friends can watch them play," Wilkinson said.

"You know KU's recent track record. The kid doesn't want to play for a losing program," Woolard said.

Quickly, it was arranged for John Hadl to make a visit to the OU campus.

Wilkinson understood what Woolard was implying. In contrast to the KU teams that had competed with the Sooners for the Big Seven title a few years before, recent Jayhawk teams had suffered through long, losing seasons. When J. V. Sikes left KU after a 2–8 season in 1953, Kansas hired Chuck Mather, a coach with no experience at the college level, but he had become a high school coaching legend by winning six straight Ohio state championships at Massillon. The KU experiment proved fruitless. The Jayhawks were 0–10 in 1954, and 3–6–1 in 1955 and 1956. At the time of Woolard's phone call, the Jayhawks were 1–3–1.

Wilkinson and Woolard arranged for Hadl to visit the OU campus and see an OU game. As he did with almost all potential recruits, Wilkinson met privately with the Lawrence star. Wilkinson explained how he ran the OU football program and discussed how Hadl could fit into his plans. After the interview with Wilkinson, Hadl did what most young men who had that experience did. He committed to play football at Oklahoma.

By the time undefeated Colorado invaded Norman in late October, the Sooners were securely ensconced where they had spent most of the past four years—at the top of the wire service polls. Nearly sixty-two thousand fans (the largest crowd ever to see a Big Seven conference game) came to see OU play the Buffs, who were eager to stop OU's winning streak at forty-four games. Since a season-opening 6–6 tie with Washington, Colorado had not lost and was improving rapidly. With many of the players who had nearly beaten OU in 1956 returning, the Buffs were an excellent team.

Both teams threatened early in the game, but neither scored. Late in the first quarter, Thomas boomed a quick kick 67 yards from the OU 20. As the ball was about to roll dead at the Colorado 13, a Buff lineman tried to throw a meaningless block on one of the Sooners. His leg inadvertently brushed the ball, and the Sooners recovered. On first down, the Sooners gained 4. Then Thomas, who was playing right half with the alternates as well as the starters, was stopped for no gain. On third down, alternate quarterback David Baker pitched to Bobby Boyd on an inside reverse. Boyd sliced off right guard and dashed virtually untouched into the end zone. Baker's extra point gave the Sooners a 7–0 lead, the first time since 1951 the Sooners had scored first against the star-crossed Buffaloes.

The touchdown lead held up through halftime, but Colorado evened the game on the third play of the second half. Thomas rifled a halfback pass to Sandefer, but the ball glanced off his hands. Running up to stop the play, halfback Bob Stransky picked the deflected ball out of the air and sped 40 yards for a touchdown. Krisher overpowered the Buff blockers to block the extra point. The Sooners retained the lead, 7–6.

Later in the third quarter, the Buffs got another chance when they recovered a fumble by Carl Dodd at the OU 25 and drove to third-and-2 at the OU 7. By now, the OU fans in the enclosed north end zone were screaming for the Sooners to halt the Buff advance. Dowler raised his hands in the particular way quarterbacks do to ask football fans for quiet, but the OU crowd howled louder. Dowler tried to change plays at line of scrimmage, but the center thought it was the snap count and moved the ball.

The Oklahoma crowd had saved the day! The Buffs were penalized 5 yards for illegal motion and moved back to the 12, where Stransky slipped trying to skirt right end. Colorado coach Dal Ward decided to try a field goal from the 20. The snap was good, but the ball had barely left the kicker's foot when Thomas streaked in from the outside, leaped, and blocked the kick.

As the fourth quarter began, the Buffs were back near the OU goal again after a short OU punt. Running from the single wing, Stransky faked left, pivoted, and rolled to his right. He flipped a short pass to Dowler, who grabbed the ball at the 2 and stepped into the end zone to score. This time, the extra point was good, and Colorado jumped to a 13–7 lead.

The Sooner offense seemed dead. The Sooners did not penetrate beyond midfield in the second quarter and got no farther than the OU 33 during the third quarter. At last, Thomas came to the rescue. Taking the short kickoff at the 19, he twisted his way to the OU 47. Three plays later, the Sooners faced fourth-and-1 at the Colorado 44. Abandoning the double wing formation used earlier in the game, OU came with the straight Split T. Dodd ran the quarterback option to his left and cut upfield for 11 and the first down. Finally, the Sooners drove to a first down at the Colorado 8. There, Dodd again ran the Sooner option play to his left and pitched to Thomas. Thomas turned the corner, broke a tackle by Stransky, and outran Dowler to the goal.

The cheer for the OU touchdown was deafening. It reverberated again when Dodd's conversion sealed the Sooners' 14–13 win. The 1-point difference was the Sooners' smallest margin of victory since their 14–13 win over Texas in 1950.

There was a way to defeat Oklahoma, and every opponent seemed to know it instinctively. Stop Clendon Thomas and you stop Oklahoma. The problem was that after coaches had agonized over Xs and Os, put in special defenses, and practiced them all week, they still could not stop Thomas.

Colorado stunted its line to stop him, but he scored the winning touchdown anyway. Two weeks later, Missouri put its middle linebacker in Thomas's primary handoff hole, but he still got 100 yards. The year before, with Harris, McDonald, Thomas, and Pricer in the backfield, opponents always had to guess who would be their undoing. With no passing threat and no other great runners, the Sooners were dependent upon Thomas, and other teams knew it. Yet week after week, they could not stop him or the Sooners.

The week of the Notre Dame game, *Sports Illustrated* magazine put Thomas on the cover with the headline "Why Oklahoma Is Unbeatable."

Clendon Thomas strolled across the OU campus toward the Sooner locker room underneath Memorial Stadium. He wore a plaid woolen shirt, khaki trousers, and large shoes that befit his muscular, rawboned frame. Small cuts from the game the previous Saturday were still visible on his face. As he sat changing into his practice uniform, an eastern sportswriter sat down across from him and started to chat. Wilkinson believed the exposure to sportswriters—and the requirement to express themselves verbally—was important training for his players. As a result, he never shielded his players from the press, as some other coaches did.

The writer asked Thomas about the winning streak. Like others, Thomas tried to seem nonchalant, but the sportswriter sensed an inner discomfort within Thomas. From talking with teachers and students, the sportswriter knew that virtually everyone on campus talked about the winning streak, and they—teachers and fellow students—felt a sympathy for the players that was nearly universal. Even the most casual of football fans seemed to sense that, unlike their predecessors, the current Sooners were not a band of exceptional talents. Each bore the burden of the winning streak personally, knowing that he might be the one to make a mistake and allow an opponent to be victorious.

"Against Missouri, we just had fun for a change," Thomas said. "We forgot about the streak and played a little better."

"There isn't much fun in the streak?" the sportswriter asked.

"You're not supposed to admit you *don't* have fun if you are a college football player," Thomas said candidly. "You can sit and weep in the locker room after a game. You can walk on crutches with a broken leg and realize you will limp the rest of your life. You can look in the mirror and see the flat nose and the jagged stumps of teeth. You may go right from the stadium and lie down in your bed because you're so bruised it hurts when you stir. You may be sick with fear every minute you play, but you always tell a sportswriter it's lots of fun. That's why you play—for fun. But you also go out and play football to win. The streak's just part of it."

The Streak. The words caused an uncomfortable stirring inside the Sooner players. It was always there. None of them—other than Ken Northcutt—had been playing at OU when it began. They could only be the ones playing when it ended.

"No one mentions it in a game, but it's there," Thomas continued. "The streak was started by the guys who came before us, and we think about it a little too much. We don't talk about it at all in the dressing room, but we have to face up to it. The pressure's there. Winning is pressure, but it is better than losing."

The terrier barked as Wilkinson's doorbell rang. The same sportswriter who had talked with Thomas the afternoon before stood on Wilkinson's porch on Friday evening. The peace and quiet on Brookside Drive was broken only by the moaning of a train at the depot two miles away on the edge of downtown Norman.

Wilkinson gave the visitor a drink and sat on a stool with his back to the logs burning on the open hearth.

"The pressure must be terrific," the sportswriter said.

"The streak impresses opponents a lot, and a lot of people in Oklahoma think it would be a catastrophe if we lost, but it's just part of the game to our coaches," Wilkinson said. "These things go in cycles. We're in a good cycle, but I also have the feeling that sometime we'll get our brains knocked out. I can tell you one thing. The pressure isn't as much as if we had lost five in a row. Winning pressure is great for a coach."

"What about the kids?"

"They have a lot of pride in it and want to keep it going," Wilkinson said. "The only problem is that they played as well as they could against Colorado and won by one point, and people were shocked by the margin. They can't understand that. I've tried to explain to them that such things aren't fair, but they have to deal with it. I've told them that the fans will never remember all the victories, but they will sure remember the team that ends the streak."

The sportswriter put down his drink and pulled a notepad from inside his suit coat. Wilkinson, mindful that the sportswriter was taking notes, made an effort to speak even more distinctly than normal.

"I don't do anything special to get them mentally prepared every week," Wilkinson continued. "I don't even talk about it. They don't want to be on the team that breaks the streak. But if we lost, everything wouldn't stop. The Russians would still have Sputnik. The players know that, and they have enough pride to keep it going. I don't have to remind them, but I have told them."

The letter came amid the stack of mail that arrived daily at the OU athletic department. Throughout the year, but especially during football season, Wilkinson was the recipient of hundreds of letters from football fans across the country.

Some came from small boys. Others from parents whose sons had played at Oklahoma. Still others from those who wanted favors or tickets. This particular letter, which Wilkinson would not have time to read until the following week, was likewise from a football fan, but was differentiated from the others largely by its return address:

> THE WHITE HOUSE
> Washington, D. C.
>
> November 13, 1957
>
> To Coach Wilkinson and Members of the OU Team:
>
> For my grandson far more than for myself, but, of course, for myself as well, I thank you very much, indeed, for the football autographed by all of you. David has ardent interest in the sport and is today a member, he tells me, of what is surely the finest team in America. Now having a football bearing the signatures of the head coach and team of the University whose football record has eclipsed all others will please him tremendously. So, to all of you go his thanks and my thanks for this prized gift.
>
> Dwight D. Eisenhower

Notre Dame. November 16, 1957. This was the day football fans across America had been waiting for.

The Irish were 4–2 against a tough schedule. They had lost two straight before playing OU, but they represented a bigger threat to the Sooners than the previous year. The sophomores who had suffered through the worst season in Notre Dame history were now more experienced. They had been thoroughly prepared by Notre Dame scout Bernie Crimmins, who had seen the Sooners play three times. The Notre Dame student council had proclaimed the week "Beat Oklahoma Week." Spontaneous pep rallies had sprung up each day. Still, the Sooners were favored by three touchdowns.

More than sixty-three thousand fans were expected for the game, which had been sold out since May and coincided with Oklahoma's fiftieth anniversary of statehood. To escape the carnival atmosphere surrounding the game, Notre Dame coach Terry Brennan lodged his players in Chickasha, thirty-five miles southwest of Norman, and brought them to Norman for a light workout Friday afternoon on Owen Field's faded fall turf—now painted green for color television cameras.

The game itself quickly became a defensive struggle. Through the first quarter, Oklahoma kept the Irish deep in their own territory. Three times, the Sooners seemed poised to score. Each time, they failed. On their first possession of the game, the Sooners drove to the Notre Dame 13 before Carl Dodd's fourth-down pass to Dennit Morris fell incomplete. Moments later, the Sooners recovered an Irish fumble at the Notre Dame 34, but the Sooner alternates lost 5 yards in three plays and were forced to punt. Just before the quarter ended, Nick Pietrosante punted into the fifteen-mile-per-hour north wind, and the ball went only 29 yards before it sailed out-of-bounds at the Notre Dame 43.

Wilkinson sent the OU starters back in, and they began to drive. On fourth down at the 34, Dodd sneaked for a yard to get a first down. Three plays later, OU faced another fourth-down situation. This time, Dodd was rushed heavily by the Irish line, and he fumbled the ball, picked it up, and then fumbled again. Pietrosante recovered for the Irish 24 yards back upfield at the OU 48.

Taking advantage of the momentum and the change of ends at the quarter, the Irish moved in six plays to three first downs, the last coming on Bob Williams's 10-yard pass to Pietrosante. Three plays later, the Irish had another first down at the OU 3.

On first down, Pietrosante slammed into the OU line, but Harrison and Ross Coyle stopped him for a yard gain. On second down, Pietrosante hit the same spot. Harrison and Doyle Jennings gave up but another yard. On third down, Williams gave the ball to Frank Reynolds over the left side. Harrison rose to the occasion again. Charging forward, he and Dodd stopped Reynolds for no gain.

With one last opportunity, Williams sent Jim Just off right guard, but Harrison was ready one more time. He joined the left side of the Sooner line in holding Just out of the end zone, ending the Notre Dame threat. After three plays, OU punted, and the Irish came charging again, but the Irish offensive was blunted when Baker intercepted Reynolds's running pass in the end zone.

By halftime, it was clear to Wilkinson that the Sooners—even though they were averaging 300 yards a game on the ground—did not have enough offensive muscle to move inside on the inspired Irish. Every time the Sooners tried to go wide, the Irish would shoot the linebacker immediately to the outside to beat the Sooners to the corner. Now, the Sooners' forty-seven-game winning streak was in jeopardy, and Wilkinson knew the Sooners had to find an answer to the Notre Dame challenge. In the Sooner locker room, Wilkinson remained certain the Sooners would find a way to score at least once and win the game. The Irish had been averaging a half dozen fumbles a game, and Wilkinson was sure the Sooners would be able to take advantage of Irish errors when they occurred.

The Sooners' opportunity seemed to come early in the third quarter, when a punt by Thomas took a favorable bounce and rolled dead at the Notre Dame 4. On second down, Williams tried to run around the right end, but Harrison broke through, grabbed Williams's arm, and raked the ball loose. For an instant—in a moment that would later seem an omen—the ball lay tantalizingly on the ground, the game-changing mistake Wilkinson had anticipated. Quickly, Williams lunged to recover his own fumble. The Sooners' best opportunity was lost.

By the start of the fourth quarter, the OU fans, accustomed to seeing great offenses, were stunned. This Sooner team with its plodding, pedestrian offense had been flirting with defeat all year. Now, it seemed imminent. With the Irish linebackers filling the gaps in the Sooner line and charging on nearly every play, short passes in the flat should be open, but the Sooners simply could not complete them under such pressure.

Finally, Notre Dame took the ball at its 20 and began to drive. The Irish kept pounding the center of the OU line. From Crimmins's scouting, the Irish knew that the Sooners would key on the quarterback and pursue quickly, so they ran a play similar to a counter, in which the halfbacks would start straight toward the line, then slide to the opposite side of the center just before they got the handoff. The Sooners seemed powerless to stop it.

Alternating handoffs to Reynolds and Dick Lynch with blasts by Pietrosante, Williams moved the Irish downfield against the grudging Sooner defense. Finally, the Irish got a first down at the OU 32. Wilkinson sent in the rested alternates to stop the drive. By now, he no longer believed the Sooners would be able to score. Instead, he foresaw the two teams fighting to a 0–0 tie.

When Notre Dame got two more first downs and drove to the OU 8, the Sooner starters came back onto the field. On first down, Pietrosante got 4. On the next two plays, Harrison and Searcy plugged the middle firmly, giving up only a yard. With four minutes to play, Notre Dame now faced fourth-and-3 at the enclosed end of Owen Field. As the OU fans had done three weeks previously against Colorado, they began to yell loudly to disrupt the Irish signals. Williams raised his hands to quiet the crowd. Fired by their past success against Colorado, the Sooner fans only grew louder. Then, in one of the most remarkable displays of sportsmanship in the history of college football, the Sooner players raised *their* hands, asking the fans to give the opposition a chance to run its play. The crowd complied.

Williams pitched quickly to Lynch, then faked to Pietrosante. The big fullback slammed into the Sooner line and veered to his right. With a crushing body block, he sent Dodd sprawling and cleared the way for Lynch to sweep into the right corner of the end zone. The Irish took the lead, 7–0.

With 3:50 left to play, the Sooners still had time if everything fell into place for them. Alas, it did not. After four plays, the Sooners gave up the ball on downs to the Irish at the OU 33, but the OU defense was still determined. Stopping the first two Irish plays for losses, the Sooners forced Williams to pass. Twice, he threw incomplete, and the Sooners had the ball one last time at their own 39.

Hoping that fresh players would provide the speed needed at the end of such a grueling game, Wilkinson sent in third-string quarterback Bennett Watts and a team of reserves that included halfback John Pellow, the fastest player on the Sooner squad. If the Sooners could break him into the open, they might score in one play. On first down, Brewster Hobby's pass to Pellow was incomplete, but then Watts hit Pellow for 10 yards and a first down. The Sooner fans cheered with renewed vigor. Watts dropped back again and threw long over the middle to Rector, but the ball bounced off him and into the air. Trailing the play, Pellow dove headlong for the ball. He grabbed it and fell to the ground at the Notre Dame 30. The crowd's shouting reached a crescendo.

Immediately, Wilkinson sent in Dale Sherrod to replace Watts with a play Wilkinson thought could save the day—a short pass to Gautt, the receiver strong enough and fast enough to overpower Irish defenders and get into the end zone. Sherrod saw Gautt open near the Notre Dame goal and threw, but his pass was short. Deflected by an Irish defender, the ball sailed over Gautt's head and into the arms of Williams in the end zone. The Sooners' drive ended, and with it ended the forty-seven-game winning streak.

The gray November clouds hung low over Memorial Stadium, a silent shroud covering a massive concrete coffin. No one in the stands moved, as if by moving they would be admitting the game was truly over. They remained stationed at their seats, sure that if they waited long enough, the fifth quarter would begin, and the Sooners would find a way to come from behind for one more victory. Only a small contingent in green and gold defiled the silence, buzzing like a bothersome fly in the twilight. Meanwhile, a voice from on high confirmed the worst.

"The forty-seven-game winning streak has ended," said public address announcer Jack Ogle.

A moment later, Ogle's voice returned.

"Have you fans appreciated that streak?" he said.

Slowly at first, then growing in intensity, the sixty-three thousand responded. First a low roar. Then louder and louder. Red hats sailed through the air in tribute to the gallant Sooners. Far better that the streak end in Norman, among friends and family, than to suffer the humiliation of defeat before taunting strangers.

In the Sooner locker room, the Sooners sat in silence with towels draped over their heads. They felt they had somehow failed those who had preceded them. Tubbs wouldn't have let it happen. McDonald would have found a way. In plain truth, the players did not know what to do or how to act. Never before had they played in a losing game at Oklahoma. No one had prepared them for this. They knew how to win. You sing and you yell at each other in the showers. You speak politely and dress properly because people will judge Oklahoma by your behavior. Wilkinson had taught them all those things. He had not taught them how to lose.

At last, Wilkinson stood before them. His fatherly, handsome face was punctuated with red eyes that hinted he felt the same emotions as they, but his tears were not born of defeat. They were a measure of his love for them and his admiration for their composure in the face of adversity.

"You have done something no other major college football team has ever done or will ever do again," he said. "I am proud of you. You have been just as much a part of this as any other Oklahoma team. We could not go on winning forever. Just remember, the only ones who never lose are the ones who never play."

The following Monday, Wilkinson left his office shortly before eleven o'clock to drive to Oklahoma City for the weekly meeting of the Oklahoma City Quarterback Club. For nearly five years, the meetings had begun with the members engaging in jubilant discussion about the Sooner victory the Saturday before and ended with Wilkinson's cautious evaluation of the game ahead. Now, the pattern would be shatteringly different. For the first time since the Sooners' 7–7 tie with Pittsburgh the week after the loss to Notre Dame in Norman in 1953, Wilkinson would have to explain why the Sooners had not won. As he drove, he only hoped they, who only rooted in the stands, could accept defeat as gracefully as the young men who had actually lost on the field.

As he sat eating lunch waiting to speak, he commended the effort of the Sooners to those at the head table, but he seemed to hear the words "should have" floating around the room far more than any time he could remember. Finally, he stood to address the three hundred in the dining room.

Before he could begin, a few of the members started counting in unison.

One. Two. Three. Four. Five. Six. Seven.

As the chant continued, more and more voices joined in, and Wilkinson, visibly moved by the tribute, smiled as the counting continued. Finally, nearly two minutes later, the crowd concluded its impromptu salute to the Sooners. Forty-five. Forty-six. Forty-seven. The count concluded with a level of emotion that left every member grateful for the streak they had been privileged to witness.

In a matter of days, Wilkinson would find that appreciation for the events of the past half decade was not universal. Less than a week after the loss to Notre Dame, this letter was sent to the editor of the *Daily Oklahoman*:

> Saturday's defeat of the Big Red by Notre Dame emphasizes the need for a move that has now become inevitable—kicking coach Wilkinson upstairs to the position of athletic director.
>
> The truth is that this man can be outcoached, as proved by Bear Bryant and Terry Brennan. His day, like that of his mentor, Faurot, has passed its zenith.
>
> Today's football requires a dynamic type of coaching that is beyond the now outdated Golden Boy of Oklahoma.
>
> Let's get a young hero able to cope with modern football before the great publicity value of our football team goes into a shadow.

The letter was short, but long enough for Wilkinson to ponder one thought as he read. How could his father have been so right?

Undaunted by the loss to Notre Dame, the Sooners defeated Nebraska the following week to win the Big Seven championship and earn a trip to the Orange Bowl to play Duke, the champions of the Atlantic Coast Conference.

After John Hadl's visit to OU in mid-October, events in Lawrence, Kansas, moved swiftly. By the end of October, Chuck Mather had resigned. A month later, KU named its next head coach—former Sooner Jack Mitchell, who had just completed his third year as the head coach at Arkansas. During his time at OU, Mitchell never demonstrated much interest in a coaching career, as was the case with his teammate Darrell Royal. In fact, Mitchell was uncertain what he would do after graduation. In the end, he chose coaching mostly because of what he had learned from Wilkinson. His first job—as a high school coach in Blackwell, Oklahoma—was far from impressive, but as a former All-American well versed in the Split T, he moved up quickly. He spent one year as an assistant at Tulsa, then two as an assistant at Texas Tech. In 1953 he was named head coach at Wichita State. After a 13–5–1 record over two seasons, he was named head coach at Arkansas before the 1955 season and amassed a record of 17–12–1 in his tenure there.

Hollywood handsome, Mitchell still retained his compelling personality. His habit of running his fingers through his thick, black hair only accentuated his decided resemblance to actor Robert Mitchum. Now, he was returning to the Big Seven where he—like Royal—would be competing against teams coached by Wilkinson. Wilkinson realized Mitchell could be a formidable challenge in recruiting, particularly in those areas of northeast Oklahoma that were as close to Lawrence as they were to Norman.

Duke was a good team, certainly better than its 6–2–2 record might indicate, Wilkinson believed. The Blue Devils possessed a strong line and an impressive backfield. The Duke line was as big as Notre Dame's but slower. Neither did the Blue Devils have an alternate unit to compare with Oklahoma's. As a result, Wilkinson and his offensive assistants—Eddie Crowder and Sam Lyle—devised a plan to take advantage of those weaknesses. The Sooners would operate from their spread formation and run a lot of wide plays, trying to wear down the Duke line.

On defense, Jones had designed an equally daring plan. Instead of playing containment defense as they normally did, the Sooners would shoot the gaps in the Duke line and try to force mistakes. In the process, they might give away some big gains, but Jones and Wilkinson believed the breaks would fall in OU's favor.

The night before the game, Wilkinson addressed the team.

"Duke is a big team, widely recruited," Wilkinson told his players at Bal Harbour Hotel. "But if you will play them so hard and fast that in the second half they tire and have to play on their willpower, I honestly think you'll beat them. I think you can outgame them. If you don't, you don't deserve to win anyhow.

"Before the season began, I told you that you were a football team that inherited a lot. Now, I think differently. You are a team that has come a long way on your own. You haven't inherited anything. You are a better team now than you were at any time all season. And you have done it all yourselves."

For most of the first quarter, the Sooners and Blue Devils traded punts and quick kicks. Slowly but surely, Duke gained field position and started its fifth possession at the OU 30. The Blue Devil alternates drove to the OU 17, where Duke's quarterback George Harris tried to throw to one of his ends at the Sooner goal line. Harris's pass sailed off target to the right, where David Baker took the ball on the run and dashed down the sideline. With blockers in front of him, no Duke player could stop him. Baker raced 94 yards—an Orange Bowl record—to score the Sooners' first touchdown.

While much of the first quarter was played with the ball in Oklahoma territory, the first five minutes of the second quarter were spent entirely at Duke's end of the field. The Sooners got another break early in the quarter when the Duke center snapped the ball over the punter's head, and the Sooners took the ball at the Duke 13. Four plays later, Thomas got the ball on a double reverse and sprinted to OU's second touchdown. In seven plays, Duke marched down the field to score and cut the Sooners' lead to 7 points. At the end of the first half, OU clung to its 14–7 lead.

Among his many gifts, Wilkinson possessed an uncanny understanding of how football is played. Composed equally of instinct and long hours of study, that ability enabled him to play a football game in his mind. Like great generals, Wilkinson could sense the course a battle would take. Through the first half, the Orange Bowl game had fallen into place as he suspected it would. The big Duke line had enabled the Blue Devils to outrush the Sooners in the first half, and they had outpassed them as well. The difference in the game, Baker's long interception return, sprang from the weapons Wilkinson knew would prevail—speed and daring. Wilkinson and his assistants did make one significant change for the second half, however. The wide plays had not worked as well as they had anticipated. With a one-touchdown lead, the Sooners would play it safe and stick to basic inside running plays.

Midway through the third quarter, Dodd took a Duke punt at the Duke 49 and followed a convoy of red-jerseyed blockers to the Duke 14. Hammering straight ahead, Dodd and Thomas (both of whom were playing on injured ankles) moved the ball inside the Duke 1. On fourth down, Dodd wedged into the end zone to give the Sooners a two-touchdown lead. On the final play of the third quarter, Duke scored again to cut the Sooners' lead to 21–14.

As the team changed ends, Wilkinson called Dodd and Baker to him.

"Straight T stuff and run the ball," he told them.

Two minutes later, the Sooners made the most of another Duke misplay. On an attempted quick kick, the Blue Devils fumbled, and the Sooners recovered at the Duke 24. On first down, Sandefer swept around right end for 19 yards to the Duke 5, but a 15-yard penalty on the next play put the Sooners back to the 19 with little chance to make a first down. When two plays gained a mere 2 yards, Dodd decided drastic action was necessary. On third down, Dodd rolled to his right. As he did so, he shoveled an underhand pass to Sandefer, who was cutting across the middle. Darting behind the left side of the Sooner line, Sandefer dodged Duke tacklers to the 4.

"For crying out loud!" Wilkinson said to Jones. "That's the most dangerous play we've got!"

On fourth down, Dodd went to his right and pitched again to Sandefer, who dashed into the end zone for the Sooners' fourth touchdown.

Three plays later, the Sooners got the ball back again when Morris recovered another fumble at the Duke 29. With a 28–14 lead, Wilkinson sent in the alternates and repeated his instructions to Baker.

"Keep it on the ground and hammer it out," Wilkinson told him.

"Yes, sir," Baker said.

In the excitement of the moment, Baker ignored Wilkinson's instructions. He called a halfback pass by Hobby.

"They stopped me last time in the flank. I'll be open over the middle this time," Baker told Hobby. Baker was right. Hobby hit him with the pass, and Baker dashed into the end zone to score.

With the score now 35–14, Wilkinson could overlook Baker's lack of discretion, but he was given another opportunity to question it moments later. The Sooners blocked a Duke punt and ran it to the Duke 9. On first down, Baker called another pass from the spread. This time, he rolled to his left and threw to Hobby for the touchdown.

Wilkinson threw up his arms in resignation and smiled.

"I might as well let him call them!" he said.

In the final four minutes, Oklahoma and Duke each scored another touchdown, but the final score of 48–21 did not reflect how closely matched the two teams were. The difference was the Sooners' 27 points in the fourth quarter, which proved the Sooners worthy of Wilkinson's trust. The lessons learned of August had prevailed.

As the Duke and Oklahoma players left the field and were retreating to their respective locker rooms after OU's devastating fourth-quarter outburst, the OU cheerleaders got the Sooner faithful up for one final victory cheer. Hearing the roar, one discouraged Duke player paused momentarily in his dejection to look back toward the field.

"Good Lord, don't tell me they've scored again!" he said.

1958

A decade after Bud Wilkinson made his head coaching debut, the forty-two-year-old Oklahoma coach had created an aura around the OU football program that he scarcely could have imagined ten years earlier. Under his direction, the Sooners had won three national championships—and if the 1949 Sooners had been given their due, maybe a fourth. His teams had won forty-seven straight games, an NCAA record. His use of a bona fide quarterback option play had revolutionized the position. His success had helped make the Split T the dominant offense in football. Even the last two major single wing holdouts—Red Sanders at UCLA and Bowden Wyatt at Tennessee—eventually adopted the offense.

But Wilkinson's offensive enhancements paled beside his most important contribution, the creation of the Oklahoma 72 defense. Within a few years, the defense—also known as the "Okie Defense," 5–4, or 5–4–2—had become the dominant defensive scheme in college football because of its versatility. Because of that, even Wilkinson himself was struggling to devise new ways to attack it. Without innovations, he concluded in the summer of 1958, there was no way to move the ball successfully against it on a consistent basis.

Wilkinson realized the loss to Notre Dame the previous fall was the death knell for the "old" Split T he had relied upon for most of his coaching career. Without an overpowering offensive line and a power runner like Nick Pietrosante, the Sooners simply did not have enough offensive weapons to move a determined defense.

And the maneuver of putting linebackers in the gaps in the line, so successfully executed by Notre Dame and tried by Duke, had to be dealt with.

Wilkinson's answer was the "running spread," which contained the basic Split T play structure but utilized flankers and increased the space between linemen. By going on a quick count, the Sooners would give the defense no time to adjust and fill in the holes. And with David Baker, Brewster Hobby, and Bobby Boyd, Wilkinson had passers of sufficient talent to add passing to the team's attack.

The changes in Oklahoma's offense had not come suddenly, of course. The Split T had been evolving for fifteen years, with each coach modifying the basic structure devised by Don Faurot. Wilkinson accelerated the changes during the 1956 season and continued them into the 1957 season. From the start, Wilkinson realized there was no chance that the 1957 Sooners could run over opposing teams as their predecessors had during the two previous years. There had to be new weapons, and Wilkinson knew it, but the '57 Sooners simply did not have the talent to execute the plays Wilkinson knew were necessary.

It would be easy to say the defenses were catching up with the offenses, but the situation went beyond that. After World War II, when many college teams switched to the Split T, offenses had to attack only one or two set defenses. If they could break through those, they could score—and did so frequently. Coaches realized their defenses would have to become tougher and more sophisticated to contend with the new offensive formations. This defensive evolution continued for nearly ten years, until there were a multitude of defensive formations, most of them derivatives of Wilkinson's 5–4–2.

The effectiveness of these sophisticated defenses was noteworthy, particularly in an era marked by one-platoon rules, which limited the role of specialized offensive players. With most college teams playing nearly identical offenses, something had to change. It was time for innovation to move to the offensive side of the ball.

The NCAA rules committee realized it as well. In 1958 the NCAA made two sweeping changes that would alter the face of college football. First, a team scoring a touchdown would have the right to run or pass for 2 points or kick for 1. To make a 2-point play sufficiently difficult, the ball was moved from the 2 to the 3-yard line for the conversion try.

Second, the rules committee liberalized the substitution rules, allowing any player to enter the game twice in each quarter, regardless of whether he had started the quarter or not. Previously, a player could reenter the game during a quarter only if he had started that quarter. The rule change, seemingly minor on the surface, meant that there was room for greater use of offensive and defensive specialists.

As a member of the rules committee, Wilkinson liked both rule changes. He had championed the addition of a 2-point conversion, believing it would make the game more interesting for players and fans. It would add strategic and dramatic interest to what had become the most routine play in football. He also favored some form of liberalized substitution rule that would allow more players to participate without returning to the two-platoon system, which Wilkinson believed was not in the spirit of what college football should be about.

Shortly after Jack Mitchell arrived in Lawrence as coach of the Kansas Jayhawks, he repeatedly heard one sentiment from KU boosters. If he was serious about making Kansas a football power, he'd better begin by getting hometown star John Hadl, one of the best football players ever produced in the state of Kansas, to attend KU. KU fans knew that before Mitchell was named the Jayhawks' coach, Hadl had committed to play for Wilkinson and Oklahoma. And the number one thing Mitchell could do, the KU boosters told him, was to keep Hadl in the KU camp.

Mitchell realized that Hadl's commitment to Oklahoma was merely verbal and could be changed. Early in the spring of 1958, the weather was turning warm in Lawrence, and Mitchell believed it was time to make sure Hadl became a Jayhawk. Mitchell learned that Hadl's father enjoyed horses and bourbon, so one day Mitchell arrived at the Hadl home with *both*—a pair of saddled horses and a couple of drinks. He invited Hadl's father to go for a ride.

Jess Hadl was a mechanic who had worked hard since being taken out of school in the eighth grade by his parents. To support his family, Hadl normally held down two jobs with little time for frivolity. When Mitchell showed up at the Hadls' front door, it provided Hadl's father a chance to indulge his two favorite forms of relaxation.

On the ride, the two talked about horses, bourbon, and how the future of KU football rested on the shoulders of his son. In fact, he told Hadl—as he told parents of numerous other potential recruits—that his son might be the savior of KU football. By the time the ride was completed, Mitchell had pretty much convinced Jess Hadl of that truth. Mitchell was a great salesman. A great recruiter. But that was a given. He had, after all, seen how it was done by the best—Jim Tatum.

When the two returned from their ride, the elder Hadl had an announcement: "You're going to Kansas, and we're not talking about it anymore," he said to his son.

When Hadl called the OU football office the next day, Wilkinson was not in, so Hadl told an assistant of his decision, proud that he had been forthright with Oklahoma but grateful he hadn't had to speak directly to Wilkinson himself.

When Wilkinson learned of Hadl's decision to play at Kansas, it did not surprise him, although if what Al Woolard said was true, the Sooners could have used him. There was always room for a halfback who could play offense and defense—and was a superb punter. Not only that, at six feet tall and nearly two hundred pounds, Hadl was bigger than any halfback on the OU roster. Still, there was nothing Wilkinson could do. The Sooners would have to live without Hadl.

At the same time, Wilkinson also found himself embroiled in a series of events that bothered him much more and led to a situation he disliked immensely—a conflict with a fellow football coach. In this case, it involved former OU assistant Bill Jennings and centered around a Nebraska schoolboy named Monte Kiffin.

Kiffin, voted the outstanding high school athlete in the state, was a tall, rangy lineman who fit the OU mold. Both he and his coach wrote to Wilkinson expressing Kiffin's desire to play football at Oklahoma. Wilkinson was reluctant to pursue Kiffin, regardless of his ability, because he believed it improper to invade the recruiting territory of another school in the conference.

"I would rather not recruit in Nebraska without Coach Jennings' permission," Wilkinson wrote back to Kiffin and his coach.

When Wilkinson's comments were eventually published in Nebraska newspapers, they evoked considerable criticism of Jennings because Kiffin's interest in OU implied that Nebraska football was not good enough for a player like Kiffin. The incident might have passed at that, but Eddie Crowder talked Wilkinson into going on a recruiting trip in a university plane. One of the stops was Lexington, Nebraska, where they paid a courtesy visit to Kiffin at the request of Kiffin's parents. Pleased that Kiffin would be interested in Oklahoma, Wilkinson still suggested that Kiffin would be better off to play in his home state.

Wilkinson's visit to the Kiffins' home caused the situation to reach critical proportions for Jennings, who was not trusted by many Nebraska fans because of his strong OU ties. When knowledge of Wilkinson's visit with the Kiffins became public, Cornhusker partisans were furious. With Wilkinson's previous statements about wanting Jennings's permission before trying to recruit Kiffin, it appeared that Jennings had indeed given Wilkinson permission. And the most suspicious believed Jennings might even be trying to steer Kiffin toward OU.

Jennings knew that his selection as the Cornhuskers' head coach, after quitting coaching altogether after the 1953 season, had been an event of pure coincidence. The Nebraska job was his one and only chance to succeed in coaching. In more than the figurative sense, he was determined to fight for his coaching life. Jennings wrote to Wilkinson saying that if OU did not stop trying to recruit Kiffin, he would report to the NCAA recruiting infractions that occurred while he was at OU—including some not previously reported. What Jennings failed to mention was that *he* was the cause of the violations.

Those incidents involved the funding of recruiting visits to Norman by prospective athletes in the early 1950s. At that time, Big Seven rules did not allow schools to pay travel expenses for campus visits by athletes. This was not true in the Southwest Conference, and in order to compete with these Texas schools, Jennings, who was in charge of OU recruiting, contrived to have an Oklahoma City accountant and OU alumnus named Arthur Wood solicit funds to pay for trips to Norman by Sooner recruits.

The rule prohibiting free trips to the campus was soon abolished by the Big Seven, but before it was, Wood paid out several thousand dollars for campus visits by OU recruits. The problem was that only Jennings knew of the arrangement. The other Sooner coaches, including Wilkinson, never knew of the funding arrangement or even questioned whether the travel expenses of athletes were being subsidized.

In 1954, the year after Jennings left the Sooner staff, the NCAA began an investigation into the OU football program. At the time, Wilkinson—in good conscience—asked Jennings to testify to the NCAA investigating committee that he knew nothing about recruiting irregularities and that he did not know Arthur Wood. Jennings came to Norman and did so, knowing that both statements were untrue. Now, four years later, Jennings's letter intimated that he would inform the NCAA of the actual nature of his involvement if Wilkinson continued to pursue Kiffin.

Wilkinson, still unaware of Jennings's previous activities, regarded Jennings's letter as blackmail. With the consent of George Cross, he sent a letter to NCAA executive director Walter Byers suggesting that if Jennings knew anything, he should disclose it immediately to the NCAA and Nebraska chancellor Clifford Hardin. Wilkinson's letter, and the previously uncovered matters Jennings's letter implied, set in motion a renewed investigation of the Oklahoma football program that would continue for much of the next two years.

Kiffin, caught in a maelstrom he could not have imagined when he first contacted Wilkinson, took the path of least resistance. He enrolled at Nebraska. In time, he would become a solid, but unspectacular, performer for the Cornhuskers.

As the 1958 season approached, the Sooners seemed likely to surpass their accomplishments in 1957, which, Wilkinson believed, should not be underestimated. They had, after all, come within a touchdown of being undefeated and perhaps winning a third straight national championship. Eight starters from the 1957 team had departed, but the potential existed for an explosive offense the Sooners had lacked the year before. With confidence gained during the Orange Bowl, Baker seemed to be blossoming as the starting quarterback. Although there was no Clendon Thomas among the halfbacks, Hobby and Boyd were quick and elusive.

The most important offensive change, however, was the shifting of Prentice Gautt from left halfback to fullback. For the previous three seasons, the Sooners had been without a significant ball-carrying threat at fullback. In 1955 and 1956 Pricer had been a superb, though underestimated, fullback. His strengths, however, were blocking and defense. He carried the ball a mere five times a game, but with McDonald and Thomas, he was not needed as runner. In 1957 the Sooners relied on Dennit Morris, a fullback out of the Tubbs mold. That is, he wasn't a fullback at all. He was a center who happened to be a superb linebacker. With Harrison, perhaps the finest center in the nation, firmly established at that position, the only way for Wilkinson and Jones to take advantage of Morris's prowess as a linebacker was to do what they had done with Tubbs. Make him a fullback, the other player who became a linebacker on defense.

Gautt was different. He could block, just as Pricer and Morris had, and he was an excellent linebacker, but he could also run with the ball. With Gautt at fullback, the Sooners would no longer have to count on defense to provide the breaks for a pedestrian offense. And in Ronnie Hartline, the Sooners seemed to possess a backup that some thought might eventually be even better than Gautt.

Not surprisingly, many football experts were picking Oklahoma to win its fourth national championship, but Wilkinson knew enough about football to understand that the Sooners' high preseason rankings were more a tribute to the strength of the 1957 team than an accurate appraisal of his current team.

Schooled in Wilkinson's new offense, the Sooners opened the season against West Virginia in Norman. For the Mountaineers, even *playing* the game was a victory. For years, the school had been attempting to gain respectability in football circles. Now, merely getting on Oklahoma's schedule had given them that. Throughout the first quarter, the Sooners amazed everyone in the stands (and the press box) with a variety of formations never before seen in such proliferation—flankers, split ends, unbalanced lines. Not the least of the changes was a new Sooner huddle Wilkinson had devised that caused considerable consternation for the Mountaineers. The center, ends, and flankers would leave the huddle first to get to their positions. Then, a few seconds later, the remaining Sooners would all clap their hands and hustle to the line of scrimmage. Baker would call a quick snap count, and the Sooners would be off and running with no time for linebackers to fill in the gaps or adjust to the Sooners' offensive set. With the West Virginia defense spread all over the field, the Sooners moved the ball at will—at least until they got inside the West Virginia 10. Then, their poise would suddenly disintegrate. Three times, the Sooners drove inside the West Virginia 10. Three times they faltered, losing touchdowns to fumbles and penalties.

Early in the second quarter, the Sooners got the break they needed when they blocked a Mountaineers' punt. In five plays, the Sooners drove to the West Virginia 27. There, Baker gave the ball to Gautt on a fullback slant off left tackle. Gautt rocketed through the open hole and across the 20. At the 15, he was confronted by four Mountaineer defenders. He knocked one over, bounced off two more, outran the fourth, and kept on going. Another hit him at the 10 and bounced off, so did another at the 5. Gautt scored standing up. Hobby, delighted that Gautt had emerged from his shell of insecurity, ran to Gautt and tried to pick him up and carry him around the field.

The deluge was just beginning. In their 47–14 victory, the Sooners rolled to 599 yards in total offense, including a school record 264 yards passing. Boyd, whom Wilkinson had made the alternate unit quarterback to take advantage of his quickness and lessen the liability of his mediocre speed, hit five of nine sidearm passes, including an 86-yard pass-and-run play that end Wahoo McDaniel turned into the Sooners' fourth touchdown.

At the traditional postgame gathering at Wilkinson's home, the Sooners' new offense monopolized conversation. Wilkinson explained in his articulate manner, but with appropriate generalities, how the Sooners kept the new formations straight. The Sooner play designations were the same as always, he told his guests. The only addition had been keywords to denote the new formations.

If the quarterback said the name of a city, Wilkinson explained, the linemen were to line up in one formation. If he said the name of a country, they would line up in another. If he said the name of a bird, they would line up in a third formation. As Wilkinson described it, the system appeared amazingly simple. That is, until Jones described how the system could backfire. At one Sooner squad meeting, Jones said, Wilkinson had given the same outline to his players, describing how the names of cities, countries, and birds would be used to designate formations. At that point, Jones said, one of the Sooner linemen raised his hand.

"Coach," the Sooner asked, "what if the quarterback says 'Turkey'?"

For the Sooners and their fans, the victory over West Virginia was a refreshing return to the offensive fireworks of previous years, but for scouts of teams still on Oklahoma's schedule, the new plays and formations manifested themselves with dizzying complexity. Len Casanova, now the head coach at Oregon, which the Sooners would play in a week, sent two assistants to scout the Sooners. Both were befuddled.

"This Oklahoma offense is the wildest thing I've ever seen. You need three hands to write it down," said backfield coach John McKay. "They'll never believe me. Cas will swear I was drunk."

Darrell Royal, in the second year of what he called "Operation Comeback" to return the Texas Longhorns to football respectability, came to scout the Sooners himself.

"How am I going to defense that?" said Royal watching one of the Sooners' wide-open formations. "There are six different things they can do."

In Casanova, who had coached Santa Clara to a victory over the Sooners a decade before, Wilkinson faced a formidable rival. In a week, Casanova found an answer to stopping the Sooners. Rather than worrying about the flurry of OU players spread all over the field, Casanova realized that all the activity still revolved around the center and the quarterback. Casanova instructed the Oregon linemen not to take their positions on the line until the Sooners had gotten down in their stances. Then, the linebackers would direct the Webfoot linemen into the gaps left by the Sooners, and the Oregon linemen would gamble and shoot through the gaps.

The Oregon defensive strategy against the Sooners proved amazingly successful. The Webfoots* held the Sooner offense—so devastating in its surprise assault on West Virginia—to a mere 156 yards and one touchdown. The Sooners' narrow 6–0 victory signaled to Wilkinson that his assessment of the Sooners' ability was closer to the truth than the voters in the wire service polls, who had voted the Sooners No. 1 after the dismantling of West Virginia.

---

* The Oregon football team was designated the Webfoots in honor of the Webfoot Regiment, Massachusetts fishermen who ferried George Washington and his troops across the Delaware River during the Revolutionary War. Six decades later, descendants of the members of the Webfoot Regiment followed the Oregon Trail and settled in the Willamette Valley. At that time, Oregon became known as the Webfoot State, thus leading to the name Webfoots for Oregon athletic teams. The school's mascot was changed to the Ducks in the 1970s after a written agreement was signed between the university and Disney Corporation. The agreement confirmed a verbal agreement between Walt Disney and the university dating back to the 1940s allowing the university to adopt a cartoon mascot that resembles Donald Duck.

Even if his Sooners had been impressive against West Virginia, Wilkinson knew that their seeming success had been the result of vastly superior manpower and the element of surprise. Oregon, a good but not great team, had been able to hold the Sooners to their lowest winning total in Wilkinson's eleven years as head coach. And undefeated Texas, with an added week to scout the No. 2–ranked Sooners, would represent an even greater physical challenge even though they were 13-point underdogs.

If Royal's team presented problems for Wilkinson on the field, arrangements off the field were equally trying for Ken Farris. On most road trips, traveling with Gautt had proved no difficulty. He was accepted with the rest of the Sooners. Ironically, he experienced problems in only two locations—Oklahoma City and Fort Worth. The Skirvin, the long-standing home of the Sooners on Friday nights before home games, had refused to let Gautt stay with the team. Farris reported the situation to Wilkinson.

"Move us to the Biltmore," Wilkinson said.

Even more trying was the trip to Texas. On the week of the Texas game, the Sooners habitually stayed in the Worth Hotel. Farris had tried to get the hotel to accept Gautt in 1957, but had failed. Again, they refused, and Farris was forced to make the same humiliating arrangements for Gautt that had been necessary the year before, requiring him to make reservations for Gautt at a black hotel nearby.

Before the team left for Texas, Farris called Gautt into his office and explained the situation.

"As soon as the bus stops in front of the Worth Hotel, my station wagon will be parked just around the corner," Farris said. "As the other players are going in, just mosey around the corner and I'll take you to your hotel."

When Friday came, Farris met Gautt as planned and drove him to his hotel. He gave him enough money to buy dinner, go to a movie, buy a magazine, and get a taxi to the Worth Hotel the next morning. There, he could eat breakfast in the dining room, but had to go straight to the training room the Sooners had reserved because he was not allowed in the rest of the hotel.

"Why do you do this?" Farris asked the manager in exasperation.

"First of all, it's the state law," the manager said. "And second, if we let him stay here, we'd lose two hundred West Texas ranchers as customers."

"That's most unfortunate," Farris said. "Especially for Prentice."

At the end of the season, Farris would investigate the situation and find it was not truly a state law that prevented Gautt from staying with his teammates. The Texas state legislature had indeed passed a separate accommodations law, but it had come at the request of larger cities to prevent blacks from staying in the preeminent hotels in those cities. The legislation gave cities the discretion of applying the law or not. Fort Worth had chosen to apply it, making it more a city ordinance than a state one, but the effect on Gautt was the same.

Early in the first quarter against Texas, Wilkinson learned that his concerns about the strength of the Longhorn team were well grounded. Royal threw an eight-man line against the Sooner offense, and Wilkinson responded with a defense that put nine men near the line of scrimmage when Texas had the ball. For all the talk about new, innovative offenses, this would be an old-fashioned game of defense.

The Sooners fell behind late in the second quarter when the Longhorns got the ball at midfield. Quarterback Bobby Lackey faked a handoff to the fullback and threw to halfback Rene Ramirez for a 37-yard gain to the OU 16. Three plays later, the Sooners braced for the Longhorns on fourth-and-4. Taking a pitchout from Lackey, Ramirez ran to his left and threw to halfback George Blanch for the touchdown. After the Longhorns' success on two pass plays, Royal sensed the Sooners might be off balance. Royal ordered the Longhorn offense to line up and go for a 2-point conversion. Lackey handed off to fullback Don Allen, who bulled straight ahead over left guard to score.

In the third period, the Sooner alternates finally scored on a 38-yard drive when Boyd went to his left, faked a keeper, and pitched to Dick Carpenter, who took the ball on the run and scored untouched. The Sooners tried for two to tie the game, but Boyd's pass was incomplete. Texas retained its 8–6 lead.

Early in the fourth quarter, the Sooners again drove deep into Texas territory, but the Longhorns held on fourth down at the 24. On the Longhorns' first offensive play, fullback Mike Dowdle was stopped at the line of scrimmage and lost control of the ball. The ball slipped out of Dowdle's hands and rolled up onto his hip. The Sooners' Jim Davis, who had shot the gap and grabbed Dowdle from behind, alertly snatched the ball and ran the 24 yards to score. Boyd threw for the 2-point conversion, and the Sooners led, 14–8.

The Longhorns got the ball at their 26 with seven minutes to play. So far in the second half, the Sooner defense had dominated the Texas offense. The Longhorns were -12 yards rushing, so Royal, in desperation, sent in reserve quarterback Vince Matthews, a highly recruited schoolboy passer written off by the previous Texas coaching staff after two knee injuries. Uncannily, Matthews moved the Longhorns down the field. At last, the Longhorns faced third-and-goal at the OU 7, and Royal replaced Matthews with Lackey, who was a better runner. On his first play, Lackey fired a short jump pass to end Bob Bryant in the OU end zone. Calmly, Lackey kicked the extra point that sealed the Longhorns' 15–14 victory.

In the pandemonium after the Longhorn victory, the goalposts of the Cotton Bowl came down at the hands of the joyful Texas fans, relishing their first victory over Oklahoma since 1951. George Cross walked along the sidelines and up the asphalt ramp of the Cotton Bowl to the Texas locker room to congratulate Royal. Cross tried to find Royal among the jubilant Texas players, but he could not. Finally, he stepped outside the door that led to the Texas State Fair midway. Amid the colorful, glowing lights and the incessant din of calliopes, Cross found Royal leaning against the side of the building in the gathering darkness. Royal's face was ashen white, leading Cross to suspect that Royal had been vomiting. Cross offered his congratulations, and Royal, regaining his composure, thanked him. Royal said the pressure of the game and the tension he felt about competing against his own beloved coach had been too much.

"Somehow, it just doesn't seem right to beat Mr. Wilkinson," Royal said.

The week after the Texas game, the Sooners' second lackluster performance in two weeks, the Sooners tumbled nine spots in the Associated Press poll to No. 11. At the same time, Army—coached by Wilkinson's friend Earl "Red" Blaik—moved up to No. 1 after beating archrival Notre Dame. Wilkinson and Blaik, athletic directors for their respective schools, had scheduled a game between their teams during the 1959 season, the first time the Sooners would play the Cadets since 1946. Wilkinson called Blaik to congratulate him on his team's rise to the top of the polls.

"I'm glad we're not playing you *this* year," Wilkinson told Blaik.

"We have the opportunity to be better than I expected," Blaik said. "We've got a superior passer, several fine receivers and two extraordinary runners at halfback. Bob Anderson is the best all-around football player I've had since Blanchard and Davis, and Pete Dawkins is turning out to be a better football player than I ever imagined he could be. I suspected for a long time that he was just another 'silk stocking' prep school athlete. We see a lot of them here at the Academy. But this time, I was wrong."

Dawkins had proved it the first week of the season. As Oklahoma was dismantling West Virginia, Army was running roughshod over South Carolina, 45–8. The Cadets rolled to more than 500 yards in total offense. Anderson threw five passes from what Blaik called the "option sweep," a play similar to Wilkinson's halfback run-pass option. Anderson completed all five passes, two of them for touchdowns. Dawkins carried nine times for 113 yards and scored four touchdowns.

Dawkins and Anderson were only part of what made the Cadets so effective. Much of the attention given to Army was focused on end Bill Carpenter, Army's so-called "Lonesome End," who was rapidly becoming the most famous lineman in America. Between plays, Carpenter never returned to the Army huddle, but always seemed to be in the right place at the right time on every Army play.

Wilkinson had read about Carpenter, and Blaik explained the basics of the formation—though not the details regarding how Carpenter knew what play the Cadets were running. The two teams were, after all, going to play each other the next season. Blaik also explained how he came to devise the formation. In typical Blaik detail, the Army coach told Wilkinson that he had been on the beach at Key Biscayne, Florida, after the 1957 season when he had an idea for a new formation. The "Far Flanker," he called it. At the time, split ends were roughly 7 yards outside the tackle. In Blaik's scheme, the Far Flanker would be stationed 20 to 30 yards outside the rest of the offense to the wide side of the field, thereby creating an unbalanced line. The purpose of the formation, Blaik told Wilkinson, was to counteract the opponent's cornerbacks, who began each play stationed even with the linebackers in the Oklahoma 5–4–2 defense. This created a de facto nine-man front.

Blaik believed the Far Flanker would open up Army's attack by breaking up the nine-man front. If opponents used a cornerback to cover the Far Flanker, the defense would be reduced to eight men to stop a running play. If the opponent chose to leave the front intact and cover the Far Flanker with a safety, the opponent would be left with a three-man secondary (the two cornerbacks and one safety), and Army's Joe Caldwell was a good enough passer to exploit that weakness.

"Do you think others will copy you?" Wilkinson asked.

"They may try," Blaik replied, "but you know that no system is better than the people you have. There would be no Lonesome End if there were no Bill Carpenter. He's the one who makes it work."

Having heard the details from Blaik, Wilkinson was impressed with what his friend had devised. In fact, he liked Blaik's solution for attacking the 5–4–2 defense better than his own, but he did not have the weapons necessary to execute it. In addition, Wilkinson was happy that Blaik seemed to be enjoying another moment in the sun after an academic cheating scandal rocked the Academy seven years earlier.

Although Blaik was eighteen years older than Wilkinson, the two had become friends because they learned at coaching conventions that they approached coaching with the same orientation. That is, they were both detail-driven perfectionists. Both knew what they wanted, and they drilled their squads in organized, military fashion to achieve it. Both understood that champions make their own luck. Blaik was considered gruff and demanding. Wilkinson was more pleasant, but there was no doubt among his players and assistant coaches that he was demanding.

Blaik began his college playing career at Miami of Ohio, but transferred to West Point, where he was a star end and third team All-American before earning a commission in 1920. He spent two years in the cavalry, but quickly realized that promotions were slow in the peace time army and resigned his commission. At about the same time Blaik was making his decision, Gen. Douglas MacArthur, who had been superintendent of West Point during Blaik's years as a cadet, received new orders to the Philippines. He invited Blaik to come along as his aide-de-camp. Blaik declined the invitation, so MacArthur chose another former Army football player, Dwight Eisenhower.

Blaik began coaching as a part-time assistant at Miami before accepting a similar position at the University of Wisconsin. In 1927 he went to West Point as a part-time assistant and became a full-time assistant in 1930. In 1934 he was selected as the head coach at Dartmouth, where his teams compiled a record of 45–15–4 in seven seasons.

In 1941 Blaik came back to West Point after the Cadets suffered through two straight losing seasons (which had not happened in more than thirty years) and two shutouts at the hands of the Navy Midshipmen. In order to get Blaik to take the job, the powers-that-be at West Point dropped the requirements that the football coach be a West Point graduate on active duty and that all players meet the Academy's stringent height-to-weight standards. The latter condition came at Blaik's insistence because he believed Army was at a disadvantage because of the size of its linemen. The Naval Academy did not have the same restrictions, and so the army surgeon general was finally persuaded to drop the requirement for Army football players.

From the beginning, Blaik was successful at West Point. He did things his way and carried himself with military bearing. His players referred to him as "The Colonel," and eventually many outside the Academy began calling him "Colonel Blaik," although the title was merely symbolic.

"There can be no such thing as a football coach who is 'an easy man to play for,'" Blaik said. "Those are contradictory terms."

Blaik was often criticized for being stern and rigid, but he saw himself as doing what he had been hired to do—fulfill the Academy's fundamental mission of training winners. Thus, among some West Point graduates, the idea of recruiting great high school football players to attend West Point was not seen as being at cross purposes with creating officers for the U.S. Army. One who shared that belief was Gen. George C. Marshall, President Franklin Roosevelt's chairman of the Joint Chiefs of Staff in World War II, who once emphasized his concurrence with that belief by saying, "I have a secret and dangerous mission. Send me an Army football player."

Blaik, like Wilkinson, had a tremendous capacity for detail. Once, that tendency caused him to direct the cutting of oranges into pieces that Army players could suck on during a game. His demand for detail was so profound that he prescribed *exactly* how many segments were to be cut from each orange.

During World War II and the years shortly thereafter, Blaik reached the pinnacle of his profession. His Army teams in 1944 and 1945 were national champions. Because the war caused the dilution of talent at other schools—and the commensurate concentration of great athletes at the military academy—there were some who believed these squads were the best college teams ever assembled. After the war, Blaik became one of the first college coaches to implement a two-platoon system, using players strictly for offense or defense. Blaik was also one of the first to analyze a football game play-by-play, charting a team's tendencies on every down through the use of game film.

However, disaster struck in the summer of 1951. A number of cadets, including many on the football squad, admitted that they had helped one another by sharing answers to a weekly quiz. These were infractions that would not have been an issue at most universities, but they violated the Academy's honor code, which specified that a cadet will not lie, cheat, steal, or tolerate those who do. In all, ninety cadets were expelled. Thirty-seven were football players. All of the guilty cadets left the Academy (including Blaik's own son, Bob, who would eventually become one of Wilkinson's assistants during the 1959 and 1960 football seasons).

The two years immediately following the scandal were the most wretched of Blaik's life, and possibly his finest. Starting with junior varsity players, he rebuilt Army's football team. Blaik's biggest problem was one familiar to any coach trying to turn around a losing program. He had to convince his players that they not only could be, but *should* be, winners.

The event that demonstrated the strain Blaik was under occurred in a game when Army was trying to hold onto a 14–13 lead against Penn in the fourth quarter. Army launched a long drive to the Penn 19, where, on fourth down, Blaik ordered a substitute sent in with instructions to go for a field goal. Astonishingly, assistant Tiger Howell countermanded Blaik's order, chasing after the substitute and recalling him. Instead of the field goal attempt, the Cadets went for the first down and failed. At that time, Blaik walked over to Howell, handed him an Army blanket, and said, "Take this. You'll need it in Korea."

After ignoring Blaik's field goal order, Howell suffered through the final three minutes. When the Cadets held on to win, Howell was relieved when Blaik came over to him. "Tiger, you don't have to pack your bags," Blaik said.

Though ever loyal to West Point, Blaik never got over his resentment regarding the way in which the investigation of the cribbing scandal was handled. He was certain the scandal was fomented by a contingent of officers who believed football players were not real cadets and resented them being at the Academy.

The week after the Texas game, Colorado loomed as the last major test for the Sooners. As the two teams prepared to meet in Boulder the sixth week of the season, the Buffs were undefeated. Colorado fans—and many others in the Big Eight—were convinced that this was the year some team would finally supplant the Sooners at the top of the conference. And they were equally convinced that team would be Colorado.

That feeling had begun in the spring, when Colorado coach Dallas Ward brought Hardin-Simmons coach Sammy Baugh and San Francisco 49er defensive coordinator Phil Bengtson to Boulder to tutor the Buffaloes. Baugh promptly declared Colorado's single wing rushing attack the best he had ever seen. And Colorado fans wanted to believe it. After all, *Sammy Baugh* said it!

The problem was that Ward wasn't sure it was true. Yes, the Buffs had Howard Cook, Boyd Dowler, and Eddie Dove in the backfield for the third straight year. And they had All-American John Wooten at guard, who was good enough, pronounced Bengtson, to start on offense for the 49ers. But, Ward tried to tell Colorado fans, the Buffs had no experienced centers or ends. Not only that, the Buffs never seemed to play other teams as well as they played Oklahoma.

Wilkinson knew the quality of the Colorado team, but he also had been in coaching long enough to see signs of trouble. The Sooners and the Buffs would be playing for the Big Eight championship, and Wilkinson had no intention of losing. He knew how disgruntled Colorado fans were becoming, and he feared that a Sooner victory would cost Ward his job. As a result, Wilkinson was on edge about the Colorado game. As always, he flew the Sooners to Boulder on Thursday, but unlike other years, he closed the Sooners' final workout on Friday.

In any game, Wilkinson believed, it was important to throw the opposing team off balance. In this game, he did so by starting sophomore Bob Cornell at quarterback in place of the recently erratic Baker. Besides, Wilkinson knew, kicking can be crucial early in pivotal games, and Cornell was the Sooners' best punter. Wilkinson's intuition proved correct. When the first Oklahoma possession stalled deep in Oklahoma territory, Cornell boomed a 50-yard punt. After the Sooners stopped the Buffs on offense, Dowler responded with a 57-yard punt that went out-of-bounds on the Sooner 1.

The poor field position forced the Sooners to play conservatively, and they punted again. Settling under the Sooner punt at his 30, Dove broke into the open and returned it 40 yards before being caught from behind. Seven plays later, Colorado scored. Once again, the Buffs took an early lead over the Sooners.

In the ensuing minutes, the Sooners completed their finest drive of the year, moving 72 yards to score. They methodically moved across the 50, then Gautt burst through a hole over left tackle and raced 48 yards for the touchdown. Baker rolled to his right and hit Carpenter for the 2-point conversion and an 8–7 OU lead.

The Sooners finally put the game out of reach in the fourth quarter. Despite his magnificent punts, the tall, slender Dowler was slow getting his kicks away, and the Sooners knew it. They blocked Dowler's punt and recovered the ball at the Colorado 8. Four plays later, Baker sneaked in for the final touchdown in the Sooners' 23–7 win.

The victory, though less harrowing than others over the Buffs, was nonetheless shattering for Colorado. Yet Ward, a man of uncommon decency, hurried to the Sooner buses to congratulate the Sooners, the very players whom his inability to beat would lead to his forced resignation as the Colorado coach.

After Colorado fell, the Sooners swept through their four remaining games allowing only one touchdown. Finishing 9–1, they were ranked fifth in the nation, extending their display of continuing excellence. For a remarkable eleven straight seasons, dating to Wilkinson's second year as head coach in 1948, the Sooners had finished in the AP Top Ten, thereby tying a record set by Michigan teams coached by Fritz Crisler and Bennie Oosterbaan from 1940 through 1950. (The Michigan-Oklahoma record would eventually be broken by Bobby Bowden's Florida State teams from 1987 through 2000.)

The season marked the twenty-fifth anniversary of the Orange Bowl, and the Orange Bowl committee asked the Big Eight to suspend its no-repeat bowl rule and send its true champion to the contest. The Big Eight agreed, and the Sooners were headed to a second consecutive bowl game for the first time in nearly a decade. Their New Year's Day opponent would be Syracuse, which had emerged under Ben Schwartzwalder as one of the dominant teams in the East.

Throughout his years at Oklahoma, Wilkinson preached tradition.

"If there is any glory in wearing an Oklahoma jersey, it exists because of the men who played before you. You have to make yourself worthy of that honor," he would tell his players.

If ever there was a player on whom that burden weighed heavily, it was Baker. A talented high school athlete, Baker was recruited by three of the greatest coaches of all time. Henry Iba wanted Baker to play basketball at Oklahoma A&M. Phog Allen wanted him to play basketball at Kansas, so much so that he shared a secret with Baker that few others knew—if he came to KU, he would play with a freshman from Philadelphia named Wilt Chamberlain. Wilkinson wanted Baker to play football at Oklahoma. And Baker—like any young Oklahoman who was asked by Wilkinson to become a Sooner—could not say no. He cast his lot with Oklahoma.

Raised in a fundamentalist Christian household, Baker was more serious than most of his teammates, but he was different in other ways, too. As the son of an insurance agent, his family was not rich, but he had considerably more material possessions than many other Sooners, who were the sons of farmers or blue-collar laborers. Yet on the field, Baker quickly established himself as perhaps the best defensive back Wilkinson ever coached. He tackled with a fierce abandon that belied his sensitive nature off the field.

As a sophomore in 1956, he played alternate left halfback behind McDonald. In 1957 he was switched to quarterback behind Carl Dodd and made the Sooner alternates nearly as dangerous as the Clendon Thomas–led starters. By his senior year, Baker—a triple-threat runner, passer, and kicker—was chosen to be the starting quarterback in Wilkinson's new wide-open attack.

Even after three years as a Sooner, Baker was haunted by what he saw as his offensive shortcomings. He could not pass like Crowder or Arnold. He could not run and pass like Harris. In an effort to compensate, he would sometimes call unorthodox plays. At times, such as the two touchdown passes against Duke, these plays were wildly successful. At other times, such as running quarterback sneaks on third-and-9, they were doomed to failure.

Still, the Sooner offense was built around Baker's versatility, and the burden of living up to the offensive feats of his predecessors continued to weigh on him. Those pressures, combined with emotional turmoil brought about by girlfriend problems and the disparity between his fundamentalist upbringing and the life he was leading at OU, caused him to take irrational action. He quit attending class.

By midsemester, the situation became so serious that Baker received an academic warning. Because Baker had otherwise been a model student, Wilkinson convinced the academic dean to allow Baker to remain in school. In return, Wilkinson promised that if Baker cut class one more time, he would be dropped from the football team immediately.

Baker's frame of mind improved after the Colorado game. Stung by Wilkinson's decision to start Cornell against the Buffs, Baker responded by playing the finest offensive football of his career at OU over the final four games of the year.

Things seemed fine until the first week in December. Baker was attending classes and practicing well in anticipation for the Orange Bowl. But as they were each year, the Sooners were to be treated to a quail hunt by OU booster H. C. Hicks at his ranch near Guymon. On a Wednesday night, two days before the Sooners normally left for the hunt, several of the seniors gathered in one of the rooms in Jeff House to watch Bob Harrison be introduced by Bob Hope with the rest of the Kodak All-America team. The impromptu celebration was uncharacteristic for the normally disciplined Sooners. The popcorn was not unusual. The beer that accompanied it was. Fueled by its warmth, some of the Sooners decided they would leave for Guymon that night, giving them an extra day of hunting. Ignoring the ultimatum from the academic dean, Baker joined them on their joyride, never once mentioning a Friday morning English class he would miss.

When the Sooners returned to Jeff House on Sunday night, Jones and Robertson were waiting. They ordered Baker to remove his belongings from Jeff House. The next day, Wilkinson lived up to his half of the bargain that had kept Baker in school. Technically, the university's academic rules would have allowed Baker to remain eligible through the end of the semester and play in the Orange Bowl, but Wilkinson believed football players had to be college students first. Besides, he had given his word. Accordingly, he dropped Baker from the team. In the weeks that followed, however, Wilkinson kept in contact with Baker and even arranged for him to meet with a psychiatrist without charge to Baker. He also called Baker's mother to explain the circumstances surrounding her son's dismissal from the team.

The heir apparent to Baker as the starting quarterback seemed to be Boyd, but that solution presented difficulties. Boyd was used to playing with the alternate unit, and they with him. Besides, Boyd was not a punter. The answer was to move Cornell from the third unit to the starting team. For the first time in his coaching career, Wilkinson entered a bowl game with a sophomore quarterback leading the Sooners.

In moments of defeat as well as victory, Wilkinson never conceded that a particular play was so new or so daring that it could not be defended. There are, he would say with matter-of-fact assurance, no new plays in football. It was rather their combination or their execution at an unsuspected moment that made them effective. So it was that as Wilkinson prepared the Sooners for Syracuse, he did so by making a slight alteration to OU's offensive scheme that had been successful several years before. Traditionally, the Sooner ends ran the deep pass patterns. The halfbacks would run short routes. Wilkinson decided he would reverse that pattern for the Orangemen—just as he had against Texas in 1952.

Wilkinson also added a trick play as well. On the play, the quarterback would fake a quick pitch to the left halfback going to his left. At the same time, Gautt would move a short distance in the same direction. After the quarterback faked a delayed handoff to the right halfback, he would make a long, low lateral to Gautt. The right side of the Sooner line would peel off from its blocks and form a wall down the left side for Gautt. The play, which depended upon Syracuse's defense responding to the misdirection fakes rather than concentrating on Gautt, would give the Sooners a chance to get their most explosive runner loose in an open field. But the timing had to be right.

Those would be the only special changes Wilkinson would make for the game. As always, the Sooners' prospects for victory rested upon speed, conditioning, and flawless execution because, Wilkinson knew, blocking and tackling were still the heart of football. Just as they had the year before against Duke, the Sooners would attempt to wear down the larger Syracuse starters by alternating two quick units.

The defensive strategy Jones developed also contained elements of the plan used against Duke. The Syracuse line was so much bigger than Oklahoma's that the Sooners could not confront them head-on. As against Duke, the Sooners would gamble on stunting to penetrate the Syracuse forward wall. Then, if they got the lead, the Sooners would shift back into their normal containment defense to prevent the long gain.

By the time the Orange Bowl game finally arrived, Wilkinson decided the special play would be most effective early, while the Syracuse defense was still gaining its confidence. The first time the Sooners got the ball, Wilkinson told Cornell to run the play. On the Sooners' first play, Cornell ran the new play to the right. Gautt gained 10 yards.

Immediately, Cornell came back with the same play to the left. This time, it worked as Wilkinson had drawn it on the blackboard. The fakes froze the Syracuse defense, and Gautt exploded into the open down the left sidelines. The right side of the Sooner line formed a corridor for Gautt, who raced 42 yards to score. Barely two minutes into the game, Oklahoma was already ahead.

At the end of the first quarter, the Sooners scored again. Hobby took a pitch from Cornell on the halfback option to the left. Confused by OU's changed pass routes, the Orangemen left Ross Coyle open short, and Hobby hit him. Coyle turned upfield, broke into the clear, and rambled 79 yards to score. A 2-point conversion gave the Sooners a 14–0 lead. In the third quarter, Hobby fielded a Syracuse punt at the Oklahoma 40. He caught the ball at the right hashmark and took off without waiting for the blocking wall to form. Hobby weaved his way through the Syracuse defenders and dashed 60 yards to score. The rest was left to the Sooners' defense. Although Syracuse powered its way to a statistical advantage (311 yards in total offense to 245 for the Sooners), the Orangemen did not score until early in the fourth quarter as the Sooners prevailed, 21–6.

As he had all season, Wilkinson tried to explain to all who would listen that the Sooners were only a reasonably good college team, which—in Wilkinson's own understated manner—suggested that the Sooners were, nevertheless, better than most teams in the country. In the end, the 1958 Sooners, like their predecessors of the year before, became living proof of the validity of Wilkinson's belief that defense was the key to victory. The 1958 Sooners, voted the fifth best team in America in the final AP poll and the last in a string of great Wilkinson teams, proved to be the least productive offensively, scoring fewer points than any Wilkinson team to that time.

1959

Jim Tatum was gone. Only forty-five, he had succumbed to a mysterious bacterial infection that wracked his massive body, leaving a void in the ranks of college coaches as large as Tatum had been in life. And if the man on the street did not fully understand Tatum or appreciate his genius, Bud Wilkinson did.

James Moore Tatum was the youngest of nine children born to a merchant banker-farmer in McColl, South Carolina. He was sent to the University of North Carolina by an uncle to play football for Carl Snavely, one of the South's first great coaches. Tatum was not graceful, but at six-foot-three, two hundred pounds, he was big and tough.

By the time Tatum was a senior, he was good enough to be named honorable mention on some All-America teams and for Snavely to offer him a job as an assistant coach. When Snavely went to Cornell, Tatum followed. There, he met Wilkinson, then a young assistant at Syracuse.

By the early 1940s both Wilkinson and Tatum had left the Northeast. Wilkinson returned to Minnesota as an assistant, and Tatum, three years older and with three more years' experience, went back to his alma mater as head coach.

In his first year at North Carolina in 1941, Tatum revolutionized college football. Recalling the humid heat he had experienced during fall workouts as a student, Tatum changed the first practice during two-a-days from midmorning to prebreakfast before the sun had heated the morning air. The change proved so successful it would eventually be copied by almost every football team in America. However, the dew made the footballs so wet that Tatum and his staff had to have a second set of footballs for the afternoon to replace the waterlogged balls used in the morning.

The football gods smiled on Tatum in his coaching debut against Wake Forest, a team favored to beat North Carolina by two touchdowns. It rained throughout the game. Wake Forest, unable to handle the slippery ball, fumbled repeatedly. But Tatum's Tarheels, used to handling a wet ball each morning during practice, never fumbled and won, 6–0.

After the 1942 season Tatum enlisted in the U.S. Navy and was assigned to the coaching staff at Iowa Pre-Flight under Don Faurot. Watching Tatum then and later in his career, Faurot would come to regard Tatum as the finest recruiter and defensive coach he ever saw.

At the end of the war, Tatum was the head coach at NAS Jacksonville, where he met Jap Haskell, the athletic director at Oklahoma. When Haskell returned to Oklahoma and the call went out for a new head coach, Tatum got the job. Enthusiastic and organized, Tatum poured his soul into coaching the Sooners. By September, he had done all he could to prepare the Sooners to meet Red Blaik's heavily favored Army team. So determined was Tatum that nothing would spoil the Sooners' debut, he arranged to have two airplanes to fly to West Point—the first and third teams on one, the second and fourth teams on another.

"If one plane crashes, we'll still have enough to play the game," Tatum told Wilkinson.

When the bus driver got lost taking the Sooners from the airport near West Point to their hotel, Tatum figured it was a psychological ploy to unnerve his team.

He paced the center aisle of the bus trying to whip his players into a frenzy.

"This driver is nothing but a Blaik agent!" he shouted.

Most of the Sooners only chuckled to themselves, just as they did the day of the game when the game itself was delayed for thirty-five minutes waiting for President Harry Truman, but Tatum was incensed.

"Why delay a football game for a president?" he fumed.

As great a recruiter and organizer as he may have been, Tatum became excitable and unpredictable during a game. Neither he nor his players knew what he would do next.

Against Army, Tatum decided that to stop Glenn Davis and Doc Blanchard, a third guard—Norman McNabb—would replace quarterback Jack Mitchell on defense. Tatum had Mitchell and McNabb seated on either side of him as Darrell Royal started the game on offense. They were seated in the middle of the Sooner bench with their helmets between their knees—as Tatum had carefully instructed all the Sooners.

When the Sooners gained little on their first two plays, Tatum was on edge.

"I'll get McNabb ready," he said through the headset to Wilkinson, who was stationed in the press box.

"Get ready to go in," he said, nudging McNabb.

When the Sooners were forced to punt after one more play, Tatum handed the headphones to McNabb, leaped to his feet, and started searching the bench.

"McNabb! McNabb!" he yelled in his bull bellow voice. After a few seconds, he hurried past Mitchell and McNabb, both too scared to say anything, to the opposite end of the Sooner bench. Finally, Tatum came back to the spot where he had been seated and grabbed the headphones from McNabb.

"Bud, we've left McNabb at home. How did we make such a mistake?" he said.

Just then, he looked down and saw McNabb.

"McNabb, where have you been? Get in there!"

Late in the game, the Sooners trailed, 14–7, but had driven down to the Army 4. Tatum decided the extra point would be a critical play and planned to put a couple of guards in the backfield to protect the kicker. Tatum jerked Dee Andros from the bench and started to show him how to protect the kicker.

"Pay attention," he told Andros, who was trying to look around Tatum to see what was happening on the field. Suddenly, Tatum heard a tremendous roar.

"We've scored!" Tatum said and turned to send Andros in.

But the Sooners had not scored. Royal's errant lateral had been intercepted by Army's Arnold Tucker after it hit a Sooner player or bounced on the ground. No one was quite sure which. Just as Tatum turned around, Tucker raced by the Sooner bench. Tatum took off along the sidelines after Tucker, chased him all the way to the end zone, and grabbed the ball from the startled Cadet. He held it in the face of the official trailing the play.

"Illegal play!" Tatum shouted at the official. "Illegal play!"

The game film later showed that Tatum—regardless of how silly he may have looked—might have been right, but it was simply Tatum's way of doing everything he could to win. Like Wilkinson, he realized that football was a game of emotion, and he was constantly stirring people up, fearful that he might not be doing everything he could unless someone was mad at him.

Tatum knew football, and early in their year together, he taught Wilkinson a lesson that Wilkinson would remember the rest of his coaching career. Football coaches traditionally diagrammed plays using Os to designate offensive players and Xs for defensive players. That is how Bierman had done it. Faurot, too. But when Tatum diagrammed plays, he never used Xs to designate the defensive players. He always used the players' names.

"Because an X can't do what a particular player can do," Tatum said. "And the differences are what win football games."

Despite Tatum's bravado and occasional callousness, Wilkinson liked him. Yet it was hard to imagine two personalities more diverse. All the things that Wilkinson relished—art, music, history, politics—were of little interest to Tatum. The only politics that concerned Tatum were those surrounding football, and he played them to the hilt.

After Oklahoma A&M lost star tailback Bob Fenimore to an injury, the Aggies came into the season's final game against Oklahoma with a 3–6 record. But Tatum took no chances. He brought George Cross and Snorter Luster into the Sooner locker room and had them describe the humiliating defeats administered by the Aggies in 1944 and 1945, which most of the current Sooners had not endured. Tatum's Sooners won, 73–12.

Football was Tatum's consummate passion, as those most dear to him knew only too well. They knew he would say anything, do anything to get what he wanted. He might be sorry later, but he would do it again if he thought it was necessary. Brutally frank, Tatum cared little whether he offended those around him, especially if they couldn't help him achieve his ends. After the 1946 season Tatum tried to leverage Maryland's overtures into a better deal at Oklahoma. In negotiating with George Cross, Tatum made it clear he did not want to be athletic director. He wanted his position as football coach to be autonomous and have a figurehead he picked supervise the other sports. He also wanted the university to fire basketball coach Bruce Drake (then on the way to finishing second in the NCAA tournament) and sports information director Harold Keith, sentiments that only alienated him further from other non-football employees of the athletic department.

In the end, Tatum left Oklahoma for what he saw as greater opportunity and freedom at Maryland. As he had in Norman, Tatum made the most of his new challenge. Tirelessly, he prowled the hills of West Virginia and Pennsylvania in search of rugged, brawny football players to run his Split T attack. In nine years, his teams won seventy-three games and went to five bowl games. In 1953 they were undefeated and ranked No. 1, and Tatum was selected Coach of the Year.

As Tatum aged, he seemed to mellow, if only slightly. When the success of the nationally televised contest between Oklahoma and Notre Dame opened a new world for college football, Tatum understood its power. Television, a sleeping giant, could bring millions of dollars to colleges across America through the only organization that spanned conference borders—the NCAA. Others saw its potential as well. After the 1952 season, Maryland, as one of the reigning national powers, was invited to join a sixteen-team conference that would air its own games and split the revenue among its members, leaving the NCAA out in the cold.

Tatum refused to go along.

"Ninety percent of the schools depend on football gate receipts to carry the rest of their athletic programs. They'd be starved out if the big games were televised," Tatum said. "Are the crowds going to buck the traffic to see a game if they can sit in their living room and see it on TV? With unrestricted television, they'd never sell the seats in the end zone that get you your profits."

Even if Tatum learned to accept defeat on the football field gracefully, he remained sensitive to criticism about his football program. When he gave out ninety-three scholarships at nearly $1,000 each one year, Maryland was chastised for overemphasizing football. Critics said that during his years at Maryland, an inadequate stadium became ultra-adequate, and an inadequate library became more inadequate. When the university got a new president in 1954—one intent on raising the university's academic standards—Tatum took the changes personally.

After a second undefeated season was ruined by Wilkinson's Sooners in the 1956 Orange Bowl, Tatum took a pay cut from $18,500 to $15,000 to return to his alma mater.

"I'm going back to North Carolina to die," he said with his boisterous laugh.

At North Carolina, he set to work as he had everywhere, toiling so hard that he ended up in the hospital for exhaustion. But a 2–7–1 record in his first year led to only marginally successful seasons the next two years.

In 1959 Tatum had twenty-four lettermen returning, and he believed a new day was about to dawn in Chapel Hill. Strangely, Tatum began to run a high fever in mid-July. At first, he dismissed it as a summer cold, but the fever went higher, and his body became covered with a red rash. He was rushed to the university hospital. A week later, he died.

Tatum's death shocked the sports world and medical world alike. He was a brute of a man. He was overweight and drove himself hard, but his health had been excellent until he came down with the fever. Doctors could find no reason for his death and ordered an autopsy.

Their findings were as surreal as Tatum had been in life. His body had been overwhelmed by a bacterial infection—one related to typhus and Rocky Mountain spotted fever—that afflicts many people in a mild form, but Tatum had suffered an infection of virtually unprecedented proportions that attacked his vital organs, which eventually ceased to function.

During the years following World War II, when college football emerged as a game of national scope, Tatum was a giant on the landscape. Almost single-handedly, he invented the modern art of recruiting. Every college coach since World War II owes a debt to Tatum, a debt that would not be acknowledged until a quarter century after his death when he was inducted into the National Football Foundation's College Football Hall of Fame in 1984.

As extreme as they may appear in retrospect, the things Tatum did were, by the standards of his time, within the letter—if not always the spirit—of the rules. And if, with the passage of time, his methods seem incompatible with more modern standards, it is because those newer standards are the result of—or reaction to—Jim Tatum's recruiting legacy. For regardless of what anyone thought of Tatum, one fact remained. During his career, Jim Tatum was the second most successful coach of his time. The only one to exceed him was Bud Wilkinson.

As the 1959 season approached, Wilkinson could see that the Sooners were not the caliber of team that Sooner fans thought they were. He believed the Sooners would be as good offensively as the team that went 9–1 the year before, but they could not match their defensive prowess. The 1958 Sooners may have suffered on offense—particularly when compared to the glory years of 1955 and 1956—but they were formidable on defense. They shut out five teams. They limited four more (including Syracuse) to one touchdown. Only two teams scored twice against the Sooners—Texas, in the game the Sooners lost, and West Virginia, which scored its second touchdown when the game was out of reach.

What Wilkinson hoped was that the '59 Sooners would have success early that would give them the confidence to overcome their weaknesses.

Harold Keith, the Oklahoma sports publicist, returned to his hotel room late Thursday afternoon. He had come to Chicago early in the week to talk to the Windy City's newspapers and broadcasting stations about the Sooners' season-opening game with Northwestern. Interest in the game was keen. For years, Oklahoma football had been well known in the area, not only because of Oklahoma's reputation under Wilkinson but also because of the heavy newspaper coverage the Sooners received every time they played Notre Dame.

The Sooners were also a favorite whipping boy of fans loyal to Big Ten teams. Throughout the early 1950s, as Oklahoma rolled to victory after victory, Big Ten fans would point to the Sooners' weak conference schedule and insist that Ohio State, Michigan State, Illinois, and Iowa were better than the Sooners. They were quite certain that if the Sooners played a *real* schedule, like the Big Ten teams did, they would never record so many victories.

Wilkinson's reply was always the same. The Sooners merely played the teams on their schedule. They could not be responsible for anything beyond that. They had to play their six conference opponents. Add to that the traditional rivalries with Texas and Oklahoma A&M (now called Oklahoma State and part of the new Big Eight Conference), and the Sooners were left with only two game dates free each year. On numerous occasions, Wilkinson tried to schedule teams from the Big Ten, but with a conference so large, they had even more problems than the Sooners accommodating non-conference games. However, in a desire to create a football program of national stature, Wilkinson always tried to schedule opponents of equal standing. Notre Dame. Pittsburgh. California. TCU. North Carolina. Oregon. And even if they were not scheduled, high-caliber opponents came regularly in the Orange Bowl: Maryland. Duke. Syracuse. Over the previous five years, OU had played and beaten the nation's best.

That was the message Keith tried to convey to each of the big city doubters. And look at this year, Keith would insist. How can you call Army and Northwestern—which inflicted Ohio State's only loss and came within 6 points of going to the Rose Bowl in 1958—creampuff opponents?

After Keith had completed his mission for the day, he received a telephone call from Fred Russell, sports editor of the *Nashville Banner* and the writer of the *Saturday Evening Post*'s football preview that had picked OU No. 1 in the country. Russell routinely ran the point spreads of major games in Friday's paper. This week, Russell had been shocked to find that the Sooners had suddenly dropped from 6-point favorites to 3-point favorites. Such a drop meant there was considerable money being bet on Northwestern. What, Russell wanted to know, could have caused such a dramatic shift? Keith told him that there were no new injuries and dismissed the change as evidence of bettors' high expectations for Ara Parseghian's Wildcats. Within hours, Keith would see events in a different light.

Fresh from their hotel in Evanston, the Sooners went by bus to the Chez Paree nightclub near downtown Chicago. The bus arrived shortly before seven o'clock for dinner and the early nightclub show. The Chez Paree, with its reputation for first-class entertainment, had seemed to Ken Farris a good experience for the Sooners, most of whom came from small towns in Oklahoma and Texas. When the OU party arrived, Farris was disappointed to find that the night's headliner was not a Frank Sinatra or a Frankie Laine as he had been led to believe. Instead, the Sooners would be entertained by a singer named Patrice Wymore—a capable Broadway and movie actress (and the wife of Errol Flynn), but hardly the household name Farris had expected.

As the Sooners entered the dining room, they encountered a striking young blonde woman and a couple of older men, who were positioned so that it was virtually impossible for the Sooners to pass by without talking to the members of the group. One of the men introduced himself and his daughter and said she was an Oklahoma fan.

"Please introduce yourselves and tell her what position you play," the man requested. Politely, the unassuming Sooners complied and then went into the dining room to be seated.

Soon, waiters began serving the evening's appetizer, a cold fruit cup, but they did so in a peculiar manner. Rather than going down the rows of tables as was generally done, the waiters began serving the fruit cups in seemingly random fashion. One here. Another there. Within minutes after finishing the fruit, several of the Sooners excused themselves from the table. Brewster Hobby thought nothing of it until he suddenly began feeling nauseated himself. Politely, he excused himself to find the restroom. When he got there, he found the small restroom crowded with Sooner players violently ill. Some could not wait until they reached the toilet to vomit. They vomited right on the floor, leaving a repulsive, slippery coating on the tile.

One of the team managers found out what was happening and hurried to tell Farris. Quickly, taxis were dispatched to take the Sooners back to the Orrington Hotel. On the way, the cabs had to stop several times to allow players to throw up again. The alert cab drivers abandoned their intended course back to the hotel and instead headed for nearby Louise Weiss Memorial Hospital. Their quick reaction turned out to be warranted. Third-string quarterback Bob Page, who suffered circulatory collapse and went into shock shortly after they reached the hospital, might have died otherwise.

Late that night, the police were informed, and investigations of the incident, both formal and informal, were begun. The management of the Chez Paree denied that the fruit cup could have been the cause and suggested accusingly that sandwiches the players had eaten earlier in the afternoon had been the cause. Besides, they said, other patrons ate at the restaurant that night and did not become ill—but the other patrons were not regulars on the Oklahoma football team. The explanation was further flawed because Jimmy Harris, the only OU assistant to eat with the players, had been one of those stricken. And he had not eaten lunch!

Carefully, Farris and ticket manager Red Reid tried to piece together the events of the evening and the status of the Sooner squad. In all, thirteen players and Harris had been affected. Of the thirteen players who had become ill, ten were starters or alternates. When they outlined the situation to Wilkinson, the conversation sounded like a battle casualty report. Three Sooner starters—quarterback Bobby Boyd, center Jim Davis, and tackle Gilmer Lewis—were confined to the hospital. Four players—including starting halfbacks Brewster Hobby and Jimmy Carpenter—were under the care of team physician Dr. Mike Willard at the hotel.

It was too much for coincidence. The sudden change in the point spread. The mysterious young woman, who, Farris and Reid speculated, might have been a memory expert hired to pinpoint the location of key players. The illness affecting only certain players, most of whom were regulars. When the lab samples that might have pinpointed the cause mysteriously disappeared, it added up to only one conclusion. The fix was in, and the Sooners were caught in the middle.*

On Friday night, Wilkinson tried to rally the Sooners' confidence as best he could.

"Don't tell yourself when it gets tough, 'I've got the best excuse in the world in the food poisoning.' Forget that!" Wilkinson told them. "The record won't say 'food poisoning.' It'll just give the score."

By game time on Saturday, dark clouds were moving in rapidly toward Northwestern's Dyche Stadium. The Sooners won the toss and kicked off with a strong south wind at their backs. They stopped the Wildcats on their first possession, but the Northwestern punt rolled dead at the OU 17.

---

* Now, more than sixty years after the incident, it is unlikely the full truth will ever be known regarding what happened in Chicago that week in 1959. However, investigations were undertaken at the time, and their conclusions are similar. The Sooners were made sick after apomorphine was placed on the fruit cup served to certain Sooners at the Chez Paree. Apomorphine is a drug, first synthesized in 1845, that has been used in the treatment of alcoholism and advanced Parkinson's disease. Among its chief side effects are nausea and vomiting, especially among those who have not been exposed to it before. Wilkinson's friend, Tim Cohane, sports editor of *Look* magazine, was one who investigated. He found evidence tying the food poisoning to gamblers, but the magazine's lawyers concluded the allegations were too risky to publish.

On the Sooners' third play, Boyd—who had been discharged from the hospital that morning—rolled to his left and threw to Hobby, who was a step behind the Northwestern secondary. The swift Hobby raced 50 yards before he was finally knocked out-of-bounds, but the Sooners, victims of so much distress already, had an ineligible receiver downfield. The gain was nullified and the ball placed on the OU 8. The Sooners punted and stopped the Northwestern offense a second time. Again, a Wildcat punt drove OU deep into its own territory, this time the ball rolling dead at the 9.

With the Sooners trapped deep near their own goal line, Boyd called a quick kick, but the center snap to fullback Wahoo McDaniel hit another Sooner, and the ball bounced to the ground. McDaniel tried to punt anyway, but his kick was blocked and the ball recovered by Northwestern. In two plays, the Wildcats scored. Minutes later, a short Sooner punt gave Northwestern the ball at midfield, and the Wildcats drove in for another score.

Early in the second quarter, the Sooners finally got good field position at the Wildcat 45. Suddenly, the rain began to fall in torrents so heavy that sportswriters in the press box and fans high in the stands could not see the players on the field. Nevertheless, the Sooners drove through the pouring rain to score a touchdown that cut the Wildcats' lead to 13–7. Finally, it seemed, the Sooners were recovering their poise. The feeling did not last long. Moments later, the Wildcats' All-American halfback Ron Burton ran 62 yards to score through the sloppy tackling Sooners. Then, a Sooner fumble at the OU 7 set the stage for the Wildcats' fourth touchdown. By halftime, Northwestern led, 25–7.

Although the rain stopped for the second half, the field remained slippery, and the Sooners kept making mistakes. In all, they fumbled twelve times, losing five. Four times, the fumbles took place inside the OU 40, and all four were turned into scores by the Wildcats. As the game was drawing to a close, Parseghian looked across the field at Wilkinson. There he was, his team trailing 45–13 with no chance of victory and mud splattered over his gray suit. Still, Wilkinson encouraged his players, never letting up until the game had ended. It was a sight Parseghian would never forget.

The loss to Northwestern, the most decided in Wilkinson's entire career, alerted America to the truth of what Wilkinson had been saying. The Sooners simply were not the powerhouses of old and would have to play with all their resourcefulness to continue winning.

For Jones, the challenge was perhaps the greatest he had faced in more than two decades of coaching. His linemen were the least experienced he ever had. Jones, always a heavy smoker, now seemed to be smoking constantly, in the coaches' locker room as well as his office. His ulcers—brought on by the hectic pace he and Wilkinson demanded of themselves—seemed more active as well.

During the spring and fall two-a-days, Wilkinson and his staff had worked to refine the Sooners' less-than-perfect execution. The technique drills, a constant ingredient in Wilkinson's formula for success, were never so discouraging. Even after the start of the season, when they should be perfecting *tactics* for the upcoming opponent, the Sooners were struggling to overcome execution errors that Wilkinson considered elementary. Day after day, the Sooners practiced to master the assignments that earlier Sooner teams had perfected quickly.

Football is like most games. Small matters have major implications. Nowhere, Wilkinson and Jones knew, is this more true than in the line, where patient players toil endlessly without glory or adulation. In at least one respect, the Sooners' current group of linemen was no different from the scores of linemen they had produced in their years at Oklahoma. All had received the benefit of Jones's unparalleled coaching. Wilkinson knew—and would tell anyone who would take time to listen—that properly trained, intelligent, mobile linemen are the most underrated asset in football. Jones was a master at creating "smart" linemen. Year in and year out, Jones turned out linemen who could think as they played and react to changing defenses or conditions as they unfolded. And it was they, perhaps more than the fleets of agile halfbacks, who had been the key to Oklahoma's success.

In his office, Jones kept a small movie projector on which he could review game films. Once a week, he brought the linemen into his office in small groups to review the film of the previous game. With each group, Jones would watch plays in which they did not execute as expected. Jones could show every player where a failure of technique—a step with the wrong foot or a failure to stay on his feet—kept him from making a play.

The importance of this contribution cannot be overestimated. While players on teams without Gomer Jones might know they did not make a block or missed a tackle, they had no one to tell them *why*. And without someone with Jones's eye for detail to explain what they had done wrong, they would continue to repeat the same errors. It was little wonder that Wilkinson considered his compatriot the finest *teacher* of football he ever saw. And Wilkinson could see that Jones would have to be at his best if the Sooners were to be successful during the rest of the year.

The second week of the season, the Sooners defeated outmanned Colorado, 42–12, and began to prepare for Texas. Wilkinson noticed that Northwestern and

Colorado were stacking their defenses to stop Gautt and Hartline, whom they regarded as bigger threats than the Sooners' small halfbacks. To combat that, Wilkinson added a play that called for the quarterback to fake the fullback trap over the middle, then throw to one of the halfbacks. He was convinced such a new play would be necessary against the solid Texas defense, which had already shut out Nebraska, Maryland, and California.

Early in the game, Gautt broke into the Texas secondary twice on the fullback trap play. And just as Wilkinson had expected, the Longhorns began to set their defense to stop him. Midway through the first quarter, OU recovered a Texas fumble at the Longhorn 32. In two plays, the Sooners moved to the 23. There, alternate quarterback Bob Cornell called the new play Wilkinson had installed for the game. He faked to Hartline and then hit Jackie Holt behind the Texas secondary for a touchdown. Late in the first quarter, OU scored again on a pitchout to Dick Carpenter but failed on a 2-point conversion try to take a 12–0 lead. In the second quarter, the Longhorns scored twice to go ahead of the Sooners, 14–12.

In the second half, the Sooners played the Longhorns on even terms until midway through the fourth quarter. Then, for one play only, the Sooner defense let down. The Longhorns' Jackie Collins caught a short pass at midfield, and the swift Collins outran the Sooner secondary to score a victory-clinching touchdown.

Staggering from their worst start since Wilkinson's rebuilding year in 1951, the Sooners steeled themselves for their quest to win a thirteenth straight Big Eight championship. One afternoon, the Sooners were particularly ragged in practice, but rather than drive them harder on the practice field, Wilkinson stopped practice early. The cause of the Sooners' failures, he felt certain, was not lack of practice but lack of team unity. In the locker room, he called an impromptu squad meeting.

"I'm ashamed," Wilkinson said angrily. "I don't want to be associated with some of you. A lot of you have been talking about this guy behind his back, and I want it to stop."

He pointed squarely at Gautt.

"If you're men, you'll stand up and tell him directly to his face what you've said and apologize," Wilkinson said, leaving the room and closing the door behind him.

For a few moments, no one moved. Gautt sat frozen in apprehension, fearful of what he might hear. In the three years since he arrived at OU, he had learned to be oblivious to much of what went on around him. At first, he had been paranoid about what others might be saying, but he changed his attitude once he realized such a state of mind would drive him crazy.

Now, he found how naive he had been. First haltingly, then with gathering intensity, players Gautt believed were his friends began to confess their transgressions against him. Who they were and what they said astounded Gautt.

After a few minutes, Wilkinson's mandated truth session was more than Gautt could take. He stood up. The locker room went silent.

"In no way do I want to be a detriment to this football team," he said. "I want it to be successful. If it will help team unity for me to leave, I'll do that."

Then Gautt left the room. The discussion continued as the remaining Sooners told how they felt. In the end, it became clear that there were only three players who did not want Gautt on the team. Others who had been against Prentice in the beginning admitted they were wrong. They were glad to be his teammate.

The experience, as emotional as it was for Gautt and the other Sooners, seemed to free the Sooners of the bad blood among them. Like what they said or not, Gautt at least knew where they stood. There were no longer any secrets. The Sooners were finally a team.

A week after a 23–0 victory over Missouri, the mistake-prone Sooners found themselves struggling against Jack Mitchell's young Kansas Jayhawks. Three times in the first quarter, the Sooners had the ball inside the Jayhawk 30, but missed blocking assignments, dropped passes, and a fumble kept the Sooners from scoring.

In the second quarter, the Sooners finally scored, and it was Boyd who provided the Sooner spark. A gale force north wind carried John Hadl's punt to the OU 20, where Boyd fielded the ball. Boyd cut to his right, where the Sooners formed a corridor down the sidelines. Darting and dodging, Boyd (who could run backward or sideways almost as fast as he could run forward) threaded his way through the Jayhawk defense to the KU 36. Quickly, the Sooners moved to three first downs. From the KU 3, the Sooners drove straight ahead three times. On the third play, Boyd wedged into the end zone. Davis's kick was good and gave the Sooners a 7–0 lead.

In the third period, the Sooners drove to the Kansas 4, but a fourth-down pass fell incomplete. The Jayhawks could not move, and Hadl lifted a punt high into the Oklahoma wind that carried the kick far downfield. When the ball finally landed, it took a decidedly KU bounce and rolled and rolled to the OU 2-yard line. After the 94-yard punt, the Sooners could not move and were forced to punt the ball back to the Jayhawks.

When Kansas got the ball back near midfield, Jayhawk halfback Dave Harris slashed off left guard, cut quickly to the outside, and outran the pursuing Sooners to score. Mitchell, with a chance to join Royal with a victory over his former coach, chose to have the Jayhawks go for the 2-point conversion and victory. From the 3, Jayhawk quarterback Lee Flachsbarth rolled to his right, but his pass was low and hit a crouching official in the head. The ball caromed into the air, the outcome of the game riding on its errant flight. Alertly, the Sooners' Cornell grabbed the ball and dropped to his knee, preserving the Sooners' 7–6 victory and seventy-four-game conference winning streak.

It had to end. Everyone, even Wilkinson, knew it would. There had simply been too many close calls. Too many schools in the Big Eight had now committed to improving their football teams. Scores of young coaches, Wilkinson and Jones among them, had returned from their wartime coaching experiences with greater understanding of the game and how to forge winning teams. In developing football programs of their own, these coaches—now in their thirties and forties—had listened and remembered.

The system. That was the key. If you had learned "the system" from a great coach, you could implement it yourself. Or, at least, you would get an opportunity to. Royal. Mitchell. Walker. Owens. Elliott. Jennings. The list of Wilkinson's protégés to become head coaches began to multiply by the late 1950s. And with them came not only an understanding of how Wilkinson had organized the Oklahoma program, but an aura of Wilkinson himself. If a young man had played or coached at Oklahoma, the magic seemed transferrable. And these young coaches, still filled with the energy youth engenders, were able to recruit and teach better than their predecessors.

Bill Jennings was neither the best nor the most dedicated of Wilkinson's pupils, but when Pete Elliott showed signs of reviving the Cornhusker program before leaving for California, Nebraska went looking for another coach from the Wilkinson mold. Jennings, not even in the coaching profession at the time, was available. Fortunately for him, he took over the year that Pat Fischer—the youngest in a line of brothers who were to Nebraska football what the Burrises were to Oklahoma—arrived in Lincoln.

Still, Jennings did not enjoy the success Royal and Mitchell were to discover. When his team lost its first five games in 1958, Jennings was hanged in effigy on the Nebraska campus. During the first six games of the 1959 season, Nebraska won only two. The Cornhuskers clearly could not match the Sooners in any phase of the game except kicking. Jennings, aware of how close to victory Kansas had come with a strong kicking game, decided to pin his hopes of upsetting Oklahoma on the same strategy Mitchell had used. Whenever they had the wind, the Cornhuskers would not hesitate to punt—before fourth down if necessary—to keep the Sooners from getting the ball close to the Nebraska goal. Wilkinson, too, believed the Cornhuskers had a chance, particularly if the Sooners continued to play as inconsistently as they had all season.

In the first quarter, the Sooners moved well on offense. Running from an unbalanced spread formation, the Sooners moved down the field after the opening kickoff. Seemingly, nothing could stop the Sooner halfbacks as they made large gains behind Gautt's blocking. Finally, inside the 10, Nebraska stiffened, but Boyd gave the ball to Gautt, who powered into the end zone from the 3 on his first carry of the game.

Inexplicably, the Sooners eased off, and much of the rest of the first quarter was played in Sooner territory. Finally, after two missed opportunities, the Cornhuskers scored. A pass for 2 points failed, and OU retained a 7–6 lead. In the second quarter, the Sooner alternates tried a quick kick on second down from inside the Sooner 30. The snap was high, but rather than falling on the ball and punting on third or fourth down, Cornell tried to kick the ball anyway. It was blocked. A Cornhusker lineman picked up the ball and ran it 30 yards for a touchdown. Late in the second quarter, Cornell led the Sooners on a 54-yard scoring drive, and they took a 14–12 halftime lead.

In the third quarter, the Sooners could not move on offense, and Nebraska took a 15–14 lead. Early in the fourth quarter, the Sooner alternates drove to the Nebraska 28 only to fumble the ball away. Three series later, the Sooner secondary let a Nebraska punt roll rather than catching it, and the ball stopped dead at the OU 4. When OU answered with a 54-yard punt, the Sooners escaped from their poor field position, but Fischer returned the kick 61 yards before Hobby caught him from behind. Three plays later, Nebraska scored to take a 22–14 lead.

When the Sooners fumbled the ensuing kickoff, Nebraska kicked another field goal to take an 11-point lead with less than seven minutes to play. Faced with the sobering prospect of defeat, the Sooners played with newfound spirit, marching 67 yards to score on Gautt's 3-yard slant with four minutes to play. There was still time to salvage victory.

The Cornhuskers returned the OU kickoff to their 18, ran three plays, and then punted to the OU 41. The Sooners had 2:25 to save the day. Mixing passes and running plays, Boyd guided the Sooners inside the Nebraska 30. Only seconds now remained, and Boyd had to throw long on every down. Two were incomplete. The third was intercepted by the Cornhuskers.

In the concrete dressing room, the loss—the first to a conference opponent since Wilkinson became coach twelve years earlier—was especially bitter for the Sooners. Two years before, when the forty-seven-game winning streak had ended, the Sooners played as well as they could. Notre Dame had, in every real sense, *won* the game. For each of the Sooners, there was no doubt they had lost to an inferior Nebraska team. As the players sat and waited for the baggage to be loaded for the trip back to Norman, Wilkinson addressed the Sooners.

"I must be a sorry coach, men," Wilkinson said. "I can't seem to get through to you that if you have discipline, you'll never make the ridiculous mistakes you made out there today. If I were doing my job correctly, you'd have that discipline. I've told you over and over what's the matter, but I didn't sell you, I guess. I just don't know how to get on people's backs. I don't ask you to win. All I ask you to do is play as well as you can. That's all. If you'd just do that, I'd be the happiest guy in the world. Even if we lost."

On the bus to the airport, the Sooners' ability to repeat as Big Eight champions seemed very much in doubt. Wilkinson sat with Keith and talked quietly.

"We're not a hungry team," he said to Keith. "When we get behind, we eat 'em up, but we don't play well when we're ahead. It's my fault or we wouldn't do that. I feel so bad about it that I could cry."

Two weeks later, after an easy victory over Kansas State, the Sooners were offered a chance at redemption. Army, 4–2–1 in a season filled with devastating injuries, was not the team it had been during its undefeated season in 1958. Heisman Trophy winner Pete Dawkins was gone, and so was coach Red Blaik. In January, Blaik had resigned, choosing the financial rewards—and security—of becoming a vice president of Avco Corporation, a defense contractor. Though ever loyal to West Point, Blaik believed that leaving after an undefeated season—and a victory over Navy—was the best course of action open to him.

Taking over for Blaik was his top assistant, Dale Hall, who still had All-American halfback Bob Anderson, Lonesome End Bill Carpenter, and quarterback Joe Caldwell. If the Sooners could beat Army, they could prove they were a good team that was a mere two touchdowns—and one gambling conspiracy—from being undefeated.

November 14 was not a Wilkinson day. Subfreezing cold and a bitter northeast wind were not what the Sooners were used to in Norman. Wilkinson could not remember a colder game or a more difficult challenge. Because a college team faces them so seldom, great passers like Caldwell cause enormous difficulties. Wilkinson believed the Sooners could move the ball against Army and could stop Anderson, but he was not certain the Sooners, particularly in the secondary, could maintain their poise against Caldwell and Carpenter.

During the past two seasons, Carpenter had become something of a national celebrity. He was a skilled athlete, both as a blocker and pass receiver, but Blaik's Lonesome End formation was devastating in its psychological effect because of Carpenter, who seemed to destroy the aplomb of even the most capable defenses. How does he know the plays? How does he *always* end up in the right place at the right time? The answer was simple enough: Carpenter received the signals through the positioning of Caldwell's feet in the huddle and, when it was time for a pass, Caldwell always knew where to find his favorite target. Army was sure that sooner or later, the Sooners would make a mistake, and Caldwell would find a way to exploit it.

In the first moments of the game, it appeared the Sooners were incapable of containing the Cadets. Army took the opening kickoff and drove 58 yards to score. Late in the first quarter, the momentum of the game changed with a Sooner interception. Patiently, the Sooners drove down the field to the Army 1. Boyd went to his right on the quarterback keeper. Stopped cold at the line of scrimmage, he spun free and pitched to Mike McClellan, who skirted the Cadet defense to score. The extra point was good, and the Sooners took a 7–6 lead.

Midway through the second quarter, McDaniel's punt rolled dead at the Army 7. Army tried a sweep to the right, but the Army ball carrier was hit fiercely by the left side of the Sooner line and fumbled. The ball rolled backward into the end zone. The Sooners recovered the fumble and took a 14–6 lead. Later in the second quarter, Army came back to score on a touchdown pass by Caldwell, but the Cadets failed on a 2-point conversion try, and the Sooners retained a 14–12 lead.

In the second half, the Sooners needed only three plays to take control of the game. On the kickoff, Anderson bobbled the ball and returned it only to the 7. On Army's first play from scrimmage, the Cadets fumbled, and the Sooners recovered. On the Sooners' first play, Boyd squirmed 9 yards to score. Davis's third conversion gave the Sooners a 9-point lead. On the final play of the third quarter, the Sooners recovered another fumble at the Army 20. Four plays later, Boyd sneaked over from the 1. With Davis's extra point, the Sooners led, 28–12, but there was too much game left for Wilkinson to feel confident against a passer like Caldwell.

After Carpenter returned the OU kickoff to the Army 30, Caldwell began to strike. With four completions in a row, Caldwell led the Cadets to a touchdown. A 2-point conversion cut the Sooners' lead to 28–20 with twelve minutes remaining—still far too long to suit Wilkinson—but the inspired Sooners managed to stop Caldwell and the other Cadets for the rest of the game. The victorious Sooners trotted off the field, boisterously laughing, hugging, and slapping each other on the back. As they entered the locker room, Jones greeted each Sooner.

"It was great! It was great!" he said, rubbing his hands together as he savored the victory.

Even Wilkinson, his hat pushed back on his forehead, was thrilled.

"We'll go all the way now!" he said. The Sooners shouted back in approval.

In the final two weeks of the season, the Sooners faced the prospect of struggling to outlast opponents they had customarily beaten with ease. Iowa State's Cinderella Cyclones, a band of upstarts who gloried in calling themselves "The Dirty Thirty," came into the game with a 7–2 record, considerably better than the Sooners' 5–3. In contrast to Wilkinson's other years at Oklahoma, the Cyclones were only one victory from sharing the Big Eight title with the Sooners.

The Sooners responded to the threat to their authority with a 35–12 victory, the Cyclones' dreams of an Orange Bowl trip destroyed by remarkable performances by Boyd (who quarterbacked both the starters and alternates after Cornell was injured) and Gautt, who gained 110 yards, scored twice, and led the Sooners with eleven tackles.

The defeat, discouraging as it was for the Cyclones, was a moral victory of sorts.

"They were up for us," said Iowa State coach Clay Stapleton. "And it's damn sure a change when Oklahoma gets up for Iowa State."

No less an effort was required the following week as the Sooners struggled to defeat Oklahoma State. After falling behind 7–3 early, the Sooners played the second half as well as they had all season and won, 17–7. In many ways, the victory was symbolic of the Sooners themselves—not pretty, nor particularly memorable—but a tribute to the Sooners' newfound willingness to persevere under adversity.

At 7–3, the Sooners were not a great team. They were not even a top ten team, the first Wilkinson team in more than a decade to fall from the top of the AP poll. But their 5–1 conference record enabled them to remain Big Eight champions. With the Big Eight rule against repeat bowl participation still in effect, they were forced to stay at home, unable to add another bowl victory to their record of late-season achievements.

"I'm as proud of this team as any I've ever had anything to do with—as a player or as a coach," Wilkinson said hoarsely in the Sooners' locker room. "It's very easy when so many things go wrong early in the season, as they did for us, to fold up. Instead, this team got up off the floor and played very well in the last three games. In many ways, that's harder than playing well when you're always winning."

Part V
THE FALL AND RESURRECTION

1960

By the time of the AFCA meeting of 1960, rumors were flying. The NCAA was getting ready to make a major announcement, and there was growing reason to believe the news involved Oklahoma.

Since the rift between Bud Wilkinson and Bill Jennings over Monte Kiffin—and the attendant exchange of letters about possible recruiting violations by Oklahoma—the NCAA had been busy in its investigation of OU. As a part of that inquiry, the NCAA asked Jennings to appear before the Infractions Committee to testify about his relationship with accountant Arthur Wood.

At the same time, George Cross began his own investigation into the matter. Cross even questioned Wood himself. Wood admitted he had handled a fund to assist players with travel expenses to Norman for recruiting visits from 1952 to 1954. At first, Wood said, he had paid these expenses himself at the direction of Jennings. But as the demand for this money increased after the 1953 season, he asked friends and clients to contribute. He also explained that neither the Touchdown Club—nor any other organization—was involved. Wood told Cross that Jennings was the only Sooner coach who knew about the fund and that Jennings's direct involvement was minimal. Finally, Wood said the amount spent during a three-year period was less than $6,000.

Cross passed this information to Walter Byers at the NCAA. Not content, Byers asked Wood to provide bank statements and canceled checks related to the fund.

Wood refused, saying that doing so would put him in violation of professional ethics and could expose him to criminal prosecution for violating certain sections of the Internal Revenue Code. Wood's refusal angered Byers. In early January, the guillotine fell. The NCAA placed OU on indefinite suspension. The Sooners could not participate in a bowl game or appear on television until Wood opened his records to the NCAA. Despite pressure from university officials and OU fans, Wood remained steadfast in his refusal to compromise the confidentiality of the fund.

Almost immediately, the sports world took sides on the Sooners' second probation in five years. Some believed OU had finally gotten its just deserts and that the information that had come to light was only the beginning. Others sided with *Sports Illustrated*, which said, "Bud's well-behaved Sooners, perennial champions of the Big Eight Conference, have just been slapped with one of the heaviest penalties in the NCAA records, and seemingly for no crime whatever."

To Wilkinson, such support was comforting, but immaterial. The NCAA probation was a fact, and as Wilkinson surveyed the situation, it did not appear good. Oklahoma's success in recruiting high-quality athletes had mysteriously fallen off. The Sooners were still getting most of the players they wanted from Oklahoma and West Texas, but the overall *quality* of recruits from those areas seemed to be diminishing.

Wilkinson knew such things go in cycles. He had understood all along that Oklahoma's supply of extraordinary talent would eventually ebb. He had been saying so for years, though most people had simply refused to believe him. The recruiting drought, like the NCAA probation, was a reality, but that did not mean Wilkinson had to accept it passively. He began trying to identify something that would induce the best players to come to Oklahoma and rekindle the spirit of the players already there.

By late May, Wilkinson believed he might have an answer to his recruiting dilemma—a home-and-home series with the University of Hawaii, surely an attractive lure to young men from Oklahoma and Texas who might never have been west of Amarillo. Because the president of the University of Hawaii had formerly been dean of the Graduate College at OU, discussions proceeded rapidly. The Sooners would play in Honolulu after the conclusion of the 1960 season, and the Rainbows would travel to Norman the following year.

The plan received stubborn resistance from Big Eight faculty representatives, who had to approve any game beyond the normal ten-game schedule. Reports from the meeting suggested that the Oklahoma State and Iowa State representatives had taken the lead in a movement to deny the Sooners any kind of recruiting advantages. By a 5–3 vote, the committee turned down Oklahoma's request.

In the days that followed, talk of Oklahoma's leaving the Big Eight was rampant. Even the regents, always quick to respond to conference affronts to OU's sovereignty, were caught up in the fervor. At first, Wilkinson, too, was furious, for it was clear that the vote was motivated by petty vengeance rather than rational policy. But after the sting of the rebuff eased, Wilkinson—as well as the regents—let the matter drop and began preparing for the season at hand.

At the same time Wilkinson was confronting the probation issue, a significant problem of sorts was developing inside his own household. Where should his son Jay go to college? During his sons' years at Norman High School, Wilkinson had done everything possible to keep them from receiving special treatment because they were his children. He wanted them to have identities of their own. So firmly did he believe it that once he sent word to the *Norman Transcript* that he would prefer that the coverage of the high school football games exclude any mention of his sons unless they had done something truly significant. And certainly, he told the newspaper, they were not to be mentioned merely because they were his sons.

Pat, Wilkinson's oldest son, was a reasonably good high school football player, but he was an excellent student and had given up the game when he entered Stanford University. Jay, on the other hand, seemed to have the ability to succeed in college football, and where Jay wanted to play was OU. Wilkinson would not hear of it. College, he knew, was a time for more than football. It was a time for an individual to develop independence and maturity. Jay could obtain neither at OU, where he would continue to be Wilkinson's son.

As the Sooners' lackluster 1959 season had neared completion, there came added pressure for Jay to stay at home and play for Oklahoma. The decision was not easy for Wilkinson because he believed his son was good enough to play for the Sooners. And, Lord knows, the Sooners could use him! But Wilkinson remained firm. Jay could not attend OU.

Wilkinson tried at first to interest Jay in attending one of the military academies, Stanford, or one of the Ivy League schools. Jay eliminated them all from consideration, especially Stanford and the Ivy schools. They were the only schools where financial need was still a requirement for obtaining an athletic scholarship.

"Everything else I have, you have given me," Jay said to his father. "I want to earn this myself."

"That's fine," Wilkinson told his son. "You can go anywhere you want, but you can't come to Oklahoma."

In the end, Jay chose to attend Duke—a university with a superb academic reputation located so far from Norman that Wilkinson would have to take his son to Dallas to get convenient airplane connections.

To some, the 1960 Sooners seemed likely to be as invincible as Wilkinson's teams in years past. One national magazine went so far as to rate the Sooners sixth nationally, but Wilkinson could see that the Sooners' strength was an illusion. There were more good high school teams, more good coaches, and more good players who were big, fast, and well coached. All of it meant that the pool of college football talent was spread more evenly than ever before. And the edge enjoyed by Oklahoma and a few other perennial football powers was declining.

Surely, Wilkinson knew, you could win games by setting a novel tempo, as his Sooners had done for years. But you had to play good defense and kick well, and it was getting harder for the Sooners to control Kansas, Missouri, Nebraska, and Colorado on defense. The Sooners' effective 5–4–2 defense, which had been one of Oklahoma's secrets to success in the preceding decade, was now universal, giving other teams the defensive flexibility only the Sooners once possessed.

Gone, too, were many of Wilkinson's valued assistants, who had moved on—as Wilkinson believed they should—to head coaching jobs of their own. Only the faithful Gomer Jones and the redoubtable Port Robertson remained. Through the years, Jones had been offered head coaching opportunities, notably at Houston and Southern Methodist. Each time, Wilkinson placed no pressure on Jones to stay at Oklahoma. But each time, Jones chose to remain, and Wilkinson was grateful.

The two of them could not do all the coaching alone, however, and a six-man staff demanded talented and dedicated assistants. In the place of Ivy, Elliott, and Lyle were new, capable assistants. But the knowledge of how to organize a successful program, once the province of only a few, had become widespread. The willingness of Kansas, Missouri, Nebraska, Iowa State, and Oklahoma State to upgrade their football facilities had increased the level of competition dramatically in the Big Eight.

Mitchell's Kansas Jayhawks with a backfield that included stellar transfers Bert Coan from TCU and Rodger McFarland from Texas A&M—added to spectacular native Kansans John Hadl and Curtis McClinton—seemed to be a national powerhouse in the making. So, too, was Missouri. Under Dan Devine, the football team had finally become integrated and possessed two balanced units reminiscent of Oklahoma's in the mid-1950s. Both teams were big and powerful. Beside them, Wilkinson's squad looked like schoolboys. Wilkinson knew that conditioning and morale would be critical. For the first time, the Sooners would have athletes clearly less talented than other teams in the Big Eight.

The Sooners were not short of spirit, however. Jimmy Carpenter, only five-foot-nine and 165 pounds, was highly competitive, and Wilkinson hoped Carpenter would be able to move from halfback to quarterback to make the most of his leadership abilities. In high school, Carpenter had played on teams that won forty-nine straight games and three state championships. Carpenter knew how to win, an attribute Wilkinson valued. He believed such players understood the sacrifices necessary to be a champion, and they would be willing to make them at OU. Unfortunately, Carpenter had played little as a Sooner. As a sophomore in 1958 he had started at left halfback, but at the start of the 1959 season, he had suffered a debilitating hamstring injury and had been lost for the season. In the spring, he had reinjured his leg and missed half of the twenty days the Sooners had to practice. Only Carpenter's competitive nature offered Wilkinson the prospect that Carpenter would be ready to play at full speed once the season began.

From a similar mold came Monte Deere. Deere knew he was shorter on talent than the Sooners' bigger halfbacks and spent the spring and summer of 1960 working on a rigorous training program. His regimen included running, handball, and lifting weights, all designed to give him a conditioning advantage over other Sooners.

Wilkinson was proud of the character his players demonstrated, but he was uncertain how much effect it would have. One-platoon football, Wilkinson estimated, was composed of morale, conditioning, and skill in equal thirds. His team could be well conditioned and spirited, but without athletic ability, they would be fighting at a disadvantage.

The Sooners of five years before had been blessed with tremendous natural ability and highly refined skills. For them, morale and conditioning were ingredients that enabled them to win national championships. The 1960 Sooners, Wilkinson could see, were woefully short on natural ability. Spirit and conditioning—the traits Carpenter and Deere embodied—were not enough, but they would be necessary for the Sooners to win more games than they lost.

Most of the key offensive backs from the season before—Bobby Boyd, Prentice Gautt, Brewster Hobby—were no longer wearing crimson and cream. Neither was Jerry Thompson, the Sooners' only All-American in 1959. Wilkinson could see that through Jones's meticulous training, the line was acceptable, but for the first time since he arrived at Oklahoma, Wilkinson was without a lineman of All-America caliber.

In the backfield, the situation was even less encouraging. It was the weakest Wilkinson could ever remember. There was no Buddy Leake standing in the wings to replace a Billy Vessels. The best seemed to be Mike McClellan, who had been the object of a heated recruiting controversy three years before. The Texas high school one-hundred-yard dash and broad jump champion in 1957, McClellan was recruited by Oklahoma and several SWC schools. He chose Baylor, but soon became disenchanted because of the hazing inflicted upon incoming freshmen. Although freshmen at Oklahoma had to endure razzing from upperclassmen and the disciplinary lessons of Port Robertson, physical hazing as it existed at many schools was not tolerated by Wilkinson and his staff. McClellan understood that and transferred to Oklahoma at the end of the first semester. Immediately, officials at Baylor accused Oklahoma of tampering with one of their football players.

Wilkinson denied it, as did McClellan. Much of the uproar seemed to be politically motivated, however, so it continued. To clear the air and eliminate any hint of wrongdoing on the part of Oklahoma, Wilkinson refused to give McClellan an athletic scholarship. McClellan left OU and returned home to Stamford, where he went to work in the oil fields. For months, Wilkinson and his staff left McClellan alone, making it possible for other schools to recruit him or for him to return to Baylor, which is the course his family preferred. In September 1958 McClellan enrolled at OU to stay, and Wilkinson gave him a scholarship.

A sure tackler and able pass defender, McClellan's greatest asset was his tremendous sprinter's speed, which came with limitations of its own. Standing upright and running in a straight line, McClellan was a world-beater. Cutting from side to side and dodging tacklers, he was probably not as effective as Boyd.

Early in the season opener against Northwestern, the Sooners did something they had not done against the Wildcats the year before. They got ahead. The Sooners took the opening kickoff and drove 53 yards, where Karl Milstead kicked a 35-yard field goal. But the tenor of the game—and the season—was established in that opening drive. A bobbled third-down snap forced the Sooners to settle for Milstead's field goal instead of driving for a touchdown.

The Sooners' second drive into Northwestern territory was ruined in a similar manner when the Sooners were penalized 15 yards for having an ineligible receiver downfield. In the second quarter, the Sooners were again driving deep into Northwestern territory when an errant pitchout caused the loss of 17 yards and the ball. Costly errors every one. Instead of leading by two touchdowns at halftime, the Sooners trailed, 9–3.

By the fourth quarter, the Sooners trailed, 12–3, but the game was winnable. Wilkinson knew it. Inside, the Sooners knew it, too, but they could not make it happen. Fumbles ruined two drives. Poor conditioning, leaving the Sooners without the physical reserve to execute their assignments when they were tired, caused the Sooners to fall a yard short of a vital first down and with it, any chance of winning the ball game.

After the 19–3 loss, the Sooner locker room was restrained. Wilkinson closed the dressing room to the press while he tried to explain the terrible truth.

"Gentlemen, you are not a bad football team, but neither are you a good one. You stand at the crossroads. You can either get tough and fight hard to win, or you can become mentally soft and never develop the character required to defeat a good opponent. The choice is yours," he said.

Wilkinson could not tell which route they would choose, but he believed fervently that without physical conditioning, discipline, and mental toughness, no team can reach its potential.

Though it had been nearly a quarter century since he had played at Minnesota, Wilkinson could still recall the lessons he learned from Bierman: Don't settle for the type of football that defeats mediocre teams. Meet the standards necessary to beat the best. You can't fool a good team. The good ones don't take the fake. You have to block them, so prepare accordingly. If you are going to be a champion, you have to be willing to pay a greater price than your opponents will ever pay.

Bierman ran his teams that way, and the results proved him right. Wilkinson could still remember the torturous training Bierman put his teams through, including one raw, cold day when the Gophers were practicing in the field house. Bierman had them running wind sprints time after time. They'd run. Then rest. Then run again. Wilkinson could recall his burning lungs and aching legs, but with that memory came an equally clear recollection of beating Iowa, 52–6, the next Saturday.

That was what it took to be a champion. When you are clearly better than your opponent, such discipline is immaterial. But when two teams have equally talented players who are well conditioned and smartly coached, the difference is mental toughness. After years in football, Wilkinson was still not sure where you got it, but a team *had* to have it.

Wilkinson also knew that unless your standards are high in everything, the entire team will retrogress to the lowest level. That was why the Sooners' uniforms were the best money could buy and why they always traveled by airplane. If you are going to be a champion, you have to act like one. That was why the Sooners had no written training rules. The Sooners were expected to meet and master temptation on their own. Wilkinson believed a player who stays up till 2 A.M. in the middle of the summer or takes one drag off a cigarette in the off-season had not hurt himself physically, but he had permitted a small crack to form in his own mental armor. Yes, if you wanted to be a champion, you had to be willing to pay a greater price than your opponent. And for fourteen years, he had taught his teams to beat their opponents down so hard they wouldn't pay the price in the fourth quarter. Then, a champion finishes the job.

"The fourth quarter is ours," Wilkinson always told his teams. Until now, they had believed him, but with each week it seemed that "Play Like a CHAMPION Today" was just a hollow catchphrase.

A week after the loss to Northwestern, the Sooners played Pittsburgh. Wilkinson was sure he and his staff would know the type of season that awaited them once the Sooners faced the Panthers. With five minutes left to play in the third quarter, the Sooners trailed Pittsburgh by a touchdown after taking an early lead in the first period. It was exactly where they had been the week before against Northwestern. Now, the powerful Panthers had a first down at the OU 7. If they scored, Wilkinson feared an entire season would be lost.

On first down, Pitt quarterback Jim Traficant tried to turn left end behind massive Mike Ditka, the Panthers' All-American end, who possessed size and speed in a combination never before seen in a player at his position. But Billy White came charging from across the field, sliced past Ditka, and hit Traficant hard, stopping him for no gain. On second down, the Panthers went wide to the opposite side, but White was there again and held the Panthers to a 3-yard gain. From the Sooner 4, Traficant tried the right side again and picked up 3.

On fourth down, the ball rested a mere 18 inches from the Sooner goal. One last time, Traficant tried to wedge into the goal. Running to his right, he cut upfield in a seam behind the tackle. Ronnie Payne would not be blocked. He grabbed Traficant and held on until help came up to drag him down.

The Sooners had held. There might be hope.

Now, the Sooners had the ball, but it was 99 yards from the Pittsburgh end zone. Playing as Wilkinson believed they could, the Sooner starters drove to the Pitt 34 before being forced to punt. But the 65-yard drive changed the complexion of the game. Wilkinson sent in the rested alternates, hoping they could seize the moment. On fourth down, the Sooners blocked the Pittsburgh punt and recovered the loose ball at the Pittsburgh 11.

Two plays later, the Sooners scored. Trailing 14–13 with eleven minutes to play, Wilkinson chose to go for two to win the game. To line up in the T would give away their intentions, so Wilkinson went with a play that would disguise them. Milstead concentrated on the goalposts as Bennett Watts kneeled and called signals. Watts took the snap from center and rose to his feet as Milstead faked a kick. Milstead swerved to the outside and Watts followed. At the corner, Milstead crashed into Ditka, drove him back out of the play, and Watts raced into the end zone. The Sooners emerged victorious, 15–14. Wilkinson was delighted, but surprised. It was the kind of effort he hoped the Sooners would give, but he had not been certain his hopes would be realized.

After the Sooners looked particularly ineffective against Texas in a 24–0 loss, Wilkinson still could not tell what lay in store for the Sooners. Each week, they would meet a team that had waited years for the chance to defeat the Sooners decisively, just as Texas had. With the Sooners' illusion of invincibility destroyed, Wilkinson's players would have to learn to make a total, unrelenting effort on every play of every game if they expected to survive.

The next week, the oddsmakers favored Kansas by 9 1/2 points over OU, the biggest spread ever against a Wilkinson team. The reasons were obvious. Defensively, the Jayhawks had held OU to a single touchdown the year before, and most of KU's best defensive players returned. On offense, the Jayhawks were even more impressive. Mitchell had moved Hadl from halfback to quarterback to make room for Coan and McFarland. McClinton also returned at fullback to give KU potentially the best backfield in America.

The Sooners took the opening kickoff, and Carpenter returned it to the OU 35. Relying on Hartline and McClellan, Carpenter directed the Sooners down the field. In thirteen plays, they scored as McClellan sliced into the end zone over left tackle.

For the rest of the first quarter and into the second, Hadl's punting kept the Sooners deep in their own territory. Once he punted 50 yards out-of-bounds inside the OU 1. The next time, he punted out-of-bounds at the OU 10. The deep kicks limited the Sooners offense dramatically. For more than ten minutes, the Sooners' offense consisted of virtually nothing but short keepers by Carpenter and Cornell in keeping with Wilkinson's field position strategy—the upshot of the Sooners' loss to Notre Dame seven years before. Against the Jayhawks, ball control was particularly crucial. With the lead—and a team that had limited ability to come from behind—Wilkinson told his quarterbacks to play it safe.

Near the end of the first half, the Sooner defense could no longer contain the talented Jayhawks. Starting from the OU 39, they drove to score running nothing but power plays between the tackles. Then Jayhawks' kicker John Suder, who had been perfect on extra points in the Jayhawks' previous games, missed. Miraculously, the Sooners went to the locker room ahead, 7–6.

Choosing to take the benefit of a fifteen-mile-per-hour wind, KU kicked off to begin the second half. Just as they had at the start of the game, the Sooners started to drive. Hartline, taped firmly by trainer Ken Rawlinson after a knee injury in the first quarter, continued to roll through the Jayhawk line. First to the left side. Then to the right. Carpenter engineered the Sooner drive as Hartline began to amass more rushing yardage than the entire Kansas backfield. After gambling and getting a first down at the KU 35, Carpenter rolled out and passed to McClellan, who ran to the KU 11. The next three plays lost 2 yards. Facing fourth-and-12, the Sooners lined up in field goal formation with Milstead to kick. Carpenter took the snap, and Milstead drove his leg forward. As he did, Carpenter rose to his feet and rolled to his right. The Jayhawks poured in after him, but Carpenter gently lobbed a screen pass over their heads. McClellan caught the pass behind a wall of blockers and dashed down the sideline to score. Milstead's extra point try was blocked, leaving OU with a less-than-comfortable 13–6 lead.

The daring Sooners refused to give ground and forced fumbles that ended KU's next two drives. Finally, the Jayhawks quit trying to run against the inspired Sooners. Hadl threw long to McClinton. Running at full speed, McClinton lunged forward to grab the ball with his fingertips. He fell headlong to the turf but held onto the ball for a 41-yard gain. From the OU 10, KU scored in two plays. The extra point tied the game.

With 2:33 left, the Jayhawks got the ball one last time at midfield. Hadl threw to Coan for 14 yards and a first down at the OU 31. A second pass to Coan earned another first down at the 20. With time running out, Sooners rushed Hadl hard, but he slipped through left tackle for 13 yards to the Sooner 2. With fourteen seconds remaining, Mitchell sent in Suder for a field goal that would win the game. Suder chunked the kick, and it sailed up and off to the right. The Sooners had tied the Jayhawks, 13–13.

In the locker room, Wilkinson congratulated his players warmly. The Big Eight title, conceded to KU or Missouri early in the season, now seemed very much up for grabs.

The following week, the Sooners manhandled Kansas State in the usual manner, 49–7, and found themselves going into the Colorado game with momentum and a chance to beat the Buffaloes, who were leading the conference with a 3–0 record.

As always, the Sooners flew to Colorado early. On Thursday, they practiced hard in Denver. Wilkinson and his assistants ran the Sooners through a heavy dose of wind sprints, driving their bodies to help them adjust to the altitude and the effort Wilkinson believed would be necessary on Saturday. Unlike the teams coached by Dal Ward that featured high-powered offenses, the Buffs' greatest strength under Ward's successor, Sonny Grandelius, was defense. With a great middle linebacker in Joe Romig and outside linebacker in Jerry Hillebrand, Colorado had held K-State, Iowa State, and Nebraska to a touchdown apiece.

On Friday evening, Wilkinson met with the Sooners in the top of the Park Lane Hotel. As he always did, Wilkinson tried to inspire the Sooners to play their best. In most years, that had generally been good enough to win easily. He was not so sure about this team.

"Most of us are five times as good at anything as we think we are," Wilkinson told them. "Several years ago, Brutus Hamilton, who coached the U.S. Olympic track team, said that no one would ever run a four-minute mile. Then along came one guy who had enough guts to fight himself and do it. Once the barrier was broken, it was clear that it could be done. Others reached the same level of achievement. The first year after it was broken, three guys broke the four-minute barrier. The next year, 16 did it. The biggest hurdle in achieving *anything* is believing you have the capacity to do it. And, gentlemen, if you will believe in yourselves and want to beat Colorado badly enough, you can do it!"

The Sooners did as Wilkinson asked, but to no avail. The bigger Buffaloes overpowered the Sooners, holding them without a first down until late in the second quarter. Yet the Sooners fought hard on defense, stopping the Buffaloes on the ground. They lost only because Hillebrand made two clutch receptions in one drive, catching a deflected fourth-down pass at the OU 19 and another pass at the OU 1. The 7–0 final score, which marked the first time the Sooners had been shut out in a conference game since 1942, was all that Wilkinson could have realistically hoped for.

On Monday at the weekly Touchdown Club meeting in Oklahoma City, Wilkinson was asked why Hartline wasn't used when the Sooners had a first down on the Buff 5 after a 68-yard run by Watts.

"Colorado's defense was packed to stop Hartline on every play," Wilkinson explained. "In that situation, I think it was better to fake to Hartline and call on other players. As a coach, you try to do the very best you can. Since coaches are subject to the human quality, the same as anyone else, this is no guarantee that what you think is best is always correct. You make the decision in light of your best judgment. When you win, you gain confidence in your judgment. When you lose, you do some soul searching. The validity of your judgment is then not so apparent."

The members of the Touchdown Club listened politely, but Wilkinson could tell by the whispering in the room that the wisdom of his judgment was indeed not apparent.

A week later, the Sooners lost again, but this time they let victory slip through their hands. Leading Iowa State 6–0 at the half, the Sooners were hounded by mistakes in the second half. Three times they fumbled. Twice they failed to make first downs because of motion penalties. These were mistakes the Sooners could not afford. Iowa State tailback Dave Hoppman ran for 152 yards and guided the Cyclones to the winning touchdown with three minutes left in the game. The 10–6 victory was Iowa State's first over Oklahoma since 1931.

Missouri, 8–0 and ranked No. 2 in the nation, came to Norman the following week. Perhaps the finest Missouri team ever assembled, the Tigers led the nation in defense against rushing, and their opponents had yet to score a touchdown on the ground. The arrival of such a traditional rival and the smell of an upset victory lured two thousand students to the Sooners' practice on Thursday afternoon. When Saturday brought a sunny, seventy-degree afternoon, the Oklahoma spirit of autumns past was rekindled. After playing the national anthem, the OU band broke ranks, ran toward the Sooner bench, surrounded the Sooner huddle, and began playing "Boomer Sooner."

The Sooner players responded. On the third play after Oklahoma received the kickoff, Carpenter faked a handoff to Hartline, the Tiger defense converged on him, and the Sooners trapped the Tigers' right tackle. McClellan slid through the open hole and broke into the clear. Using his sprinter's speed, McClellan outran the Tiger secondary on a 70-yard touchdown run.

The Tigers stormed back. The Missouri juggernaut, like Sooner teams of old, drove relentlessly up and down the field, scoring on a 2-yard dive, a 30-yard draw play, a 77-yard sweep, and a 33-yard field goal. Yet the Sooners would not fold. With 8:33 left in the first half, the Sooner alternates broke Melvin Sandersfeld on exactly the same trap play that enabled McClellan to score. At halftime, the Sooners trailed, 24–12, but they were playing more inspired football than they had all season. A tremendous victory was still possible.

Early in the fourth quarter, McClellan intercepted a Mizzou pass at the OU 26 to stop a Tiger drive. Immediately, the Sooners began to move by running inside against the heart of the Missouri defensive line. On the fifth play of the drive, Hartline burst straight up the middle for 26 yards to the MU 37. Then the Sooners moved to three more first downs to put the ball at the MU 1. On the next play, Carpenter sneaked in. Hartline kicked the extra point, and the Sooners were within a touchdown of the Tigers.

The OU fans could sense a new stirring in the Sooners, and when Missouri was stopped after three plays and got off only a 12-yard punt, Oklahoma had the ball at the Missouri 35. In three plays, the Sooners drove to the 30, but a fourth-down pitchout to Sandersfeld went awry, and the Sooners lost 10 yards. In a fleeting moment, the dream was over.

On the first play of the fourth quarter, Norris Stevenson got outside on Missouri's "Student Body Left" sweep. He raced 60 yards to score and sapped the Sooners' momentum. Two more Sooner fumbles resulted in a touchdown and field goal, giving Missouri a 41–19 victory (the Sooners' first conference loss in Norman since 1942 and the first loss to MU in fourteen years).

Wilkinson was justifiably proud of the Sooners' effort, but to him, the story was the same: Twelve possessions. Four fumbles. Three interceptions. You cannot make that many errors against the nation's No. 2 team and hope to win.

The next week against Nebraska, the score was closer, but the outcome was predictable: Flashes of brilliance one minute. Fumbles and frustration the next. The Sooners jumped to a 14–0 lead and then wilted. The Cornhuskers scored 9 points in the fourth quarter to win, 17–14. The trait that Wilkinson valued above all—the will to give sixty minutes of all-out effort—simply was not there. The silence in the Sooner locker room after the defeat was mute testimony that the Sooners understood that, too.

In the final game of the season, the Sooners found themselves in the unlikely position of having a worse record than Oklahoma State. Yet the game was important to both teams, for pride, if nothing else. From studying game films, Wilkinson and Jones discovered that the Cowboys were tipping off their plays by the position of the wingback. Together, they devised a gambling defense to stop the Cowboys. They stationed ten men in set assignments and left Phil Lohmann to roam from side to side according to the position of the OSU wingback.

Sandersfeld gave the Sooners a first-quarter lead on a 5-yard sweep to conclude a 78-yard drive, but late in the first half, the Sooners lost Carpenter, McClellan, and Sandersfeld to injuries. At halftime, Wilkinson had to reshuffle his backfield. Cornell would have to quarterback both units. Deere was moved from left halfback to right halfback, and Jerry Pettibone, a fourth team halfback who had played only sparingly during his four years at OU, was promoted to the starting unit.

OU took the second half kickoff and drove 77 yards for the touchdown with Cornell scoring on a 3-yard sneak. Milstead kicked the extra point to make it 14–0.

The Cowboys finally scored with eleven minutes to play after driving 80 yards against the OU starting line, but they failed on an attempt to run for the 2-point conversion. The game—and Wilkinson's unblemished record against the Aggies—lay in the balance.

Part of the tradition Wilkinson instilled in the Sooners—and one that passed from class to class—was the belief that each player must give 100 percent in practice every day. Such dedication was necessary, regardless of a player's position, because Wilkinson knew that great football teams are built on the practice field—and they are built from the bottom up, not vice versa. The will to prepare each day every week of the season was the key. In fairness to all, Wilkinson and Jones designed the Sooner practices so that every player was given equal attention and had equal opportunity to demonstrate his skill. And if a player on the fifth team improved, it behooved all the players ahead of him to improve as well.

Pettibone was living proof that the system worked. For four years, he had practiced diligently, if anonymously. And when his time came—with less than a quarter left in his college career—Pettibone was ready. OSU prepared to kick off, and Pettibone, standing at the Sooner goal, prayed the ball would not come to him. It did. In his one brief moment in the sun at Oklahoma, Pettibone took the kick at the OU 3 and ran straight upfield. He saw an opening to the left and cut toward it. Suddenly, he was free down the sidelines, running past the Sooner bench with Wilkinson matching him stride for stride.

"Run, Jerry, run!" Wilkinson shouted.

Pettibone was finally bumped out-of-bounds at the OU 48, but he had done his job. He gave the Sooners field position when they had to have it.

With 1:52 left, Hartline kicked a 24-yard field goal to seal the Sooner victory, but what had made the victory happen—and pleased Wilkinson more than the triumph itself—was that the Sooners, in their last game of a 3–6–1 season, had run sixty-five plays without losing a fumble.

Why, after so long, did Oklahoma lose? Mostly, it was just a matter of time. The other Big Eight schools, forced to improve their football programs to compete with OU, finally reaped the benefit of their efforts. Texas schools began to recruit more intensely. And, most critically, the pool of players in the area Wilkinson regarded as Oklahoma's natural recruiting territory was no longer sufficient. Wilkinson believed that if he had eight players from each recruiting class of forty-five playing productively as seniors, he could field a good team. Eight from each class produced a core of twenty-four players, just a bit more than the number of regulars—the starters and alternates—that Wilkinson regarded as The Team. Wilkinson knew there would be attrition within each class: Injuries. Academic failures. Mistakes (that is, players recruited by OU that were not good enough or did not develop sufficiently to play at the level Wilkinson expected). Add all those factors together, and for the first time under Wilkinson, the teams at Missouri, Kansas, Colorado—and, yes, even Iowa State—were better than OU.

Above that, Wilkinson was now sandwiched between two of his finest protégés—Royal to the south at Texas and Mitchell to the north at Kansas. Technically, the most successful of Wilkinson's former players at that time was Jim Owens, who took over the Washington Huskies after Royal left for Texas. Owens' Huskies finished 10–1 in both 1959 and 1960, were a top ten team both years, and won two Rose Bowls with a gutsy one-eyed option quarterback named Bob Schloredt. Owens, however, was one thousand miles from Norman and no recruiting threat to Wilkinson.

Royal and Mitchell, on the other hand, were close by, and both had the ability and charisma to get the players they wanted—as Mitchell had proved with Hadl. Suppose, if but for a moment, that Chuck Mather had remained the coach at Kansas and Hadl had followed through with his plan to play college football at Oklahoma. Imagine the impact a triple-threat, two-time All-American might have had on the fortunes of the undersized Sooners.

In truth, the Sooners' difficulties, as Wilkinson himself finally came to realize, occurred because *he* was late in understanding that all of America was changing. The airplane and television were altering the face of college football. Wilkinson had assumed that a good player would *always* go to the best school close to his hometown, as Hadl finally chose to do—but only after Kansas hired Mitchell and he turned on his charm. Certainly, football was still a regional game, but there were schools, and Oklahoma was one of them, that could draw talent from anywhere it chose.

Monte Kiffin, who was prepared to leave his home state behind to play for Wilkinson, was symbolic of the legions of young men, perhaps nationwide, who would have answered Wilkinson's call to come to Oklahoma, had Wilkinson only done so. Wilkinson's unfailing devotion to the football virtues he had learned from Bernie Bierman—the very source of his greatest strengths—had blinded him. He did not see clearly that college football had shed forever the innocence Wilkinson so loved.

Surely, there were other young men with talent, young men with character, who longed to be Sooners. Wilkinson vowed to find them. Together, he and Gomer would lead the Sooners to the top again.

1961

Late on the morning of January 9 the NCAA announced at its annual meeting in Pittsburgh that it was lifting the indefinite probation of OU. Walter Byers and Arthur Wood had found a compromise solution that allowed the NCAA to see the appropriate records without releasing the names of his clients. As a result, the banishment of Oklahoma had ended.

At the same time, there were persistent rumors that Wilkinson was getting ready to retire from coaching, that at forty-five he wanted to run for public office, perhaps governor, in 1962. The rumors were untrue. After all that Wilkinson had accomplished in football, he had no intention of leaving coaching after a losing season.

Armed with the good news of OU's removal from probation, Wilkinson and his assistants hit the recruiting trail with renewed intensity. They traveled to places they never visited before. They ignored no lead on a promising prospect. They signed two players from Illinois, one from Colorado, and one from Missouri. They even invaded south Texas, long the stronghold of the Texas Longhorns, but lost the prime prospect, Johnny Roland of Corpus Christi, to Missouri. In Washington, D.C., they found John Flynn, a tough and talented end. In Farmington, New Mexico, they found Ralph Neely, a giant tackle blessed with speed and intelligence.

Ironically, as Wilkinson and his staff began to look beyond the recruiting territory that had been so good to them for so long and then gone fallow, the region again blossomed with talent. From Muldrow came 227-pound end Glen Condren. From Tulsa's Washington High School came Ed McQuarters, who weighed 230 pounds and was a state heavyweight wrestling champion. McQuarters had gone unnoticed by the Sooner coaches until they saw him outrun one of the halfbacks in training for the Oklahoma All-State game.

Under their very noses, the Oklahoma staff found Lance Rentzel—a big, speedy halfback from Casady High School in Oklahoma City who was an honor roll student and accomplished pianist—and Tommy Pannell, who had quarterbacked Norman High School to the state championship. From Purcell came Rick McCurdy, a single wing tailback who would have to find a new position, but that did not concern Wilkinson and his staff. They were not recruiting players for positions. They were recruiting athletes. They would find positions for them later. Perhaps most exceptional of all was Jim Grisham, a rugged fullback and linebacker from Olney in the heart of north-central Texas, where Wilkinson had previously found two of his greatest linebackers—Tubbs and Harrison.

Taken individually, the Sooner recruits were extraordinary prospects. Together, they represented one of the best classes ever recruited at Oklahoma. The help, Wilkinson knew, could not come too soon. In the past four years, Oklahoma had only one All-American lineman—Jerry Thompson in 1959—and the Sooners had not had an All-American back since Clendon Thomas in 1957.

Just before the start of spring practice, Wilkinson received a long-distance call from Ted Reardon, the executive assistant to President John Kennedy. Reardon explained that Kennedy was looking for someone to become Special Consultant on Youth Fitness and asked Wilkinson if he would come to Washington to visit with the president about the position. Wilkinson said he would.

After the two exchanged pleasantries and the White House photographer posed them for the ritual photo session, Wilkinson came immediately to the point that had worried him most about the possible presidential appointment.

"Mr. President, how important is this program to you?" Wilkinson asked.

Privately, Wilkinson feared that youth fitness—a subject dear to his own heart—might be to the newly elected president a politically expedient program that no one could criticize. Wilkinson was surprised by Kennedy's answer.

"I don't believe there is anything more important," Kennedy said. "The mechanization of our society has virtually eliminated for the majority of our citizens enough physical activity in their daily lives to maintain physical fitness. Escalators, lawnmowers, automobiles are all developments of the last 60 years. We have reached a state where muscular activity has been virtually removed from our lives. School children no longer walk to school. They are bussed."

Wilkinson listened carefully and nodded his assent.

"I do not consider myself a student of history," Kennedy continued, "but from my reading I have reached the conclusion that nations do not respond to challenges unless the population, as a whole, has great vigor and vitality. These qualities are based on the individual physical well being of the citizen."

Pointedly, Kennedy asked Wilkinson, who was only two years older than he—but considerably grayer—if he would accept the position.

"Yes, I would be pleased to do it," Wilkinson said.

Eager to get a youth fitness program in motion, Kennedy suggested to Wilkinson that he resign his position at OU and come to Washington to serve on a full-time basis.

"I'm not certain that would be wise, Mr. President," Wilkinson said. "I think my ability to address the fitness problem with the proper media and public support is enhanced by the fact that I am an active coach. If I resign that position and come to Washington, I become nothing more than a member of the bureaucracy. I believe my coaching is an important asset."

The president could not quarrel with Wilkinson's logic.

When Wilkinson returned to Norman, he discussed the matter with George Cross and the regents. He assured them the commitment would not interfere with his coaching duties, and they gave unanimous approval. The reception to Wilkinson's prestigious new assignment was not universal, however. News of Wilkinson's pending presidential appointment caused some OU fans to fear they were losing Wilkinson permanently. Others thought Wilkinson could not do both jobs well. To allay such concerns, Wilkinson wrote a letter to each member of the Touchdown Club describing how he intended to handle the situation.

"The government understands the limitations on my time," Wilkinson wrote. "Briefly, I will be here for spring practice sessions. After spring practice, I will be on call to the government until the first of August, at which time I will again devote my efforts to our team in preparation for the coming season."

Explanation of the situation seemed to settle any uneasiness among most Oklahoma fans, the coaching staff, and the players. For most of the summer, Wilkinson was in Washington or on the road, giving speeches to spur awareness of the need for physical fitness, particularly among young people. One of the statements that seemed to please his audiences most was his definition of a football game. It is, Wilkinson said, twenty-two people on the field desperately needing rest and 100,000 people in the stands desperately needing exercise.

In 1961 OU faced a stiff non-conference schedule—Texas, Army, and Notre Dame—and a stronger Big Eight conference. Wilkinson was also forced to prepare for the season amid the worst rash of injuries he could remember. In addition, there was a growing realization among some of his players that life would require them to look beyond each Saturday.

One was senior center Jim Byerly, who chose to forgo his final year of eligibility. Married and forced to weigh his life in economic terms for the first time, he came to understand that college football was, in reality, a business. Viewed in that light, a football scholarship represented very cheap wages. Byerly had seen former OU players return to the campus after a year or more in pro football. Pro linemen were paid approximately $7,500 a year, and the former Sooners routinely showed up with a new car, but no money in their pockets. Byerly wanted no such future for himself. He decided to quit football and go to work managing restaurants that his father-in-law owned in Oklahoma City. Uncertain how Wilkinson would react to such a decision—and fully aware of Wilkinson's powers of persuasion—Byerly left OU without giving Wilkinson a chance to talk him out of it.

Like other Sooners, Byerly knew Wilkinson frowned on his players investing important years of their lives in pro football. Those years only put them at a disadvantage in competition with others in their real careers. There was, he was careful to teach them, life after football. Some Sooners, especially those most enamored of pro football, believed Wilkinson could not understand the lure of a career in the National Football League. What they and Byerly did not know was that Wilkinson had made his own decision about the value of pro football a quarter century earlier. After starring in the College All-Star game, Wilkinson was offered $3,500 a year by the Green Bay Packers. He was offered $3,600 to coach at Syracuse. He went to Syracuse.

An Oklahoma–Notre Dame football game is news, so you can expect it to be nationally televised any time it occurs. It is a credit to the traditions of both schools that the season opener between these two teams in 1961 was televised coast-to-coast from South Bend, perhaps the only time that such attention has been accorded two teams that finished the previous season with records of 3–6–1 and 2–8, respectively.

Early in the game, the Sooners looked like a transformed team. Operating from wide-open formations to take advantage of the slower Irish linemen, the Sooners began to move. Led by Bill Van Burkleo, a sophomore quarterback from Tulsa who had been the Oklahoma schoolboy sensation of 1959, the Sooners drove into the strong wind. Van Burkleo hit Mike McClellan for 16 yards. Phil Lohmann, moved to fullback for his senior year, gained 14 through the middle of the Irish line. Van Burkleo passed to McClellan in the left flat, and he dashed 26 yards before being knocked out-of-bounds at the Irish 16. The drive finally stalled at the 10, and Milstead lined up to try a 32-yard field goal. It never crossed the line of scrimmage. Nick Buoniconti broke through the Sooner line and blocked the kick. The ball rolled back to the Notre Dame 41, where the Irish took possession.

Wilkinson sent in his alternates. Two plays later, the Irish blockers opened a hole in the right side of the Sooner line. Angelo Dabiero sped through and cut to the outside. Several Sooners had shots at tackling him, but Dabiero twisted away from all of them and raced 51 yards to score. The Irish missed the extra point, and that seemed to provide some measure of inspiration for the Sooners.

After the Sooners returned Notre Dame's short kickoff to the Notre Dame 28, the alternates scored in seven plays as time expired in the first quarter. Unfortunately, the teams had to change ends of the field at the quarter, and Milstead's extra point try against the fierce wind was also no good.

The Irish scored another touchdown in the second quarter, but the Sooners again blocked the extra point try. The half ended with Notre Dame leading, 12–6. In the third period, the Sooners played gamely, holding Notre Dame scoreless. But the Irish dominated the fourth quarter. The Sooner alternates let Dabiero get free on runs of 22 and 30 yards, and the Irish scored to clinch a 19–6 victory.

In the end, Wilkinson saw the game as a case study in the Sooners' lack of depth. The starting team, which played 80 percent of the game, fought the Irish on virtually even terms. The alternates, in the game for only eleven plays on defense, gave up 160 yards. With defense like that, it is almost impossible to win.

The following week marked the nadir of Wilkinson's coaching career. In the first quarter, Iowa State scored three times to take a 21–0 lead. Despite losing six fumbles and throwing an interception, the Sooners fought back and held the Cyclones scoreless the rest of the game. But the 21-point handicap was too great to overcome. The Sooners lost, 21–15.

Their success during the final three quarters against Iowa State seemed to encourage Wilkinson and the Sooners. Though still hamstrung by mistakes, the Sooners played with a tenacity that Wilkinson admired. Yet he knew that spirit can make up for only so much. Against a tremendously fast Texas team, the Sooners were simply overmatched. The 28–7 final score was as close as Wilkinson could have hoped. At the end of the game, Wilkinson hurried to the middle of the field to congratulate Royal, but there followed more than the ceremonial shaking of hands. The two embraced briefly. Their friendship, nurtured over fifteen years, meant more to both than any bounce that football fortunes might take.

Wilkinson was tremendously proud of his former pupil, who had taken a once-proud program, broken and in disarray, and rebuilt it into one of the finest teams in America with the very fundamentals Wilkinson had preached—speed, execution, daring, and spirit. The Longhorns might be wearing burnt orange, but they bore Wilkinson's unmistakable hallmark.

A student of military history, Wilkinson again and again emphasized to the Sooners that no one remembers losers, but he knew there were exceptions. The world remembers the handful of Spartans who stood their ground at Thermopylae, not the thousands of Persians who overcame them. The Hebrew zealots who died at Masada, not the Roman legions that outlasted them. The 180 men who defended the Alamo, not Santa Ana's soldiers who massacred them. As the Sooners prepared to play Kansas, the preseason favorite to win the national championship, Wilkinson hoped his players would display that kind of valor against tremendous odds.

The Sooners did not disappoint him. Seven times, the Jayhawks drove into Sooner territory and were rebuffed, twice inside the 5, but that is not what many saw. What they saw was an impotent Oklahoma offense that gained only 98 yards and crossed the 50 only twice. Unable to block effectively, the Sooners had to abandon the option play, leaving the once proud Oklahoma Split T in shambles.

Disappointed with the Sooners' 10–0 loss (the second time in two seasons the Sooners had lost four straight games), many fans left Memorial Stadium dazed that a conference opponent had shut out the Sooners. They had never seen it at home before. But Mitchell and others who knew football appreciated the game the Sooners had played. Injuries had destroyed any semblance of depth in Jones's line. The backfield—other than McClellan—had virtually no speed. For the second week in a row, the overmatched Sooners had played a great team as well as they could.

On Monday morning, the *Daily Oklahoman* carried a column by sports editor John Cronley analyzing the game of two days before. Bearing the headline "Yes, Kansas Is That Good, OU That Bad," the article—from a man who had been Wilkinson's friend and confidant for nearly fifteen years—cut deeply into the psyches of the staunchest OU fans. In letters to the newspaper and in angry conversations among themselves, they accused Cronley of being a traitor to the Sooner cause.

To the surprise of many, Wilkinson defended Cronley at his weekly press conference on Monday.

"I think people are too critical of the press," Wilkinson said. "A columnist's number one priority is to be read. If he doesn't write something controversial or interesting, he won't be read. A columnist has as hard a job as a football coach. He has to go to the wall every day and write something people will read. That is not easy. I personally don't get overly concerned as long as the information published is accurate."

What Cronley wrote was, in essence, accurate. Wilkinson could not disagree, but what the article neglected to mention was what Wilkinson and his assistants could see taking place each day in practice. The Sooners were getting better, not worse. They had played two of the best teams in America on successive Saturdays and, since halftime of the Texas game, had been outscored only 17–7. Unlike the Sooners of the year before, there was no failure of willpower. In fact, no team Wilkinson coached ever tried harder. As Wilkinson knew, losing teams are the easiest to coach. Ridiculed or politely ignored by the fans and press, the players band together in self-protection and develop a unique closeness. The coaching staff has no morale problem to confront. The coaches' problem is one of building confidence. The players must continue to believe in their coaches. And above all, in themselves. Fans, mindful only of the scoreboard, could not see that. Nor did they see the Sooners' practice the afternoon that the Boomers, OU's magnificent freshman team, scored five times against the varsity. *That* was what Wilkinson saw and what excited him about the Sooners' prospects for the future.

Undefeated Colorado, ranked in the top ten in both polls, came next. Twice the Sooners fought their way into the lead, holding a 14–10 advantage over the favored Buffaloes as the game entered the fourth quarter. It was not enough. An inspired Colorado touchdown drive and the Sooners' failure to recover the ensuing kickoff allowed the Buffs to score two times in the final period and to escape with a 22–14 victory.

"Oklahoma is the best 0–5 team I've ever seen," said Colorado coach Sonny Grandelius.

Not only was the defeat the Sooners' fifth straight, but it was their ninth loss in the past ten games. Oklahoma, the school that had won more games than any team in college football during the previous fifteen years, was a shadow of its former self.

If some fans deserted the hard-luck Sooners, one who never did was Morris Tenenbaum. Tenenbaum had served as a not-so-silent volunteer sentinel outside the Sooner dressing room since 1935, the year Biff Jones arrived at OU. Through the intervening quarter century, Tenenbaum became a well-known figure around the OU campus, but one whose past remained shrouded in mystery.

The details were sketchy, mostly the result of what Tenenbaum told people about himself. Born in 1897, he came to the United States from Poland after escaping from the Germans in the early 1900s. With him, he brought only a Bible and an American penny. By the time he arrived in Oklahoma City in 1914, he had lost the penny but still had the Bible, which he kept in his living room. A tailor by trade, Tenenbaum opened a secondhand clothing store in Norman in 1923 and made his living buying and selling used clothes and shoes. He would start at the gate of the university and proceed down fraternity row buying old clothes from students in need of money—often for trips to Dallas for the Texas game. By the end of his trek, Tenenbaum would have a bundle of clothes in his arms and three or four hats on his head, which he would take home, mend, and resell.

As a younger man, Tenenbaum wore natty straw boaters and some of the finest old suits he bought, but as he aged, he became less sartorially splendid and more eccentric. He often wore a felt hat pulled down tightly over his large ears and an old wool sport coat, even on the hottest days. These idiosyncrasies merely endeared him to generations of Oklahoma football players. On practice days or game days, he would be in his assigned spot outside the Sooner locker room. As gatekeeper to the OU locker room, a position he fulfilled as tenaciously as Cerberus, Tenenbaum admitted no outsiders to the OU dressing room before, during, or after a game.

His instructions from Wilkinson were direct: "I don't want *anybody* in here!" Wilkinson told him. Tenenbaum took his charge seriously, especially after seeing Wilkinson run his own brother out of the OU dressing room at the halftime of a Texas game.

It was not Tenenbaum's ritual attendance on game days that inspired the loyalty of the Sooners. It was his unfailing devotion on practice days, when the Sooners slaved through the endless technique and conditioning drills, far removed from the crowd and the band. It was as if he and Wilkinson shared an unspoken bond about what was important in football—and life. He, like Wilkinson, would never fail to support his boys even when no one was watching.

Each day—rain or shine, hot or cold—they knew Tenenbaum would be outside the door as they went out to practice. In his later years, Tenenbaum could not keep track of every player's name. He called them all "Roommate" or "Shickosha All-State."

"Hey, Roommate, you want some Chiclets?" Tenenbaum would say to each player as he left the locker room en route to the Sooners' practice field. He would dig into his trouser or coat pocket and produce a ration. Technically, they were not Chiclets, but rather sticks of gum. For most, it was spearmint, but to his favorites he offered wild cherry. Each of the Sooners, in turn, would call Tenenbaum by his first name and thank him. Those who knew him best—often the ones to whom he offered the wild cherry gum—would often tease him in return.

"Thanks, Maurice," they would say, giving his name an exaggerated French pronunciation.

After practice, he would wait as they left the stadium.

"Hey, Fraternity Brother, you want some sleeping pills?" he would ask and give each player some pieces of hard sugar candy from his pants pockets.

At night, Tenenbaum would return to the small house where he lived alone with his cherished mementos of living four decades in the shadow of the university. Tenenbaum's modest home was decorated with the photos of Sooner players and others he had met. OU coaches Tom Stidham and Bud Wilkinson held places of honor, as did Harry Truman. On one wall hung a piece of fabric with the letters "OU" arranged in buttons. Brightly colored curtains, cut from the scraps of material from secondhand skirts and blouses, adorned the windows. In his bedroom hung a large quilt. Each square was made of the fabric from a different tie, and the quilt had been sewn with a Singer sewing machine that dated to his arrival in America.

In the beginning, Tenenbaum had been entranced by the excitement generated by Biff Jones's inspired teams. After more than a quarter century, football had lost its allure. He was drawn to Memorial Stadium not by the game itself but by his love for the boys. And they knew it. Tenenbaum also knew the troublemakers when he saw them. Not a few were the Sooners he would privately counsel.

"The world is yours. Just go ahead and hunt for trouble and see how long you last," he would tell them.

Away from the practice field, Tenenbaum was quick to defend his charges and the game they loved.

"It's not football that hurts those boys," he would say to a passerby. "It's college girls. They dream about them all night."

Eventually, Tenenbaum became well known for his volunteer service to the Sooners, so much so that he printed a small booklet that contained pearls of his unconventional wisdom. On the flyleaf was a short note:

"One Dollar for My Private Opinion and Reputation. If anybody could prove that their opinion and reputation is better, I will pay the difference or I will compromise and split the difference. The reason I made a success is because you haven't got anything I am crazy about. I am a good American citizen. I am not poisoned with prejudice, selfishness, nor jealousies. I would appreciate it if you learn to spell my name correctly."

Just as Tenenbaum would be there for the Sooners on practice days, they knew they could count on seeing him on Saturdays sitting inconspicuously in the southwest corner of Owen Field. That is, as inconspicuous as a man with a deer horn-and-silver dollar ring can be. During the game, Tenenbaum would sit at the end of the Sooner bench or on the tarp behind it, a cigar or cigarette clenched firmly between his teeth. On rainy days, he would wear a red fireman's hat pulled over his old felt hat with the words "Chicken Inspector" emblazoned in red on the front.

Through Wilkinson's great seasons, Tenenbaum and his peculiar talismans became good luck omens for the Sooners. In the fall of 1961 neither he nor his good luck charms could rescue the boys he loved, but the small secondhand clothing merchant never let the Sooners get matters out of perspective. Tenenbaum had known poverty and oppression. He had seen world wars and a depression. A football game was minor. As each defeat piled upon another, the Sooner locker room became like a funeral parlor with relatives standing outside crying.

Tenenbaum, though sympathetic, was philosophical.

"You can't play the game without losing or without winning," he would tell them. "If you can't afford to lose, don't play."

At the Sooners' weekly squad meeting on Sunday morning after the loss to Colorado, Wilkinson shocked the entire team.

"If you play with the intensity you have shown so far, I believe you will win all the remaining games on our schedule," Wilkinson told them.

For the rest of the day, the Sooners were in disbelief. Then, Wilkinson repeated the same statement during his weekly television program that afternoon. The poor man has lost his mind! The losses have affected him more than we thought, people said to themselves.

After nearly thirty years of college football, both as a player and a coach, Wilkinson could see what was not apparent to the average fan—or even to the Sooners themselves. They were improving, and when their level of skill coincided with their level of effort—which had always been excellent—they would start to win. Buoyed by Wilkinson's confidence in them, the Sooners began to feel like winners. They were ready to sacrifice anything necessary to be successful.

The following Saturday, the Sooners led Kansas State, 10–6, with four minutes to play, but many of the Sooners were playing scared. And for an Oklahoma Sooner, there was no feeling more haunting than to be in danger of losing to Kansas State after losing the first five games of the season.

With the ball at the OU 28, quarterback Bob Page called the option play and ran it with textbook precision. He faked to the halfback and moved laterally to the corner to test the Wildcat end. The end charged. Looking directly at the end to freeze him, Page pitched back to the trailing halfback. Immediately, he sensed something wrong. The halfback was not there! Page had run the wrong way. The ball rolled free for what seemed an eternity before the alert Carpenter fell on it at the Sooner 19. Now faced with second and 19, Page called what his sessions with Wilkinson had trained him to call—the fake quick kick, which Wilkinson and his staff had added to the playbook for the game.

Wilkinson always preached that the true test of team morale is whether a player would rather sit on the bench and win than play and have the team lose. Few OU teams had been in position to test that hypothesis. These Sooners had, and they passed the test. The Sooner reserves, though unlikely to play at the end of such a close game, stood along the sidelines cheering loudly for their teammates on the field.

Page took the snap and lateraled to Carpenter, who took one step back and swung his leg upward. As he did, McClellan came behind him and took the ball. Before the Wildcats understood what had happened, McClellan, a 9.6 sprinter, was gone. He dashed 82 yards for a touchdown that assured a 17–6 Sooner victory, perhaps the sweetest in OU history. Certainly, the most appreciated.

Missouri had installed a new wide-end, six-man line defense designed by Al Onofrio, Dan Devine's defensive assistant, and the Tigers—ranked among the nation's top teams with a 5–1–1 record—were holding opponents to less than a touchdown a game. Wilkinson analyzed the Sooners' upcoming game with Missouri carefully. It was unlikely the Sooners could score twice against the Tigers, who returned many of the players from the team that had almost won the national championship the year before, but the Sooners could probably score once. To win, they would have to play defense.

"In every football game, a team gets the ball first-and-10, twelve to fourteen times," Wilkinson explained to the Sooners. "If you can stop Missouri twelve times, not let them score, make them give up the ball, we'll win."

Executing Wilkinson's plan would not be easy, especially with Billy White, who was playing with near All-American brilliance, out with a hip pointer. Jones and Wilkinson put Dennis Ward in White's place, backed up by George Stokes (a six-foot-five free spirit who, at sporadic intervals, would yell "It ain't agonna work!" across the line of scrimmage at the opposition on offense).

An intermittent rain fell on Columbia most of the morning, but MU's tarp kept the field dry until game time. A record crowd of over forty-five thousand filled Memorial Stadium and spilled out onto the grassy hill at the closed end of the stadium.

Early in the first quarter, the Sooners were tested. Missouri quarterback Ron Taylor threw 40 yards to Conrad Hitchler to the Sooner 3, where Monte Deere made a touchdown-saving tackle. Now, for Wilkinson's plan for victory to work, the Sooners knew they had to hold. On first down, the Tigers got 2 yards. On second and third down, the Sooners stopped Mizzou for no gain. On fourth down, the Tigers sent left halfback Vince Turner on the Tigers' "Student Body Right" sweep with both guards pulling to lead interference.

Ward, making his first start, remembered what Jones had drilled into the Sooner linemen in goal line situations: "Eat dirt and grab legs!" Ward made a strong, low charge, split the Tiger blockers, and tackled Turner for a 2-yard loss.

In the second quarter, the Tigers fumbled at the MU 43, and the Sooners recovered. Two first down plays moved the ball to the Missouri 14, where Page tried a play series Wilkinson had suggested on the sidelines to thwart the aggressive Tiger defense. On first down, McClellan went wide to the left on a sweep and lost a yard. Page then came back to the opposite side with the halfback pass option, hoping to draw the Tigers in. Page pitched to Carpenter going to the right, and the Tigers reacted as hoped. They charged Carpenter so hard he barely had time to catch the ball, but he was able to get his pass off before the Tigers knocked him to the ground. His pass was complete to McClellan at the 5, where McClellan broke away from the Tiger cornerback and scored.

At halftime, the Sooners retained their 7–0 lead and had stopped Missouri on defense seven times. Five more times, the Sooners told themselves. If they could stop the Tigers five more times in the second half, victory was theirs.

Early in the third period, the Sooners' resolve was tested. The Tigers drove to the OU 8 before Van Burkleo broke up two straight passes to end the Missouri threat. Later in the quarter, the Sooners forced Missouri to punt at midfield.

"Nine!" the Sooners shouted in unison, just as they had announced their success at the end of each of the Tigers' eight previous possessions. Three more times. The Sooners had to hold just three more times.

Three minutes into the fourth quarter, OU forced Missouri to punt and then held the ball for one series before punting the ball back to the Tigers. On the next series, Lohmann intercepted a Tiger pass at the MU 40 and ran 22 yards before being stopped. When George Jarman missed a field goal that would have given Oklahoma a 10-point lead, the Sooners went on defense for the twelfth time with seven minutes to play.

Mixing runs and passes, Taylor moved the Tigers toward the Sooner goal. With 3:16 left, Missouri got a first down at the OU 31. On first down, Taylor's pass was incomplete. On second down, he threw long, but Deere intercepted the pass to preserve the Sooner victory.

The Sooners had done it. Twelve times, they had stopped Missouri. All that remained was for Page to run out the clock.

At the final gun, Wilkinson could not contain his joy. He raced onto the field with the Sooners, leaping and clapping his hands. Linebacker Johnny Tatum, who had worked diligently to strengthen his knee after having surgery in July, grabbed the game ball off the ground and raced for the Sooner locker room.

"I'm going to keep it!" Tatum shouted. "As long as I live, I'm going to keep it!"

New York loved the Sooners. Wilkinson, with his urbane manner and sophistication, had always appealed to eastern tastes. And OU's weekly "filmettes," with the film highlights of each Sooner game—dutifully scripted by Harold Keith and edited by Ned Hockman—made sure that television and movie audiences in New York and across the country could keep up with the Sooners. During the forty-seven-game winning streak, New York sportswriters loved the Sooners, too. They provided relief from the eastern schools they normally covered and gave them the opportunity to make not-so-oblique references to surreys with fringe on top and winds sweeping down the plain.

The writers, and New Yorkers as well, were less excited about the prospect of seeing the Sooners play Army in Yankee Stadium, where the New York Giants held sway as one of the best teams in pro football. When the OU-Army game was scheduled in 1956, it promised to be a remarkable coup. When the game day finally arrived in mid-November five years later, it seemed merely a contest of tarnished titans even though the Black Knights of the Hudson were 6–2 and had won five straight.

Bob Ward, an All-American guard for Jim Tatum at Maryland who had joined Wilkinson's staff in 1960, scouted Army against Detroit and William & Mary. He presented Wilkinson with a fascinating piece of information. On defense, Army always used a closed huddle, well behind the line of scrimmage, and routinely came back slowly to the ball. Wilkinson designed a play to take advantage of the Army weakness.

Technically, Wilkinson had not designed the play he had in mind. It had been devised by none other than Gomer Jones's coach at Ohio State, Francis Schmidt, who had been one of the phalanx of young coaches who brought college football to the forefront of American sports during the 1920s. Schmidt lettered on the Nebraska football team in 1905 and eventually obtained a law degree from the same school. Then, he joined the army in World War I and became a captain. In 1919, he became the head football coach at the University of Tulsa. In his first season, his team compiled a record of 8–0–1 and outscored opponents 592–27.

Schmidt was so successful that he was hired by the University of Arkansas before becoming the head coach at TCU and then Ohio State. During this time, his teams became known for using outlandish trick plays involving multiple laterals and unusual formations (hence, the shroud of secrecy surrounding the playbook that Jones had experienced firsthand). Sportswriters extolled the success of Schmidt's razzle-dazzle offense and, because Schmidt's teams were known for running up the score on hapless opponents, they began calling him "Close the Gates of Mercy" Schmidt.

Schmidt's years at Ohio State coincided with Wilkinson's years at Minnesota, so Wilkinson was quite familiar with Schmidt's trick plays. And, believing as he did that few things in football were truly revolutionary, Wilkinson chose the Army game to use one of Schmidt's finest creations—the Swinging Gate formation.

As with nearly all of Wilkinson's trick plays, the Swinging Gate involved deception. The play actually had two phases. First, Page would hand off to Carpenter, who would run to the right. After gaining 2 or 3 yards, he would slip down or let Army tackle him, making sure not to make a first down that would necessitate moving the chains or otherwise disrupt the flow of the game. Then, the Sooners would line up without a huddle and run the Swinging Gate play to the opposite side with virtually the entire line in front of the swift McClellan. Timing was critical. Wilkinson did not know when the Sooners would use the play, but they would wait for the right psychological moment to spring the trap.

The right moment came early—on the Sooners' second possession—when an Army punt rolled dead at the OU 12. Now, before the Army defense gained confidence, was the time, Wilkinson decided.

Page called the first play in the sequence. Carpenter took Page's handoff over the right side, but there were no Army defenders to stop him. Carpenter could not control his instincts. He kept running and gained 11 yards for a first down. In the huddle, Page called the sequence again. This time, Army was ready, and Carpenter slipped down after gaining 2. As he headed back toward the Sooner huddle, he handed the ball to the referee, who had been warned that the Sooners had a trick play planned. Instead of huddling, the Sooners merely pretended to walk back to their huddle, while the Cadets went, as expected, into their closed defensive huddle.

The Sooners drifted into an offensive line formation with six men grouped wide to the left. When the referee placed the ball down, center Wayne Lee crouched over it with Carpenter behind him. When the referee dropped his arm to signal the ball was ready for play, Carpenter waited two seconds, as the rules required.

"Set. Hike!" he yelled.

Lee snapped the ball to Carpenter, who tossed a long, low lateral to McClellan. Startled, the Cadets hurried from their huddle and chased after McClellan. But it was too late. McClellan dashed 75 yards untouched to score.

For the next two quarters, neither team threatened seriously, but late in the third quarter, OU drove to the Army 1. The 2,200 Cadets in the stands refused to quit yelling as the Sooners tried to call signals, so Page went to a delayed count trying to get the Cadets to jump offside. They did. Twice. Finally, the Sooners snapped the ball on a quick count and scored. Late in the fourth quarter, Army scored, but the 14–8 triumph on national television kept intact Oklahoma's reputation as a "television" team.

Red Smith of the *New York Times*, home with a cold, watched the game on television and wrote cogently of the game:

"Chances are the military leaders of tomorrow learned more Saturday about the value of surprise to an attacking force than they had absorbed in three years of lectures at the Academy."

The lesson was not lost on the generals, either. At the end of the season, Hall would be removed as the Army coach, and Wilkinson would be saddened, certain that the Sooners' surprise play contributed to Hall's dismissal.

When the Sooners returned from New York, more than three thousand fans came to Max Westheimer Field to welcome them. It was like old times, as if the first five games of the season never happened. The Sooners were winning again.

The following week, the Sooners' good fortune of the previous three weeks seemed to desert them. They trailed Nebraska, 14–0, at the half and were lucky that the game was as close as it was. On two occasions, wide-open Cornhusker receivers dropped passes from quarterback Dennis Claridge. In the Oklahoma locker room, Wilkinson criticized the Sooners for their lackluster effort, particularly in the line. He pointed to Carpenter, who sat with his nose bleeding from the punishment he had taken from the Cornhuskers in the first half.

What had gone wrong was clear. On offense, the Sooners had failed to make a critical first down that had cost them a possible touchdown. And on defense, they had failed to control the line of scrimmage and let Nebraska dominate the course of the game. If the Sooners were to win, Wilkinson told them, they would have to stop Nebraska and control the ball in the second half.

In the third quarter, the Sooners did as Wilkinson instructed. They began to dominate the line of scrimmage and scored twice, tying the game at 14–14 just before the end of the quarter. In the fourth quarter, the Sooner defense remained immovable, forcing Nebraska to punt again. The ball, caught by the south wind, sailed long and kept bouncing toward the Sooner end zone. Finally, it rolled dead at the OU 2. Slowly, patiently, the Sooners began to drive. After twenty-two plays, the Sooners got a first down just inside the 2 of the frustrated Cornhuskers.

After two quarterback sneaks by Page, the Sooners were still a yard from the goal line. Page, anticipating a call from Wilkinson, hurried back to the huddle. No messenger came from the sidelines. Wilkinson was going to let Page make the most important call of the game. Page chose to go with speed and courage: Carpenter to the outside. Page took the snap, faked to Lohmann, and flipped a pitchout to Carpenter, who dashed to the corner to score.

The Sooners leaped jubilantly, surrounding Carpenter, his pale, freckled face still bloody from the pounding he had taken. When the final gun sounded five minutes later, Wilkinson leaped in exhilaration and bounded onto the field to greet his players.

"You are a *great* team. You are a *great* team," he shouted again and again.

Jennings walked from the Cornhusker bench perfunctorily toward Wilkinson. They met in the center of the field, not even breaking stride as they shook hands.

"Nice game," Jennings said.

"Thanks," Wilkinson said.

Jennings walked alone toward the Nebraska locker room, his college coaching career at an end after five losing seasons.

The next Saturday, the Sooners beat Oklahoma State, 21–13, to complete a remarkable five-game sweep in the second half of the season—just as Wilkinson had predicted.

With the football season completed, Wilkinson resumed his duties in Washington, trying to develop a widespread youth fitness program. When he returned to Norman, he was discouraged. He told George Cross that people with whom he talked seemed more inclined to talk about the congressional appropriations necessary than to discuss the project itself. They talked about millions of dollars. Wilkinson thought a successful youth fitness program could be accomplished with little federal money. He was appalled at how little attention government bureaucrats paid to saving money in doing their jobs. Frugal by nature and accustomed to operating on a limited athletic budget, Wilkinson was increasingly critical of government agencies that seemed to spend federal funds wantonly. He became emphatic that citizens should demand an end to the waste he saw every time he went to Washington. For the first time, Wilkinson seriously considered the idea of entering politics.

"Who knows? I might switch my registration to Republican and run for the Senate," Wilkinson said to Cross in jest.

1962

As Wilkinson and his assistants prepared for spring practice, they were guardedly optimistic about the 1962 season. The biggest problem, as Wilkinson saw it, was that the Sooners had only two experienced starters. For the rest, they were depending on the promising—but untested—sophomores from the previous year's recruiting class. The two returning starters were both linemen, center Wayne Lee and guard Leon Cross. Lee, a talented linebacker, had become a starter as a sophomore in 1960 because of his defensive play, but he and Gomer Jones had worked hard to make him proficient on offense as well. By the spring of 1962 Jones believed Lee was in the same class as Bob Harrison as an offensive blocker.

Cross, on the other hand, had lost two entire seasons, 1958 and 1959, to injuries. His teammates often teased him about his persistence in the face of those obstacles, calling him "Old Rugged" Cross. However, his experiences had a more serious side. Through redshirting and an injury hardship ruling from the NCAA, his eligibility was extended over six seasons, meaning that by the time he was a senior, there were Sooner players who could say truthfully that Cross had been there when they arrived and was still there after they left.

Wilkinson and his staff were pleased with the development of the previous year's freshman class, especially Jim Grisham, who seemed certain to be the first sophomore to start at fullback since Leon Heath. In all his years at Oklahoma,

Wilkinson had never started the season with a sophomore at quarterback, but Tommy Pannell seemed to be the exception. He could run and throw better than any OU quarterback since Jimmy Harris.

In addition, Ralph Neely offered the prospect of being exceptional, while Glen Condren and John Flynn appeared likely to make significant contributions as sophomores, as did halfbacks Charles Mayhue and Wes Skidgel, who were the two front runners at left halfback. The team would be bigger and faster than 1961, but there were still significant problems. The Sooners had no runner with McClellan's breakaway speed and no capable punter. As far as the backfield was concerned, it looked like 1959 all over again.

Enter Joe Don Looney.

In 1961 Looney had carried Cameron Junior College in Lawton, Oklahoma, to an undefeated season and a victory in the Little Rose Bowl. Word of Looney's ability quickly spread to Norman, and throughout the season, Jay O'Neal (in whose recruiting territory Lawton was located) followed reports of Looney's football prowess. After the season was over, O'Neal went to Lawton to study film of the promising junior college star and to meet Looney in person. The films showed that Looney was blessed with abundant athletic talent—a genetic gift from his father, who had been Davey O'Brien's favorite receiver at TCU. Looney also had magnificent strength, which he had developed himself through hours in the weight room.

To recruit Looney would be a significant break in policy for Wilkinson, who had never accepted a junior college transfer into the Sooner program. Before having O'Neal pursue Looney further, Wilkinson went to Lee and Cross, the Sooner co-captains, to ask their opinion. They understood Wilkinson's concern about embracing a player who had not been molded by Port Robertson. At the same time, they said, Looney's apparent level of ability seemed to make the risk worth taking.

On the surface, Looney seemed to have only two problems. The first, given his natural ability, might be overlooked. That is, O'Neal discovered, Looney had never played organized football before enrolling at Cameron. The product of a broken home, Looney had been forbidden to play football by his mother. His only previous athletic experience had been limited to track.

Looney's second—and more serious—problem was his grades. O'Neal explained to Looney that Wilkinson would accept him, if he could make nineteen hours of B in the spring and summer to graduate from Cameron. If so, there would be a scholarship for him the following fall at OU. Through determined effort, Looney did it.

Because of the recruiting freedom Wilkinson gave his assistants, he never actually saw Looney until two-a-days began in August. On photo day, Wilkinson was standing next to O'Neal when Looney trotted onto the field for the first time. Wilkinson, who after twenty-five years of coaching could recognize great athletic ability instinctively, was shocked.

"Who in the world is that?" he asked. Looney looked like the kind of back OU had needed for three years.

"That," O'Neal told Wilkinson, "is Joe Don Looney."

Looney quickly demonstrated his remarkable athletic ability, but along with it came a decided propensity for independence. Looney would not go to the training room for treatment. He was sometimes late for practice. And he might go days at a time without shaving. Looney was intelligent and pleasant, however, so the coaches accepted his behavior as the price they must pay for having a player that Robertson had not groomed for them. Looney's teammates also came to accept his unusual manner, although his disdain for shaving—and his massive weightlifter's arms—caused the other Sooners to nickname him Bluto, after the villain in Popeye cartoons.

Looney might have been uncomfortable at Oklahoma with its rigid but unwritten code of behavior had it not been for Flynn, who proved to be a perfect running mate for Looney. Flynn did not like to wear shoes and paid little more than casual attention to Wilkinson's training regimen. He would often be in the wrong position on defense, but his natural ability and desire enabled him to recover in time to make a tackle or interception because of his innate sense of where the ball would be.

At the start of two-a-days, Wilkinson and his assistants believed the Sooners would be better than the teams that had preceded them in 1960 and 1961. To be sure, they were inexperienced, but they were talented and unimpressed by supposedly superior manpower. They had beaten the alumni by three touchdowns in the spring game, and such bravado would be necessary against a schedule that included three bowl champions and Notre Dame in the first four games. Realistically, the Sooners appeared to be a year from contending for the Big Eight championship.

Eight days before the opening game, the Sooners' hopes for the new season received a painful blow. In practice, Pannell suffered an ankle injury that would keep him out for the entire season. With barely a week to work, the coaches scrambled to find a successor to Pannell—and to find him fast. They chose Monte Deere, who had played primarily on defense, but had two years' worth of game experience.

In the first game, the Sooners faced Syracuse, which had won the Liberty Bowl the previous season. The Orangemen had lost Heisman Trophy winner Ernie Davis to graduation, but they were similar to the big, rough Syracuse team the Sooners had encountered in the Orange Bowl four years earlier. The primary difference was, they were *bigger* and *rougher*, with All-American end John Mackey and Jim Nance, a 220-pound sophomore fullback.

The two teams played rugged defensive football for most of four quarters, but Syracuse held a 3–0 lead. Late in the game, the Orangemen were driving toward the OU goal and threatening to score a touchdown that would put the game out of reach for the Sooners. On fourth-and-inches at the OU 27, the Orangemen gave the ball to Nance, who started wide and then cut upfield. Johnny Tatum came up fast from his linebacker spot and hit Nance solidly at the knees. The massive Nance had only to fall forward to make the first down, but Paul Lea came up quickly, hit Nance high, and pushed him back. The ball went over to the Sooners with only 2:57 to play.

There was no room for error, no time for wasted plays. If the Sooners were to win, they would have to drive nearly 75 yards against the rugged Syracuse defense. As the Sooners went to the line of scrimmage on first down, Looney paced the sidelines near the Sooner bench.

"Coach, put me in. I'll score a touchdown for us and win the game," Looney said to Wilkinson. On second down, Wilkinson sent Looney in to replace Grisham. On his first carry, Looney picked up 5 yards to get the Sooners a first down at their own 40. After an end run was stopped for no gain, Looney returned to the huddle with his eyes glazed. To Deere, they seemed to be on fire.

"Give me the damn ball. I'm gonna score," Looney said.

Deere, not desiring a fight, called a fullback sweep to the left.

The Syracuse end crashed through and tackled Deere as he pitched to Looney. Looney turned the corner and broke into the Syracuse secondary, where he was soon swarmed by orange-and-blue jerseys. Looney stumbled but did not go down. Miraculously, he emerged from the congestion on his feet and burst into the open field. With his sprinter's speed, it was a foot race to the goal. Looney won the race easily, and with it, the game. With the New York media—including Red Smith—at the game, Looney's 60-yard run made him an instant national celebrity.

Now winners of six straight games, the Sooners played host to Notre Dame. With the wind blowing from the south at twenty-five miles per hour, the Sooners won the toss, and Wilkinson chose to take the wind. Logically, the decision made sense, but the wind became immaterial when the Irish drove the length of the field to score on the inexperienced Sooners. The Sooners proved their mettle, however, when they came back to score on a 58-yard drive.

Choosing to receive the second half kickoff, the Irish drove the length of the field to score again, this time going 89 yards in 19 plays. Six times, the Irish faced third-down situations during the drive, and each time, Irish quarterback Daryle Lamonica found a way to keep the drive alive. The Irish missed the extra point, leaving the Sooners an opportunity for another fourth-quarter comeback.

Taking the ball at the OU 28, the Sooners drove steadily down the field. Hoping to catch the Irish a step slow on defense, Wilkinson put Looney in for Grisham for the first time since early in the second quarter. Looney responded. With Looney carrying seven times for 27 yards, the Sooners drove to a first down at the Notre Dame 3. From there, the Irish defense stiffened, and on fourth down at the 1, Deere made a bad pitch to Grisham, ending the Sooner drive.

Wilkinson and his staff viewed the 13–6 loss to Notre Dame with mixed emotions. Defensively, the Sooners were playing well, but they needed to learn how to score on offense. And Wilkinson was not sure what to do to teach them.

When two-a-days started six weeks earlier, there were one hundred guys out for practice. By the end of two-a-days, there were only sixty-six left. Lance Rentzel was one of them, and he owed it all to a broken hand. Just when he was ready to quit, his hand had been fractured in a scrimmage. After the doctors put Rentzel's hand in a cast, all he had to do was dress in gym shorts and trot around the practice field for four weeks. Now, it was the third week of the season, and the doctors finally removed the cast. Rentzel was ready to play, but he knew he wouldn't. Fifth teamers never play against Texas, especially when the Longhorns are ranked No. 1 in the country.

Rentzel and another sophomore named Ronnie Fletcher, a small quarterback blessed with a powerful arm, knew that Wilkinson regularly jogged around the football field every day after practice. They decided they would try to impress him by practicing a long pass play designated "58-Special." Their stratagem worked. Wilkinson noticed the swift Rentzel and the rifle-armed Fletcher and talked to both of them the next day at practice.

"Lance, you're pretty fast, and I think we're going to put in that special play against Texas to take advantage of it," Wilkinson said.

Rentzel listened as Wilkinson explained how the play would be run. Rentzel would line up at flanker, and Fletcher would line up at the other halfback spot. The quarterback would pitch out to Fletcher, who would throw the ball deep to Rentzel behind the Texas secondary.

"What pattern should I use?" Rentzel asked.

"Use whatever pattern you want," Wilkinson told him. "The important thing is for you to outrun Texas's deep coverage. Fletcher will find you."

In practice that week, the Sooners tried the play several times in practice. It never worked. Still, Wilkinson insisted that he intended to use the play if the situation was right.

"Lance, we don't have room on the team plane for you, but if you can arrange your own transportation to Dallas, there's a chance we may use you," Wilkinson told him.

As a result, Rentzel rode with a friend halfway to Dallas before the friend's car broke down. From there Rentzel hitchhiked the rest of the way and made it to the Cotton Bowl in time to suit up and run down the Cotton Bowl ramp with the rest of the Sooners, still unsure that he would play.

The game, played in eighty-five-degree heat, was a defensive battle. Neither team could mount a drive in the first quarter, but early in the second, Deere pitched wildly to Skidgel, and the Longhorns recovered. Texas made one first down, but then the Sooner defense held. The Longhorns were forced to settle for a 26-yard field goal. Seven minutes later, Deere made another erratic pitchout that rolled into the Sooner end zone, where it was recovered by the Longhorns, putting the Longhorns ahead, 9–0.

With 1:30 remaining in the half and the Sooners at their own 27, Wilkinson looked along the sideline.

"Rentzel. Fletcher." Wilkinson called.

Rentzel walked over to Wilkinson in disbelief, now uncertain he was prepared to play in such a big game.

"Excuse me, Coach. I thought I heard you yell for Fletcher and me," Rentzel said.

"I did. You're going in," Wilkinson said.

Rentzel looked at Fletcher, whose eyes now seemed as large as saucers, and they ran onto the field.

After Deere's ball-handling difficulties, Wilkinson had installed Norman Smith at quarterback. Smith called the Sooners' special pass play, and Rentzel took his assigned spot flanked to the right side. On the snap count, he broke from his stance quickly to get behind the cornerback. Rather than backpedaling, the Longhorn defender turned and ran with Rentzel, keeping with him stride for stride. Finally, Rentzel realized he could never get behind the cornerback and turned. As he did, Fletcher's pass hit him in the chest for a 39-yard gain.

The OU fans cheered wildly. What a genius that Wilkinson is, putting in a trick play with players who aren't even listed in the program!

Trotting back to the huddle, Rentzel looked to the sideline, expecting to see Wilkinson wave him out of the game. He did not.

"Turn it over! Turn it over!" Wilkinson yelled.

Smith called the same play, but to the left side. Rentzel lined up as the flanker on the left side and dashed downfield. This time, Rentzel got behind the secondary, and Fletcher whipped the ball to him. Rentzel caught it at the 2 and fell into the end zone. The Sooners missed the extra point, but headed to the locker room trailing by only 3 points.

In the second half, the respective defenses took over the game. Neither team scored, and Texas won, 9–6. Rentzel was elevated to the third team after his performance, but he would not catch another pass all season.

After the Texas game, Wilkinson heard rumors that Looney was planning to quit school. Sooner players had found Looney packing his bags and asked why he was leaving.

"The grass is growing up around my feet," Looney told them. "I've got to be moving on."

Unable to understand what could be troubling Looney, Wilkinson invited Looney to his house. They sat down in the living room, and Wilkinson came quickly to the point.

"Do you like Norman?" Wilkinson asked him.

"Yes, Coach, I like it very much," Looney said.

"Do you like the University of Oklahoma, Joe Don?"

"Oh, yes, it's the best school I've ever attended."

"Do you like the boys you play with?"

"I sure do, Coach. I've been around with a lot of teams, but these are the best boys I've ever played with."

"Do you like to play football, Joe Don?"

"Yes, sir, I enjoy it more than anything else I've ever done."

"Well, then, Joe Don, why in the world are you talking about leaving?"

Looney's eyes began to bulge with emotion. "I can't stand going to class. I don't have time to get my laundry out."

Wilkinson could not believe what he had heard.

After regaining his composure, Wilkinson got Looney to agree to stay in Norman five more days.

"Then if you want to leave on Sunday, go right ahead. I'm with you," Wilkinson said.

Wilkinson did not claim to be a psychiatrist, but he had studied psychology in college, and he quickly surmised that Looney had psychiatric problems. He was not violent. He was probably harmless to other people, but he seemed to have curtains in his mind. Three months with a good psychiatrist could straighten him out, but that was easier said than done.

So, unfortunately, was finding a way to utilize Looney most effectively. Looney simply could not take defeat of any kind, but Wilkinson could see he was not the super player he appeared to be in the Sunday morning papers, and that made things difficult. The unvarnished truth was that Looney's reputed speed was not football speed. It was track speed. The best way to use him would be to do what Wilkinson did against Syracuse and Notre Dame—wait until the defense was half a step slow, when his exceptional straightaway speed would allow him to do what he did against Syracuse. The problem was that such a plan would cause sportswriters to be critical of him or Looney—or both. That would not bother Wilkinson, but he knew it would damage Looney's tender psyche even further.

When OU met Kansas in the fourth game of the season, KU was slightly favored to win. The Jayhawks had a sound line and a great backfield. Hadl and McClinton were gone, but in their place, the Jayhawks had a phenomenal sophomore halfback named Gale Sayers. Born in Wichita but raised in Omaha, Sayers played tackle football in his neighborhood park with twenty-year-olds when he was still a teenager. By his senior year, Sayers had seventy-five scholarship offers. He looked at the major schools close to home that had a history of playing black football players. Originally, Sayers intended to go to Iowa (where a black player had been on the team in the 1890s) but changed his mind when Iowa head coach Jerry Burns decided he didn't have time to meet with him on his campus visit. In early 1961 Sayers verbally committed to Iowa State, where Jack Trice had starred in the 1920s. After graduation, Sayers changed his commitment to Nebraska. Three months later, he announced that the pressure from the boosters of the Cornhuskers had offended him and chose Kansas, where Homer Floyd (a black fullback who came to KU with Chuck Mather) had been a star.

Once the game began, it was KU's defense rather than Sayers that most impressed Wilkinson. It held the Sooners without a first down in the first quarter as the Jayhawks took an early 7–0 lead. Seeking to solve the Sooners' offensive malaise, Wilkinson tried something new. He inserted Looney at left halfback in the same backfield with Grisham. Before the Kansas game, Looney had been playing fullback, so he and Grisham alternated. In analyzing the first three games of the season, Wilkinson realized that the team's most dependable runners were Grisham and Looney. The Sooners' fast but light halfbacks had been generally ineffective, especially when yards got tough against teams with big defensive lines. The answer seemed to lie in going with the biggest pair of backs ever to play at Oklahoma, but even that did not seem to work. The Sooners had been stopped short of a touchdown late in the first half with both in the game and still trailed 7–0 at the half.

In the Sooner locker room, Wilkinson was disturbed by his players' lack of intensity. He was particularly disappointed in Looney, who never seemed to perform well unless he felt under pressure. Wilkinson grabbed the big running back by the shoulder pads and shook him, hoping to apply enough pressure to awaken the competitive spark in him.

"Joe Don, you're not playing as well as you can," Wilkinson said. "Now, get with it!"

After Wilkinson's challenge, Looney's expression seemed to change. In Looney's eyes, Deere saw the same look he had seen in the huddle against Syracuse.

Early in the second half, OU got the ball at its own 39. On first down, Deere called a halfback trap play to Looney. Looney faked to the outside, then cut back over left guard. The hole was wide open, and Looney raced 61 yards to score. Butch Metcalf's extra point tied the game with 8:48 left in the third quarter.

Late in the quarter, OU began to drive from its 44. Deere threw deep to Flynn, who made a superb catch over his head at the KU 28. Then, Looney and Grisham powered the Sooners to a first down at the KU 6. On first down, Grisham gained 3 over left tackle. On the next play, Deere faked to Grisham and kept the ball around the left end and scored untouched. His touchdown would be the difference in the Sooners' 13–7 victory.

Wilkinson was delighted. For the first time all season, the Sooners had earned a victory. The Syracuse victory he counted as the greatest of good fortune. But the KU win had been earned, and the youthful Sooners—who easily could have been 0–4—stood 2–2. They were developing faster than Wilkinson ever thought they could.

As it had for the 1961 Sooners, Kansas State marked a turning point. Able to perfect their skills against the overmatched Wildcats, the Sooners learned how good they could be. They held the Wildcats to 10 yards rushing and 73 yards in total offense while rushing for 488 themselves. Wilkinson cleared the bench in the 47–0 victory. The following week, Colorado presented the same type of opportunity. Weakened by heavy graduation losses and reeling from the dismissal of Sonny Grandelius over recruiting improprieties, the Buffaloes were 1–5. The night before the Colorado game, Wilkinson spoke to the Sooners.

"The difference between being good and being great, and we are approaching being great, is extra effort. You have to take pride in doing the very best you can on every play," he said. "If each of you will do that, then you'll know that every player on the whole team is doing that, too. And nothing can beat you. You can go as far as you want to go. Nobody can stop you but yourselves. You're Oklahoma, 1962. Nobody else is. It's your team. You can make it as good as you personally want to make it."

The Sooners dominated the Buffaloes the way they had manhandled Kansas State. The defense, particularly against running, was formidable. And Deere, who had completed only six passes for 74 yards previously, enjoyed a record-setting day passing. As good a leader as he was, Deere was far from a picture passer, and the Sooners knew it. They told him his passes floated like dead quail falling out of the sky. Yet Deere, despite his aesthetic shortcomings, experienced a day that statistically exceeded anything Arnold, Crowder, or Harris had achieved. Deere hit five of six passes for 246 yards, throwing touchdown passes of 32 and 83 yards to wingback Virgil Boll and 41 yards to Flynn.

Each week, Sooner fans worried that the Sooners' dream season—so welcome after the trials of 1960 and 1961—could not go on, but the Sooners' success continued based on the improbable combination of precocious sophomores and one unpredictable junior college transfer who happened to be leading the nation in punting. The Sooners defeated Iowa State, 41–0. Then they held Johnny Roland to only 9 yards and beat Missouri, 13–0. They exploded to overpower Nebraska, 34–6, in the game that decided the Big Eight championship. Finally, they gained 610 yards in total offense in dismantling Oklahoma State, 37–6. Throughout the final weeks of the season, the Sooners remained impenetrable on defense and explosive, if not always consistent, on offense. But if Looney faltered, as he did against Missouri and Nebraska, the always reliable Grisham responded with 100-yard games.

For the first time in four years, the Sooners returned to the Orange Bowl. The No. 7–ranked Sooners were pitted against No. 5 Alabama. The Crimson Tide squad, which had finished behind undefeated Ole Miss in the Southeastern Conference, was similar in makeup to the Sooners. Both teams relied on hard-hitting defenses and solid, ball-control offenses. The Sooners were bigger, approximately five pounds heavier per man across the line, and the Alabama backs were size-wise no match for Looney and Grisham. The Sooners, second in the nation to Ohio State in rushing with 265 yards a game, had experienced two separate seasons. During the first four games, the Sooners had ranked ninety-third in the nation in rushing with barely over 200 yards per game, but after Wilkinson shifted Looney to halfback, the Sooners had averaged 471 yards per game over the last six games. No similar reversal in form had taken place in college football in years, if ever.

The greatest differences between the two teams were experience and passing. The Crimson Tide starting team included eight seniors who had played on Alabama's national championship team of 1961, two juniors, and one sophomore. The sophomore was Joe Namath, a quarterback who had broken the Alabama record for passing yardage and tied the record for touchdown passes. In contrast, the Sooners had sophomores in key positions and relied on Deere's incredibly effective—if not artistic—passing. Still, Deere's ability to gain yardage through the air could not be denied. He had hit 60 percent of his passes for 768 yards, thrown nine touchdown passes, and had not been intercepted all season. Three times during the season he had thrown three touchdown passes in a game.

On defense, the Sooners had stopped four great backs. They held KU's Sayers to 23 yards in 9 carries, Iowa State's Dave Hoppman to 23 yards in 16 carries, Roland to 12 yards in 9 carries, and Nebraska's Bill Thornton to 32 yards in 11 carries. Perhaps more important, they ranked third in the nation in defense against scoring. The Crimson Tide had finished the season 9–1, losing only to Georgia Tech, 7–6, and possessed a defense even stingier against scoring than Oklahoma's. Throughout the season, OU had given up 44 points. Alabama 39.

The Tide was also blessed with two exceptional leaders, Namath on offense and senior Lee Roy Jordan on defense. Jordan, a quick, rugged linebacker from Excel, Alabama, was so confident of his ability that he often seemed asleep at his position before a play began, but once the ball was snapped, there was no question he was among the best linebackers in America.

Leaders. Poise. Those were the biggest differences Wilkinson could see in the two teams, but those two factors had Wilkinson concerned. Alabama had proven leaders and a roster of players who had already won a national championship. The Sooners, on the other hand, were dependent on sophomores and a junior college transfer whose performance was sometimes unsteady. Yes, the defense had been great against running plays, but the Sooners had not faced a passer of Namath's caliber all season. On top of that, there was Grisham's injury. During practice the week before the Orange Bowl, Grisham hit a seven-man blocking sled. Unlike sleds at OU, this sled had no springs, and Grisham suffered a separated shoulder. His readiness for the bowl game was still questionable.

Seldom do bowl games generate the anticipation that surrounded the 1963 Orange Bowl, but seldom is there a game where the teams are led by coaches who are regarded as the finest of their generation. The Orange Bowl, matching Wilkinson and Bryant for only the second time in their careers, promised to be a textbook in coaching preparation.

Oklahoma versus Alabama. Wilkinson versus Bryant. To football fans, it seemed a battle of titans, but to the coaches themselves, the game was a contest of friendly rivals. Even if the fans of the two schools were not on speaking terms, Wilkinson and Bryant had become close personal friends since their previous meeting in the 1951 Sugar Bowl. In the activities surrounding the first meeting of their respective teams, Wilkinson had come to know Bryant well. They had been only casually acquainted during World War II, so Wilkinson found for the first time that he and Bryant had much in common, not the least of which was a warm friendship with Red Sanders. Before the war, Sanders had been the head coach at Vanderbilt University. On his staff was a former end from Alabama named Paul Bryant.

With their friendship with Sanders in common, Wilkinson and Bryant grew to trust each other quickly. Each appreciated the skills the other possessed. Kentucky was playing better defense than Oklahoma at the time, while Oklahoma's offense was more advanced than Kentucky's. Both young and ambitious, the two agreed they could benefit by offering each other counsel during the off-season. And since their teams were unlikely to play each frequently, they could be remarkably open in their discussions.

During the summer of 1951, Wilkinson and Bryant took a suite in the Peabody Hotel in Memphis and spent a week talking football. The arrangement was Spartan. Each had a separate bedroom connected to an open living room, where they had a blackboard brought in. Each morning, they would awaken early, go to the coffee shop for breakfast, and adjourn to their room. Then, from midmorning until they broke for dinner, the two lived in a world of football: How do you organize practices? How do you motivate players and the coaching staff? How do you defense a great passer? How do you handle overzealous alumni?

Wilkinson looked forward to his meetings with Bryant, which took place each summer for seven years. When Bryant was at Kentucky, they found Memphis a convenient location. After Bryant became the head coach at Texas A&M, the site moved to Dallas. But the location was unimportant. Through the years, the bond between Wilkinson and Bryant grew stronger, even though they seemed on the surface to have little in common.

Almost three years older than Wilkinson, Bryant was the eleventh of twelve children born to Wilson and Ida Bryant, who worked a small vegetable farm in Moro Bottom, Arkansas. Actually, there was no such town as Moro Bottom. It was just a stretch of bottomland bordering Moro Creek where the Bryants raised turnips, black-eyed peas, and watermelons they sold in nearby Fordyce. With her husband bedridden much of the time, Ida Bryant farmed 260 acres with the help of her children. As a small boy, Paul would awaken at 4 A.M., feed and water the mules, hitch them to the family's wagon, and take the older children to school.

By thirteen, Bryant was virtually full grown and chopping cotton in the fields to help support the family. One evening, he and three friends walked the seven miles to Fordyce to see a movie, which cost a dime. Outside the theater was a sign reading: "One dollar per minute for anyone who'll wrestle the bear." For the young Bryant, it seemed an opportunity to earn money the family could use desperately.

At first, Bryant got the best of the bear. Then, when the bear had reversed their positions and gotten on top, its muzzle came loose. The bear bit Bryant on the ear. Bryant squirmed loose and ran headlong from the stage. He was so shaken by the experience, he bumped into the theater seats, leaving marks on his knees that would last all his life. As a result of his exploit, which immediately became the talk of the town, he was nicknamed "Bear."

The next year, the family moved to Fordyce. One fall day, Bryant happened to be walking by football practice at the high school. The coach, noticing Bryant's size, asked if he wanted to play. Bryant told the coach he did not know how.

"It's easy," the coach told him. "All you do is try to kill the man with the ball."

Bryant took to the game instantly. A week later, he played in his first game for the Fordyce Red Bugs.

Football practice postponed Bryant's daily chores, but he was good at the game, and it provided him relief from his deep-seated feelings of inferiority. Later, Bryant learned he could go to college by playing football. Unfortunately, with no books at his house, Bryant had always been an indifferent student. Through sheer willpower, Bryant persevered and got his diploma. Football became an escape from the poverty he had always known.

Offered a scholarship to attend Alabama, Bryant played for Frank Thomas, a coach little given to innovation but a demanding taskmaster. And Bryant, like Wilkinson, would later develop a coaching style that owed much to his own mentor.

During Bryant's years playing with the Crimson Tide, he would become known as Alabama's *other end* because most of the attention was focused on Bryant's roommate, Don Hutson. Together, they led Alabama to victory in the 1936 Rose Bowl. In 1937, as an assistant coach, Bryant returned to Pasadena with the Crimson Tide and was offered sixty-five dollars a week by a theatrical agent who believed Bryant had a future in motion pictures.

Bryant turned the agent down and spent four years at Alabama before joining Sanders's staff at Vanderbilt. Then, at only twenty-eight, he was invited to interview for the head coaching job at Arkansas. Driving back from Fayetteville to Nashville, Bryant learned of the bombing of Pearl Harbor on his car radio. Patriotic and grateful for an America that had let him rise from the poverty he had known as a boy, Bryant immediately enlisted in the navy.

Like Wilkinson and most full-time coaches then in the navy, Bryant was selected to participate in the navy's Pre-Flight program and coached at North Carolina Pre-Flight. When the war ended, Bryant was released from the service in time to become the head coach at Maryland, which had suffered through a 1–9 season in 1944. With seventeen military players Bryant brought with him, the Terrapins went 6–3 in 1945. But the situation at Maryland became tenuous when the university's president, Dr. Curley Byrd, fired one of Bryant's assistants over Bryant's objections. His authority eroded, Bryant resigned. Three days later, he became the head coach at Kentucky, where he faced another major rebuilding task.

Bryant believed that discipline, firm but fair, was necessary to make a football program successful. So, when a young lineman named Pat James was late for practice one day, Bryant ordered him to remove the cow manure from the field where the team practiced. The next day, when Bryant was late for practice (some say by design), he picked up the shovel, loaded manure onto a cart, and wheeled it off.

Like Wilkinson, Bryant knew that you could not field a good team without good athletes. And also like Wilkinson, he was receptive to anyone who showed he could play the game. On the first day of practice in 1948, a brash young man named Walt Yowarsky showed up wearing a zoot suit and twirling a watch on a gold chain.

"Where's the Bear?" the young man said.

Despite Yowarsky's appearance, Bryant gave him a chance to prove himself. Two years later, Yowarsky would be voted the most valuable player in the 1951 Sugar Bowl.

To both Wilkinson and Bryant, recruiting was one of the least attractive aspects of college football. Both preferred the strategic decision-making and the relationships with their players and members of the coaching staff, but both realized that recruiting was necessary in order to win. "Hell, Bud, you can't make chicken salad without the chickens," Bryant would frequently say to Wilkinson.

Both competitive, they mastered different styles. Wilkinson smooth and urbane. Bryant straightforward and direct. But Bryant was anything but simple. Wilkinson received great credit for his study of psychology, but it was Bryant who arranged the furniture in his office so that the couch for visitors was lower than his desk.

When Bryant first arrived at Kentucky, he had to try everything to convince recruits that Kentucky could be a winner. One of the players he pursued seriously was a big tackle named Bob Gain. Gain attended a Catholic high school in Chicago and was receiving pressure from family and friends to enroll at Notre Dame. Bryant hired an actor and dispatched him—dressed as a priest—to Gain's home with but one message to deliver: "My son, I want you to know the Church does not care whether you go to Notre Dame or Kentucky." Gain went to Kentucky.

Wilkinson heard all those stories about his friend. And he heard the not-so-flattering stories of Bryant's first year at Texas A&M, when he took a weak, poorly disciplined squad to Junction, Texas, and drove them until they dropped. Those who could take it stayed to become the nucleus of Bryant's rebuilt Aggie teams. Those who could not were of no interest to Bryant. "Be good or be gone," Bryant would tell his players coldly.

The "Junction stories" were circulated widely at the time of the last summer meeting between Wilkinson and Bryant in Dallas. Wilkinson believed those stories were spread by those without the physical and mental toughness to make Bryant's team—or those who did not understand that one of the virtues of football was its molding of courage.

Wilkinson understood that discipline was the primary requirement to achieve success in any endeavor, even football. He had enough confidence in his friend to believe Bryant did merely what was necessary to achieve discipline—in a way that was natural for him. Discipline was essential to the success of any football program, Wilkinson believed. But how to achieve it was always different from coach to coach. Michigan State's Duffy Daugherty, another of Wilkinson's closest friends, did it through humor. Bryant through intimidation. Either way, it has to spring from within.

If Bryant was so intimidating in staff meetings that he frightened his own assistants, so be it. If he could get the attention of a young, cocky Joe Namath by lifting him off the ground by his face mask, so be it. That was merely Bryant, and Wilkinson had confidence in his integrity, his motives, and his genuine concern for the young men he coached.

What was right for Bryant was not right for Wilkinson, and he left it at that. He was certain that Bryant's gruff, fearsome exterior was at least partially the product of Bryant's harsh childhood and the demands of rebuilding three football programs. Life had spared Wilkinson both, and he was grateful.

After Bryant became the head coach at Alabama, their yearly retreats ceased, but united by their love for football, the son of a Minneapolis mortgage banker and the son of an Arkansas dirt farmer remained lifelong friends.

In the years that followed, the two would visit when they could. Once, Wilkinson came to Alabama to speak at Bryant's spring clinic for high school coaches. At the clinic, Wilkinson turned the attention of his audience from the Xs and Os that seemed to mesmerize some members of the coaching fraternity and talked about the indispensability of discipline, conditioning, and spirit. They were, Wilkinson told them, the factors that decided the outcome of a closely fought contest.

When Wilkinson finished his lecture, Bryant stormed up toward the stage. "Bud, why in the hell did you tell them that?" Bryant said angrily. "I didn't want them to know that stuff!"

Bryant, who forbade profanity by members of his coaching staff yet paid his share of quarters into the "kitty" established for that purpose, was a man of immense appetites. Cigarettes. Scotch. Games of chance. He loved them all, but he was careful to enjoy them discreetly so he would not influence young people—or let his mother find out.

At a coaches convention in Las Vegas, Wilkinson and Bryant once shared a suite. Early one morning, Bryant was returning to his room after shooting dice throughout the night, a timetable he often followed to ensure privacy. Wilkinson had just arisen.

"Pablo, look at your ankles!" Wilkinson said.

After a night of standing at the dice tables, Bryant's ankles were swollen to twice their normal size. Immediately, they got Bryant an appointment with a doctor, who diagnosed the circulatory ailment that would eventually cause Bryant's death.

Bryant would achieve his greatest coaching triumphs during the succeeding two decades, in part because his love of football would keep him going when nothing else could.

"Without football, I'd be dead in a week," Bryant would say, which was, of course, an exaggeration.

Without football, Bryant would last four weeks.

In the locker room, Wilkinson stood in shirt sleeves addressing the Sooner players in an effort to bolster their confidence.

"You have to know your enemy to defeat him. Here's Alabama. They aim to beat you by making no errors—and I don't think they'll make any. By out-toughing you. And by out-maneuvering you. We have more good football players. They have a few very fine, dedicated ones, but we should be smarter, more dedicated, and more confident. I know you can out-tough them and beat them."

Wilkinson surveyed his players to be sure they were following what he was saying.

"Defense," he continued. "They haven't thrown a screen pass all year, so you can be sure that the first thing they'll do in the game is throw one. The key is if their quarterback fades farther than 5 yards. If you'll keep them from hitting the home run play, a long run or getting a receiver behind you, then I honestly don't think they can score on you. I don't think they can move on you. We have to protect our punters. They think they can block it on you.

"Alabama bases its offense on the short pass. And like every team that does, they'll hit some. If they hit the first three, don't freeze. Namath is a great passer in every respect but one—he throws the interception. If he throws thirty-six passes, we'll intercept one in five if we do three things—rush him hard, hold up their receivers, and cover them when they throw. I know we can get to him if we'll just put the pressure on him.

"They are sure to quick kick if they have long yardage on second down. They never do it on third down. If they are behind their 30 with second-and-nine, they'll do it. We'll alternate two pass defenses, one of them with four deep backs. We haven't used four men back this year. They may expect it. Our linebacker is the man who can nail Namath. The biggest key to their offense is when he rolls out left or right. If he does, you can be pretty sure it's going to be a pass.

"You have to attack on every play. Attack like you lead by three and they are on your one with ten seconds left. You know how you'd do it then. You will need that attitude on every play."

As one o'clock approached, the Sooners were ready, but President Kennedy, late in arriving for the game, had delayed the entire timing of the Orange Bowl.

Finally, only a few minutes before the game was scheduled to start, Wilkinson entered the locker room escorting the president.

"I wanted to see if my physical fitness man could keep his own men in shape," Kennedy joked amiably.

The president spotted Larry Vermillion, who had a slight paunch, and patted Vermillion on the stomach.

"Is this man okay?" Kennedy asked with a smile.

The Sooners roared with laughter.

Then he smiled at Vermillion.

"Good luck," he said.

The consummate politician, Kennedy started going down the line of Sooners, shaking hands with each player and asking where he was from.

At last, Wilkinson felt compelled to break in.

"Pardon me, Mr. President, I don't think there's time for that," he said.

When the game finally started, Alabama won the toss, chose to receive, and drove into OU territory before Melvin Sandersfeld skidded headfirst across the turf to intercept Namath's first pass. Alabama countered by holding OU on three straight plays, as Jordan personally took control of the Crimson Tide defense. Looney punted 49 yards, but Cotton Clark broke free to return the kick 19 yards to the Alabama 39.

Quickly, Namath moved Alabama to three first downs, mixing running plays with short passes. At the OU 25, Namath sent split end Richard Williamson on a Z-pattern. Williamson got behind Mayhue, and Namath hit him with a touchdown pass.

Coming back, the Sooners ran a three-play series in which they did not huddle. Grisham got 3 over right tackle. Then he burst through the left side for 24 yards for a first down at the Bama 36. As Alabama went into its defensive huddle, the Sooners got back over the ball for the next play. Expecting to catch the Tide unprepared, Wilkinson had inserted the rifle-armed Fletcher at halfback. The Alabama defenders crowded the line of scrimmage waiting for Grisham or Looney. The ball was snapped. Allen Bumgardner slipped behind the Alabama secondary as Deere pitched to Fletcher, who threw long for Bumgardner. He caught the ball at full stride along the sideline before being caught from behind at the Alabama 6.

From the 6, Deere gave the ball to Grisham. Normally, Grisham kept a solid grip on the ball, but his injury from the week before had required trainer Ken Rawlinson to tape Grisham's shoulder and arm thoroughly. Grisham found that he could not raise his arm very high, and he had little strength to hold the ball. When the Alabama defense met Grisham at the line of scrimmage, one player managed to put his helmet into the ball. It popped into the air, and the Crimson Tide recovered.

Moments later, OU threatened again when the Crimson Tide fumbled and the Sooners recovered at the Bama 31. Grisham carried for 4 yards and then for 2. Jordan, ranging from sideline to sideline, made both tackles. Facing third-and-5, Deere gave the ball to the redoubtable Grisham again. Grisham plowed over left tackle and then ran over Jordan for 5 yards and a first down. Two plays later, Grisham gained 10 more yards over Jordan. Grisham's forward motion was stopped, but he was sliding laterally. He heard a whistle and dropped the ball to go back to the huddle. An Alabama player fell on the ball immediately, and the referee signaled first down for Alabama.

"What about the whistle!" Grisham complained. But the officials would not listen. Another OU drive had been lost.

In the second quarter, a 45-yard punt by Clark pinned the Sooners inside their 10. When Looney was forced to punt the ball back, Alabama returned the kick 13 yards to the OU 34. Namath hit Williamson again for 20 yards to the OU 14. Two plays later, Clark circled the Oklahoma flank to score.

Late in the half, Looney punted high and long from midfield. The Alabama safety waved for a fair catch and then let the ball go, expecting it to sail into the end zone. But it bounced short, and Flynn raced in to down at the Alabama 1. The Sooners had at last gained a field position advantage, but time ran out before they could take advantage of it.

The two defenses took control in the second half, keeping Alabama comfortably ahead. Trailing 17–0 late in the game, the Sooners twice drove inside the Crimson Tide 20, but Deere was thrown for a loss on fourth down on the first penetration, and Looney was stopped short on another fourth-down play with only seconds left in the game.

When the final gun sounded, Wilkinson hurried to the center of the field to congratulate Bryant.

"Your team played great defense, especially when we were in scoring position," Wilkinson said.

"Sure," Bryant said matter-of-factly. "They didn't have to worry about you throwing on us. We could jam you up."

"How did you know that?" Wilkinson asked, stopped short by Bryant's comment.

"I remember one summer you told me that no team could stop you if you had a first down inside the five," Bryant said. "I figured that meant you'd run and dare us to stop you."

After the game, Wilkinson stood in the quiet of the dressing room. As he had known all along, Alabama had a better team. Their line, though smaller than Oklahoma's, was quicker. And Jordan, protected by a defensive scheme that shielded him from Sooner blockers, had made thirty-one tackles and played as good a game as any linebacker Wilkinson had ever seen. Pablo had done a tremendous job.

That night at the Orange Bowl party, the Sooner players were introduced one at a time. When Grisham was introduced, Bryant left his place with the Alabama players, walked across the stage, and shook the young Sooner's hand. Like Wilkinson, Bryant knew a football player when he saw one.

1963

On New Year's Day of 1963, Robert S. Kerr, the uncrowned king of the United States Senate, died. An ambitious country lawyer, Kerr parlayed his rural Oklahoma background into one of the most powerful positions in the world. Partly because he shared a southwestern heritage with Senate Majority Leader Lyndon Johnson and Speaker of the House Sam Rayburn, Kerr gave Oklahoma influence in the Senate far beyond the state's political base.

In a state populated with self-styled "yellow dog Democrats" ("I'd sooner vote for a yellow dog than a Republican," such voters would say), Kerr was the leader of a political machine that held a virtual monopoly on all important state offices until 1962, when Henry Bellmon, a rancher and state senator from Billings, did the impossible. He was elected governor, defeating brash, red-haired J. Howard Edmondson, who had swept to office in 1958 on the strength of a reform-oriented "Prairie Fire" campaign. Edmondson, only thirty-six, did what he set out to accomplish and ended prohibition in Oklahoma. It was a victory that surprised many, especially those who believed with Will Rogers that Oklahomans would vote dry as long as they could stagger to the polls. As a result, Edmondson was popular in the larger cities, but he was unpopular in rural Oklahoma—precisely where Wilkinson had found many of his greatest players and where he, unlike Edmondson, was practically revered.

After Kerr's death, a new senator had to be appointed, and time was short. In two weeks, Bellmon was to take office. Edmondson quickly arranged with

Lieutenant Governor George Nigh, also a Democrat, to be named to the Senate seat. The appointment would be good for nearly two years, until Oklahoma law required the state's voters to select a new senator at the next regularly scheduled general election.

Wilkinson's growing fascination with politics and his desire to make a contribution on a larger scale than football were now free to bear fruit. The unassailable Kerr was now gone. Like many Oklahomans with Republican leanings, Wilkinson had registered as a Democrat to be able to cast a vote in Democratic primaries, where the real election of officeholders took place. A change of voter registration would be required, but Wilkinson's path was now clear, if he chose to take it.

As he spent the summer fulfilling his youth fitness responsibilities, Wilkinson considered his possibilities. Running for the Senate as a political newcomer had its risks, but Wilkinson—and others around him—believed he had the name recognition to be successful, if he chose to run. By the end of the summer, Wilkinson had not decided for sure what he intended to do, but he was back in Norman on schedule eager to develop the potential of his Sooners.

Two weeks before the start of fall practice, Jay O'Neal received a long-distance call from Joe Don Looney.

"Is it all right if I come back weighing 227?" he asked.

In the spring, Wilkinson and his staff had given Looney a target weight of 205, so O'Neal was not pleased. Looney explained he had worked all summer on a weight program prescribed by the trainer at LSU. (Formalized weight training for football was first instituted at LSU in 1958. At that time, there was no weight training program at Oklahoma because Wilkinson believed it made players muscle bound and slowed down their coordination and agility. That was one of the reasons Wilkinson liked to recruit farm boys and others who had developed their strength through manual labor.)

"At 227, you'll be slower," O'Neal said.

"No, no," Looney said, "I'm faster than ever."

When the Sooners arrived for two-a-days, Wilkinson and his assistants ran the Sooners through the standard conditioning drills. It quickly became apparent that Looney was telling the truth. He was slimmer, faster, and punting even better than he had the year before. Imagine! An *improved* Joe Don Looney!

During the Sooners' final scrimmage a week before the season opener with Clemson, Wilkinson was disappointed. The Sooners, though blessed with talent approaching that of the national championship teams in 1955 and 1956, were not performing like their predecessors. The Sooners, mindful of their physical abilities and spoiled by their success the year before, lacked concentration and intensity. They also lacked an experienced quarterback, and Wilkinson knew he had to find the leader who could move the team consistently.

In the first half against Clemson, the Sooners played just as they had practiced. They lost three fumbles and gave up two touchdowns to the determined Tigers in the humid, ninety-degree heat. Only a 26-yard touchdown run by Jim Grisham just before halftime narrowed the Clemson lead to 14–7. In the second half, the Sooners improved dramatically. On their first possession of the half, quarterback Mike Ringer—the first sophomore quarterback ever to start the season for a Wilkinson team—called the option play to the left. Just as he was hit by Clemson's defensive end, Ringer pitched to Lance Rentzel. Rentzel dashed down the sideline, then cut back to score.

The 49-yard run established the tone of the second half and gave the Sooners the momentum they had been missing. Equally important in the withering heat, the Sooners' third-team line was able to play head-to-head with the Clemson starters. With the additional rest the three-team rotation provided, OU's starters and alternates outscored the Tigers, 24–0, in the second half to maintain the Sooners' top ten status. The Sooners' victory also set up a battle with USC, the defending national champions, who were again ranked No. 1.

The Trojans were coached by John McKay, an assistant at Oregon when OU played the Webfoots in 1959 and a renegade among college coaches in his time. He believed in passing. He astutely found that through an attack based on running and short passes, the Trojans could control the ball as effectively as a team like the Sooners that relied on a running attack. In fact, McKay found that his team could make *more* yards per play—and control the ball more effectively—passing rather than running. So effective was the Trojans' extraordinary attack that they won the national championship the year before, only McKay's third as a head coach.

The Trojan offense ran from several variations of the T formation, including the I formation (which was popularized in the 1950s by Tom Nugent, who coached at Virginia Military Institute and Maryland). The I formation positioned the fullback and a tailback directly behind the quarterback. The remaining halfback was stationed to either side as a blocker or pass receiver, much as in the Wing T the Sooners were using with increasing frequency.

The Trojans' I formation relied on two highly skilled players to make the offense go. One was the tailback, a halfback who combined speed and power and could, from his position behind the quarterback, go to the right or the left with equal facility. The other key player was the quarterback, who had to be an accomplished passer and capable runner. The USC passing attack was of considerable concern to Wilkinson, since two of Oklahoma's three deep backs from the 1962 season were gone, and the secondary was woefully inexperienced.

The Trojans had beaten Wisconsin, 42–37, in a frantic Rose Bowl and faced the Sooners with many of the same players. Starting tailback Willie Brown possessed 9.6 speed in the one-hundred-yard dash, and reserve sophomore Mike Garrett was only a step slower. Pete Beathard—who threw four touchdown passes against Wisconsin—returned at quarterback. Also back was Beathard's favorite receiver, Hal Bedsole (who at six-foot-five stood a half foot taller than the Sooners' defensive ace, Charlie Mayhue).

The day after the victory over Clemson, the OU players gathered in the squad meeting room on the second floor of Jeff House. Wilkinson showed movies of the game the day before and voiced his concern over the Sooners' lack of speed and consistency. They had beaten Clemson solidly, but had earned only eight first downs. Much better effort would be needed against USC, he told the Sooners.

Bobby Drake Keith, who had joined the OU staff from Alabama, scouted the Trojans against Colorado. USC was an exception among college teams, Keith explained. The Trojans could pass or run with equal effectiveness. The key was Beathard, who was deadly on a play the Trojans called the "sprint out pass," which forced the defense to react much more quickly than the standard T-formation rollout. To stop Beathard, the Sooners would have to cover the field laterally all the way to the sideline, which meant considerably more running than they were accustomed to. The Trojans also used a draw play, a running play seldom used in college, in which Beathard would drop back as if to pass and then hand the ball to the tailback, who would cut back against the grain.

Keith identified Bedsole as an additional threat. He ran sideline pass patterns so well that defenders often overplayed to the outside. When they did, Bedsole would break upfield past them for a long gain. To counter that, O'Neal had developed a special pass defense for the Trojans. From films, he saw that Brown ran the deep routes and Bedsole ran the short ones (mostly hook and square-out sideline patterns), so the Sooner secondary would play loose on Brown and tight on Bedsole, bumping him relentlessly as he tried to run his patterns.

On Monday, the Sooners reported in sweat suits for practice, which was limited primarily to calisthenics and running to relieve the soreness the steam room had not eased. After thirty minutes, the players lined up for conditioning drills, which they called "Gomer Sprints." Jones, as always, insisted that the Sooners run them his way. He would have the players sprint 10 yards, then sprint back the same distance without resting. Then he would lengthen the distance to 15 yards. Then 20. Then 50. Then 100.

Monday night, the team assembled again, and the coaches passed out a ten-page scouting report on Southern Cal. Also in the briefing folder were thirty plays Wilkinson expected to use against USC, along with detailed diagrams of USC's three most common defenses. For the game, which would be nationally televised, Wilkinson developed ten new plays, including a couple of reverses and a forward pass off a reverse. Wilkinson knew that all the new plays would not be used, but he did not tell the players which ones so they would work equally hard to perfect all of them. Wilkinson drew the plays on the blackboard and reviewed the blocking assignments. The players dutifully copied the plays into their notebooks.

In terms of talent, Wilkinson could see that the Sooners were clearly outmanned. OU's strategy would be to control the ball on the ground, keeping it away from USC's high-powered offense. Then, when the Trojans were drawn in tight to stop the Sooners' bread-and-butter running game, the Sooners would spring a reverse.

"Study these plays until you know your assignments without thinking," Wilkinson told the Sooners.

On Tuesday afternoon, Wilkinson drew the three defenses the Sooners would use against USC, then sent his players out for the hardest practice of the week. At this stage of the season, the Sooners never scrimmaged. Practices might have been physically draining, but they consisted of drills and running plays against blocking dummies. There was little, if any, contact. At Minnesota, Bernie Bierman had followed such a regimen, which was unusual for the time. Most teams practiced by scrimmaging. As a result, Bierman's teams, neither worn nor suffering from midweek injuries, were at full strength on Saturdays. Often, they won games they were not expected to win because of it.

Bierman's wisdom was not lost on Wilkinson. He knew that most teams were "over practiced" and took steps to prevent that from happening to the Sooners. "No team ever lost because it was too fresh," Wilkinson would tell his assistants.

By Wednesday afternoon, the players had picked up their individual defensive assignment sheets. On the sheets were drawn the three basic defenses the Sooners would use. Guards received a special sheet describing their assignments on each USC play or any special situation, such as an unbalanced line or motion. At 3:30 practice began and lasted ninety minutes. For a while, the Sooners practiced Wilkinson's new plays against dummies. Then, the freshmen and reserves ran USC's plays, with centers John Garrett and Carl McAdams calling defensive signals to see how the Sooner defense reacted. Then, the starters and alternates ran offensive plays against the freshmen holding dummies 5 yards off the line of scrimmage. This practice, devised years before by Jones, prevented a chronic problem with linemen. Often, after they had made contact with the defense, they would go to their knees and lose their footing. With the dummies 5 yards away, Sooner linemen could not let up after a few steps. They learned to fire out at full speed.

During most weeks, Thursday practices called for one hour of work on the kicking game—punts, kickoffs, conversions, field goals, and kick coverage and returns—and final refinement of goal line defenses and new plays. Not this week. Wilkinson read in the newspaper about record-breaking 110-degree temperatures in Los Angeles, the hottest the city had experienced in one hundred years. He decided it would be best to fly to Los Angeles on Thursday morning and practice in the heat on Thursday afternoon. It had been ninety and humid for the Clemson game, and now the Sooners were facing the possibility of playing in weather twenty degrees hotter.

The Sooners' chartered DC-6 arrived in Los Angeles about noon. Instead of going to the Rose Bowl, where OU was supposed to work out, Wilkinson called a 3 P.M. practice on the lawn at the hotel so that the Sooners could feel the afternoon heat. Surprisingly, the low humidity, caused by the wind blowing off the desert, meant the weather did not seem as hot as in Norman. McKay, on the other hand, chose to have USC practice at night. In fact, he wanted the game itself postponed six hours and played at night to avoid the heat. But the Sooners were more accustomed to extreme heat than the Trojans, and Wilkinson saw a day game as being to the Sooners' advantage.

That evening, the Sooners met to watch film of the 1962 USC-Navy game. The Sooners began to feel their defense might be able to contain Beathard and company and that the USC defense might not be good enough to stop them. The inside running game with Grisham and Looney appeared particularly lethal.

Friday morning, Wilkinson assembled the Sooners in a large meeting room in the hotel to rehearse the offensive and defensive alignments while sitting in chairs. Wilkinson was determined that the Sooners would not lose the spring in their legs.

"Don't even stand around in the lobby," Wilkinson told the Sooners. "Save your legs for Saturday."

At Jones's instruction, players on the third team put their chairs in a formation like the Trojan offense. The first and second teams took turns sitting opposite them in OU's defensive formations. Jones would then call the defense, and the players would point to the holes they were to cover or the direction they would stunt. They also practiced a new signal Wilkinson and Jones had devised for the game. As soon as the Sooner middle guard saw the Trojan tailback or wingback go in motion, he would yell "motion right" or "motion left," and the line was to stunt in that direction.

After the chairs were rearranged, the third team assumed the role of the USC defense. The first and second teams took turns assuming the Sooners' offensive formations. When Wilkinson called a play, the Sooners were to point to the man they were to block.

After more than fifteen years, the lesson Wilkinson learned from Henry Iba had not lost its immediacy. Through repetition, he and his assistants would ingrain in the Sooners automatic reactions that would not fail them under game conditions on Saturday. Wilkinson knew the game could be won if each player concentrated on defeating the man opposite him. If every Sooner could accomplish that task, the result would be victory for the team.

In the afternoon, the Sooners worked out at the Coliseum. Wearing shorts and T-shirts, the Sooners loosened up and ran offensive plays the length of the field twice. After twenty minutes, they retired to the Coliseum's air-cooled dressing rooms. The Sooners went back to the hotel to sleep for two hours before a team meeting at 5:30 during which Wilkinson endeavored to get the Sooners prepared for the game the next day.

"Once when Ben Hogan was at a banquet at a major golf tournament, he sat in his chair paying no attention to the other people there," Wilkinson said. "About that time, someone asked Hogan why he was such a successful golfer. Here's what Hogan said:

'We're all at the banquet now, but tomorrow we'll all start playing in the tournament. I'm already in the tournament. I've been sitting here at the table playing the course in my mind. I've played it—every hole—three different times in my mind.'"

Wilkinson paused for the meaning of Hogan's statement to sink in.

"You can't just go out there on Saturday and play a football game," Wilkinson said. "You have to think about the game all week, what you're going to do in every given situation. You've got to play the game in your own mind."

Wilkinson knew there is little a coach can do on game day to prepare his team to win. In fact, it is possible that anything new or different a coach might do would hurt his team more than help it. As a result, Wilkinson made sure that whatever he said to his team would reinforce what they had already heard before. He knew there was comfort in familiar routines.

Still, Wilkinson saw one beneficial change that could be made in the Sooners' pregame routine. He saw no need for the Sooners to go out into one-hundred-degree heat and warm up in full uniform. It served no purpose. As a result, the Sooners went onto the floor of the Coliseum to loosen up without shoulder pads or helmets. Then, the Trojans came out in their dark red, long-sleeved game jerseys. After watching the Trojans warm up in full uniform, the Sooners felt cool by comparison—an impression Wilkinson hoped was not lost on the sweating Trojans.

Back in the Sooner dressing room, the Sooners sat on benches and practiced snap counts. Each quarterback called two plays, and the linemen clapped hands together at the instant they would charge. Repetition and discipline, Wilkinson knew, could make up for a lot in a close game.

"Don't fumble," Wilkinson told the Sooners before they took the field. "Try to intercept some of their passes and block their punts. And don't let them intercept our passes or block our kicks."

At game time, the temperature on the floor of the Coliseum was 115 degrees, and special wicker shades had been installed over both benches to provide the players some respite from the scorching sun. Rawlinson brought out a milk can of salt water, which he could dip out with paper cups to give to the Sooners, and he instructed the trainers to put ice packs on players' necks to keep their body temperatures down. This contest, Wilkinson knew, could become a game of survival.

The Trojans received the opening kickoff, but could not move the ball and punted to the Sooners. The Sooners' Virgil Boll mishandled the kick, and OU was forced to start at its own 2. Page and the alternates drove the Sooners 34 yards before he fumbled, giving the Trojans excellent field position. On USC's first play, the Trojans fumbled, and the Sooners recovered.

Tenaciously, the Sooners began to march toward the Trojan goal. At the USC 40, the Sooners ran a double reverse to Larry Shields, who swung around right end for 20 yards. Unfortunately, the gain was nullified by a holding penalty, but Wilkinson was now certain the Trojans were indeed vulnerable to reverses. The Sooners would be using every misdirection play they had.

Keeping the Trojans off balance, Sooners got a first down when John Porterfield picked up 9 on an end-around option play. Three plays later, the Sooners faced third-and-10 at the USC 19. The Sooners' call was daring, a naked reverse to Looney to the wide side of the field, but the Trojans fell for it. When Looney got the ball, he cut up inside a huge hole with only Ringer in front of him. The USC safety stood motionless at the goal line waiting for the thundering Looney.

Looney gave him a hip fake, the Trojan defender went the wrong way, and Looney scored untouched.

Undaunted, USC came back and scored on a 67-yard drive capped by a short plunge by fullback Ernie Pye. The Trojans missed the extra point when the center snap was wild, leaving OU ahead, 7–6.

Wilkinson knew the Sooners could not go straight ahead against USC. The Trojans simply had superior manpower. To overcome it, the Sooners continued to run more razzle-dazzle plays than a Wilkinson team had ever used. Boll completed a double reverse pass to Looney for 18 yards, and a second end-around by Porterfield was followed by a third only two plays later. A fourth-down gamble at the USC 24 paid off as Rentzel completed a halfback pass to Porterfield for 10 yards to the USC 14. Three plays later, Ringer faked a handoff to Grisham and followed him through the hole. Ringer fell into the end zone for Oklahoma's second score.

Late in the half, the Sooners drove to the USC 7 with two minutes to play. After a wild pitchout, an incomplete pass, a 15-yard penalty, and a 1-yard loss trying to pass, the Sooners faced fourth-and-goal from the 27. George Jarman came onto the field to try a 43-yard field goal, the longest of his life, and he drilled the kick through the uprights. The upstart Sooners now led the defending national champions, 17–6.

The Sooners took the second half kickoff and continued to control the ball and the tempo of the game. In sixteen plays, they drove 79 yards to the Trojan 1. There, the Sooners tried one more piece of deception. As the Sooners took their stances, one Sooner halfback stood up and took a step backward (which a player in the backfield can do).

"Hold it!" he yelled.

The center snapped the ball, and Page handed off to Grisham, who powered into the end zone. Unfortunately, a Sooner lineman had also moved during the play, and the Sooners' touchdown was nullified. The illegal motion penalty against the Sooners moved the ball back to the USC 6. Jarman tried another field goal, but Bedsole blocked it to stave off the Sooner threat.

With eight minutes left in the game, the Trojans scored again but missed a 2-point conversion. On the ensuing kickoff, Looney turned the game's momentum back in favor of the Sooners. He took the kick at the OU 3 and sprinted back 50 yards to the USC 47. The Sooners drove to the USC 25 before fumbling, but the OU defense remained overwhelming. Three times Beathard tried to throw, but each time, a Sooner defender broke up the play. The Sooners took the ball at the USC 24.

Needing to maintain possession for the final two minutes, the Sooners stayed on the ground for three plays but gained nothing. On fourth down, Jarman came onto the field, and the Sooners lined up for a field goal that would put OU ahead, 20–12. Ringer took the snap from center, but then he rose to his feet and rolled to his right. Damon Bame, the Trojans' All-American linebacker, broke through the Sooner line and grabbed for Ringer, but Ringer outran Bame to the corner and threw on the run to McCurdy. The pass was low, and the Trojans' Garrett rushed in to knock it away. Instead, Garrett tipped it up into the air. McCurdy lunged forward, grabbing it with one hand, for a first down.

Victory belonged to the Sooners!

That night, the five thousand Oklahomans who came to Los Angeles for the game could be found at almost all the area's famous watering holes, singing "Boomer Sooner" repeatedly, as they had since Thursday night. The joy was overwhelming because they had seen—and the national TV audience had seen—that Wilkinson and the Sooners were back. Most could not have imagined the *lifetime* of football knowledge Wilkinson brought to bear on the Trojans—the timing of workouts, the understanding of the importance of fresh legs, the courage to send the Sooners forth with a staggering assortment of reverses and misdirection plays that were merely a flashy version of the Sooners' traditional ball-control offense.

In talking to sportswriters, Wilkinson was diplomatic and said complimentary things about the defeated Trojans. McKay returned the compliment. "They block and tackle. That's what they do best."

Looney was more succinct. "This was no upset," he said.

Wilkinson's strategy had worked. The Sooners had controlled the ball, running ninety-seven plays to USC's fifty-one. And the Sooner secondary, so questionable at the outset of the season, limited Beathard and the Trojans to a mere 112 yards passing. Using its punishing pass defense, the Sooners did not allow Bedsole to catch a single pass, bumping him unceasingly so that he dropped three passes. Throughout the rest of his college career, no team would intimidate Bedsole like the Sooners.

The following Monday, the Sooners were voted the No. 1 team in America. Wilkinson had done what he vowed to do. The Sooners were on top again.

Yet Wilkinson could see the Sooners were not a great team. If one looked closely, they were not fast, nor were they quick enough in the line. But perhaps most serious, they did not burn with the desire for greatness that Wilkinson's national championship teams had possessed. Wilkinson believed he would know the measure of his team in two weeks, when the Sooners played Texas.

The greatest problem now facing Wilkinson was the loss of Ringer, who had injured his elbow before the USC game when he accidentally stuck it into a fan while studying. The injury did not bother Ringer against the Trojans, but it soon became inflamed and required surgery. He would never be the same. Neither would the Sooners.

In addition, Looney was becoming more uncontrollable than ever. From studying game films, Wilkinson knew that Looney's so-called "great" plays—other than the run against Syracuse—always happened because the rest of the Sooners did their jobs correctly. Looney was simply the beneficiary of their effort. In fact, Wilkinson did not particularly want Looney back for the 1963 season. Looney's ability to contribute on a consistent basis was questionable, and his notoriety diverted attention from Sooners who executed their assignments unfailingly. More important, Looney's attitude was potentially disruptive.

In addition, his eccentric behavior of the year before was becoming more extreme. Unknown to Wilkinson and the coaching staff, Looney kept a submachine gun in his room. When a teammate questioned him why, Looney seemed surprised anyone would notice.

"Doesn't everybody?" Looney said quizzically.

At first, Looney worked hard in two-a-days, but finally his unwillingness to go full speed all the time caused problems. Criticized by Johnny Tatum, now a graduate assistant, Looney lost his temper. A brief shouting and shoving match ensued. The incident, trivial as it was considering the emotion and intensity associated with two-a-days, seemed to take on greater significance because it involved Looney.

Soon, Looney lapsed into the behavior patterns he had exhibited at times in 1962. In drills, he would perform magnificently the first time, but would grouse like a bored child if he were asked to repeat them. On some days, he would even complain that his legs were tired and would refuse to practice at all. Early in the season, Wilkinson wanted to dismiss Looney and Flynn, who only compounded each other's recalcitrant tendencies. But he left the matter to a squad vote, and the Sooners chose to put up with the pair, if only because Flynn never let his lifestyle interfere with superior play on Saturdays.

Against the Sooners, Texas was magnificent. The Longhorns took the opening kickoff and drove 68 yards in thirteen plays to score on a fourth-down play from the OU 2. In the second quarter, they scored again on a 12-yard run and increased their lead with a touchdown in the third quarter, when Rentzel fumbled a pitchout and the Longhorns recovered at the OU 18. Seven plays later, in a crucial fourth-down situation, Texas wingback Phil Harris outran the Sooners' wide coverage to the corner of the end zone. The Sooners finally completed a 62-yard drive to score in the third quarter, but Wilkinson watched grimly as the Longhorns scored their final touchdown on another fourth-down play.

The Sooners were thoroughly outplayed by the Longhorns, and Wilkinson was discouraged by the 28–7 loss, primarily because it confirmed his fears about the mental toughness of the Sooners. To make matters worse, Looney had been unforgivably lazy and gained only 4 yards in six carries.

During conditioning sprints the following Monday, Wilkinson lost his patience. Looney was loafing visibly, and he seemed intent upon incurring the wrath of the Sooner coaching staff. Finally, Wilkinson reached his limit. First, Looney had refused to practice when he suffered minor injuries. Next came his altercation with Tatum. Then he had not hustled against Texas. Now, this.

"Joe Don, we're going to try it one more time," Wilkinson told Looney in a firm, matter-of-fact tone. "If you don't try this time, you might as well keep on running because you're off the team."

Looney lined up with the rest of the Sooner backs for the next sprint. One of the Sooner assistants blew his whistle, and they took off. While the others ran, Looney trotted down the field like a sullen child. When he reached the spot where the other Sooners were hunched over trying to regain their breath, Looney trotted past them silently toward the Sooner locker room.

That evening, Wilkinson called Garrett, one of the Sooner co-captains, into his office.

"Go tell Joe Don he's off the squad," Wilkinson told Garrett.

Garrett went to Looney's room and found him lying on the bed. He told Looney the news, and Looney seemed shocked.

"Who did it? Why?" Looney asked.

"The coaches and players feel you are more of a detriment to the team than an asset," Garrett said.

"What can I do to get back on the team?" he asked.

"I don't have any answers," Garrett said. "Talk to Coach Wilkinson."

Looney knew the situation was hopeless. He packed his bags and disappeared, but in his place would reside a legend that would not diminish as the years passed. In years to come, it would bewilder Wilkinson—even irritate him—that the player fans asked about more often than any other was not Royal, not Vessels, not McDonald, not Harris, not Tubbs, not Thomas, not Gautt. It was Joe Don Looney.

With Looney's disruptive influence removed, the Sooners began to play with greater spirit. The Sooners twice came from behind to beat KU, 21–18, which set the stage for convincing victories over Kansas State and Colorado. Then, on successive weekends, the Sooners outlasted Iowa State and Missouri, both games in which the Sooners' ability to dominate play in the second half was crucial. By late November, they stood 7–1 and were scheduled to face Nebraska in Lincoln in a showdown for the Big Eight championship for the second straight year. The Sooners flew to Lincoln on Thursday afternoon in anticipation of their customary light workout at Memorial Stadium early Friday afternoon.

About the same time the Sooners were leaving Norman to fly to Lincoln, President John Kennedy was making final preparations for a campaign trip to Texas. The trip was one he did not relish, but it was a necessity. To solidify his support for the 1964 election, he would need Texas, which had voted for Richard Nixon in 1960. The president, comfortable that all was in order for his trip, walked from the Oval Office and stopped briefly to visit with aide Ted Reardon.

"They tell me Bud Wilkinson is interested in politics," the president said to Reardon. "I'll have to give him a call when I get back from Dallas."

When the Sooners returned to the Cornhusker Hotel after their Friday afternoon workout, they were met by news of Kennedy's assassination. For Wilkinson and the Sooners—as it did for the rest of the nation—time seemed to stand still while they absorbed the impact of the events in Dallas. Wilkinson liked Kennedy, and his death shook Wilkinson so deeply that he had to retrieve wartime memories from the *Enterprise* to cope with the unexpected loss. How do you carry on in the face of death when you have no choice but to carry on?

Throughout the country, college football games and other events were being canceled in honor of the slain president, and the officials at both Oklahoma and Nebraska were uncertain what course they should take. At dinner, Wilkinson sent Ken Farris to call Oklahoma governor Henry Bellmon to elicit his opinion. Bellmon said he would accept whatever decision Wilkinson and George Cross thought appropriate. When Farris returned with Bellmon's answer, Wilkinson excused himself to call Reardon and ascertain what the Kennedy family would prefer. Ninety minutes later, the answer came. The Kennedys believed the game should be played.

Standing in the hotel, Wilkinson talked with Bill Connors, a sportswriter from Tulsa who had started covering the Sooners about the same time Wilkinson became head coach. Through the years, they had become close acquaintances. Both were shocked by the news of the president's death.

"Suddenly, this game doesn't seem quite as important," Connors said.

"It never was," Wilkinson replied.

Many of the players wanted to go back to Norman and return to Lincoln in two weeks to play the game. Some of the Sooners, especially those who had met Kennedy at the Orange Bowl, felt they knew him personally. Since January, Wilkinson had often brought some personal word from the president to the squad. Talking with his players at the hotel that Friday night, only six hours after the assassination, Wilkinson told them he knew it would be difficult to play, but that this had been the official decision based on the Kennedy family wishes.

"There will be a football game tomorrow," Wilkinson told the Sooners, "but unless you can discipline yourselves to concentrate on the game, you will not win it. Life goes on. It's short. We don't have much time to do the things we want to do. About all there is to life is what you do with your opportunities. If you'll go after this team hard, reducing the game to a test of heart and courage, these guys can't stay up with you."

As the Sooners dressed for the game on Saturday, the OU locker room was extraordinarily quiet. The Sooners had read the newspapers, and they knew this might be their last season—perhaps even their last game—with Wilkinson. And that suspicion, combined with the trauma of Kennedy's assassination the day before, placed the Sooners in an emotional turmoil.

Wilkinson could see it taking place and tried to calm the young Sooners, but at game time he realized his players were too emotionally wired to play their best football. Once the game started, Nebraska's opening kickoff sailed high and long on the strength of a twenty-mile-per-hour wind, and Shields—who had raced 65 yards for a touchdown on a perfectly executed punt return against Missouri—fielded it 5 yards deep in the Sooner end zone. On the sidelines, Wilkinson sensed that Shields might try to run with the ball. Unconsciously, Wilkinson gave his head an exaggerated shake, punctuating his belief that the Sooners should be satisfied to take the ball at the 20.

Wilkinson's instincts were right. Fired by events of the past week, Shields was determined to run the kick back. He charged out of the Sooner end zone and headed upfield. The Cornhusker coverage was too good, stopping Shields at the OU 15, achieving at least momentarily some psychological advantage. As Shields trotted toward the sidelines, he knew he had made a mistake. Wilkinson walked onto the field to meet him, but instead of berating Shields, Wilkinson hugged his determined halfback for a brief moment and patted him on the shoulder pads. Desire, he knew, could make up for many youthful mistakes.

Shields's lapse in judgment was an omen of things to come. Throughout the first half, the rest of the Sooners played with the same emotional fervor. Twice on the first series, Tommy Pannell overthrew open receivers. When McCurdy's punt into the wind was short and bounced backward to the OU 39, the situation looked dire. The Cornhuskers moved to a first down in two plays, but the Sooner defense stiffened and forced Nebraska to try a field goal, which was wide to the left.

Four more times in the first half, Nebraska took possession in OU territory, but the Sooners left the field at halftime trailing only 3–0. Defensively, they were playing magnificent football, but on offense, they had earned only two first downs. On their six possessions, they had fumbled or been forced to punt after running only three plays.

In the third quarter, what emotional discipline the Sooners had demonstrated in the first half deteriorated. Three times, they fumbled to the Cornhuskers inside the OU 35. They ran only seven plays during the quarter and were fortunate the Cornhuskers held only a 10–0 lead. But the last of the three fumbles led to a Nebraska touchdown early in the fourth quarter, and the Sooners found themselves trailing, 17–0.

Suddenly finding their composure, the Sooners moved to the Nebraska 22. Three plays later, the Sooners were still at the 22, and their hopes for a final Big Eight championship for Wilkinson seemed to be evaporating. On fourth down, Wilkinson sent in Fletcher, who continued to work his own form of magic. Fletcher started to his right, faking a sweep. He stopped, turned, and threw back across the field to Flynn, who was wide open and raced into the end zone. Jarman's extra point cut the Nebraska lead to 10 points with 12:43 to play.

Soon, the Sooners' aplomb evaporated completely. Twice, Sooner interceptions led to Nebraska touchdowns that gave the Cornhuskers a 29–7 lead. On the kickoff following the second Nebraska touchdown, Pannell fumbled, and the Cornhuskers recovered. The Sooners now faced the prospect of humiliation. Five times they had fumbled away opportunity. Twice, they had thrown it away. If this was to be Wilkinson's last season, this was no way to bid him goodbye.

On the Cornhuskers' first play, the Sooners forced a fumble. Mayhue recovered, and the Sooners set out to regain some measure of dignity. Contained all game long, the Sooners scored two quick touchdowns to narrow the final score to 29–20. The Sooners' rally, futile as it may have been, pleased Wilkinson, for he valued spirit above all, and he knew that many teams would have given up in similar circumstances.

After the game, the Bluebonnet Bowl issued an invitation to the Sooners, but Wilkinson did not want to go. His brother's recent death—a personal tragedy he had not shared with the Sooners—weighed heavily upon him. The urgent need to put his brother's affairs in order left little time or energy to prepare for another football game. He saw it only as an added burden. Still, Wilkinson felt a responsibility to the team that had played so hard under such trying circumstances.

"If the team wants to go, I'll go," Wilkinson told captains Vermillion and Garrett on the airplane back to Norman.

In Norman, the squad—sensitive to the joyless nature of Wilkinson's acquiescence—voted against going to a bowl and prepared to end the season with OSU. The Cowboys were likely to be tough, having lost to Nebraska only 20–16. If the Sooners won, they would be 8–2, which might enable them to finish in the top ten for the second year in a row.

In the final game of the year, the Sooners performed remarkably well. In the third quarter, the Sooners took a 14–10 lead on Grisham's 1-yard smash. Early in the fourth quarter, Grisham did it again. He pounded the OSU line for 65 yards in an 88-yard drive that moved the Sooners ahead, 21–10. Then, the Sooners began to play with even more feverish intensity. After an OSU fumble, Grisham burst 20 yards up the middle to score. On the Cowboys' first play after Grisham's touchdown, Ed McQuarters forced another fumble. Four plays later, Grisham scored yet another touchdown.

By the time the Sooners had completed their 34–10 victory, Grisham had amassed 218 yards rushing to surpass the previous Sooner record of 215 set by Buck McPhail in 1951. It was a remarkable performance, one that Wilkinson would treasure. From the sidelines, Wilkinson marveled at Grisham, who excelled in so many aspects of the game. A rugged linebacker. A devastating blocker. A capable pass receiver. A vastly underrated ball carrier. Like only a few other backs Wilkinson had coached. Grisham was a truly complete football player.

As the crowd dwindled out of the stadium, Wilkinson gazed up at the rows upon rows of empty bleachers in the massive brick-and-concrete edifice that dominated the OU campus yet teemed with life only five days a year. Wilkinson walked up the ramp into the Sooner locker room for the last time. In the past five seasons, his teams had lost more games than they had during his first twelve. They had been beaten by Nebraska, Colorado, Kansas, Missouri, and even Iowa State. But never in seventeen years had they lost to Oklahoma State.

Amid the end of the season and dealing with his brother's estate, Wilkinson's time was limited. In early December, Wilkinson went to George Cross's office in the OU Administration Building. He told Cross he was undecided about running for the U.S. Senate, but he could not continue as football coach.

"I am no longer able to get myself in the proper frame of mind to prepare for a football game," Wilkinson explained.

He told Cross he would be resigning as head football coach within a few weeks, but he wanted to retain the position of athletic director at least temporarily. On January 11, Cross arranged for a meeting of the board of regents. At that time, Wilkinson submitted his resignation as the Oklahoma football coach.

In the week that followed, rumors swirled around the campus regarding the board of regents, politics, and the naming of the new football coach. Quickly, Wilkinson perceived that the regents—most with Democratic Party allegiances—were holding up the naming of a new head coach until it was clear what his political intentions were.

Never had Wilkinson felt so powerless. He no longer wanted to coach, of that he was certain. The coaching of football—so intriguing to fans but, in truth, so repetitive and mundane—now seemed insignificant. He wanted to be free to pursue the siren song of politics and government, but the regents were determined not to allow him to follow the plan he had so carefully crafted.

Wilkinson knew the position of football coach was emotionally charged. His father had warned him of that a quarter century before, but being athletic director was not supposed to be so contentious. Now it was. If he did resign, he would be cut off without income for months before the senatorial election, which seemed to be the regents' goal. If he announced he was running as a Democrat, all would be forgiven. But if he did, he would be compromising his principles before he was even elected. His values told him the state needed a viable second party. Henry Bellmon, an astute and principled man, had proved it. But Republican was just a label. It didn't define him. Why, when he was willing to serve the people of his adopted state, was he being held captive? There was no ransom he could pay, no deal he could make in the face of such a power play. If he did not resign as athletic director, the regents—in their pettiness—would ensure that Gomer Jones, his loyal Sancho Panza for seventeen years, would *not* become the next head coach at Oklahoma.

For years while working with Wilkinson, Jones had not desired that title coveted by so many. Now, Wilkinson could see that Jones had lost that sense of self. As good a coach as Jones was, Wilkinson knew Jones was not emotionally equipped to be a head coach. And he knew that Jones also knew it. But with the kingdom the two of them had created there for the taking, Jones could not sit idly by and abdicate it to another who had not earned that right. Wilkinson believed Jones had earned that right, and though he could foresee a tragic ending, he could do nothing to forestall it. If he did not do what the regents wanted, the head coaching job would be given to another candidate out of spite. If he yielded to their power play, the position would be given to Gomer, and events—good or ill—would be put in motion. But, Wilkinson concluded, Gomer *deserved* his chance.

With that in mind, Wilkinson acceded. Certain it was not the proper course of action, but equally certain he had no other alternative, Wilkinson announced that he intended to resign as athletic director and recommended that Jones be named football coach without delay. Wilkinson knew it was the only thing—the only *right* thing—he could do.

The next afternoon, Wilkinson drove to the campus to attend a meeting of the board of regents. The meeting, held to interview four candidates for the head coaching position, was to take place in the north end of the stadium. At one o'clock, Wilkinson met with the regents briefly. He submitted his resignation, which was accepted, and left. Walking down the steps from the second floor, Wilkinson could not help wondering if it would be the last time he would ever do so. For more than a decade, he had climbed these same stairs, sat at the same metal desk, and directed the fortunes of a football program that now ranked with any in the country. As he pushed open the heavy metal-frame doors and stepped into the cold January air, Bud Wilkinson faced the day he always knew would come. The day he would have to prepare himself, as he had prepared scores of young men, for life after football.

Index

Page numbers in *italics* indicate illustrations.